Brace yourself for an epiphany! Peter Kline has given us a gold mine of his insights, experiences, and strategies. *Why America's Children Can't Think* is a proactive, compelling, and thoroughly inspiring challenge that ignites learning and inspires teaching. He draws upon the highly successful work of some of the most innovative but overlooked seminal thinkers, and applies breakthrough findings from neurologists, cyberneticists, optometrists, and audiologists to reach the genius inside each child.

Kline bridges the gap between scientific research on brain functions and their "added value" in creating successful and joyful learning experiences. With the mandate to "leave no child behind," the book provides insightful and compelling strategies to liberate and inspire young minds through the "free play of the intellect." We are challenged to sharpen our "intense personal radar" to first understand, and then to teach to, the uniqueness of each child.

Why America's Children Can't Think is a brilliant book that is essential reading for all those interested in cultivating excellence in teaching and learning.

Linda Tsantis, Johns Hopkins University

Why America's Children Can't Think

Why America's Children Can't Think

Creating Independent Minds
for the 21st Century

Peter Kline

INNER
OCEAN

Inner Ocean Publishing, Inc.
P.O. Box 1239
Makawao, Maui, HI 96768-1239

Cover design: Bill Greaves
Cover photo: Getty Images
Interior page design: Bill Greaves
Typography: Debra Lordan
Copy editor: Kirsten Whatley

189 6840
Publisher Cataloging-in-Publication Data

Kline, Peter
        Why America's Children can't think :
creating independent minds for the 21st
century / Peter Kline. --Makawao, Maui, HI
        : Inner Ocean, 2002

        p. ; cm.

        Includes bibliographical references and index.
        ISBN 1-930722-10-9
        1. Creative thinking - - United States. 2.
        Critical thinking - - United States. 3.
        Thought and thinking. 4. Educational tests
        and measurements - - United States. 5.
        Educational Psychology. 6. Education and
        state - - United States. I. Title.

LB1062 .K55 2002
370.118/0973 - - dc21   CIP

Printed in Canada by Friesens

9 8 7 6 5 4 3 2 1

For Margaret Park,
who contributed so very much
to this book.

Contents

Preface

Recently three public schools near me shared the media spotlight as they received significant monetary rewards for raising their standardized test scores. Principals, teachers and students applauded themselves for a job well done. Indeed such success is a laudable result of much hard work. Hopefully, the money received will be used to bring these schools yet more success.

But merely raising scores on standardized tests and believing that to be the primary indication of success in solving the problems of our American educational system is like applying a small adhesive bandage to a gaping wound. It is too small to staunch the loss of the lifeblood of the nation's much-needed talent pool of critical-thinking and problem-solving abilities. These are a *sine qua non* of student achievement because they are based on generating answers to new questions rather than on the information that falls below the threshold of what's really relevant and needed in today's world. It's time we started preparing students to face the adult world they'll have to cope with—which will be most unlike the world they're living in now.

The national focus on test scores, which too easily leads to the result that teachers teach not much more than test answers, is more likely to lower the median level of national intelligence than raise it.[1] It invites the kind of lockstep education that was out-of-date even two centuries ago.

In a memorable passage in one of his novels, Charles Dickens describes a teacher who seemed bent on prying open the lid of a student's head, pouring in a certain amount of knowledge and then slamming it shut. Unfortunately, this bit of muckraking is as relevant in today's world as when Dickens wrote about it. Far too many think that knowledge is something you can force teachers to teach in such a manner that everyone learns the same thing.[2]

It can't be done. The result is that the best teachers are forced into pedagogical straitjackets that restrict them from using their wisdom as their life experience tells them it should be used. This leads to social conditions in which "the best lack all conviction, while the worst are full of passionate intensity."[3] This is what happens when students are forced into thinking that negatively impact their future performance.

Long ago in a faraway land and a distant time there may have been such a thing as a "body of knowledge." Today, however, the amount of available information in all fields is growing at more than a billion times the rate it was in 1950. By the year 2010 it will be continuing to expand at more than ten times that rate.[4] As a result, the knowledge you can memorize is out-of-date before you hear about it for the first time, which means that the only hope for developing a meaningful relationship to information is to be free to explore it in a subjective manner. The best course is to chart your own unique path like a frontiersman through a seemingly infinite jungle of ever-proliferating facts that no mind will ever encompass, while at the same time learning tools of communication so that a reasonable amount of wisdom can be shared.

While we must have a sense of history, including the history of science, mathematics and the arts, history itself changes rapidly as new discoveries are made and new interpretations of past events become relevant and meaningful. All too often nearly everything that we think we know about a subject turns out under closer examination to be based on assumptions that are either only partly true or patently false.

The process of teaching students to read, using a conscious method that connects directly to the formation and exploration of their individual thoughts, interpretations and values, needs to begin in the first grade and be well established by the third. This is in no way unrealistic. At this age, children are constantly making interesting observations about practically everything. But too often, teachers attempt to respond to them only on the basis of whether or not they happen to agree or find the ideas relevant to the immediate discussion. That's one reason why younger children live in a world filled with a context so much wider and richer (though obviously less detailed) than their parents and teachers. Furthermore, children's ideas are not necessarily trifling. I find that many of the things I believe and develop in my work today are based on thoughts I remember having before I entered kindergarten. Most people I talk with who can remember those years have a similar sense that they have not abandoned the integrity of their earliest intimations, or even have had to return to these later in life. Failing to encourage children's richness of thought and imagination removes the advantage of teachable moments. It is certainly a form of child abuse; but it also endangers our freedom and perhaps even our species by reducing its creativity.

In the "fill 'em up" approach to education, if we assume that children are born with nothing on their minds, and that it is the business of education to fill those minds with the things that Everyone Should Know, as if we were programming computers, then there might be some sense in a lock-step curriculum. However, the human mind is fundamentally different from a computer in that respect, because all of us are born with the ability to compute and create language genetically encoded in our brains. It has also been established that no two people learn in exactly the same way. And indeed, many, if not all, of us seem destined for our own special kind of knowledge, skill, experience and creativity.

That's fortunate, because in the new world of the future we are rapidly moving into, no two people will be required to do exactly the same things with their lives. As automation replaces production lines and even line workers are expected to solve complex problems, the need for a highly developed capacity to think and respond in an original manner is becoming a requirement for all citizens everywhere.

The framers of the Constitution built the foundation for a democratic government in the hope that an electorate would choose its representatives wisely. However, an electorate that does not understand the issues on which the quality of life depends cannot hope to do any such thing. In today's electorate, too many do not bother to vote at all, while too many others cast their votes in response to emotional trash so transparent that thoughtful and concerned citizens can easily see through it.

It is thus extremely important to the future of our society that we educate all citizens to read and interpret information thoughtfully and thoroughly to serve the needs of the body politic in its entirety. This is an enterprise from which no one is expendable. It means that the largest possible majority should be able to get an accurate picture from a page of print that represents not only what it says literally, but also what its meaning and value might be. That, at present, the majority of high school graduates cannot do either of these things satisfactorily is the greatest crisis of our age.

Surely the founders of the views on which our society is based—men like Thomas Jefferson, John Adams, Alexander Hamilton and George Mason—would, despite all their differences, have agreed on this. The exchanges of ideas that informed the Constitutional Convention should have set the tone for those heard in the halls of government ever since, though few would assert that such an outcome has been achieved.

Instead, we have recently seen a "watering down" of journalism, our fourth estate, so that less and less of what it has to offer is challenging and stimulating—or, in many cases, even remotely true. As a result, potential voters usually see and hear little of what they need to know in order to form valid opinions.[5]

It's possible that the rise of yellow journalism in recent years was a by-product of the end of the Cold War. It's often said that if aliens were to attack Earth, all the nations of the world would unite in harmony to fight against them. We certainly saw the makings of such a transformation in the response to 9/11, but, persuaded that patriotism requires us to continue living as before, we have not greatly departed from our previous mindlessness.

That's not quite the atmosphere of public discussion we had during the Cold War, which split our country into factions over whether it was better to be dead than Red. Nevertheless, because the potential destruction of the globe was at stake, there was an imperative in the back of everyone's mind that led to a reasonable amount of intense exchange between opposing points of view.[6] Since members of the opposition to the government's position were highly motivated to banish the threat of nuclear extinction, and a large segment of the population shared their concern, the sale of serious books on serious subjects was widespread.

Today, by contrast, we seem to have entered the Era of Intellectual Pabulum. Nearly all the publishers who used to give us a steady stream of thoughtful essays about the nature and future of society and the body politic, as well as thoughtful analyses of the arts and sciences, have abandoned any sort of crusade for the life of the mind. Instead, too many insist that we choose between blockbuster bestsellers (many of whose authors are celebrities that are not real writers) and nothing at all.[7]

Meanwhile, many millions of children have set off for their first day of school with thousands of hours of television under their belts and zero books read to them. As author of *Endangered Minds* Jane Healy and others have pointed out, this rewires the human brain so that an entirely different kind of thought process emerges, one that cannot compute the importance of thoughtful discourse and discussion.

The burden of this combination of too much television and too little exposure to books has fallen upon the schools. It means that today's teachers have to teach many things that previously were learned at home. Reading teachers have to teach today's children what their grandparents knew intuitively, namely that a good book can be transformed by the mind into something like the private showing of a deliciously wonderful movie that gives rise to significant food for thought.

The visualizing capacity of the mind, if it is not stimulated by parents reading to children or by an environment of storytelling, has to be developed pedagogically, or it may never develop at all.

All this being so, we are in imminent danger of making extinct the fine art and gentle pastime of reading good books for one's own pleasure and enlightenment—a pastime that, for several hundred years, our ancestors and those of the citizens of other nations have reveled in.

This is doubly unfortunate since, in the opinion of most good readers, there are few pastimes that can equal a quiet evening with a good book.

And obviously those who read good books will also read newspapers that appeal to their intellectual predilections.

For many years I taught high school students how to read and write deeply and critically. In fact, it was not uncommon for me to spend an entire class period having the students debate the subtle implications of a few lines from Shakespeare. No one seemed immune to the charms of this greatest of all writers when they understood the literal meanings of the lines and could thus go on to consider their figurative and implied meanings, which can run very, very deep. However, even the literal meanings, it must be admitted, are not always evident at first even to the most experienced readers, since Shakespeare added more new words to the English language than the collected efforts of most of the literary geniuses who came after him.

In fact, over the years I have heard repeatedly from many of those students (including some who didn't do very well at their studies generally) that getting to know the delights Shakespeare's writing could offer was one of the most important rewards of their entire education. Certainly this has never surprised me, since it was also true of me.

Some years ago, Mortimer J. Adler edited a remarkably well-indexed edition of the *Great Books of the Western World*, and included with it a volume entitled *The Great Conversation*. This title captures for me, more than any other single phrase, what reading should be.

I think you, as a reader, should begin by conversing with the author of the book. Finding the areas of agreement and disagreement that you have with the author brings the book radiantly to life.

When you've sufficiently engaged your mind with the author's, it's time to reflect on what it means to be able to converse in this manner with many of the most brilliant thinkers who have ever lived.

What this means is that we must teach reading thoughtfully from the very beginning, and in the spirit of conversation. Trying to control that process with standardized tests seems only a means of freezing it out of existence. I've found that when real learning is taking place in the classroom, everyone is aware of everyone else's learning. That's because the learning informs the conversation and the informed conversation invariably glows with a quickening energy as it discovers its possibilities.

And if it's the discovery of possibilities we're talking about, how can those be tested?

It's not that evidence of reading and thinking skills can't be gathered somehow. But since no two readers function the same way if they're moving toward their own unique rewards to be had from their reading, no standardized test could possibly frame the right questions for everyone.

There is perhaps one essential key to the art of reading, and that is listening intently to the inner voice that is aroused by what the author has to say. In that conversation between reader and author a marvelous web of thought is spun out, which can lead in completely new and previously unimagined directions.

By basing your reading on your previous knowledge and adding to that knowledge with the careful consideration of what each new book has to offer, you can unfold to yourself your own private world, each thought evolving out of the previous thought. This is the manner in which the universe has unfolded itself. It has always done whatever it needed to realize the possibilities opened up by what it has previously experienced.[8]

If you learn to listen to yourself and assess all that you have already done, you will inevitably see golden possibilities opening up before you.

A precious few of us have mastered this technique. Shakespeare was perhaps the best at it, and therefore is perhaps the best writer for teaching us how to practice it. The rest of us aimlessly wander in a dark wood obsessed by one or more of the following:

What am I supposed to do?

What is expected of me?

What's the assignment?

What's going to be on the test?

How can I make the most money?

How can I stay out of trouble?

How can I stir up the most trouble?

How can I please my parents?

How can I frustrate and disappoint my parents?

How can I most effectively get back at those who have done me in?

At any given point in our lives, we can do what needs to be done—or we can do something else. We mostly do the "something else."

The study of complexity theory at the Santa Fe Institute has focused on the process by which the universe creates itself as a self-organizing system. (To the extent that this implies that the universe is intelligent, it does not lead to atheistic conclusions, but instead corresponds rather closely with the underlying philosophies of most of the world's great religions.)

You and I are (or can become) self-organizing systems. We do this by paying attention to our own thoughts about what is going on around us and developing our responses from an evolving awareness unique to our experiences.

Those of us who do this will become self-actualized individuals whose lives can make a difference to those around us. Those who do not will become part of the entropic background noise that keeps things disorderly.

The trouble with school, as I see it, is that it encourages most children to stop listening to themselves but never tells them what to listen to instead. Both the traditional instructional methods and the tests used to determine the results of teaching fail to focus on a learner's success in developing a consistent interpretation of his or her life experience.

Ever since universal public education shifted, mid-nineteenth century, from an ideal to a practical experiment, visionaries have been trying to reform schools. Horace Mann was the driving force behind the establishment of the public school system in the United States. He has sometimes been accused of pilfering the Prussian military system for his model of classroom discipline, but in fact his philosophy was more like that of philosopher John Dewey or educator John Holt than the parlance of most histories of education usually suggest.

Early in the last century, Gary, Indiana, was a stronghold of public school reform. There the rather abstract approach to education that had developed up to that point was challenged by a more practical, hands-on approach, which New York City tried, but ultimately failed, to replicate. Critics of the Gary schools felt that they had abandoned liberal education in favor of training their students in vocational skills. This problem served as a springboard for debate about the Ivory Tower approach to education versus the anti-intellectual approach. Throughout most of the century, the debate about the role of education as a means of producing the responsible citizenry needed to make democracy work waxed and waned. The question of whether or not all students could be brought to the level of achievement that the elitist Ivory Tower, or perhaps, better said, the Ivy League, set as a standard for the measurement of a cultured mind was widely debated. In recent years these views have been re-invoked by Allan Bloom and others, who have argued, largely from a doom-and-gloom perspective, that educational standards are far too low, and that much of the great tradition of Western thought is being sacrificed in the melee.

Throughout the century, there were mainstream attempts to change things, like the progressive movement promulgated by John Dewey, or the turmoil of the sixties, during which brilliant classroom teachers like John Holt and Jonathan Kozol had a great deal to say. On the sidelines and never mainstreamed were reformers like Rudolf Steiner, Maria Montessori, Kurt Hahn and A. S. Neill. However, their awareness that all children learn differently provided, in the end, a chorus of voices crying in the wilderness. We are still, as I write, convinced that standardized tests are the magic formula that can save us.[9]

The implications of this for our nation's future are obvious. Since reading is the platform on which an education must be built, if our schoolchildren don't learn to read thoughtfully, critically, with joy and with their whole personalities, then everything else we might hope to do for them will be more or less hopeless. Therefore I hope educators, as well as those charged with the formation of educational policy, will read this book. Above all, I hope that we, as a nation, will stop trying to make the finger in the dike a rolled-up collection of standardized tests and will start meeting headlong the challenge that anti-intellectualism inevitably poses to the future of a free and thoughtful society.

Historian David McCulloch's biography of John Adams should help fuel public debate on the subject. Ask yourself, when considering any public policies, laws or programs for school reform, whether Adams would have approved. Adams, an inveterate reader himself, was, more than any other single individual, the architect of the kind of government and society we have today. If we want to make him and the other Founding Fathers proud of what they wrought, we must consider the challenge of creating an educational revolution as prelude to the renaissance that they envisioned. That means we will have to start doing things very, very differently. The current catastrophe in public education is assuredly the most compelling crisis before us, and it concerns me that we have, as a nation, adopted the policy of the insane: What we have done so far hasn't worked, therefore we must do more of the same.

However, that subject is not the main thrust of this book, which propounds some thoughts and experiments that will lead to more satisfactory experiences in reading. This book shows how reading can be taught so that (1) everyone learns to do it and (2) young minds are liberated and inspired in the process.

It's in the way we teach reading that we can make the most difference between enchaining young minds to outworn creeds, ideas and traditions and showing them how to become intellectually free and able to function as effective citizens in a democratic society.

If our attention is focused on listening to our own thoughts in relation to what's going on around us (which includes the thoughts of others), there will be no limit to how far our thoughts can reach.

It is my hope that, within my lifetime, public schools will discover how to be the chief instruments by which people can learn the fine art of freedom and discover the awesome responsibilities that implies. For we can be said to be fully conscious only when we are acting in unpredictable ways based on the integrity of the lives we have thoughtfully crafted from the sum totality of our experiences—whatever those may be. Any other sort of life cannot be said to be fully conscious—in the sense that Thoreau meant when he said, "I have never met a man who was fully conscious—for how could I look him in the face?"

Acknowledgments

Frequently enjoined by bumper stickers to thank my teachers if I can read, I am trying to recall their names. Mrs. Hoffman, my kindergarten teacher, didn't teach reading as such, so far as I can recall. However, she did create a post office in our classroom, thus allowing us to write letters to one another, so we must have known how to read and write. I remember lousing up the system by sending letters to people with nothing in them and then watching the disappointment on their faces when they opened them. Clearly I could write their names in order to accomplish this.

I don't remember anything about my first grade teacher, but I do remember that I started out in the lowest reading group and finally made it into Stephen's group, which was the highest. Mrs. Thomas, the second grade teacher, was great fun, and Mrs. King, who taught me third grade, became such a good friend that I corresponded with her during my freshman year in college. After that things went rapidly downhill. In the sixth grade my mother caught me with unsigned papers that were supposed to have been signed by her, and I was consigned to doing my homework at the kitchen table under her watchful eye, which reversed the direction of my falling grade point average.

Which brings me to thanking my mother, who read T. S. Eliot in the hospital while waiting to give birth to me. This may account for the fact that Eliot became my favorite poet (or one of them) after nearly becoming a stillbirth in my literary experience.

My mother, Susan Kline, believed that the unexamined life is not worth living and often insisted that I acknowledge that. So I have written this book partly to assure her (even in the better place to which she has gone) that I continue to dedicate myself to the awesome challenge of confronting the examined life.

I must also acknowledge my Uncle Dean (my father's youngest brother) for rescuing me when, not yet five, I fell all the way down the stairs. He was the only one with me at the time and did his best to comfort me. This consisted of sitting me in a chair and giving me a world atlas to distract my attention from the residual pain I was feeling. It struck me recently with blinding insight that he was more uncomfortable than I, not knowing what to do with my crying self. I was so deeply touched by his attempts to rescue the situation that I look upon that atlas as a symbol of one human being reaching out to another against all odds. I have since decided at that moment, my immoderate and indeed somewhat dangerous love of books was born. I said as much at his funeral recently, but found it hard to get the words out as the tears streamed down my face, so I know it is true.

Both my mother and father read aloud to me often. My first true love among books was *The Jungle Book*, which so impregnated my imagination that I invited a group of its characters to camp out on the roof of our house every night. I impersonated them for the entertainment of my younger brothers, who may have been naive enough to think that those creatures—Mowgli, Ka, Baloo and even Shere Kahn—were actually talking to them, but I can't be sure of that. That probably has nothing to do with the fact that my brothers are both, like me, published authors, but it does suggest that my mother touted literacy to our family with remarkable effectiveness.

I skip now to the teacher (I've forgotten her name) who had us dramatize *Evangeline* in the eighth grade. Though only one of the scenes I wrote made it into the version we eventually staged, it was my first experience of being a playwright, and a most remarkably satisfying one.

What with one thing and another, though, I read very little that wasn't assigned from about the middle of the sixth grade until my junior year in college, because my eyes needed the help of an optometrist. In 1955, when Dr. Amiel Francke came to my assistance, the excitement of books reentered my life in full Wagnerian splendor. The end result is that my house is now so overfull of them that nothing except rebuilding it will help.

Another deeply treasured friend along the way was Paul Scheele, who invented PhotoReading. I was on the scene when he concocted the idea of teaching people to read twenty-five thousand words a minute. I was also in one of his first classes, and as a result of Paul's course, I greatly increased the number of books I read and the rate at which I read them. Today, Scheele's course is sweeping the country. I hope it catches everyone, because it is one of the best ways I know to increase one's reading pleasure and profit.

Undaunted supporters of the reading program on which this book is based include Jane Norton, my brother Michael Kline, Edie Crane, Jan Folkmeier, Dr. James Easton, Dot Feldman, Warren Gifford, Sam Weidner and Sue Welling.

For helping me get this book into print I am deeply indebted to Mark and Margaret Esterman, Carol Banner and Jane Hale, all friends who have profoundly shaped my life.

Those who have influenced the writing of this book in its final version include Dan Dizon, Paul Messier, Barbara Kapinus, Carolyn Breedlove, Dr. Don Helms and Dr. Steven Ingersoll.

Chapter 22 is a special case, and for that I must thank David Lloyd Kreeger, Charlton Ogburn, Peter Kreeger, Ira Zinman, Monty Diamond, Aaron Tatum, Jack Shuttleworth, Tom Searcy, Amy Cofield, Dennis Jelalian, Barry and Linda Morley, and Warren Gifford.

Time to mention my children, none of whom are children anymore. I know that children seldom if ever learn anything from their parents, but I am certain that parents learn a great deal from their children. My eldest, Stephanie, has taught me the virtues of saying exactly what one thinks and not mincing words. Stephanie is certainly one of the gentlest, most honest people I have ever met, and it is no wonder that her daughters, Grace and Molly, are, as their wonderfully exotic father puts it, "card-carrying angels." As a teacher, she gives first graders the best start in life that any-one could have.

Maureen, who came next, has been both a literary critic and champion, and a spiritual teacher. I remember when she was four how she said, "I love everyone in the world, including the people I don't know." The amusing thing is, she still feels that way. As a reporter on economic issues, writing in both English and Italian, she dispenses profound wisdom on contempo-rary issues, and as a mother she is raising Nicholas and Ricardo, who tend to both be either athletically amazing or totally engrossed in books: a rare combination.

Wendy, my youngest, has reached the pinnacles of academic achieve-ment with a thesis published as a book. Added to this glory is her profes-sional violin playing, which was briefly understudied during a bout with carpal tunnel syndrome by a leading role in *As You Like It*. At present the apple of her eye is her little Max, already at two showing an inclination for mathematical brilliance.

The eldest of my two stepsons is Seth, whose diary, written at the age of eight, was so fascinating it seemed to cry out for publication. Now Seth is well on his way to a career in sales and marketing because he knows and can explain his products so well that everyone wants to buy them.

Jonathan, on the other hand, showed no flair for reading at all, though he demonstrated a penchant for practically everything else. As a dancer he resembled the young Michael Jackson. As an artist he drew pictures that people wanted to buy. As a friend he quickly seemed to get mistaken by his peers for a psychiatrist. Books, however, for a long time were not for him. If you read to him he wanted to get up and run around. So what a surprise it was when in the seventh grade he jumped seven grade levels in reading, and developed a passion for *Much Ado About Nothing* and *Hamlet*. Today, he says he wants to be a photojournalist.

Watching all these children grow up has taught me that no two people are even remotely the same, that we all have unique ways of learning, but also that one can carry on a deep conversation with a child of any age if one chooses one's words well, and that the disdain some of us have for children is the deepest form of oppression among the many oppressions that imprison the world.

As a high school teacher for twenty-five years, I developed the most profound respect for the minds of young people. My students invariably taught me more than I taught them. It is to the future health of such young minds that this book is directed.

Finally I must mention the publishers for whom I wrote several books, including this one, until they decided to specialize in the kinds of books that I don't write. Nevertheless, Margaret Park, to whom this book is dedicated, gave it the most loving editorial ministrations a book can have. Her husband, Mark Esterman, was also a profound influence not only on my writing, but on my reading as well.

When Roger Jellinek took over this book for Inner Ocean, he proved a most delightful person to work with, offering suggestions that were precisely targeted to improving the book yet further, and putting a crown on the whole writing experience, for which I am exceedingly grateful.

When the ball was passed to Kirsten Whatley, she lovingly and skillfully attended to the myriad details that must be right if a book is to be worth printing. And John Nelson has, at the end, exhibited a wonderful bedside manner as the book's midwife in taking it to the stores.

Last, but (I'm afraid) most, my wife, Syril, is not just a life partner, but a book partner as well. We share books, both in the reading and the writing of them, particularly in relation to Shakespeare. Not a day goes by that I don't learn something new from her (or from the television set that she continually corrupts my too-bookish nature, by making me watch). And on those occasions when I seek only to find a pillow for my head and she regales me with the rare delights of yet another obscure Elizabethan romance, I lovingly acknowledge that I have more than met my match.

There is no frigate like a book
To take us lands away.

—Emily Dickinson

Part One

Building
the Foundation

*What are all the mechanisms necessary
in order to become a good reader,
and how should we deal with them?*

1

The Great
Conversation

How can we, as a civilization, move from a traditional
body of knowledge to the use of the World Wide Web
to create an ongoing conversation that will be
brilliantly enlightening and life enhancing?

Nothing defines our humanity more than the art of reading.

Now that I've written that statement, I invite you to read it with me.

To do so, you must subject it to critical analysis. A number of antithetical possibilities have probably occurred to you already:

We are toolmaking animals. Nothing defines our humanity more than our toolmaking ability.

We are social animals. Nothing defines our humanity more than our social complexity.

We are political animals. Nothing defines our humanity more than our political systems.

The question is, how good are these definitions and others like them? Is the definition of human distinctiveness I have offered more satisfactory than any of these?

The Scope of Reading

See how you and I have started a conversation? You cannot have read this far and remained passive. You are now a participant in a discussion, collaborating with me to see whether or not what I am telling you is true, whether it applies to your life, and perhaps what use you can make of it.

Why America's Children Can't Think

The spider is a toolmaking animal. The web it spins is a miraculous killing machine, as lethal as some of the most advanced products of modern technology.

Ants and bees are social animals. Their very existence is defined by their social activities; so much so, there is a real question whether the organism we should be thinking about is the individual ant or bee (which is monumentally stupid) or the ant hill or hive as a whole (which is remarkably intelligent).

When the male lion executes the cubs of the leader he has just overthrown, he is acting politically, like the chimpanzee, which can be equally ruthless with the babies of a hapless female. Politics, as we know from relatively recent animal studies, dictates the laws of the jungle as much as it dictates behavior in Congress or in the Balkans—and they can be spine-chillingly similar.

No species other than our own, however, has any conceivable use for a library. Within the pages written by a favorite author we can explore whatever far corners of the universe he or she has chosen to think about in print.

It is the library that frees us, the library that opens new worlds to us, the library that allows each member of our species to discover and define a unique way of being and confronting the world.

In saying all this, I am nevertheless implying a broader definition of reading than is usually meant in a pedagogical context. Reading neither begins nor ends with books. Under some circumstances it can be fully accomplished without them. Reading, however, in the sense meant here, centers around books and the unique relationship each reader builds with each book. For no reader will ever read the same book another has read. Half of the experience is, of necessity, in the individual reader's mind. What's important about any reading experience is the nature and quality of the change that takes place in a person's thinking as a result. While understanding the meaning of words, sentences and ideas is a *sine qua non* of reading, it's interpretation, not comprehension, that is the point. That's why it's so crazy to think that multiple-choice questions can reveal anything significant about reading comprehension. Any meaningful investigation of the quality of reading requires a discussion with the reader about impressions of what has been read. Often such discussions are essential to complete the reading experience itself. If you return to the first sentence in this chapter and what follows it, you'll be reminded of the fact that everything about the reading of that sentence depends not just on what it literally means (if, indeed, it can have a purely literal meaning at all) but on how you interpret it. Structural linguistics guru Noam Chomsky's investigations into the deep structure of the pyramid of meanings that underlies even the simplest conversational exchange should have taught us all by now that the concept of literal meaning is little short of an oxymoron. The simplest statement we can make has layers of hidden meanings.[1]

There's a mechanism in the neural structure of the brain that is designed to proofread and correct the following sentence: "I cat read." The actual sentence itself remains ambiguous, but your brain tells you almost instantaneously that the sentence should have said either "I can read" or "I can't read." That's because there's instant recognition that the word "cat" doesn't fit into the meaning dictated by the other two words, partly because the word "I" requires a verb following it.[2]

Some impulse deep within us, closely related to this proofreading capacity built into the DNA of our neurology, should go to work on the following sentence: "The Department of Defense has announced the development of a clean bomb for the arsenal of the future."

The notion that a bomb can be, in any sense, clean is anathema to our most basic experiences. This is language being used to create the same kind of double bind that would occur if a mother asked her child for a hug and then barked at her because she smelled bad. It is language being used to say something that should never even be thought.

To say that, in reference to the bomb, is not to take an antiwar position. It is simply an insistence that we acknowledge that a bomb that, for example, kills people without destroying buildings is still not "clean" since the result would be dead bodies in the bombed sites. This reflection, in turn, leads to speculation about the conditions under which it makes sense to kill off a large population while preserving the buildings. Are buildings really more valuable than people?

The fact that language has been used in this way without automatically provoking responses of the sort I've outlined here is evidence that as we grow older we become insensitive to the implications of what we are saying. We have learned to accept the literal meanings of words and sentences without requiring even the most rudimentary logical analysis of what has been said. We have deadened an instinctive response to language that is so basic it is programmed into our brains from birth.

A Good Movie about Reading

One of the best movies about reading devotes only about one percent of its footage actually to showing books on the screen. This is *October Sky*, which is set in the mining town of Coalwood, West Virginia, at a time when the future of the mine is in question and the town's very existence is at stake. Those who live there are little different from domesticated animals. They are born and grow up to work in the mine; and they die in the mine, or from its effects. In Coalwood, anyone who seeks another kind of life is branded a traitor or a misfit.

This true story opens with the launching of Sputnik in 1957, and tells of four boys who escape from their animal-like fate by winning college degrees that will open up careers for them far away from home. Early in the film you see the eyes of the townspeople fixed on the night sky. Across it blazes a single point of light. Immediately a symbol is created: The townspeople resemble the background of "fixed stars" against which the new phenomenon of alert and active boys will streak across the cultural firmament, creating havoc and excitement with their rockets as they force their way out from under the oppressive limitations of their heritage.

You hear the voices of the townspeople: "What's that thing for?" "Isn't it wonderful?" "Are they spying on us?" "Will they bomb us?" And the conclusion: "What a waste of a bomb that would be!"

But the mind of one boy in the crowd, Homer, marches to a different drum. "I want to build one of those things myself. I want to take my country into the sky and catch up with the Russians. I want to assist Dr. Wernher von Braun."

In the struggle that follows, Homer must learn to read a great many things. He must read the faces of the people he deals with to determine whether they will help or hinder him. He finds allies in three fellow students, in his teacher, in his mother, in some adults with needed knowledge and abilities; and, as the denouement approaches, even in his father, who has until then been his main antagonist. The drama takes place all around him, but in his private war for liberation the chief weapon is the knowledge contained in books. In his case, this knowledge is mostly mathematical. He must learn the equations that will help him understand the forces that drive and guide rockets. He must calculate these forces for himself in order to turn the failures of his enterprise into successes. Only in books can he find the resource that will help him realize his dream.

Books store the collective wisdom accumulated by our species, turning us into a giant organism that thinks for itself, beyond the guidance or wisdom of any individual.[3] The miracle wrought by books infuses Apollo 11, the Constitution of the United States, the plays of Shakespeare and *The Diary of Anne Frank*, for none of these could have been possible without the aid of our collective cultural heritage.

The mechanism of all this is recorded in the film: the pictures that young Homer sees in books. Whether the cover of an antique volume of Jules Verne's *From the Earth to the Moon* or the diagrams in technical tomes, Homer translates these pictures in his mind into real things that change the world: specifically, the rocket he sets off in an area near his town that ultimately wins first place at the national science fair, along with the hearts of his townspeople. Then Homer looks forward to lending his assistance to that ultimate giant step that will help transform all such primitive rockets into the achievement of Apollo 11.

Books, then, can not only take us lands away, they can reconstruct our world. They are the tools of freedom and transformation, the liberators of the mind. This much is noble and poetic, but there's something more sinister that we must also face, for there's a dark side to everything, even to the free and widespread access to information.

Our species may live or die via the Internet. We have now embarked on a worldwide conversation that needs to include every human being. That conversation requires universal reading and writing skills carried to a level never before believed possible. In the future, no one who cannot read and write e-mail will be included in the games people play. The word that appears on the computer screen must be read and evaluated much as you and I together have read and evaluated the first sentence of this book. This process requires the mental ability to decipher and understand the printed or transcribed word, and the critical ability to interpret it. Unless we can thoughtfully evaluate the messages we constantly confront, many of which will appear in our lives suddenly and without discoverable context, we will be unable to defend ourselves in a jungle of exploding communications, new information and changing rules that is unlike anything any species has ever confronted before.

Pandora's box has been opened and can never again be closed. The World Wide Web shelters hate groups, plots to infect the earth, porn industries, and the devastating waste of intellect gone wrong in the trivia of vacuous web chatter. No one will ever control the Web. It will either destroy us or elevate us to the heights of our potential. We must prepare for it now, if not sooner, and we must not leave anyone out. In the near future everyone will have to master the art of reading: thoughtfully, critically and imaginatively.

Soon the Web will make universally available every book, paper or document that is unguarded and extant. It will deluge us with information trillions of times more profuse than the sum total of all that was known a century ago. It will present us with the maximum conceivable challenge to our ability to select and judge wisely.

If you have e-mail and are a Net browser, you must have reacted many times to false alarms sent flooding through the wires, warning of this or that impending catastrophe. No doubt you've forwarded these to friends, only to be embarrassed a day or two later when you found out the alarm was only a hoax.

Meanwhile, though, real trouble is brewing as never before. Morose and sinister people once isolated can now contact each other in great numbers and brew their plots together. We cannot sit back and let that reshape our lives. We must use the new knowledge and technological prowess that has been unleashed by the Sorcerer's Apprentice to build a better world, a community of people who care enough about their species to want to preserve it.

To do this we must all become effective and critical readers who can separate the good from the bad, the true from the false, the inane from the brilliant, the relevant from the irrelevant, and the uplifting from the degrading.

The Growth of Complexity in Human Society

Once upon a time our species lived and worked organically in small, intimate communities. There was a kind of equality then, for opportunity was equally available to everyone. All used their wits, and the witless did not survive.

Then civilization arose and a few leaders gained a corner on the sources of power, keeping most others close to the level of slavery. A widening gap grew between the rich and poor, the haves and the have-nots, the privileged and the underprivileged. About twenty thousand years ago when the hunter-gatherers settled into farming and began to cultivate land, an uninterrupted battle for dominance began and has remained in force ever since.[4]

Now, however, thanks to the immediate access to all information that the Internet provides, power can pass from hand to hand with lightning speed. A single person operating out of a spare bedroom can challenge the financial supremacy of General Motors. The rules change so rapidly and drastically, those in power may lose all in a single day, while millionaires may be created overnight.[5]

In the process, the resources needed to produce, for everyone, a healthy and satisfying existence that does not threaten the environment are being created and are, for the most part, now assembled. We need only understand and use them.

A prerequisite for all of this, though, is universal literacy. And that doesn't mean simply the ability to recognize a word when seen. It means the sophistication of understanding needed to play in the world game. The latest statistics tell us that right now only 17 percent of people in the United States have that level of reading skill. The other 83 percent must catch up or be left out.[6]

All this is happening at a time when 20 percent of humanity still has so much trouble learning to read that illiteracy amounts to a national (and international) crisis. Why this 20 percent can't learn to read in grade school is open to a great deal of speculation, but the numbers hold true no matter what statistical method you use, or what theory of brain activity you entertain.

Of those who haven't learned to read by the third grade, 1997 statistics tell us, seven out of eight will never be adequately literate.[7]

In the world of tomorrow, this will be a horrific problem—one which I shall address from a very special perspective, because I know experientially what it means. I was one of the 20 percent. As a youngster I was blocked from learning to read well enough to make reading the central core of my life, which I wanted it to be. By the time I was a junior in college, I had only enough books to fill a single shelf, and my reading ability measured somewhere around fourth grade level.

But I was fortunate. I finally joined the one out of eight. With the help of Dr. Amiel Francke, a developmental optometrist, I bootstrapped myself into the top one percent of college-educated adult readers as the world of books opened up to me with awesome majesty and endless delight.

I became committed to sharing that delight with my students and, by 1997, had developed a program that seemed able to end illiteracy for all those who couldn't read, regardless of age or background. Interestingly enough, in developing this program, I improved my own reading even further.

Because reading is an organic process—a process the mind was designed to value but not specifically equipped to learn—I want to give you a sense of how that process works. There has to be continuity from the first halting steps of recognizing the letters of the alphabet to the sophisticated interpretation of other people's ideas in a context that is uniquely your own, that defines you as a person, and that provides you with tools to transform the world. What happens to you in first grade can profoundly affect whether or not you get a doctorate and, if so, what kind it will turn out to be. The primer you cut your reading teeth on profoundly shapes your mind. If it bores you and trivializes life for you, it may leave in its wake a potential devastation of one of life's greatest pleasures. If it makes reading magical for you, it will set you up for a lifetime of enjoyment and discovery.

A major literary movement, the Theater of the Absurd, was launched when the Romanian-French playwright Eugene Ionesco set out to learn

English. So vacuous was the primer he used that it inspired his first play, *The Bald Soprano*, which is about the death of language. In it we meet Mr. and Mrs. Smith, their maid, Mr. and Mrs. Martin, and the Fire Chief. They engage in a lengthy discussion of whether or not, when the doorbell rings, there is someone there. After much argument they arrive at the pontifical truth that "when the doorbell rings, sometimes there is someone, and other times there is no one."[8]

The absurdity that language takes on when it becomes disconnected from the honest need to communicate something of value is dramatized with hilarious effect in this play. Behind the hilarity lies the real tragedy of habitual obfuscation degrading our communications with what Byron called the Living Lie. Too many speak, yet say nothing. Too often language is shaped to conceal the truth. Too much of life is lived in the shadows of assumptions that lure us away from all that is good for us. Universal thoughtful literacy could change all that. Widespread suspicion about the lie beneath the word could stop the obfuscators and drive them reluctantly toward truth. Truth, of course, may never be found in all its brilliant clarity—at least language may never encompass it—but it's a good idea to be looking for it anyway.

Our lives are too often run by people who are victims of the absurdity encoded in the first grade primers from which they learned to read. In their book *On Learning to Read*, Bruno Bettelheim and Karen Zelan take us deep into the thoughts of children as they struggle with print for the first time.[9] All the awesome peculiarities of life are hanging there, poised for consideration, and their young minds shape the innocuous words before them into hidden meanings that teachers overlook and deride. Dick, Jane and Sally, or whoever the current icons may be, have too much interest in the superficial sitcoms of life to propel into consciousness any of the real dramas that lurk in the child's mind. As a result children are often taught to read with a reflex action that suggests language "sort of communicates something." They learn to use words the way they use Kleenex—primarily for discharging the waste products of their minds. The respect for language as a means of making things either precisely or poetically clear is not developed in school, and so remains largely absent from our culture. It wasn't absent, though, a couple of centuries ago, when children were treated like adult readers as they learned to wrestle with the more serious philosophical questions in life.

That is why these days so many things are all muddled up. That is why we have so much trouble establishing priorities that will support our continued existence on this earth. That is why people almost always misunderstand each other, which results in a very high divorce rate, endless lawsuits, and bad feelings galore. The phrase "tell me about it" is not usually a request for information; it is, rather, a cynical suggestion that we are at the end of the road in trying to understand whatever is under discussion at the moment.

This is too bad, because our human business is to transform the world, not just to litter it with the waste products of our miscommunication. All of us are designed by nature to change our surroundings; we must do so whether we want to or not.[10] Anyone who does not transform the world has never lived. If you don't believe me, look at the walls in the bedroom of any teenager and compare what you see there with the walls in the living room of that same household.

Reading Is Both Necessary and Universal

We are born to raise families, furnish our homes, drive our cars around polluting the environment, struggle for dominance in our social groups, earn a living, run for president, invent a better mousetrap, or write an immortal poem. All of us grow up with dreams and ideals for our lives. All of us meet life-threatening challenges that we must use our brains to surmount.

All of us must read because we cannot help it. The people looking at the sky as Sputnik streamed across it were reading the sky. The hunter of a hundred thousand years ago tracking a deer through the woods was reading the woods. The baby cooing at you is reading your facial expression.

These forms of reading supply the mental background and exercise for reading words. I can "read" the words I hear as I listen to you tell me something. But reading words on a page or a screen is a different kind of experience. When you tell me something out loud, 7 percent of your message is conveyed in your words, 38 percent in your tone of voice, and 55 percent in your body language.[11]

When words hit the page they carry none of the fixin's with them. The words alone have to do 100 percent of the communicating.

So, enter literary style. It's something that's rarely encountered in speech, though a few charismatic people manage to talk in prose now and again. How many, though, go around saying things like "The quality of mercy is not strained" or "In matters of grave importance, style, not sincerity, is the vital thing" or "It is a far, far better thing . . ."? The voice of a good author can speak to us uniquely in print. You can tell Hemingway from Fitzgerald in a paragraph, Shakespeare from O'Neill in a sentence. The voice of the artist dominates the work of art, even though all literary artists cultivate multiple personalities that attempt to settle things among themselves via the printed page. Even philosophers do that—or should I say, especially philosophers?

The art of the actor via the playwright brings text to the printed page. Literature begins as poetic drama, then separates into drama and poetry. Eventually it becomes nonfiction and ultimately even mathematics.[12] What they all have in common is the goal of rendering on paper some conceptual (or conceived or contrived) part of the universe.

Then the collaboration begins. As a reader you must do far more with a printed page than you ever have to do watching a movie, listening to a conversation, or speculating on things all by yourself. The printed page becomes an invitation to the movie of the mind, a private reverie inspired by the author, but uniquely your own. "The girl got on the bus," writes the author, but you know the shape of the girl and the color of the bus. The author who does too much for you by overworking the details leaves you cold, or perhaps fatigued. You want to collaborate, to fill in what's not spelled out. The book is as much yours as the author's, and may become so much yours that you remember it long after the author has forgotten it.

I know things about Shakespeare that Shakespeare never knew, about Robert Frost that Robert Frost never knew, and about John F. Kennedy that Kennedy never knew. Already you know things about me that I may never know. I cannot possibly guess or imagine what you will do in the privacy of your mind with the thoughts that I put on paper. I have learned through bitter experience, though, that sometimes interpretations concocted in my readers' minds will reach out and bite me, inflicting wounds that may take some time in the recovery room. This is true of all writers. Some have been executed for what they wrote, some ostracized or reviled, some elevated to the level of saints, and some worshipped for a while and then retired into oblivion.

One writer, when asked, "How do you know when you have written well?" replied, "You never do." The habitat of the writer is in a life doomed forever to uncertainty. The plight of the reader is never to know absolutely what a book really says or means.

All we can do is grasp at meanings and do the best we can with them.

The Economic Need for Good Reading Instruction

Formal education necessarily begins with the teaching of reading, and for some time I have devoted most of my energies to building a system of reading instruction that can produce close to a 100 percent success rate in teaching the mechanics of learning to read.

There's no use at all in this, however, unless the process engages the mind so that the result in later years will be intelligent behavior of the type that is both commercially viable and morally and ethically acceptable.

It might surprise you to think of the teaching of reading as an economic activity. It will perhaps surprise you even more to learn that in some places they calculate the future need for prison cells based on the reading scores of first graders.

Whether we end up as rich, poor, beggars or thieves has everything to do with how well we learn to read. If we learn to read well all kinds of other opportunities open up for us and our lives are enriched in every conceivable way. If we do not, the chances are we'll live much more isolated and less satisfying lives. So depriving people of the opportunity to learn to read, for whatever reason this happens, is one of the most abusive things a society can do to its citizens.[13]

Schools are going to have to train people not just to get jobs, but to serve the larger community with wisdom and insight. The development of wisdom and insight has never before been a function of public education, which has concentrated mostly on teaching people to follow directions, show up on time, and avoid rocking the boat. Now, however, many public schools are awakening to the challenge that is inevitably going to be required of them, and they are beginning to teach wisdom and insight with a great deal of success in some areas. Their future, however, necessarily requires that they succeed in this mission with all of their students.[14]

So a different way of reading, thinking and communicating must now come to the fore, one that, in many respects, reverses what has been taught in the past about reading and about the teaching of reading. We can no longer afford to read for information alone, we must now learn to read in order to become wiser.

All that I have said above is meant to explain why what you will find in these pages sometimes runs counter to the current wisdom about reading instruction. I say that with reservation, since the reading program I and my colleagues have developed for use in schools makes instant sense to most reading experts and seems to them to meet a need that has been unfulfilled until now in the teaching of elementary reading skills.

What's missing, and what's needed, is, first, a completely reliable way of developing word attack skills. This must be accomplished in such a way that the progression from decoding words through spelling analysis to sight recognition can progress as efficiently as possible. The second thing needed is a guarantee that throughout the process of learning to recognize and read words, there's never any doubt that comprehension of meanings is always being explored as well. The purpose of this book is to provide some guidelines for meeting such a goal so that, from the beginning, we can build the foundation that will take us all the way to the height of our potential. This book is for everyone who cares about reading, how it happens, what it can accomplish, and how it can be improved. That should include parents, teachers, policymakers and everyone else who has ever picked up a book and become lost in it, only to wonder why that isn't possible for everyone. Reading, more than any other single activity that we engage in, enables us to grow and improve ourselves in unpredictably wonderful ways.

2

A Civilization Challenged to Literacy

Why do so many of us have trouble learning to read, and why can this problem so easily be fixed?

You and I live in a world so defined by language that without it we are helpless. Just how much language defines and even controls our world is something that we seldom pause to appreciate. The physical environment seems real and pervasive. The environment created by the mind seems little more than a phantom or a dream.[1] Yet outside of the mind's environment, human beings can barely exist. The passages to heaven or to hell are paved not with stones but with words. Consider what happens when you step across the border between the United States and Mexico. In doing so, you take one small step with your body and one giant step with your mind. Your body has merely moved a few inches, a few feet or part of a mile. Your mind is forced to redefine itself and its surroundings almost entirely. You were in your own country, now you are a foreigner (or vice versa). The language in which you are expected to communicate is no longer the same. With the language go all kinds of hidden dimensions determined by cultural expectations that words themselves can scarcely reveal, even though they are the carriers of them. The laws that govern your actions are different, as are the political and social conditions. It may be that you can no longer read many of the signs or newspapers or books.

The change in the mental landscape as one passes back and forth between two radically different countries and cultures is far less significant, however, than the differences in the mental landscape for those who can read versus those who can't.

A person who cannot read cannot access most of the delights that civilization makes possible. Such a person cannot participate in the dialogue carried out among people all over the world, whether it's through the letters to the editor in the local newspaper, through e-mail on the Internet, or in the form of a college seminar on some arcane but fascinating topic. For such a person rich communication is possible, but only within the local community.[2] The average person has had to deal with written texts only since the invention and subsequent widespread use of the printing press; so really, reading things that are printed is an activity that became a concern for most people only about five hundred years ago.

Problems with Early Reading Instruction

Reading problems can be understood only by realizing that reading text is a process of interpreting an extremely subtle code. This requires skills that human beings as a group have known about for less than ten thousand years and have used widely only in recent history. Because reading is a human skill that is very, very new, it is hardly understood at all. That's one of the reasons why learning to read is so much more of a challenge than learning to speak your native language. It is an activity to which your body-mind system is not yet very well adapted. That's why nearly all of us are relatively poor readers compared to what we might have become.

Over and over again I have reviewed the very expensive materials developed by publishers to introduce children to reading. I have been appalled at them for their insensitivity to the inherent problems of confronting print for the first time. What is obvious to the experienced teacher is often confusing to the beginning reader. Teachers and curriculum designers should know this, but for some reason it isn't widely understood. Too many who produce books designed to teach reading have never developed the ability to imagine what it's like actually not being able to read.

In many cases people with poor reading ability are not strong in the kind of intelligence that is most likely to dominate the teaching and curriculum-development professions. A high percentage of those who fail to learn to read are kinesthetic learners. A very low percentage of teachers and curriculum developers are kinesthetic learners. So there is a mismatch of learning/teaching style; and the sad thing is that educational research has studied this mismatch so very little that it goes mostly unnoticed. The result is that primary reading materials tend to become more unsuitable as they become more expensive.

A simplified form of this dilemma was revealed in Bettelheim and Zelan's book mentioned in the previous chapter. In it they discuss the pattern that developed when it was discovered that the old and very interesting "McGuffy Readers" weren't successful in teaching everyone.

In order to increase the success rate, the vocabulary of primers that came along later was simplified and the subjects made more vacuous. As a result, fewer people learned to read. So the publishers simplified vocabulary still more and made the stories even more vacuous, and success rates went down even further.

No one thought to ask why.

One of the causes of this phenomenon was that learners take reading very seriously, but if the content itself is boring or trivial it disappoints them and they lose interest. That's not the whole story of what happened with these readers, but it indicates the level of insight that goes into most commercial products developed for schools for use with beginning learners.[3]

This hasn't improved over time. Recently I watched a first grader working with a computer program designed to teach the skill of categorizing things. Pictures of birds appeared on the screen, and the student was asked to pick out all the birds that were green and put them in a trash can.

The educators who designed this program evidently thought that a child who can select the green birds understands the concept of "green." It did not occur to them that the child is also learning that what you do with birds is throw them away—a strange way to think about our respectable fellow creatures or about ecological issues.

Hidden Confusions in Print

But even beyond the inadequacies in educational theory, print itself seems designed to confuse the young reader. The average primer gives beginners no idea what particular letters are doing in the words in which they appear and why. It distracts the reader with all sorts of irrelevant issues. It attempts to seduce the reader into wanting to read, not realizing that all children, by virtue of their humanity, want to read, if only they can figure out how to do so. Trying to seduce a child into the act of reading is intellectual harassment.[4] Whenever I have sat down with an elementary school principal and we have gone over such materials together, the principal has revealed to me that he or she has always wondered why all those confusing pictures and boxes and other patterns are necessary in beginning readers. It usually hasn't occurred to him or her that that's so the publisher can charge more for the books.

Training in reading instruction is even worse, however. Teachers are instructed to do so many different and often contradictory things in their classes that it is impossible to imagine how any rational human being could keep it all straight. Certainly the emphasis on a wide range of confusing techniques has the effect of blinding the teacher to any possible communication with the minds of the students in front of her. She is far too busy trying to remember what the teacher's manual said to do next. She might get it all straight after she has taught the course about fifty times, but by then it will have gone through endless modifications as teaching trends and fashions change with the political climate.

Learning to read is essentially a very straightforward process of matching graphic symbols with sounds. Complicating it with all sorts of ingenious tricks like looking at pictures for clues, or looking at the beginning and ending letters and trying to guess what's in the middle is nothing short of madness. It shows that the people who thought up these techniques have no memory of what they had to do themselves in order to learn to read, and have allowed themselves to fantasize that children are a species quite inhuman.[5]

All of this confusion is perpetuated by teachers' colleges loaded down with "experts" who promote conflicting theories about reading, which no two people seem to agree about unless they have made a political arrangement to do so. Whatever the research one camp of experts offers, another finds fault with it immediately, so that an innocent bystander can only conclude that reading instruction is a subject about which the experts are constitutionally unable to make up their minds.[6]

This same situation existed in 1942 when I was being taught to read. I remember my mother complaining about it when I was a child. The difficulty seemed to have arisen toward the close of the nineteenth century when reading instructors began to speculate about the relationship between early experiences with print and adult reading. It seemed as if adults read by recognizing whole words. Thus, they reasoned, children ought to be taught to read that way from the beginning.[7] As this heretical notion spread, large numbers of teachers dispensed with the boring drills on phonics that had always been used before. Scarcely anyone noticed that, as a result, a sizably larger proportion of the student population developed reading difficulties.

The system used to teach word recognition needs to be the best that can be discovered. However, the problem of illiteracy is also a good deal more subtle than the failure to teach individual word recognition. There remain two other stumbling blocks to the development of engaged, imaginative reading skill.

The first concerns reading readiness and how the eyes may easily get out of whack if they undertake the wrong kinds of activity too soon.

The second concerns the difference between the way children learn to speak and the way they are almost always taught to read. That difference boils down to the power of creating one's "self." As an infant, I created language for myself out of the background noise around me. Every new word I acquired was the result of an attempt to communicate that originated deep inside of me. I was (like all children) hungry for new ways to say things. Everything I said, or that anyone said to me, seemed to be of the greatest importance and central to my experience of life.

As I grew older, my mother read to me frequently. She was an extremely literate person who believed that a child should absorb the niceties of prose and poetry at an early age. The children's book authors I listened to were classics: Robert Lewis Stevenson, A. A. Milne and P. L. Travers, author of the *Mary Poppins* trilogy. One of my most vivid memories is of Mary Poppins flying in on an umbrella for her job interview with Mr. Banks in brilliant black-and-white on the page of the book.

The way my mother read to me and the way she conveyed her deep appreciation for the *bon mot* inspired in me an early desire to be a writer myself. I was not, however, one of those children who automatically learned to read just by being read to. I had to get formal instruction in first grade.

Unfortunately, though, the books I read in first grade were nothing like the books my mother had read to me. For one thing, they had pictures in vivid color, pictures that had nothing of the droll humor of those in the books I'd experienced at home, which inspired the most vivid fantasies by their suggestive incompleteness. No, the pictures in my schoolbooks were of boys and girls supposedly like those in my neighborhood, except that they were so synthetic and so lacking in the details of character that distinguish all real people and characters in good books they couldn't possibly have had a governess that flew in on an umbrella or toys that talked and got their feelings hurt. Those children did the most mundane things imaginable, and while they were superficially like the children in my neighborhood in that they were white and lived in houses with yards like mine, they were no more like me beneath the surface than if they had been manufactured by Sears.

Nothing that happened in first grade inspired me to deal with the process of learning to read the way I had learned to talk. I was expected to sound the words correctly, but nothing was said about their meanings; or if it was, the meanings were so boring that there was nowhere for the mind to take them.

As a result I formed a habit then that I am still trying to get rid of now. I learned at a very basic level that reading is purely a matter of recognizing words. So if I can recognize all the words on a page of print, my mind tells me I have read that page, even if I haven't the slightest idea what it says.

What Needs to Be Fixed in Reading Instruction

It is time for a reassessment of this kind of instruction. We should, from the very first word that we read, be engaged by what it has to say about our personal experiences. No child should be asked to read a sentence that doesn't lead to a discussion and speculation about its personal meaning.

Recognizing all the words on the page is a *sine qua non*, but there is a lot more to it than that. It isn't about whether the building described in the paragraph is eight or ten stories tall, it's about whether that building is a thing of beauty and a joy forever. It's about whether in that building you will discover the answer to a question that has always troubled you. It's about whether in the process of trying to answer that question you will be held hostage by dragons that are hiding in the cellar. In short, it's about how that building, and everything else in that paragraph, plays out its role in the fantasies it inspires while you read.

If nothing is going through your mind except words, then reading practice has been deadly. We should never have to confront print without being invited to ask what it has to say. And we should always understand what we are looking at before we go on to something else.

If reading is, at the same time, a totally logical experience and one that inspires the growth of the soul, then it has been well taught. If not, then something is lacking from the methods that taught us how to read.

Larger Consequences of Inadequate Literacy

Evidence that something has been lacking is all around us. As a nation we live as if we didn't understand even the most fundamental questions that affect our well-being. We accept language usage that is appallingly free of any kind of logical structure or coherent meaning. The kind of language usage that George Orwell predicted in his anti-utopian *1984* is all around us. It is an indication that, from the perspective of our culture as a whole, scarcely anyone is thinking well about anything. This language is a product of a nation that has been taught to read without attending to the implications of the text that is under consideration.[8]

We have come to the point where our survival as a species is at stake. We must learn to use language much more effectively than we do now, and this means that we must all learn or relearn to read so that we are critically engaged by everything that our eyes confront. Otherwise we have used the ideal of public education only to dull the minds of an entire nation.[9]

As things stand now, reading instruction is usually chaotic because of a paucity of reasonable hypotheses about how people can and should learn to read. We need to test those hypotheses and find out which methods of teaching reading work in the most difficult cases. Those methods should be universally adopted.

Only when this has happened will our nation solve its reading problems, which are at the root of all the rest of its problems. I believe that such a solution is within reach, and that therefore the present generation has the potential of producing a Golden Age that may well prove superior to any such age that has existed or been imagined. We shall not have anything like that, however, if we continue to behave in the nonthinking ways that characterize what social critic David Halberstam has identified in his book *The Best and the Brightest*.[10] Both leaders and ordinary citizens must learn the proper relationship between words in print and what may take place in the mind that contemplates them.

3

The Birth of
Awareness

*What are the components of awareness, and how do
they unfold themselves?*

"I am."

These two words express the profoundest mystery and the greatest miracle in the universe. They suggest the experience of fundamental awareness that precedes self-consciousness, an awareness merely of existence itself. Try to imagine that first instant in your life when you became aware, without any idea of what it was you were aware of—or even who you were. Surely this moment, emerging gradually out of nothingness, happened at some point before you were born. You were simply there, without yet any notion of what it meant to be you, as opposed to something or someone else.

Then, over time, the sentence "I am" got connected with another word: "me."

"I am me," you could think, and know that there was something out there that was *not* you. This something may have been your mother, who emerged into your awareness as more than just a source of warmth, food and physical contact. Your mother became known to you as an entity that you could not control. When she was unavailable, you cried. This was your means of telling the world that you were separated from something you wanted. For the world of you was automatically under your control (or at least you had that illusion), but the world beyond you was not. As soon as you found out there was something you could not control, you were determined to try your best to control it. The "I" reached out into the surrounding world and staked out its territory by any means it could think of.

In a sense, that's the end of the story. Our world is there, complete and furnished, once we've distinguished the world that is "me" from the world that is "out there." That's how people have lived for most of the time they have been on this earth. They grew up into a world that was externally defined for them, and they stayed there. As far as they were concerned, their world was the entire world. That's why strangers were so threatening, for they came from an alien world beyond understanding. The rules and customs of that world were beyond their ken, so the only way to treat aliens was to exterminate them.

But eventually a time came when individuals could write down their experiences and tell of the different worlds in which they had lived. Over the centuries this built up cultural awarenesses that extended farther and farther beyond the tight little awareness of the immediate community. Now what had to be learned was not just the tribal customs that stretched back unchanged for thousands of years. It was an historical record full of much that was strange and different, for the world of the past and future was no longer conceived to be exactly like the world of the present. This world beyond what could be immediately experienced became a world apart from the self and the community, an expanded third world. With the dawn of each new age, it became increasingly important to understand what that expanded world was like, how far it extended, and how one should relate to it.

Information about that third world had to be learned either from books or voyages of exploration. For a long time after writing was invented it was practiced and valued only by the privileged few. These were the people who understood the secrets of life as recorded in sacred books and epics. They frequently used them to exert power over others.

Finally, though, with the invention of the printing press, this third world became accessible to everyone who could learn to read, so reading came to be perceived as essential to a full and successful life.

This book is about that third world, how we learn to enter it, what we can do with it, and how we might want to think about it. It is about a new kind of control that extends outward from ourselves, outward beyond our community, to a body of knowledge that can be grasped with our minds. This body of knowledge may be traced back for thousands of years. Each of us can stake out territory to be brought under personal control. It is no longer necessary to conquer some little plot of ground to prove our supremacy—we can become the world's greatest experts on a certain type of cheese, on how craters form on the moon, or on pre-Raphaelite art.[1] This conquerable territory that is accessible to each of us is part of the landscape of the mind. Our brains are designed to encompass it, and in the earliest years of our childhoods, we begin to reach out to do just that.

So as we grow older, we learn not only about the furniture in our houses and the people on the street where we live, but also about the stories that are told or read to us, stories about fantastic things happening in far away places; and we come to know some of them so well that we can repeat them word for word. We learn that the geography of the mind contains something of real geography, and something of the geography of the imagination. The Land of Oz may seem more real to us than China.

Expanding Our Territories

Let's explore, beginning with an infant's awareness, how intellectual territory begins to take shape. For it is an expression of the territorial imperative that was born in the minds of our primate ancestors, which now can be conquered bloodlessly and without malice as we move into all that lies waiting to be understood by our grasping minds.

One way to exercise control is to hold onto something and cry if it is taken away. By mastering the great range of emotions we can deploy in our human interactions, we learn how to have an influence on the world around us. As infants, we notice that when we cry, someone usually tries to console us. So we use our emotions to control the responses of others, pushing their buttons much as we might push the buttons on an elevator. At first these emotions are simple and direct. But crying and being consoled is only a small part of the infant's experience, for emotion is undifferentiated and nondescript without language to plot the features of its geography. Over time, with language development to guide them, our feelings become subtle and finely shaded. When we express our emotions persuasively and distinctly, we can move other people to action. We learn that our emotions may have an even greater impact on others if we express them as poetry and painting than if we express them directly.

But our emotions have no meaning in isolation. They must be compared with those of others. From the poets, the novelists and the dramatists we learn what it is possible to feel. The expression of authors feeds the language of our internal dialogue. Their means of reaching out inspire in us new skills for making our own conquests of experience.

If you know all about the sufferings of characters such as the Bobbsey Twins, Becky Sharp and Hamlet, your own sufferings are no longer isolated. You are part of a great community of characters who have addressed the problems you have addressed and solved the problems you intend to solve. If you have fought with the Teenage Mutant Ninja Turtles, Ivanhoe and King Henry V, you can feel the taste of victory, the scorn for the vanquished, and the satisfaction of having done what you set out to do. Through reading you can explore the depth and breadth of emotion that words can convey, and thus enhance your power to communicate with and influence others.

Another way to exert control is to give something to someone and then to take it back. Here is the difference between aggression and sharing. As babies, we lure those around us into practicing negotiation. We give and take and ask for more, and sometimes we demand more. Our elders seek to appease us by redirecting our attention away from whatever, at the moment, we cannot control and onto something within our grasp. Thus we learn about our limits. We also learn that suffering is acting and acting is suffering, that we need not stay isolated in our interior pain but can reach out into communally shared mutual support as we claim our rightful place.

The grasping, giving and taking are at first expressed only in gesture. But the gestures become platforms on which to build language. Reaching out toward something is gradually transformed into the sentence "Give me that toy."

Watch a newborn infant in the crib, and you will see that the process of learning control is already underway as the foundations for language are being built. The baby is thinking, "There is something floating out there in space: my hands. Gradually these get connected to me as I learn that I can control them, and in fact that I am controlling them."

What we see the infant seeing is the object that appears to be floating: the hand, getting gradually connected to an awareness inside the self that is truly the sixth of our seven senses. This is the body's knowledge of where in space the hand is located. Our muscles have internal sensory mechanisms for this.

Consider the simple act of reaching out for an object and grasping it.

You can see where it is with your eyes, but how do you make your hand go to that place?

To get a feel for the problem, close your eyes and walk around the room. Without your eyes to guide you, your body has to grope its way.

But how do the eyes and body coordinate their efforts?

There are two ways of assessing space—one with what the eyes see, and the other with that internal sensory process in the muscles called *kinesthesia*. Kinesthesia is not even listed among the five senses you learned in school. It is not the tactile sense; it's not connected with touching. It is the sense of knowing where a part of your body is. When it operates perfectly, your hands know, without knowing how they know, where the baseball is as you move in to catch a pop fly.

Kinesthesia, Balance and Synesthesia

Connecting vision with kinesthesia is a first exercise in *synesthesia*: the awareness that two or more of the seven senses (did I forget to mention that balance is one of them, too, different from kinesthesia?) can be perceived as one. Early experiments with your body and how it interacts with the world serve to establish a great deal of synesthesia (which means, literally, "sensing together"). While vision and kinesthesia are becoming one, so are taste and smell. Color and sound gradually get connected, and some colors get connected with some tastes. There are even cross-references within a particular sense, such as "sky-blue pink."

The sense of balance, which is engineered by the body's vestibular system, is the source of most of our attention in those early years of life, during which we learn to rock, then to crawl, and finally to get up on our legs and move about.

It turns out that the two senses we didn't learn about in school are actually our two most basic senses. The first of the two, kinesthesia, is the first sense of which the infant can become aware. We start to notice it when we begin to kick and suck our thumbs at about the fetal age of seven months. The other, balance, becomes the most important sense of all during the period we are learning to stand and walk.

In fact, the sense of balance is so fundamental that it is synesthesized not only into all our other sensory perceptions, but into all our concepts as well. So all-consuming is this endeavor and its resulting discoveries during the period in our development when awareness is shaping the intellectual world for the first time, that everything in life eventually gets compared to that primary urge to keep our balance while walking, running and jumping. There is no idea about anything that is not somehow infused with the sense of balance. It is this sense (far more important in our development than in that of any animal that walks on all fours) that pushes the mind toward becoming human. It underlies the notion of fairness, which is the first moral concern a young child develops. Eventually it becomes fundamental to the construction of a sentence containing both a subject and a predicate, to the composition of a painting, to the balance that is heard in harmonic proportions; to the notion of a balanced diet, the balanced personality, or the balance of powers in government.

When we approach the world looking everywhere for balance, we define ourselves as human. We do so because we are two-legged creatures who impose the awarenesses resulting from our greatest, most difficult developmental struggle upon everything that we see around us. Balance may or may not be the primary concern of the universe itself, but because we are incapable of conceiving of a universe in which it is not primary, this is the universe we have discovered, and the one we continue to explore.[2]

Everything you do, everything you think about, every relationship you have, even every bodily process you become aware of, is an exercise in self-awareness. This awareness is perhaps the greatest miracle of all that nature has accomplished, for it is synthesized out of an impossibly large number of separate and discreet elements. It is truly an experience of *e pluribus unum* without which you could not exist.

If you examine the brain closely, you will find that it is made up of an indescribably large number of subsystems, all of which have to coordinate their efforts with one another. As you imagine a movie in your head while reading, you're developing a huge synesthetic tapestry. You can see characters moving around up there on the screen, balancing themselves and their concerns in a world that includes music and logic, interpersonal and intrapersonal issues, all of it spun out with naturalistic patterns and philosophical implications that you have recognized and captured from the real life being lived out around you.

Confronting the expression on the face of a new baby, you interpret its contortions as if they are linguistic and logical statements. You hypothesize its future as if it were a part of the developing socioeconomic culture of its time. You observe the colors of its clothes merging in your mind with the music of its babbles and the myriad acceptances and rejections it gives you personally as it does or does not grab onto your finger.

The World Order in the Brain

Imagine for a moment what it would be like if every person in the world were to become capable of working in complete harmony with every other person. Imagine a world with no wars, political conflicts, uncooperative people or dissidence of any kind. Imagine, too, that it all governs itself, without anyone having to keep anything in line. There are no punishments, no prisons and no executions.

Such a world could come about far more easily than the human brain has, for the six billion people that make up the world population are a tiny smidgen compared to all the cells in the human brain that have to get along just about perfectly in order for you to establish a sense of self—of being one person. Furthermore, each of these brain cells "knows" a great many more other brain cells than you know people. The social discourse among them is incredibly complicated, even from the point of view of a single neuron. Some live next door and are contacted with jumps of electrical impulses across synapses. Others live across the brain and are reached by a chemical spray shot out into the community of cells.

There's no accident in this analogy. The social struggles we go through in life are largely an attempt to re-create in the social world the kinds of things that are happening in the neurological one inside our skulls. Social ecology is remarkably similar to that of the neurological world. Social conflicts bear a remarkable resemblance to neurotic conflicts. Societies that destroy themselves are not dissimilar to people who destroy themselves.

Now, just as in the social world, we have experts in the sciences and the arts, outstanding athletes, brilliant mathematicians, great poets, fine psychotherapists and so on; in our brains we also have "experts" in all these different areas. Portions of the brain are finely tuned to see the world logically from the point of view of a football player, a poet or a symphonist.

And just as the physicist may double as a poet, and the musician may be an engineer, so the parts of our brains that specialize in these skills communicate in an overlapping way with parts of the brain that specialize in other skills. The result is synesthesia, the coming together of different sensory inputs like elements forming a compound. When Keats wrote the phrase "tender is the night," he used a synesthetic poetic image. Our minds could not grasp it if much of our brain activity did not operate synesthetically.

In fact, without synesthesia, we could not have self-awareness, for that is the ultimate synesthesia. Self-awareness arises from a process that takes all the different kinds of sensory experiences we learn to value and melds them into a single entity that learns to say, "I am."

When, in infancy, you begin to take in the pieces of your environment: Mommy, the stove, the dog, the television set, pretty things, clouds and so on, you at first see all of these as separate entities unto themselves, but over time they become blended into a synesthetic world, which is the world you create for yourself to live in. This world, for example, probably does not include the recognition that insects, being in plentiful supply, are an excellent food source and might be delectable coated with chocolate. You probably don't live in a world in which respect for the dead is best paid by allowing them to decay in your backyard long enough so you can drink the liquid that accumulates in their shrunken bodies in order to enhance your personal strength.

Because your world doesn't include these things, you either don't consider them, or, if you do, you regard them with revulsion. And so your world comes to include them in a negative sense. But that's your world. You created it, and if you want to, you can change it.

Expanding the Environment

Books are among the primary means by which you can learn to change your world. Books allow you to explore what it would be like to change the synesthetic units you have built and incorporated into your sense of self, in order to see what it might be like to be someone a little different. Perhaps in the past you listened to some music, looked at some paintings, or read some poetry that you really didn't like. But later you discovered the beauty in these works of art. You learned to love them. You learned something new about beauty, and began to sense the kind of beautiful world in which the artist who created each of them had lived. Thus your way of feeling changes and grows with new experiences, some of which teach you to perceive things differently.

Changes also occur in your conceptions of the world and your motivations in life. You might, for example, read the autobiography of a great artist and decide you'd like to be one, too.

You might read about life in a foreign country and decide you'd like to go there.

You might read about a new way to dress and decide to redesign your wardrobe.

You could learn about all these things in other ways, too, but books are the most immediately available resource for doing that. Every time you are struck by something new in what you read, you have a chance to expand your synesthetic mental models—to hear something, for example, in terms of its color, to imagine moving in a way that is more logical, or to consider that the taste of a new kind of food might transform your spiritual experiences.

In a way, language itself is a synesthetic experience. Through language you can represent and mentally re-create a multitude of sensations. You have heard the babbling of an infant. This is primarily a musical experience. The infant is exploring the creative possibilities of sound. Eventually some of these sounds mimic those used by others and become tools for communication. A word that was a sound may turn into a tactile experience: "sticky," or a visual experience: "green" or "green truck," or a visceral experience: "yucky" or "I get chills just thinking about it"—this last example is not a word, but a cliché, which is a sort of extended word.

The green truck may become a kinesthetic experience as you move it around with your hand and then move your body like a truck. Then it all returns to sound again, as you make the sounds of the truck.

Images into Words

Language, starting from abstract sound, quickly becomes the tool for keeping track of and filing away all those experiences, so much easier to remember when they have names. The words stand for and invoke things, and eventually almost *become* the things. The words also invoke images in the mind; so, as words are heard, images arise. These can then be manipulated into new forms and cause a child to spout new words, never heard nor spoken before:

"Me want truck."

(Looking at a torn photograph): "Mommy is broken."

(After a balloon pops in the distance): "Green all gone," or "Bye-bye, green."

The child invents language more than imitates it, and then aligns the inventions with what is socially acceptable. That's why no two people speak exactly the same language. You can tell your favorite authors apart because (if they're really good) the language they use is unique to them: "groovy," "the peripatetics of long-haired aesthetics," "it is miching malecho, it means mischief," "just the facts, ma'am, just the facts," "yadda, yadda, yadda."

In using language to reach out and grasp the world outside in order to put it inside, we invent the world. The world inside is the one we have created for ourselves. We are constantly improving on that invention, but that world is, for us, the only reality, and we will believe in it and act on it at the expense of everything else.

So gradually, through repetition and repeated association, words take on many of the qualities of the things or ideas to which they refer. Over time the use of words in laws and governmental systems is sufficient to provide whole structures and series of actions that exist only as language. There is no such thing, for example, as a corporation, except insofar as it is a series of letters arranged in a certain way on a piece of paper or preserved in some other medium. Yet corporations, which exist purely in the collective imagination of the people who read certain arrangements of words, can make tremendous fortunes and can do a great deal of good or harm in the world. Eventually the statement "I am" is transformed into "I am the word." Language, it seems, becomes the primary instrument of defining who you are.

Human beings consider it noble to die for the world they believe in. They often do not believe they have committed a crime when they are sentenced to life imprisonment because, in the context of their world, what they did wasn't a crime, or didn't happen at all. If you refuse to let something into your awareness, it simply doesn't exist.

To Galileo the mountains on the moon existed. To the Pope they did not. This wasn't a dispute. It was the inevitable consequence of the fact that they lived in different worlds with different realities, and each of them lived in the only reality that could possibly exist. There was equal integrity on both sides of the argument.

Your self will build its own reality. You might want to consider keeping that flexible, because you'll have more fun that way and be less likely to die for a cause that everyone else thinks is absurd.

No matter how flexible you learn to be, however, you'll find that you cannot look upon or do anything without connecting it somehow with yourself. You've probably already pointed out to yourself that you don't eat chocolate-covered cockroaches. But now their image is inside you. The picture is indelible. You can't get rid of it. It is part of the alien world you choose not to enter: the antithesis of you, which is as much a part of you as the world you welcome into yourself. Some of us may even become more those things we resist than ourselves simply because we allow them into our awareness. Think, for example, of the Salem witch-hunters.

The Fraud of Objectivity

As quantum physics have been trying to teach us for a long time, the notion of objectivity that supposedly underlies science and education is a fraud. We are, in fact, creatures who reach out into the world from the privacy of our own experiences. Our thoughts and our language are based on that, and it is with considerable effort that we become socialized enough to share experiences that seem to have common ground, giving rise to the illusion of objectivity. It is out of this struggle to socialize our inner experiences that the impulse to create language is born. And it is out of this urge to construct ourselves that we read.

Aside from the very primitive use of language that some primates have been taught to engage in, and the even more primitive use of it that pets use in communicating with people, humans are the only creatures that can symbolize the outside world in millions of ways and thus bring it inside themselves in a form that can be manipulated independently of whatever might be happening on the outside. They use language to do this. Whether it seems to describe what they can imagine seeing directly before their eyes, or takes them off into speculations that may lead to the creation of things never heard of or thought about before, language is a tool by which the mind is able to make these transformations.

The average person can recognize the meaning of about sixty thousand lexical units.[3] Shakespeare, the English writer with the largest vocabulary, used about thirty thousand lexical units. Sir Walter Scott, the runner-up in the big vocabulary sweepstakes, used slightly over half as many words as Shakespeare.[4] Most writers use about five thousand words or fewer in their entire output. Making and using words is a human instinct. If we have the sense of hearing, we learn to do this with sound. If we do not, we learn to do it with signs that can be either seen or felt.

Obviously, we can recognize many words that do not show up in our ordinary conversations. For example, we may know what an azure sky is but may be unlikely to point out to a friend that "the sky is particularly azure today."[5]

In writing the phrase "amber waves of grain," I find myself realizing, for the first time, that "amber" means the kind of yellow we see in actual amber, so the word is almost a metaphor when it refers to grain. I am able, when I put my attention there, to work out the meaning of "amber" in this most familiar phrase, but I have never consciously done so until this moment in writing about it. Until now "amber waves of grain" was a group of words that resounded in my mind more or less the way the sound "el-em-e-no" does in the mind of a child singing the alphabet song, who has not yet disentangled these sounds to refer to particular letters. A year ago I noticed, for the first time, that "cigarette" means "little cigar." It took me more than half a century of familiarity with these words to happen to notice this connection between them.

Our Different Vocabularies

Everyone has at least three different vocabularies. First, there are the words used for their sound values alone, which have no meanings apart from that. These words occur only in the phrases in which they are normally used, and their meanings are more visceral than conceptual. Few, for example, can define the actual meaning of "good-bye." *Webster's Third New International Dictionary* tells me that it is a contraction of "God be with you," but I disagree because its source is more closely connected to the evolution of our language. The contraction occurred when people were still saying, "God be with ye," otherwise we would say, "Good boo" or "Good bew." Also, at the time the contraction appeared in the language, "God" was pronounced "Gud."

In contemporary usage, though, the phrase "good-bye" has no meaning at all. It is a conventional sound made at the end of a visit or a telephone conversation, and has no more referential meaning than a handshake or the period at the end of a sentence. It is a kind of non-referential conversational syntax. This tells us something about how language got started in the first place. I am constantly reminded as I listen to the noises my dog makes of how human they sound. They are expressive in the same way a baby's sounds are expressive, or even those of an adult who is too overcome with emotion to use words at all.

Next, there are the words we can use to express ourselves without thinking about word choice. When only these words are used, they flow from the mouth without our thinking about how to organize them. We say what we have to say, and often don't know what we are going to say until we have said it.[6]

And finally, there are words we can recognize but cannot use without straining to recall them, consulting a thesaurus, or otherwise looking for them. These words are not yet fully incorporated into the self, and many of them never will be. They are often distancing words—words used by others, which we would not use ourselves, because they are in the wrong dialect, because they are more erudite than we are, or for many other reasons. So there are the words of the self and words used only (or primarily) by others.

In addition, language uses two general kinds of reference in communicating. One is to external objects and ideas, like "table," "door," "theory of relativity" or "supercalifragilisticexpialidocious." (No one knows what this last word means, but everyone gets the general idea that it refers to some quality of experience, the way "delicious" does.)

The other kind is about the self referring to or describing its experience of an outside element:

"I could just kill you."

"You are as sweet as peaches in the juice."

"Why are you making the night hideous?"

These examples show language used to refer to an inner state, often with metaphors drawn from external objects or ideas. Whenever I try to tell someone how I feel, I am in a different position from pointing out something that we can both see, or have a shared experience of.

The situation gets even more complicated when I observe external clues that inform me of another person's internal state:

"The king is angry. See, he gnaws his lip."

This distinction between language that seems to refer to objective realities and language that attempts to express mysterious internal states is far more significant than we might think. In many political situations, efforts are made to disqualify statements that refer to internal states as if they had no meaning or value at all. The behaviorist school of psychology of the early 1900s denied the existence of subjective feelings. The political system in the Soviet Union attempted to deny the individual the right to have personal feelings. And in the corporate world it's sometimes considered bad form to tell anyone else how you feel.

By engaging in the myth of objectivity we sometimes attempt to eliminate from consideration the possibility of subjectivity, and this can have grave consequences. The human being who has no feeling, no internal state, no personal set of values, becomes an automaton, totally at the mercy of those who seek control.

Freedom and Objectivity

The object of a democratic society is not to control people, but to make room for their freedom. So education for democracy must necessarily balance subjective values with those that appear to be objective (even though they never are completely so because as observers we always see through our own subjective lens).[7]

Understanding that fact is fundamental to understanding how we learn, how we think, and how we read. The biggest fault in the educational system, beginning with the process of reading instruction, is the fraudulent notion of objectivity. It is a myth that was developed two and a half thousand years ago by the Greeks and has misled philosophers and scientists ever since. Modern physicists are well aware that there is no such thing. They know that the universe is a self-organizing system, and the most astute of them are beginning to notice that a universe that is not self-conscious cannot exist at all, for the notion of blind chance and accident cannot account for the development of the world we see around us.[8] If we continue to teach reading as if the minds of the students were superfluous, we will never be able to help our students read thoughtfully.

4

The Mystery and Miracle of Language

How do we develop our awareness of spoken and written language, and how are these awarenesses developed differently?

The greatest miracle in the universe is the miracle of language. Indeed, the universe itself might be said to consist of nothing but language.

In the beginning, everything that is now spread out through a trillion galaxies and a realm of space with a diameter of thirty billion light-years was once crowded into a space so tiny it could not be seen by the naked eye. This means that all of the matter, or "hard stuff," that comprises the universe can theoretically fit inside the head of a pin and get lost there. Everything else consists of active relationships that exist between the tiny, tiny particles that make up everything we think we see.

These relationships are governed by rules that are never broken, and the rules, taken all together, constitute a very complex language. This language is used to form the ninety-two elements found in nature, plus any additional ones that have been constructed in the laboratory. It is used to form the compounds that arise from relationships between these ninety-two elements. And it is used to form organisms that arise from the compounds. The organisms themselves are governed by a set of rules conveyed in a language that is called DNA. This language makes up a set of instructions used to create everything living, including your body and your brain.

You and I are, in some sense, microcosms of the universe. The capacity to learn the language we speak was programmed into our brains by our

DNA, and it embodies some of the rules that govern the structure of the universe itself. One of those rules dictates relationships between things or entities that have stability as well as the activities in which these entities may engage.

We can imagine the long process by which, over time, humans constructed more and more elaborate names for things and then began to articulate relationships by the order in which the names were arranged: "Me, Tarzan. You, Jane."

A simple sentence like "The dog ran down the street" conveys a relationship between two entities and one activity. The dog and the street are the entities, and the activity is running. The relationship is specified by "down," so the street exists for the dog to run down.

Any sentence we can think of can be broken into these relationships, which mirror the structure of relationships between the stable structures and activities that fill all of space. We exist in a world of dynamic relationships and our lives can continue only by understanding the activities of the world around us and within us. Ultimately we read in order to define and collect more and more examples of dynamic relationships and whatever stable patterns we can find in these relationships to allow us to chart a course in life. Fortunately, human language is a viable means to freeze and grasp relationships long enough for the mind to examine them consciously.

The Emergence of Linguistic Awareness

We use language to make us conscious of ourselves and of how we relate to those elements of the universe we become aware of. We do this by a process of gradually emerging awareness that begins prior to birth.

When a child is born, it already knows what a human face looks like, and it seeks out the face that will provide it with what it needs. It knows also that it has a body, because it has been using that body for several months to move around in the liquid that has surrounded it. It is already familiar with some of the sounds of language, heard in the background of the ever-present mother's heartbeat.

Music is an interplay between a series of sounds and a rhythm that gives them structure. The most basic rhythm is that of the heartbeat, and all other rhythms are variations on that. The individual notes rise and fall to convey feelings.

The basic feeling patterns that music and language share can be heard in the sounds of animals and cooing babies. You can tell the feeling conveyed in the sounds of a dog, a cat or a horse, and if you listen closely you will hear in them some of the patterns that form what we call "proto-speech."

Proto-speech is the flow of sound that later makes distinctions that we will come to call words. Babbling infants build their own vocabularies. They begin this process by instinctively perceiving a large number of sounds that delight them. Gradually they notice that a particular sound produces a desired response of some sort. This begins with cries and laughter. The hearing centers of the brain select out the sounds of language from a background of other sounds and interpret them according to a growing internal vocabulary list, which is based on the recognition of words the infant may not yet be ready to articulate.

An infant's babbling is similar, in many respects, to the sounds that other animals make, but much more versatile. Most animals can't encompass with their vocal apparatus many of the sounds that humans can make. Language begins, then, with vocal expressions of feeling, akin to the language of music. An expression like "oooey gooey" tells of a feeling. So does "yuck!" or "ouch!" There are no meanings here except the feelings directly conveyed in the sounds.

Visualize a child who wants something. The arm is outstretched, the fist clenched; the child whines aggressively, insisting on being given that thing. The sounds of the whining will survive into adulthood, greatly enhancing the meanings of words like these:

I want that.
Don't you dare.
Give me that.
Please.
Dad!
Dad?

Dad!!!

Stop!

Excuse me.

If you can, fit baby noises to these words; next, listen more carefully to dog and cat noises and, later, the noises of other animals, and you'll hear them there, too. Proto-speech is all around us. It is the expression of the spirit that longs to communicate something. Language is what the spirit is reaching out for, and what it finally produces.

As you try out in your imagination the words and phrases listed above, you can hear all sorts of different melodies that can accompany them to give them a variety and range of emotional meanings. There's the command, the pleading whine, the matter-of-fact statement, the expression of terror, and the seductive lure.

Thought and Word Order

A basic sentence expressing need and feeling might be: "You give me that." "You," "me" and "that" are the entities, and "gives" is the activity. The relationship this time isn't in a separate word, like "down" in the sentence about the dog. Rather, it's in the order of the words, which imply the relationship. "You" comes first, to get your attention. "Give" comes next, to state what must happen. Now as with the dog running down the street, "me" following "give" implies the direction of the action; in other words, the object ("that") must flow along a path that ends in "me" the same way the dog runs down the street. So "give" has two elements: It's the action you're going to perform and the direction that action will take. "That" identifies the object, but only when there is an external part of the sentence present. The person speaking has to point out what it is he or she wants, or "that" remains a mystery. For instance, "Give me that" written on a piece of paper is meaningless, for there is no way to know who "me" is, or what "that" is.

So when we use language, we normally use words to refer to something outside of what the words represent; and either word order or changes in the forms of words are used to indicate the relationships that exist among them. The rules of word order and the rules for changing the forms of words, such as when to use "I" and when to use "me," are coded into the brain instinctively.

In the sentence "I give you the book," the words "I," "give," "you" and "book" refer to objects or actions. "The" further defines "book." But if the sentence were written, "I give the book you," it would have a different meaning, and then another meaning after that.

Reading the first sentence, we visualize me passing the book over to you. The book receives the main action, but you complete it. The relationship between you and the book is defined by the order of the words, which is called "syntax."

In the second sentence we may visualize me handing *you* over to the book. This, under normal circumstances, doesn't make sense. The brain then makes the following observation: "This speaker is a foreigner who does not properly understand English syntax, so the sentence should read, 'I give you the book.'"

Culture and Instinct

Everyone learns to use language according to certain rules that define stable relationships. Children learn this unconsciously, while adults learning a foreign language must learn it consciously. No one knows exactly how this language instinct works, but we know that it works the same way in all human beings that have intact language functioning in their brains.[1] You don't have to teach a child its native language, it will instinctively learn it just by engaging in social relationships and mentally observing and implementing the patterns of language that guide them. Some errors in the use of language result from dialectical differences and are commonplace. For example, in Standard English "Me and Jimmy went to the movies" is incorrect because good manners dictate that just as I should hold the spoon in my soup so it faces away from me, so should I mention Jimmy before I mention myself. Modesty dictates this. And secondly, "me" is in the objective case, meaning it cannot be the subject of the sentence.

However, a dialect is possible in which "Me and Jimmy went to the movies" is correct, because the rule of modesty is regarded as silly, and everyone knows a word that begins a sentence has to be the subject. These distinctions are of a dialectical nature. They do not reflect on the language instinct itself. However, no native speaker of English will make the mistake of saying, "I give the book you." Only a foreigner who has not yet absorbed normal English syntax would make this mistake. In such a case a syntax learned in one language is superimposed on another.

In the same way, everyone knows that "Dog bites man" is not a newspaper headline and "Man bites dog" is. Each word order infers a context, or set of circumstances, that surrounds the sentence. No sentence can exist entirely by itself because the imagination of the listener or reader will rush in to fill the gap in meaning, painting a complete picture where before there were only a few strokes.

Sometimes we can play games with this tendency, writing sentences that have an impossible context, like "This statement is not true." This is the verbal equivalent of a print by M. C. Escher, which seems to have no beginning and no end.

Enter, Context

Language is not only about relationship; it is about relationship as it is defined by a particular set of circumstances, called the context—the many things that happen in the mind external to the spoken sentence that add to its meaning.

So we go from proto-language, which is a reaching out toward communication, to words that identify objects or actions immediately visible ("the dog is running down the street") to sentences that imply a context that can be imagined outside of the immediate realm in which the communication takes place ("I could easily guess who ate my chocolate pudding"). This progression is instinctive. It is a developmental process implied by the existence of the brain, just as an acorn implies an oak tree, or a combination of gases implies an explosion.

All children can develop language, but only if they are with other human beings. A child raised by animals in the woods will be unable to develop language. The opportunity to learn it is provided by the developmental process only for a relatively short period, and the developmental process can occur only in relationship to someone else, who can also invent and use language.[2]

But so instinctive is language, so much a part of the natural process of development, that children can develop it even if there are no adults around to teach it to them. A group of children from different cultures gathered in one locale will create a language of their own, which will be as rich and complex in its inflections as any language. Such a language is called a "creole." One example of it is Hawaiian Creole, which came into being when workers from many different foreign countries were brought into the same place. The adults under these circumstances learned a crude form of pidgin English, but the children invented their own highly inflected language.[3]

So language is an instinct that constitutes the means by which we can make the structure of the universe conscious of itself. There is a direct link between the language activities in the Big Bang, out of which the universe came, and the utterances of an infant as it is gradually transformed into the poetry of Shakespeare. Viewed retrospectively, such development appears logical and inevitable.[4]

Synthesizing Activity in the Brain

In order to learn language, the brain must connect speech, hearing, vision and kinesthetics in such a way that they coordinate perfectly. The speech centers of the brain cause the vocal mechanism to produce sounds selected from a vocabulary list and arranged according to rules of syntax. This comes about in the same way a child learns to identify details of the environment. At first everything is more or less a blur, aside from the human faces that are so important to survival. Gradually, with repeated exposure to the environment, distinctive visual patterns emerge from the blur and are connected with kinesthetic and tactile patterns as the child examines his or her surroundings with a mixture of delight and the greatest care.

Objects develop identity and acquire names. Close observation of children learning language reveals that the identity of an object and its name may be learned at the same time, or the name may be learned after the identity of the object has been experienced. However, it makes no sense to introduce the name and then show the object.[5]

For example, a child sees and experiences a chair and then learns the word for it. Or a parent may hold out an apple and say, "This is an apple." The parent, however, does not say "apple" several times and then produce an apple. That's because the word must be seen as a property of the object or experience, not the other way around. The word without the object is like a grin without a cat. The mind can't handle it.

This is a very important distinction because it reveals why so many people fail to learn all sorts of things, including how to read.

It's all too common for a teacher to say, "Today, children, we're going to learn about apples. Can you say 'apple'? Here's how apple is spelled." And so on.

Eventually the apple is produced, but by that time the name has taken on its own shape in the child's mind and no longer corresponds very well with the apple that is supplied. Teaching about relationships, such as why the apple turns brown when cut, presents even greater difficulty, if the person has no experience of the relationship under discussion.

Our knowledge of relationships is built up from a foundation of concrete physical experiences that we accumulate from birth. If we understand relationships we can express them with language. As our competency with language grows, the relationships implied by the words and word order emerge easily into understanding. It's when we don't understand the implied relationships that we have difficulty with interpreting speech and reading.

Teaching Concepts Experientially

All writers are familiar with the aphorism "Don't tell, show." By the same token, the teacher who gets up in front of the classroom and says, "Today we are going to learn about entropy" cuts off learning. We need to see and hear and experience entropy before we can talk about it. Otherwise, we never quite feel we understand it. So the teacher might say, "Today we are going to learn about why your room tends to get messy if you don't clean it up, which is a universal tendency called entropy." Now the word is plugged into personal experience, and it's possible to think about it and follow the lecture and ensuing discussion.

In teaching foreign languages we build up vocabularies in which words are used to define other words, and gestures are used to indicate relationships. As certain patterns are repeated, the words take on meanings to the point where they begin to invoke the thing or relationship itself. Eventually, the qualities of the thing can be transferred to the sounds representing it to such an extent that doing violence to the word itself is often equivalent to having done the deed. For example, if you're checking your bags in the airport, just try saying, "There's a bomb in my bag and I'm going to blow up the plane" and see what happens to you. You probably won't end up in the electric chair, but you won't be getting on the plane very soon either.

Experiential learning of this sort seldom occurs in the teaching of mathematics, where concepts must be experienced in terms of the self before they can be understood abstractly. A child who has cut a pie into equal-sized slices understands intuitively about division. But a child who has been told about division and taught to manipulate numbers without making a connection between what's happening with the numbers and the act of cutting the pie, dividing the marbles, or measuring the floor to determine what size rug to buy will never quite get the idea of what numbers are all about. That's why only 6 percent of the people who are taught mathematics ever really understand it.

You may have experienced the problem of learning the name before experiencing the object when you have heard a person's name many times, perhaps talked to that person on the phone, and then finally met the person. By that time you have an impression of what the person looks like and may be surprised by the face and body shape you actually see.

So the name should, whenever possible, accompany or follow the experience of the thing. This is the natural way that children learn language, up to the point when they begin to learn to read. It's only when they start reading that they begin the process of rather frequently encountering words that refer to things they have not experienced.

This is part of the problem that stands in the way of making a smooth transition from the spoken word to the written word.

Differences Between Language and Reading

By the time we are ready to start reading (which is long after we have begun using language in rather sophisticated ways), we have formed very complex relationships with a great many words. We know what they mean. We have images for them. We know their sounds.

Now we have to match up an additional set of symbols developed from the letters of the alphabet. But in English, there is only a chance relationship between these letters and the sounds they make. The problem is further complicated by the fact that the names of the letters often have little or nothing to do with the actual sounds they make. All the names of consonants, for example, have vowels in them, but the consonants don't make vowel sounds, at least not in English.

So the transition from spoken to written English is difficult if we equate letters directly to sounds. The best way to learn to read is to sense the logical development of a sentence and then to associate the visual impression of each written word with the corresponding spoken word. However, this requires that the visual system be well developed when the child first attempts reading. Otherwise, the process of teaching the child to read becomes complex, and may fail completely.

Before we go on to reading, though, it's time to take a step backward.

Human beings have been using language for perhaps a million years. But the part of the brain that internalizes and interprets what we see has been around a lot longer, maybe several hundred million years longer. Therefore, the ability to visualize is far more basic and far more securely anchored in the brain than the faculty for language is. Indeed, some researchers think that language is an intellectual appendage, growing out of the capacity to visualize, the way the hand grows out of the arm.

In any event, we cannot properly understand language unless we first understand the complex and miraculous process of visually incorporating what we see into a mental world that can remember faces, mountains and

things that go bump in the night, sometimes well enough to draw recognizable pictures of them.

5

Visualization

Is there anything we can see that is really "out" there?
Why not?

When Michelangelo carved the **David,** he worked like any ordinary skilled craftsman operating a well-designed computer. The computer, of course, was his own mind-body continuum, and, in his case, it was extraordinarily well designed. His task was to knock marble away from the piece of sculpture that was waiting inside to be liberated. The procedure, as Michelangelo himself described it, involved holding a particular image in his mind for four years with such accuracy that he could eliminate every piece of marble that covered it up. The accuracy, however, had to be to within the tiniest fraction of an inch.

I remember the awe with which I first viewed another Michelangelo opus, *The Two Captives*, in the Louvre. I had seen them shortly before in London, but those had been expert reproductions. The originals, defined by the amazing finish of their surfaces, are remarkably different from the reproductions.

Michelangelo didn't know why he was able to form an image in his mind and maintain it for such a long period of time any more than you know how you digest your food while you're doing so. He knew only that he did, and that his task from that point on was comparatively simple and straightforward, as it would have been for you or me or anyone else, had we been inside his mind.

What we see is not "out there" nor is it even in the action of the optic nerves. It is a creation of the mind's ability to interpret a given report from the optic nerves in the light of remembered experiences unfolding as a developing and coherent whole. When you raise your eyes from this page of print and look around the room, what you are seeing is hallucination.[1] There is nothing out there that bears the slightest resemblance to what you think you see. All that surrounds you is a slightly compromised version of otherwise empty space. It extends outward in three dimensions, whereas what you see is a flat surface with a slight hint of the third dimension. It has no property that could be called color, only the property of absorbing some wavelengths of light more than others.

The seeing takes place inside your head, but you hallucinate a projection of it into the room that surrounds you. There is nothing about this hallucination that would distinguish it from an image produced entirely in your mind without external reference points, as, for instance, when you dream. The only way to be certain of what's out there is to coordinate your sense of sight with your sense of touch. If you can put your hands through what looks like a solid object, then it's not there.

But, of course, the sense of touch can also be hallucinated. So there's really no direct evidence that there's anything out there at all.

The Nonmaterial Nature of the Physical World

Since the nervous system responds consistently to stimuli from the outside world, it's possible to set up a relationship with your environment that behaves consistently, and thus to create images in your mind that have the capacity to predict what will happen to you as you move through the world.

The fact that you bump into things has nothing to do with what you call the "solidity" of material objects. It has to do with the energy fields in your body being incompatible with the energy fields in the objects surrounding you, thus creating an impenetrable boundary.

Once we can accept the idea that what we see around us is all internal mental constructs and has little, if anything, to do with the actual nature of what we are looking at, we will then be able to operate in the world on the basis of its electrical wave motions rather than its supposed "solidity."

Think for a moment about why what I have just told you has to be true. We know, from a century of scientific research, that if we were to descend to the subatomic level we would observe phenomena that have little relationship to the phenomena we think we see in the macro-world. On their own scale, these phenomena would be extremely widely separated from each other. The electrons that orbit the nucleus of an atom are tiny compared to the protons and neutrons, and are quite distant from them. The atoms themselves are quite distant from one another, relative to the size of their internal structures. So almost everything that could be observed at the subatomic level would be empty space—space so empty that a tiny neutrino taking a voyage through a bar of lead would find, just as the spaceship *Voyager* is now doing, that interatomic (or interstellar) space is mostly completely empty.[2] The main difference is that macro-space just looks empty, whereas micro-space looks bubbly, like Swiss cheese. There are huge amounts of what ought to be space that isn't even space. It's just emptiness that doesn't even have space in it.

In case you think that everything I've said so far in this chapter is nonsense, you might want to verify it by reading a few contemporary physics books. Otherwise, bear with me, and let's see what all this has to do with reading. Our view of the outside world seems to be very stable and well structured only because we have spent most of our time every day since birth creating mental images of it based on electrical impulses traveling through the nervous system. In the areas in which we have plenty of practice, the structure is "solid" and predictable. In the areas in which we have little practice, such as the interpretation of optical illusions, which rarely occur in everyday experience, or the interpretation of greatly enlarged photographs of familiar objects on a scale we rarely encounter, it's highly unpredictable and can easily confuse us.

The Unavoidable Sophistication of Visual Interpretation

People who are born blind but have had their vision restored after they reach adulthood usually can't learn to interpret visual stimuli in any meaningful way. For them, the information carried to the brain by the optic nerve is like the static you hear on the radio when you're trying to catch the program underneath it.

Some people who, through surgery, have been given access to their sense of sight for the first time as adults have been so distracted and confused by the experience that they have committed suicide.[3] One woman, however, was prepared from early childhood for the possibility that she might someday gain the capacity to see. After her operation she did learn to see. The expectation of success seems to have been a key factor in her case.

Even those of us who have seen clearly from earliest childhood see very differently from one another, as becomes evident when we consider special cases in which the power of vision has developed in unusual ways.

For example, when J. S. Bach looked at the markings on a piece of music paper, he didn't "see" anything. He heard a musical composition that his hands could play with no difficulty at all. Most randomly selected people would have none of the neural structure that Bach had in his head when looking at that piece of music paper, but most professional musicians have it, at least to some degree.

You, on the other hand, could not be reading this book unless something akin to what happened in Bach's head happens in yours while you are reading. There's a good deal more "hearing" going on than "seeing" when some people read.[4] I can get you to "see," however, if I ask you to pretend that as you drive down the street in your neighborhood on an icy road your car slides out of control and hits a telephone pole. Chances are you just "saw" that telephone pole with some degree of vividness.

The telephone pole, however, doesn't look nearly as clear as a real telephone pole because, since birth, you have spent an almost infinitesimal fraction of your time reading sentences like the one I just threw at you. Most people don't read sentences like the ones in this paragraph the way you read the sentence that left you wondering how you were going to explain the telephone pole to your insurance representative. Michelangelo, however, read marble that way, and the main difference between him and the rest of us is a powerful motivation to see in a certain way, combined with years of practice.

For a reason that's not clearly understood, visual artists get a lot more practice storing images in their brains than the rest of us do. For example, someone skilled at drawing caricatures can look at any human face, translate certain key features into a code, run that code through their brains and exaggerate those features, producing a sketch that looks, in a funny way, just like the subject. We now know how to program computers to do things like that, too, with the result that we can get them to interfere with the inalienable allegiance to accuracy of representation that the camera used to have.

The reason most of us can't do the kind of visualizing Michelangelo could do is that we were taught in school that there was something out there that was much more important than what was in our heads. We were expected to get the "right" answer instead of give our own considered opinion. We were told that our "right" answer had to agree with everyone else's, even though there's literally nothing that everyone agrees about.

If you were in school over five hundred years ago the "right" answer was that the world is flat, and you got in trouble if you said it was round, whereas today you get in trouble if you say it's flat. What you're almost never encouraged to do is say why you think it might be one or the other.[5]

Children are in the habit of inquiring about the images they hallucinate in their minds as a result of looking around them. They want to know all sorts of things about what they are seeing and what it all means. Adults, habituated to the idea that what they are seeing is what everyone else sees, tend to give the impression that there's no debate about many of the things the child might want to call into question. As a result, most of us spend our lives looking exclusively for the "right" answers and very seldom for the possible ones. These "right" answers fall into certain categories dictated by assumptions that are cultural in nature, and often unprovable.[6]

For example, I made reference earlier to the practice of preserving rotting dead bodies in Papua New Guinea and drinking the juices exuded by them. The assumption behind this practice is that strength can be passed from the dead to the living.

It might be possible to prove that random sampling of such "juices" could infect a person with disease, but so far it has not been possible to prove that some sort of unidentified energy could not be passed on in this way. We merely assume that it could not be, which is one of the reasons we embalm our dead as quickly as possible.

Our assumption that not keeping dead bodies around too long generally promotes public health is most likely correct. Our assumption, widely held in the 1960s, that if a particular nation converted to communism the nations around it would fall like dominoes, turned out not to be correct. Yet we sacrificed our national unity, stability and economic security to that unproved assumption.

A typical Papua New Guinean can look at a dead body and see an appetizing fluid collecting there, which is guaranteed to strengthen his or her own body. A U.S. State Department official could look at a map and see a series of dominoes. Bach could look at a piece of music paper and hear a concerto grosso. Michelangelo could look at a piece of marble and see a statue inside.

What we see when we look at something is determined by the expectations and experiences we bring to it. That's why no two people ever see exactly the same thing.

You might say that Michelangelo was different in that he could look at a piece of marble and see the possibility of a finished sculpture inside of it, whereas you and I are smart enough to know better. It might be argued on the contrary, however, that Michelangelo's way of looking at things is more natural than the one we have learned. In the subatomic world there's no "reality" out there, only possibility. An electron doesn't "exist" in the way an automobile seems to. It only has the possibility of existing, expressed by scientists as a probability that manifests itself when, for some reason, the electron feels a need to exist inspired by the inquiring eye of a scientist.[7] You could imagine this process as the eye beam of the scientist reaching down through a microscope and infusing the outstretched arm of the electron with life and existence. That, at any rate, is what Michelangelo might have done with this information.

Hallucinating What's in Books

You are doing much the same thing when you pick up a book and imagine that inside it is a story. If you have had several experiences of reading books and finding stories passing through your mind, the results of your various experiments are impeccable and prove the point conclusively, so far as you are concerned. Yet the reading you have done to get those stories is one of the most mysterious miracles in the universe.

So the possibilities that you see in your mind's eye are, in a sense, more real than the "certainties" you think you're seeing around you. Indeed, almost everything you do leads in the opposite direction from the reductionist truth that twentieth-century intellectual politics has, in so many cases, routinely, unthinkingly and arbitrarily argued is all there is.

All over America proud parents look at a newborn infant and say to each other (or used to, in gentler and kinder political times), "Maybe she'll grow up to be president someday."

That, of course, is hallucination, because what they're doing is looking at a baby who can't even talk yet and imagining a future for her that has only one chance in about 100 million.

Publisher's Clearing House has made a fortune on the fact that so many of us engage in this kind of hallucination without any willingness to do the math that would reveal the odds involved. Your chances of hitting the jackpot in a nationwide contest do not make it a wise investment to purchase a postage stamp to find out whether or not you have won. It's not wise to purchase even one, let alone dozens of them, and certainly buying a lottery ticket is statistically way off the charts as far as wise investment is concerned. When you buy lottery tickets, of course, what you're buying is short-term dreams, and there's nothing wrong with that if it makes you feel good. It's better than destroying brain cells with alcohol. It is very definitely a wiser investment, though, to set yourself a goal of doing something like Michelangelo did. That involves introducing feedback into the equation.

Michelangelo posed the possibility that any given marble contains a piece of sculpture. He then tested the possibility by using a hammer and chisel to reveal the piece of sculpture it contained. His experiential tests eventually proved he was right. Those statues were in there. It was just a matter of his knocking the excess marble away so other people could see them.

Look around the room now and try to find something in it that was not, at one time, merely a figment of someone's imagination. Everything made by humans had to be imagined before it could be created in physical form. Similarly, the world that we see around us may have had no physical existence five billion years ago, and six hundred million years ago had no life that could transform the landscape.

Just as Michelangelo's visual vocabulary could be used to create the *David*, Bach's musical vocabulary the *St. Matthew Passion*, and Shakespeare's literary vocabulary *Hamlet*, so the vocabularies that exist within your mind can create many things that only you can imagine.

What point is there to life itself, then, other than to imagine and, from imagination, to create reality?

The Reality of Imagination

Imagination is, in a sense, delusion. If you tell the world your imaginings before you have thought them through sufficiently, and sometimes even after you have, you will usually be laughed at. But when you have brought your imaginings to the neighborhood in the form of the house you've built, to the movie theater in the form of the film you've created, to the drugstore in the form of the medicine you've concocted, or to the stock market in the form of the corporation you've designed, the last laugh may be yours.

So life is about dreaming up the realities of the world we intend to inhabit.

And what is reading, if not a structured form of dreaming? What is reading, if not practice in creative visualization?

We read so that we can imagine, so that we can write, or so that we can create other things.

The practice in visualization that we get from reading cannot be achieved by watching television, movies or looking at the natural world. It cannot be achieved from conversation with others, for there is insufficient continuity or stability in most conversations.[8]

Reading must become a habit early in life if it is to be a lifelong source of enrichment and vicarious experience. In order to help create this habit, we must tell our children stories and read to them as often as possible.

The current habit of plunking them down in front of the television set has none of the benefits of reading to them, for the mind accepts the images on the screen passively and mistakes them for reality. But the mind of the listener who is being read to has to create the images described and thus relate to them actively as a collaborator in the story. The difference between reading and watching television is like the difference between taking a vigorous walk to build up your stamina and muscles and lazily riding around in a car.

Children's stories are designed to get young listeners to see the pictures that the stories describe. All of us know what Little Red Riding Hood, her mother, grandmother, the wolf and the woodsman look like. We can even talk about the furnishing of the two houses in the story and describe, in some detail, the woods in between. Those of us who read well paint beautiful pictures in our minds. The brushes and paint we use are provided by the authors that we read, but the paintings we construct are very much our own.

6

How the Brain Learns to Read a Text

What are the pathways through the brain that are activated when we read, and how may these be used to distinguish poor readers from good readers?

We have Sally Shaywitz and her husband to thank for the fact that we know quite a bit about how the brain processes text when a person is reading. Shaywitz, codirector of the Yale Center for the Study of Learning and Attention and professor of pediatrics at the Yale School of Medicine, finds symptoms of dyslexia in about 20 percent of the population.

In a research project led by Shaywitz and her husband, Bennet Shaywitz, functional magnetic resonance imaging (MRI) brain scans were used to measure the response of the brain in dyslexic and normal readers. The MRI shows differences between oxygen-carrying blood and oxygen-depleted blood. An active area of the brain uses fresh supplies of oxygen-rich blood, so an MRI can give us a picture of the brain areas involved in performing a task.

The dyslexic readers showed most of their brain activity in "Broca's area," which is associated with speech. Normal readers, on the other hand, had more activity in the visual areas of the brain, where language is translated into visually encoded forms of meaning. These include the simple impression of what a word means, the ability to see the image in relationship to other images, the sense of motion that is imagined, and the associated images that arise in relationship to those described.

The MRI brain scans show what areas of the brain are activated at any particular time. Therefore the researchers can eavesdrop on their subjects' brain responses as they read. Good readers show typical patterns of visual involvement when reading. Poor readers do not. As poor readers are trained to become good readers, these patterns should change, so the Shaywitzes' team believes that curing dyslexia will likely bring about changes in brain activity measurable by MRIs.

The experiment involved twenty-nine adults with dyslexia and thirty-two who could read with ease. These subjects performed a hierarchical series of reading tasks designed to show what is involved in progressing from letters to sounds and words. First they had to recognize letters, then they were asked to make judgments, such as which letters' names rhymed with each other. Then they had to decide whether certain nonsense words rhymed, a task that required readers to sound out the words.

People with strong reading skills can read even nonsense words without having to dissect them into their component letters. Thus it's easy for them to make a judgment about whether or not, for example, "geat" and "lete" rhyme with each other. Dyslexics, who have not achieved ease in word recognition, cannot make such a judgment without further analysis.

As the experimental subjects moved from one task to the next harder one, the Shaywitzes watched the pathways of their brains light up. In normal readers, the pathway involved fingertip-sized regions on the surface of the brain and moved from the back of the brain to the front, showing that the brain was actively processing the material read by creating images that gathered structure and specificity as they moved through different areas of the brain. While the patterns noted by the Shaywitzes were interesting, they did not fully reveal the brain at work in reading, as in this experiment there was no report of an MRI being applied to the normal process of reading as such. Good readers do not read in order to translate the words that they perceive into sounds. They read to translate them into images. However, if I ask you to pronounce the word "cat" you will almost inevitably see a cat in your mind's eye, and that will give rise to further images as memories of experiences with cats occur to you.

The images the Shaywitzes studied were of two general types. When you respond visually to the word "cat," you see a static picture of a cat. When you respond to the whole sentence, "The cat purrs as it lounges on the couch," you get a sense of the cat at rest, and you marry the picture of the cat in a particular context to the sound of its purring and hence to an emotive quality, which probably connotes happiness. In the process, more areas in your brain are accessed as the synesthetic aspects of the experience are activated.

Speaking Versus Listening

The Shaywitzes do not appear, from the reports of their experiments, to have examined the process of reading for content or for comprehension. Were they to do so, we would expect to see many more areas of the brain lighting up: those that activate mental imagery of various types in different sensory areas of the brain.

Translating the Shaywitzes' research data, we can say that during the time you're learning to sound out words, your attention is devoted to matching the sounds of the words as you speak them with the letters in the words you're trying to decode. Most of this activity occurs in Broca's area.[1]

If students learn to read in a chaotic way, they develop problems in recognizing words and remain stuck in Broca's area, unable to move from there to the visual cortex, which allows them to interpret and store in memory the information contained in what they are reading. They don't even, necessarily, listen to the sounds they make when they read the words, for listening is not processed in the same area of the brain as speech. Thus we do not necessarily listen when we speak, and must actually learn to do so. Evidence of this is the often self-contradictory statement, "I am not raising my voice!"

You can read aloud from a book you do not understand and your audience still can understand what you have read. Your lack of understanding is not just because the book might be in a foreign language you do not know, or may use words whose meaning is not familiar to you. It is also because you can read the sentence, "Jimmy and I went to the store" and not listen to yourself reading it. So in reading instruction, it is important to teach people how to keep their minds on the words they are sounding and to interpret what they have read. Most elementary reading teachers do not teach this skill. The only way to achieve it is to learn to read with material that is interesting and significant to the beginner, to discuss its meaning frequently in class, and to have the students process it by acting it out, illustrating it, and determining its impact on their personal lives. All this must be practiced from the very beginning while they are still learning to sound out very basic words.

In addition, it's important to teach reading in such a way that the words are never ambiguous and can always be sounded out reliably on the basis of what has already been learned. The lower the ambiguity in the spelling of the words, the less chance there is to develop reading problems.

Combining Structure and Choice

There's a paradox here that applies to all learning. In some respects, early learning of any kind must be carried out in an environment and with materials that provide a high degree of structure and predictability. In other respects, since learning is an instinct that is internally motivated, there must also be a great deal of room for choice on the part of the learner.

In simplest terms this means that new readers should learn to read with texts that are easy to decode because the words themselves are never ambiguous. At the same time they should be open enough in meaning so the student can decide on a personal interpretation that has maximum relevance to his or her experience.

This combination of clarity and openness to interpretation is no different in principle from the stimulation offered by reading experiences at a more advanced level. For example, in approaching a new work of art, you want to be stimulated to the highest level of your capacity to interpret the work, without having difficulty perceiving the work itself. You don't want to listen to a symphony on a radio plagued by static and interference. You don't want to be seated behind a pillar at the ballet. You don't want to look at inadequate reproductions of paintings. You don't want to read poetry from an indecipherable page of print.

In addition, if you are learning about something that is conceptually new, you want the information in a form that involves you completely, inter-

acting with your full intellectual capacity, but you don't want the concepts themselves to be more confusing than they really are.

These facts about learning should be basic and universally accepted in all educational contexts. In fact, they are so rarely attended to that they amount almost to heresy.

Finding Your Way More Easily

Let me approach this problem in terms of an analogy. When you're trying to find your way in a strange place you depend on road signs and other landmarks. Nevertheless it is a rare city council that will see to it that road signs are always visible and easy to read, that major intersections are always clearly marked enough in advance to make it easy to turn into them, and so forth. This is either from pure negligence or stems from the fact that the people responsible for making the signs are already familiar with the area they are marking, and are therefore unaware of confusions a stranger might experience in that area.

I believe it should be required by law that all road signs be designed and placed by people who are strangers to the area they are signposting. After the signs are up, they should be required to find their way around in the area by using the signs they have put up. Such a policy would save a great deal of gasoline and driver frustration. It would radically reduce the number of times a driver goes several miles out of the way as a result of missing a turn.

By the same token, learning materials should be designed, or at least checked out, by people who are not already familiar with the subject matter. They should be so clear that no one could possibly mistake what they mean.

Creating an Electronics Course

I was once asked to write a text for beginners in the study of basic electronics. Since I did not understand basic electronics myself, I got a lot of very simple textbooks to help me do this. I used, for example, *The Little Golden Encyclopedia*, *Barron's Guides* and similar books aimed at beginners.

Why America's Children Can't Think

After reading about eight of these I began to get some idea of how basic electronics works and what one needs to know about it. I then wrote an explanation of what I had learned from my studies. I explained things like polarity, ohms, amperes and watts, and other concepts that are essential if one is to understand how an electronic circuit works.

I then spent several hours with a person who knew nothing about the subject. We looked at what I had written on a computer screen, and whenever my friend didn't understand what I had written well enough to answer a question about it, I rewrote the material.

When this explanatory text was complete, an instructor in a corporate training class used it. By studying the text and discussing it thoroughly, the students became so clear about basic electronics that the instructor was able to reduce the delivery time of the course by 40 percent. He also found, to his great frustration, that his students understood the subject so well that they began to raise questions and introduce problems much earlier than his lesson plans called for teaching them.

When he had adjusted to the new, more efficient learning that resulted from a basic text that was really clear, he was able to reduce the time it took to teach the course even further. In addition, the students understood the material at the end of the course much better than they ever had in earlier classes, and they remembered what they learned much longer.

So the importance of clarity in early instruction cannot be overemphasized. Unfortunately, however, it is very hard to find. That's why so many students have trouble in school. Teachers who already know the material, and who can't remember how difficult it is to learn, are teaching them.

Traps in English Orthography

The English language seems as if it were specifically designed to make new readers feel stupid. In addition, many people end up feeling that the language itself is crazy.

That is not the case, however; the craziness can be removed from it almost entirely.

The English language is in fact a stratification of a thousand years of changing pronunciation. For example, the word "knighte" in Chaucer's *Canterbury Tales* is pronounced exactly the way it was written. The "k" is sounded, the "gh" is guttural, as in German, and the final "e" is pronounced as a separate syllable that may sometimes be dropped. The "i," which is followed by more than one consonant, is short.

All spellings that survive in English today reveal something about how a word was pronounced at some time in the past, even though it may not be pronounced that way now. The challenge facing the new reader is to make sense of all these archaic spellings and match them up with actual sounds that may, at first, seem to be quite unlike the word that is being spelled out.

To top it all off, the new reader is constantly confronted by new words that have to be sounded out before they make sense. The emphasis on sounding out for new readers tends to keep them in Broca's area, trying to make a match between the sounds suggested by the letters and the sound of some actual word that may be intended.

I am now going to help you revisit this problem, which all new readers face, so you can get a little taste of what they are experiencing, since you may have forgotten having that experience yourself. Sound out the following word, and say it clearly and rapidly: abrashaunighligormantupsychosis. What you'll notice, as you try to perform this task, is the confusion you face in attempting to keep the different syllables straight and remembering what you've got so far, as you add new sounds. Your attention is entirely on the relationship between sound and syllable, so you are operating in Broca's area, which pairs printed words and letters with units of sound.

Gestalting

Once you have established a system for accessing the units of a word and pairing these with units of sound, you are able to sound out words fairly easily. When you have sounded out a word several times, that word will enter your reading vocabulary, and you will feel that you instantly recognize it when you see it, as you probably did with "supercalifragilisticexpialidocious," which I used earlier. At that point, your handling of that word will change, and will thus be able to shift to the primary visual cortex, which treats the word as a *gestalt*. A gestalt is a combination of elements that the eye sees as a single unit, like a square, a circle, an apple or a cat. If you are trying to distinguish between an eight-sided and a nine-sided figure, you are probably not gestalting those two figures, so you have to analyze them.

Except for their ability to recognize the structure of the human face instantly, infants are born with relatively few gestalts ready-made by the mind, and have to work them out gradually by reexperiencing the same complex phenomena many times. The infant watching her hands move through the air in the crib is creating a gestalt to help make sense of the visual experiences, while integrating them into a synesthetic relationship with the kinesthetic sensations.

The same thing must be done with reading. The problem with 95 percent of so-called dyslexics is that they have no easily accessed formula that helps them turn unfamiliar words into gestalts. Their eyes, in traveling across the page, have roughly the same experience you might have driving down a road full of potholes. Many words leap out at the dyslexic that are ambiguous because they have never been properly gestalted.

Part of the reason for this is that the dyslexic may have had experiences leading to right-brain dominance. Since the right brain does not deal with language, except on a very elementary level, a person who has become right-brain dominant is less likely to process language in a systematic way.

Some dyslexics, however, have become left-brain dominant, and their problem is completely different. A person who is extremely left-brain dominant expects things to unravel systematically. Such a person is frustrated by rules that do not apply consistently and, upon encountering such rules, may give up and decide the subject is impossible to understand.

A right-brained person would read the sentence "I may have to save space for Dave in the race," and not notice the pattern that the "e" at the end of the words makes the "a" say its own name. The left-brained person, on the other hand, would get stuck on the fact that "have" is a violation of that rule, and would wonder why "may" isn't written "maye." Both of these readers could end up with serious decoding problems, but for different reasons.

Anyone who encounters confusions of either type, and does not resolve them, finds it difficult to adopt a smooth motion of the eyes across the page, routinely taking in one word or phrase at a time and then moving on to the next. Right-brained people are far more interested in the larger picture than in a routine and boring examination of its details. They may simply lack the patience to form good word attack skills without being carefully taught to do so. Left-brained people may stop and linger over words that do not fit the pattern, reading them several times to try to figure out what is causing the inconsistency.

In either case, the eyes will not learn to track smoothly across the page. You can learn a lot about this by watching people's eye movements as they read. Most dyslexics show irregular eye movements with a lot of back-tracking over the words. The dyslexic will typically look at a particular word and go on, then backtrack because there is some doubt as to what that word really was. Dealing with words in this way tends to keep them in Broca's area. They stay there because they have not yet developed the habits of eye movement that will take them beyond the process of puzzling over individual words. They have trouble getting to the stage where they can take words for granted and can move rapidly through an unfolding of their various meanings. The result is that they are so busy trying to match up the printed words with appropriate sounds that they have no energy left over to pay attention to the meaning of the text.

The best way to move out of Broca's area is to learn good word attack skills. This, of course, can happen only gradually. But as students become increasingly comfortable with the texts that they are reading because they can easily recognize all the words, they switch from trying to match words with sounds (Broca's area) to simply recognizing the words and moving on to interpret their meanings.

Moving Text Through the Brain

The path of text through the brain moves naturally like this: We start by seeing the words (primary visual cortex). Then we move on to "the visual association area," or angular gyrus, where the recognized words are strung together to make cohesive language units. Here we find what is sometimes called the "clean up area." By fitting the words together into semantic units that make coherent sense, the angular gyrus reconciles any mistakes that may have occurred.

For example, let us say that you think you saw the words "The cot was purring." This information is passed on to the angular gyrus, which makes the words in the semantic unit fit together and make sense. It then corrects "cot" to read as "cat." (Some readers may have automatically made this correction when reading the above "incorrect" sentence. If you had to read this paragraph over to find the word "cot" when it first appeared, your angular gyrus worked so well that you corrected it to "cat" without even knowing you were doing so.)

Assuming that the sentence has been correctly translated to read, "The cat was purring," the sentence now moves to "Wernicke's area," which takes the sounds of language and converts them into words. This is also called the "superior temporal gyrus." If it performs its function correctly, it makes it possible for you to read the sentence aloud and understand what it means.

The Shaywitzes found that people with dyslexia made too little use of this "normal" reading pathway in the brain.

For a century the essential role of the angular gyrus in reading has been reported by doctors who noticed that when this area of the brain was damaged, the ability to read was destroyed. In an article in *The Scientific American*, researchers examined the neurological process of reading by proposing a hypothetical set of pathways through the brain. They then explored errant pathways that could be characteristic of what is called "deep dyslexia."

Deep Dyslexia

Deep dyslexia comes in several different forms, whose behaviors can be explained in terms of the hypothetical pathways that the researchers mentioned they were able to program into their computers. When they disrupted these computer-simulated pathways, the computer made the same kinds of mistakes in reading that people with deep dyslexia do. A person with deep dyslexia may have a flaw in the circuitry that interprets the sentence about the purring cat, and will focus on the individual words without reference to their collective meaning. The reader then may sense an error in the word "cot" and replace it with "bed," which has a similar meaning. The result is that the reader cannot move out of the confusion created by misreading the word, and must therefore become much more skilled at recognizing every word correctly in the first place.

The model built by these researchers differs in important respects from that which shows up on the MRI research of Shaywitz and her colleagues. But it is also true that Shaywitz, in her own previous writings, has not distinguished between different types or levels of dyslexia, and asserts that dyslexia can be found in about 20 percent of the population, unlike deep dyslexia, which is found in fewer than one percent.

Clearly a distinction has to be made between the most frequently occurring kinds of dyslexia and deep dyslexia, which has a far more disruptive effect on reading. Whereas the evidence is very strong that deep dyslexia is caused by a relatively severe form of brain damage, the more common form of dyslexia may actually be learned, as Diane McGuinness strongly asserts in her breakthrough book *Why Our Children Can't Read*.

The Malleable Brain

The research of Marian Diamond and others shows that, with practice, neural network patterns can be considerably altered, and the alterations can occur rather suddenly.[2]

This is because the brain is extraordinarily malleable, so when new experiences are sufficiently compelling, old neural pathways can be immediately replaced by new ones. For example, a person who is very fond of a particular sport may have a serious accident and, from then on, lose all interest in that sport. That's a negative example, but positive ones occur as well. In *Growing Up*, Russell Baker writes of his experience in learning to fly a plane during his Air Force training. In less than a minute he went from being the worst pilot in his class to the best. Suddenly the skill of flying gestalted in his mind and all his difficulties disappeared.[3]

Why America's Children Can't Think

I myself had a profound experience of this positive transformation in brain circuitry after the age of sixty.

As a child I had great difficulty reading, and as a junior in college, I was reading at about the fourth grade level. That year I began the process of developmental optometry that transformed my reading from very poor to outstanding. Nevertheless two problems continued for me. One was that if I tried to read in a moving vehicle for more than a couple of minutes, I would end up with a combination of a splitting headache and nausea, which would last for about a half hour.[4] The other was that I found it utterly impossible to read when someone was talking near me. This made reading in airports extremely frustrating, since my attention was constantly distracted by loudspeaker announcements or loud conversations.

In October and November 1997, I spent several intensive weeks developing the reading program I am about to describe to you. When I had finished, I noticed, to my great surprise, that both of these problems had inexplicably disappeared—and they never came back. Now I can read quite comfortably in a moving automobile or an airplane that is taking off or landing. And unless I am very interested in the conversation taking place near me, it doesn't interrupt my reading at all.

I wondered for a long time why this had happened, and then an answer came to me. As a child who was severely dyslexic, I had had great trouble learning to gestalt words. As a result I formed the habit of fixating on most words longer than necessary to register what they were. This meant that I would hold my gaze on the word long enough so that if the page moved I had to move my eye with it. Our vision plays a part in the complex system by which our bodies maintain equilibrium and the sense of where they are in space (erect, sideways, upside down, at rest or in motion). A mismatch in visual intake and bodily position (for instance, eyes still and body moving rapidly) can lead to disequilibrium and feelings of nausea.

In developing the reading program I had to pay close attention to the spelling of every word that I used. In the process I became much more certain of how all the most basic words are spelled. My old habit of fixating too long was replaced by a new assurance that allowed me to recognize each word easily with a single glance. As a result, my eyes no longer clung to each word too long, and so were no longer bothered by the motion of a moving vehicle.

In addition, I was putting far less effort into determining what the words were, with the result that the energy available for interpretation of the text was greater. I now felt that the voice inside my head that was reading the text was loud and strong enough to override the voice heard when someone near me was talking. As a result, my enjoyment of reading increased significantly, and I also found that texts that previously had been somewhat difficult for me became easier to understand.

Transformations like this can take place at any age, and there is therefore reason to assume that anyone can become an excellent reader, no matter how many years of failure and frustration may have gone by.

Advantages of Being a Late Developer

The long-term failure to read well can actually be an advantage. At least it turned out that way for me. Since I had so much trouble learning to read, I honed my information-gathering skills in other ways. I became an expert guesser when I did not have complete information, thereby filling in the lacunae of the text that I had not attended to while reading it. I learned to take what I knew from a variety of different sources and blend them into a coherent logical pattern.

The key to being an excellent reader is to become habitual in your word attack skills and to learn to recognize most words at sight. When you have sounded them out often enough, the focus on sound is replaced by acceptance of the word at sight, which allows for focus on the information being interpreted in the visual cortex, and consequently on meaning.[5]

In plain English, we must learn to pronounce words first, then to hear them, and finally to interpret their meaning in visual and other sensory responses. Shaywitz's analysis of how we read, recorded in a number of different research reports over the years, strongly suggests that the ability to gestalt printed words instantly, so there is no ambiguity about what they are, is the strongest single means of progressing from the awkwardness of the beginner to the fluency of the experienced reader. Dianne McGuinness also believes this to be the case, asserting that readers who can recognize all the words in a book will have no trouble reading it well in all other respects. While the research of the Yale group is still in an early stage, one would expect that in their future research they will find significant changes in brain activity in formerly at-risk readers who have learned to read comfortably and well and can score high on comprehension tests.

Dyslexia Is Curable

Thus, in the sense of a permanent brain-function disability, there may be little or no true dyslexia. Not in reading, anyway. Even deep dyslexia should be curable by so thoroughly training the eyes to see all words correctly the first time that mistakes in word recognition disappear almost entirely. If this result is indeed attainable, then the problem is only an absence of the kind of instruction that adequately emphasizes the left-to-right progression of the eyes across the page. To the extent that a learner is invited to look randomly around inside a word to see whatever it is that might be there, he or she has no reliable method of making sense of print. I have often seen the results of this kind of teaching in adults with reading problems. Such readers might construe the word "grandmother" as "gaudy mouther." They look at some of the letters and guess what the others must be. Because they read so slowly and are so confused, they never get enough sense of the context of the sentence to guess words that would make sense in that context. The best cure is to teach them to progress one letter at a time right through the word until its letter pattern becomes familiar. Then the words can be shown on flash cards until they are seen with a single glance.

7

Visual Problems
in Reading

*How can we tell if someone has visual problems that
may inhibit reading?*

Our vision was developed for use in the wild. We have eyes that are used
to scanning the near and far horizons, processing information that may arise
anywhere within the visual field. Whether we're surveying distant vistas in
search of possible enemy attack or scouring details of the woodlands to
track a deer through the underbrush, our eyes must take in details from the
entire visual field and sort through it for the useful ones.

There are few tasks in observing our environment that require the systematic study of detail in any prestructured way. The eyes rove freely, but
have their purposes and pause where they find what they are looking for.
On the freeway or in heavy traffic, you must pay attention to events all
around you. You must notice, by looking in the mirror, that the car behind
you is getting too close. Before you can pull into a different lane to escape
a potential accident, you must make certain that nothing is in the way on
that side. You must also be sure that someone on the other side is not about
to swerve in front of you and complicate the process of changing lanes. You
have to be vigilant in a visual field of 360 degrees, half of which is broken
up and must be assembled by looking in three different mirrors.

There is no particular eye motion required here. Your eyes move
randomly in response to stimuli provided by changes in the way cars are
moving around you. Sometimes you look up to watch for the change of a

traffic light. At other times you inspect the road in front of you, watching for an oil slick or a sheet of black ice. Survival depends on how well you integrate all these observations.

One thing you are almost never required to do while driving is move your eyes from left to right in an even straight line. In fact, the only time you are ever likely to do that is when you are reading something. The eye motion reading requires of you is unlike any other. It is also unlike anything your ancestors of over five hundred years ago were likely to have needed to do.

No wonder that a high proportion of those who attempt to learn to read have a difficult time. It's not just that you're asking your eyes to follow a line of print from left to right in regular patterns—something they weren't designed to do and are not comfortable learning to do—it's also that your eyes work best and most comfortably when you're looking at things at least twenty feet in front of you. At that distance the eyes look directly out, along virtually parallel lines. However, as you focus on objects that are close, your eyes have to work harder to maintain focus. You'll notice this if you gradually bring your finger toward your nose while trying to keep it in focus. Pretty soon your eye muscles will start to hurt, and when your finger gets too close, the strain will force them to double the image.

Reading Readiness

When you read, you're usually focusing on a target about two feet away. Over time, this can be stressful to your eyes. For one thing, since the lines of sight are no longer parallel, each eye forms a picture distinctly different from the other. You'll see how pronounced this difference is if you look at this page first with one eye and then the other, switching them rapidly. Maintaining those two rather different images as one single image is the source of the stress, though just how much that is differs from person to person.

If you teach a child to read or perform similar near-point tasks before the eye muscles have developed the capacity to focus properly, you may be training the eyes to do something for which they're not ready. That's what happened to me, and it was why, at the age of nineteen, I had to undertake a rigorous course of visual training to teach my eye muscles better coordination. So it's better not to teach reading until the child has seen a developmental optometrist, who can evaluate whether or not the eyes are ready for the challenge. If stress sets in during the early stages of learning to read, the result may be that one eye simply turns in or out, which produces a tendency to become either cross-eyed or walleyed. In addition, the stress of too much reading at too early an age can make a person nearsighted.

Another reason for a vision test: Some children may already have defects in their vision, causing them to need special glasses for reading, and perhaps even different glasses the rest of the time. Ignoring this problem could produce a lot of trouble in the visual system, and even make reading so painful that the child avoids it as much as possible, or gives up altogether.

If all goes well, the new reader won't have too much of a problem learning to focus so that each eye makes an equal contribution to the image of the page. If the two eyes are working at the same time, but their inputs are not well coordinated, the brain may be uncertain of what is happening. For example, one eye might be looking at the first line of print and the other at the second line. If this happens, the brain has to decide which to choose, and it may not do that consistently. The result will be visual chaos.

Testing for Glasses

In working with elementary school children I have sometimes noticed that the student will start reading a page rather well but will be stumbling over words by the bottom of the page. That indicates a probable need for reading glasses to relieve the visual stress. Again, a developmental optometrist should be consulted. An optometrist or ophthalmologist who is not specifically trained in developmental reading problems will not know what to do and may prescribe glasses that actually increase the problem. I have worked with some students who read better without their glasses. This is easy for you to check if your child seems to be having reading problems. If your child wears glasses, have him or her read a page first with the glasses and then without them. If the reading gets better when the glasses are removed, you'd better get a new prescription, at least for reading. To be sure you're getting good information, try this experiment repeatedly at different times in the day. A child who is feeling good and is fresh may show no stress from the glasses, but may show it later, when tired.

Of course, if the reading is better when the glasses are on, that's a good sign, though you still can't be certain you have the ideal prescription. Only a qualified professional can judge that.

I've asked you to have the child read first with the glasses and then without, because if the reading improves with the glasses off, that's an indication that even the buildup of stress in reading over time is less significant than the stress of the glasses. If you reverse the process, and do the reading first with the glasses off and then with them on, and the reading deteriorates with the glasses on, this could merely mean that the child is getting tired of reading. In general, though, if a child is tiring that quickly, visual assistance may be called for.

Occasionally I've asked students to try wearing my reading glasses, and have found a great improvement in their quality of reading. Since my glasses probably aren't the right prescription for them, that's very significant and indicates that their need for lenses is quite strong.

The function of the lenses is to compensate for the stress of focusing at near point and having to reconcile two rather different images. The proper prescription for reading glasses could prevent eye problems later, such as the development of nearsightedness or possibly even of diseases like glaucoma. So proper eye care is extremely important for children who are asked to do a great deal of reading. The way we learn to approach the printed page may be as important in taking proper care of our eyes as the kind of help we receive from a doctor.

The rules for reading a line of print are comparatively simple. The eyes must travel across the line in a steady motion, recognizing each word in turn, accumulating them into larger patterns that the brain can assemble and interpret. It must be subliminally aware of each letter in each word and, at the same time, compute the developing thought of a sentence conveyed by the combination of all those letters and words, which, in most cases, is unique to the line of print in view at a particular moment.[1] Even slight mistakes in this perception can throw the process off. Skipping the word "not," for example, can skew your perception of everything else in a message.

Eye Movements in Reading
Should Be Simple

A teacher needs to make sure that students use a strict left-to-right eye motion that dwells equally on every single letter whenever a new word is encountered. This is a purely left-brain sequential skill that is in no way improved by asking people to guess. Their chances of guessing wrong are much greater than of guessing right, unless they are already such good readers that they easily make the logical word choice and spontaneously guess without being taught to do that. Diane McGuinness gives many examples of the intellectual mayhem that comes from being taught to guess what a word is.[2] It's almost as bad as teaching cash register clerks to make change by guessing. Try running a retail outlet with clerks who are creative guessers.

By forming a strong relationship between the recognition of words at sight[3] and the auditory and visual-kinesthetic images that may arise from those words, we can significantly increase our brains' involvement in reading. Some of us can do this based on our own imagery and some of us have to recall the pictures in the books that did all that wonderful work for us, thereby weakening our vision-making neural networks. Just as practice is the key to giving stability to the objects that we think surround us in reality, so it is the key to giving stability to the images that are invoked as we read.

Unfortunately it's not always so easy to learn how to do all of this. The child at play never rehearses such eye movements. So when first confronted by print, the child may have no idea what is expected.

If you'd like to get a sense of what the child who is just starting to learn to read has to contend with, get out a page printed in Chinese or Hebrew (assuming you don't already read the language you've selected). Then ask yourself what you ought to do first in order to interpret it. The answer will not come quickly, nor do answers come quickly for children who have not yet learned to deal with print.

These problems are far less likely to be severe in children who have been read to while looking at the printed page. In the process they will have picked up many clues about reading, even if they didn't learn to recognize actual words. The children who have the most trouble learning to read are those who have no experience looking at print at all, as happens in many families where books are seldom opened.

Many of the visual problems that slow down the process of learning to read are developmental. These need to be dealt with on their own terms. However, there is a specific way to eliminate some of the visual confusion that can develop in the course of learning to read. That's by teaching reading in a way that organizes the spelling patterns of words into a sequence of gradually accumulating complexity. In the next chapter I'll explain how that is possible.

8

Decrazifying English

What makes so many people think the English language is crazy, and what can be done about it?

It's natural to wonder why so many who can accomplish the incredibly complicated task of achieving fluency in their native languages cannot transfer that skill to the related problem of interpreting the same words in print. This will become clearer, however, if we look at the situation through the eyes of the beginning reader. A beginning reader cannot be expected to recognize any word in a line of print, and therefore has no way to approach the task of reading a simple sentence.

The ideal way to read is to fixate quickly on a word or group of words, know instantly what you are looking at, and move on without ever backtracking.

That statement is simple enough, but its implications are profound. What it means is that the goal is to transform the process of reading into something very close to the process of listening.

When you listen to someone speaking (say, on the radio, where you're getting information through your ears without anything added visually) there's a stream of sounds flowing through your brain that is translated into thoughts and impressions, usually including visualizations, often with a kinesthetic component.

"There he goes. Into that drugstore. He's stepping on the scales. Weight: 245 pounds. Fortune: Danger!"

That was the introduction to a popular radio series from the 1940s entitled "The Fat Man." The words were carefully selected to draw your attention into the program that followed.

Here's another example: "From out of the past come the thundering hoofbeats of the great horse Silver. The Lone Ranger rides again!"

In each case, the first impression is of motion. The picture gradually shifts from a blur to the identification of the subject. The subject in each case is engaged in an activity that is both vague and dramatic. Each of the introductions invites you to imagine something thrilling. You're going to be listening further to discover what new twist might come in the next episode.

In one case the motion is slow and deliberate, in the other it is rapid. But in both, motion is the focal point, because it captures your attention most easily.

The progression of ideas, images and impressions in these examples is effortless. The words flow into the brain, where they are accepted and interpreted in such a way that you forget you're even listening. You're completely wrapped up in the impressions you get from the sounds you hear.

If this doesn't describe most, or all, of your reading experiences, then there's room for improvement in your reading.

All Reading Can Be Thrilling

But wait a minute! you say. There's a vast difference between reading a thriller, which moves more or less the way the above sentences do, and studying complex scientific or technical material.

Not necessarily. The flow of ideas in each case can be remarkably similar.

Remember my first example of reading, which was captured in the movie *October Sky*? Homer, a high school boy, is studying a book on rocketry that consists primarily of math problems. As we watch him studying, though, we're caught up in a thrilling set of actions. We want to see how he will deal with the challenge he faces when he has given up school and has gone to work in the mine in order to supply the additional income his family needs to survive. When he gets off work, he's exhausted but, nevertheless, stays up all night working math problems.

The situation he's in is, in fact, a detective story. He's accused of starting a forest fire by shooting off a rocket. Given the distance of the fire from the site where the rocket was fired, the question is, could Homer's rocket have started the fire?

If he can correctly calculate the distance and direction his rocket would have traveled, he can not only determine whether he started the fire, but also find and reclaim his missing rocket.

This is surely as compelling a situation for a high school boy as any the Fat Man or the Lone Ranger ever faced. His entire future, self-esteem and family honor are at stake. He must find his rocket by determining the physical properties of its flight.

In a situation like this, the most arcane subject can be as dramatic and thrilling as a keep-you-on-the-edge-of-your-seat spy story. It doesn't matter what the subject is: sewage disposal, metaphysical poetry, the demographics of West Africa—you name it. A difficult-to-read book full of technical information will pull you through it as surely as any thriller ever could if you're in hot pursuit of information that means a great deal to your future because it will help you solve a problem, build a new theory, or confirm an idea you've been thinking about for a long time.

In order to turn every book into a thriller in this sense, there are basically only two things you need to do: One is to learn how to make transparent the motion of your eyes across the page so you can absorb the words as if you were listening to a voice on the radio. The second is to be very clear about what you are looking for in the book. Is it to know whether the hero escaped alive from the fire at the top of the isolated mountain, or to determine precisely how Hemingway was influenced by John Donne when he wrote *For Whom the Bell Tolls*? In either case there can be an emotional rush from discovering a missing piece of information that will save either the life of the trapped hero or the theory you've been hoping to prove in order to impress your professor and ultimately the world of literary criticism.

Basic Rules

Once again, the rules for successful reading are:

1. Remove all impediments to the smooth motion of the eyes across the page so the words are absorbed transparently.
2. Enter the realm you are reading about so fully that you feel as if something personal is at stake all the time you're reading.

If these two conditions are met, the telephone book can be as compelling as John Grisham. If you want to discover whether your long-lost twin, who lived in San Francisco twenty-eight years ago, is still there, there's no question that the phone book is for you, at the moment, the greatest thriller in the world.

Everything depends on context.

In this chapter, however, we want to explore what it is that will allow your eyes to move across the page completely without effort. That's the precondition that allows you to read smoothly and rapidly once you've established a context that will pull you excitedly through the material.

In a previous chapter I told you that, while in my sixties, I eliminated two lifelong barriers to my reading enjoyment simply by looking closely at the spellings of large numbers of words. In this chapter we're going to be in hot pursuit of the reason why that was so important to me and why it might be just as important to you, or someone you love.

Enter, Phonemes

Every language is made up of sounds called phonemes. The phoneme is like an atom of spoken language. It is the smallest unit of spoken sound that your mind perceives. That last word, "perceives," has the following phonemes: p-er-s-ee-v-z. These six sounds melt together, blending to form a single word.

There's a paradox in this, though. The phoneme in isolation from other phonemes usually sounds different from the same phoneme in an actual word. That's because the sound of a multisyllabic word is a continuous flow from one phoneme to the next, without interruption. As a result, the sounds melt into one another without a sharp break, and in between there are sounds that are neither the one nor the other, and not separable in themselves. So sounding the phonemes individually is different from normal speech.

And there's a second paradox: You can speak a language all your life without ever really identifying a phoneme, knowing what it is, or even recognizing that there might be a couple of them you don't pronounce properly, or perhaps can't even hear.

That's because you don't learn your native language as a series of units that build up into more complex structures, like bricks put together to make a building. You learn it as a continuous flow of sound, like a river, that, as you learn to examine it and its components more closely, turns out to have a lot of rocks and other things in it, around which the water flows.

If you vocalize a single note with your mouth wide open, that's like a river flowing smoothly with nothing in it. But as soon as you change that open-mouthed vocalization to the sounding of particular words, you've introduced barriers to the flow. Your breath, which carries the sound, now has to skirt around a variety of different impediments arranged for it by your teeth, your lips and the shape of your mouth.

You're unlikely to be aware of how any of this happens because, long ago, you learned to match sounds you heard with sounds you made. As time went by, you differentiated those sounds in more detail.

Still, there are times when you do not speak distinctly enough for people to understand what you're saying. That happens when you haven't differentiated all the phonemes enough to allow a listener to follow the particular words.

Actors and media people are trained to control their breathing and exaggerate their phonemes enough so their speech is always clear. Anyone who has had speech training knows that articulate speech feels at first like an unnatural way of speaking, because the sound you hear in your head seems so much more accurate and differentiated than the sound that travels out to someone else's ear. In order to discriminate the sounds well enough so a distant listener can hear all of them, you have to make sounds that, from your own perspective, seem over-discriminated.

Changes in English Spelling Rules

All the phonemes are represented, in English, by letters. That is because English is a written language that uses an alphabet. However, there are many written languages that use pictographs rather than alphabets, and the problems of learning to read them are different from those of English.

A number of languages, like Spanish and Italian, use spelling that is phonetically consistent with the sounds of the spoken language. At some time long in the past, English was that way, too. However, English has had more different languages and dialects feeding into it over time than most other languages have, so its pronunciations have changed dramatically over the centuries. Many of these changes have occurred since the language began to be written in works that are still widely read today.

If you read the anonymous eighth-century heroic poem *Beowulf* in its original Old English, you're reading a foreign language. Only a few words from Old English are still around, and even those are not particularly recognizable compared to their origins.

In 1066, William the Conqueror invaded England from Normandy and not only conquered the people but also conquered their language. For a long time after the Norman Conquest the upper classes who ruled the land spoke Norman French and the lower classes spoke a debased form of Anglo-Saxon, which is Old English.

By 1400, however, when Chaucer died, the two languages had begun to merge into one. *The Canterbury Tales* was written in Middle English. If you read it, in the original form, you can make out most of the words without prior knowledge of them: "Whan that Aprille with his shoures soote" translates as "When that April with his showers sweet."

Chaucer wrote his words with spellings that corresponded to the sounds they elicited, the same way Spanish and Italian writers do today. The word "knighte," as mentioned before, is pronounced exactly the way it's spelled. Today, the word "knight" would be phonetically spelled "nite."

The spelling in Shakespeare's *First Folio*, which comes a little over three centuries later, is quite similar to modern spelling, even though spelling was not yet standardized when it was published. By that time,

English was very similar to the way it is today. However, during that period, tremendous shifts of pronunciation were taking place. As a result, people from different parts of the British Isles often couldn't understand each other very well.

This communication barrier even within our own language has been true ever since. The dialects of English that might be spoken in a single inner city neighborhood today can range very widely because of all the different ethnic, racial and national backgrounds of the people who live there.

So there are many barriers to understanding resulting from the wide range of spellings and pronunciations that people who speak a common language must deal with. In order to make it possible to read effortlessly, we'll have to come to terms with that.

We won't get much help, though, from the pedagogical approaches that are currently in use. What we take to be reading instruction too often is actually a process that is more designed to keep people under control in a political sense than to teach them to think well enough to be good citizens. Universal literacy as a concept was not even considered before about 150 years ago, when the first public schools came into being. The idea that every member of the population should learn to read is a comparatively new one.

Dictionaries to the Rescue

The initial steps in laying the foundation for reading instruction came when Samuel Johnson, in the eighteenth century, wrote the first dictionary. In it he undertook to do four essential things that had never been done before. These were to standardize spelling, define words, give an idea of word pronunciation, and show where modern words came from in the past.

Johnson undertook his various tasks with considerable humility. He knew that the challenge demanded more thought, effort, good sense and large-scale awareness than any single individual could supply, so he assumed that armies of scholars would follow him, who would correct and perfect what he had started.

That didn't happen. Johnson's standardization of spelling was a very poor job. He made little attempt to adopt spellings that reflected, even in his time, the actual pronunciation of words, or were consistent in the way particular letters signaled particular sounds. As a result, a particular letter would be allowed to signal several different sounds when used in different words. Worse, particular sounds could be signaled by as many as twenty different letters or letter combinations.

Only two major figures followed Johnson and attempted any important improvements on his work, and even these were very minor. They were Noah Webster and James Minor, both in the nineteenth century. Webster prepared a much more comprehensive dictionary than Johnson's and changed a small number of spellings. His main contribution was to substitute "i" for "y" in a great many words, such as "wynd," "ynch" and "leysure." Other than that, he mostly left Johnson's spellings as he found them.

Minor led an enormous research project that attempted to define every word ever used in English in every way that it was used. His magnum opus, the *Oxford English Dictionary*, contained nearly half a million different definitions of about half that many words, and used nearly two million illustrative quotations. Both of these men produced works that were extremely flawed. Webster's dictionary froze, for all time, too many spellings that he should have changed when he still had the opportunity to do so. The flaws in the *OED* have been extensively documented in a recent book by John Willinsky.[1]

The point is that there is no such thing as a truly authoritative body of knowledge about the English language, how it is or should be spoken, how it is or should be written, or how to teach people to read it. For all the millions of hours that have been invested in studying these subjects, some of the most fundamental questions remain unanswered and some of the most fundamental problems unresolved.

The Futility of Standard English

There is not and never can be any such thing as Standard English, as it is in the very nature of language to change its vocabulary, definitions, pronunciations and sometimes even spellings on what is literally an hourly basis (if not at a rate that could be measured in split seconds). Attempts are made to use Standard English on network news reports, but even there, as reporters are brought in from other cultures or nations, we are exposed to a wide variety of accents.

Even without taking into account regional differences, our language remains forever in flux and is constantly developing communications problems that are difficult, and sometimes impossible, to solve. Here's one example of what I mean: When I was a child, the word "inflammable" meant that if you held the substance so identified in the presence of fire it would burn very easily. Today four different words are used interchangeably for this meaning, and no one is sure which is which, except by the context in which it is used. They are "flammable," "inflammable," "noninflammable" and "nonflammable." The first two might seem to be the opposite of the second two, but that is not necessarily true. The confusion about meaning comes from the fact that the prefix "in" has two different meanings. One is "not" and the other is "to intensify the following word, or to turn it into a more active state." So, "to inflame" means "to start or, more commonly, intensify something that is burning (either literally or metaphorically)."

There is a serious problem here, since no one can ever again be certain what means what in this array of word choices, and if someone gets the meaning wrong, the results could be tragic.

These examples are typical of changes in basic meanings that are constantly taking place in the English language (as, indeed, in most other languages as well). Among minority populations, this problem is particularly significant. "Bad," for example, is a dialect word for "good." Reversals of this sort, common in Black English (Ebonics), have been shown to create severe problems for some African-Americans in learning math, since the instructions they receive often seem to them to have the opposite of their actual meanings. Just telling children they are wrong doesn't do anything to correct this problem.[2]

Another problem is the question of what is and is not correct grammar and usage. It is interesting to note that the sign "Go slow" is correct because the word "slow" is an adverb derived from an obsolete word, "slowe," and it means the same thing as "slowly." Most people don't know this, and if they are desperately fighting the losing battle for correct speech, they wince whenever they see such a sign.

Usage Problems

Another bugbear is the question of whether or not you can use a preposition to end a sentence with. English teachers harp on this rule, which was introduced into the language by John Dryden, who derived it from Latin, which can't end sentences with prepositions. (You can write "magna cum laude" but not "magna laude cum.") So as people try to please their Dryden-inspired English teachers, they end up with such monstrosities as "This situation is one up with which I will not put." The normal and preferred form of this sentence is "This is a situation that I will not put up with," which ends with two prepositions. The preposition "up" in that sentence has no conceivable object that is a noun. You do not, for example, say, "I am not going to put up money with you anymore." You say, "I am not going to put up with you anymore." What's going on there, grammatically speaking? This is the sort of question English teachers just have to hope will not arise. A delightful essay on this subject can be found in Fowler's *Modern English Usage*.[3]

The point of this discussion is that the attempt to freeze English into some standard or perfect form is forever doomed to failure, particularly at the present time, when all sorts of other languages are suddenly getting mixed into it. If there is ever a standard English that becomes the world lingua franca, it may not be anything particularly recognizable to you and me.

The attempt to get children to speak Standard English is thus a chimera. What is very much *not* a chimera is the need to teach all children who are competent to sit in public school classrooms to read at grade level. However, reading at grade level won't get them very far in life. People who can read at no better than grade level (say that of a high school senior) do not meet the standards required for a good job in the information-based economy. They must do far better than that if they are to be successful in the more lucrative careers.

Barriers to Learning to Read

However, that dilemma fades on the horizon compared with the problem of dealing with large numbers of students who cannot read at grade level. I come now to the point of this chapter's whole discussion, which is what must be done to help people who haven't acquired that skill.

People who can't read are stymied by too many words they can't instantly recognize. So the main challenge of the reading teacher is to help young children learn to recognize as many different words as possible in the shortest possible time. No math teacher would start first graders off on the formula for quadratic equations.[4] What math teachers recognize is that first graders have to practice with simple concepts before they can go on to more complicated ones.

To review: There are two basic problems in learning to read. The first is to learn how to make the flow of words into your brain transparent. The second is to identify your own interests completely with what you're reading. Once these two things are accomplished, there's little else to worry about.

In the rest of this chapter I'll consider the first of these problems, which is to become able to recognize instantly every word you see. If there's even the slightest doubt about what the word is, the flow of your reading is slowed. Ygh tharrz eyfayn the clleightuisde dought uhbowbt whoot the uolod eax, the phlough uv iorr reoding uiz sleaud.

As you may have figured out, the two last sentences above say exactly the same thing in the same words. The second of the two uses alternate spellings derived from other words that use those letter combinations to make the same sounds. For example, "what" can be written "whoot" if you use the "oo" in "flood." "Ygh" is "if" with the "gh" from "laugh." "Eyfayn" has the "ey" from "money," the "f" from "of," and the "ay" from "says." See if you can figure out what's going on with those other spellings.

What you have just experienced is neither a trick nor a joke. It's the dilemma any new reader must face when confronting the many different ways that letters represent the same sounds. Because of the confusion that inevitably occurs in the process, many readers develop an internalized sense that the word they are fixing on at the moment is unlikely to be what they think it is.

In order to get a better sense of how this works, imagine that for years you drove a car that gave you an electric shock one time out of ten when you put the key in the ignition. That was a long time ago. Today, as you put the key in the ignition, though you know you will never get a shock, you nevertheless hold the key tenderly, gingerly, prepared to release your hand quickly, and that's why you pause just a bit before you insert the key into the ignition.

So an adult reader who is very competent may still subliminally suffer the effects of early confusion in learning to read. As I previously explained, that is what happened to me and has also happened (with different results) to several of the adults I have worked with, many of them excellent readers, who nevertheless could be reading much more comfortably.

The visual confusion accumulated through early reading experiences stays with many of us and subliminally slows down our eye motion. This produces a greatly increased tendency for the mind to wander while reading, as the ideas do not flow from the words as easily as they would if the reading process had always been comfortable. It should be obvious from this analysis that it would be extremely important to teach people to read using texts that sort out the different ways of spelling the same sound. These different ways, which I call "sound signals," should be introduced gradually, one at a time, so readers don't have to encounter enormous amounts of ambiguity as to what a word is likely to turn out to be from their very first attempts. It ought, therefore, to be one of the primary concerns of a reading teacher to do everything possible to assure that students will, as quickly as possible, develop comfortable eye movements that progress smoothly and regularly across a line without feeling a need to backtrack or pause too long over a word that ought to have become easy to recognize.

Obvious as this approach to teaching reading ought to be, I have never met a reading teacher who spent any time at all helping new readers learn to deal with this problem easily and productively. They can't, because they don't have texts that will allow them to do so. The result, as we know, is that about 20 percent of the population is dyslexic and another large segment of it is made up of people who are not nearly as comfortable with reading as they easily could be. The cost of this problem is that the reduced productivity of the workforce in today's text-oriented world is much too large.

A New Approach

The reading materials I developed in 1997, called *The Map of My Happiness,* use a system of sound signals taught one at a time. There are about two hundred spelling variants for the approximately forty-five phonemes in our language. When we teach these sound signal variants gradually, using a text that is fun to read and discuss, we find that students above second grade who have previously failed to learn to read properly make significant gains in a short time. The system is easily learned and used by teachers, and many of those who use it say that the most important thing they see happening is an enormous improvement in self-esteem as students who had thought they were stupid learn to read more quickly and easily. The text never asks them to read any combination of letters they have not already been taught.

In contrast, when I learned to read I was, all too soon, introduced to the sentence, "Mother said, 'My funny, funny family.'" Look more closely at the last three words in this sentence: "funny, funny family." Two of them are identical. The third begins and ends the same way, but is mysteriously different in the middle.

All of the words in the sentence that Mother says end with a "y." But the "y" in "My" signals a different sound than the "y" in "funny" and "family." What are we to make of this? The larger sentence, "Mother said, 'My funny, funny family,'" contains two "a's" and two "i's." None of these four vowels says its own name, and in each case the two "a's" and the two "i's" don't make at all the same sounds as each other. In fact, only two sounds are vocalized from these four letters. What's going on here? About the only place in the sentence where one notices a similarity (other than in the repeated word "funny") is that, for some strange reason, the "o" in "Mother" and the "u" in "funny" signal the same sound.

A great deal is made, in teaching children to read, of the difference between long and short vowels. In the sentence under consideration, there are no long vowels unless you think the two different "y" sounds are both long vowels—but if you do, why does that make sense? If none of the vowels are long, then they must all be short. Now that you know that, see if you can explain to yourself (or anyone else) what a short vowel is. Assuming that the "o" in "go" is long, and the "o" in "frog" is short, what is the "o" in "mother"? What is going on in the letters "ai" in "said"? Are they long vowels or short vowels, or what are they? The "u" in "funny" might be short. If that is true, what is the "u" in "busy"? What is the "u" in "buy"? It might be easier to think of the "a" in "family" as short if I hadn't already been left mystified by the "a" in "said."

The "i" in "family" is another kind of mystery, because I don't pronounce it. I say "famly." Is a vowel you don't pronounce long or short? Why or why not?

None of this would matter if we weren't all taught about long and short vowels and also taught that the "e" at the end of a word makes the "a" say its own name, as in "save" and "have" (oops!).

I have heard a great deal about what six year olds should and should not be exposed to, but no one seems to have pointed out how confusing it is to a child that age to be taught a series of rules that fail to apply to many of the most common words the child encounters. What this says about rules is that they are lackadaisical and must frequently be disregarded altogether. That's one of the reasons people behave the way they do in traffic and when filling out income tax forms. There are no rules for pronouncing words based on common spellings that can be helpful to a child (though for some mysterious reason it seems to be reassuring to adults to teach them, even if they don't understand them themselves). If a child happens to ask (as very few do), "How come 'save' and 'have' don't rhyme with each other?" The only thing a teacher can say is that "have" is an exception to the rule. Okay, then, what is "move"?

What are exceptions, and why do we have them? Why are there so many of them? Nobody knows. There are no rules that work. So we must stop teaching rules, because there's no conceivable pattern that can be derived from all the confusion I've already noted in just the one simple sentence examined above. (What is "above"?)

Let's look at another of those rules first grade teachers are so fond of: "When two vowels go walking, the first one does the talking." In the very sentence that the teacher uses to state the rule, there's only one word in which the two vowels do indeed go walking. That's "does." Which vowel does the talking in that word? Why?[5]

Breaking the Rules

Now, just for fun I'll back up three paragraphs and select every word in which two vowels go walking. Let's look at them, and see how well the rule applies (I'll mark them with asterisks):

heard
great
*deal
should
*seems
pointed
out
taught
series
*fail
encounters
about
says
they
*lackadaisical
*reasons
*people
*way
they
pronouncing
*though
mysterious

*reason

*seems

reassuring

*teach

*each

*teacher

*say

exception

*okay

Of the thirty-two relevant words that are randomly scattered through the paragraph, only fifteen exemplify the rule. That's slightly under 47 percent.

It thus may be more true to make the statement "everyone in the world is female" than to assert the above "rule" that first grade teachers proudly display for their students as a surefire guide to solving the confusing problems of interpreting English orthography. "Every person in the world is female" is 50 percent true (maybe even 51percent). Those are probably better odds than applying the commonly taught "vowel sounds" rule on the paragraph here.

Incidentally, I didn't include "reassuring" because both vowels are voiced, though the second one doesn't "do the talking" the way the first one does. "Talking," of course, implies that the vowel says its own name.

There may be some other arguments as well. For example, one might say that the "e" in "already" does the talking, because the sound is a short "e." True, but so is the "a" in "many," so who is to say which vowel does the talking here? After all, in "great," it's the second vowel that does the talking.

I have to admit I've always found the "i before e" rule useful, because it distinguishes between "receive" and "believe." It works a lot of the time, but the trouble is that the "i before e" words break the "first one does the talking" rule as well as the exceptions "with the sound of 'ay,' as in 'neighbor' and 'weigh.'"

You may think all this is funny, but really it's not. This is subliminal education. It's regularly taught in relation to our language, which is probably the most intimate part of us. Without our language, we can't even have coherent thoughts.

What I have to live with is the fact that the teachers who taught me about my language taught me that rules often (or even usually) don't apply. They didn't come right out and say this, which makes it worse. They gave me a subtle, subliminal suggestion that's sitting there below the surface of my thinking, where I have trouble unearthing it.

As a result I'm likely to feel that there's something fundamentally wrong with rules. They don't work. They're taught to me by people I ought to be able to trust but who, it turns out, are really hypocrites, albeit unintentional and unwilling ones.[6]

Undermining Respect for Rules

Maybe I'm unique in the amount of struggle I have to go through to accept rules about anything, but I don't think so. It seems to me that the younger generation tends to leave the older generation thinking that it has very little respect for rules of any kind. I'm not sure that's all the fault of the people who made up the rules for trying to decipher the English language, but I believe it's a contributing factor.

I'm all the more convinced of this as I watch what happens when my reading program, based on sound signals, is taught by teachers who believe in its value to students who have always had trouble reading. I've noticed in them a tremendous sense of relief. But I've noticed something much more significant than that, and to get at it I'd like to give you an example of a little piece of the sound signal chart on which the reading program is based.

The sound that we tend to identify with the letters "sh" can be produced by all of the following spellings: sh, ti, ci, s, ch, sci, c, ssi and ss. I've run into a good many highly literate adults who ask me, "How can 'ti' make the sound 'sh'?" to which I immediately reply, "As in 'nation.'"

We who have already learned to read are often unconscious of the spellings that we are interpreting by uttering certain sounds. We have accepted the language whole until we come to sounds we can't recognize, particularly as they show up in people's names.

However, the children who are taught to read with my program are no longer unconscious of these various ways of spelling certain sounds. Nor do they regard them as crazy, or a nuisance to have to learn. They become fascinated by variant spellings and so aware of them that they can spot mistakes in the reading program wherever they are introduced. In the early versions of the reading program almost all the mistakes were found by readers under the age of eight. They usually became aware when confronted by a sound signal that had not yet been taught to them.

An Awareness of Spelling Patterns

The young people in my program became so precisely aware of how words are put together that their reading, insofar as it involved the words being taught in the book, was in some ways ahead of the average reader. Often, for example, they noticed mistakes their teachers missed.

One of the reasons this happened was that the teaching techniques needed for the program are very simple. If the students come to a word they don't know, they cover it with their thumb and move across the word from left to right one sound signal at a time. As each new sound signal is pronounced, they go back and start again. This technique is called "word growing." Here are these two words divided into sound signals: w-or-d g-r-ow-i-ng.

Teaching students to sound out words in this way habitually builds their word attack skills quite rapidly. There is no guessing, no adding sounds not in the word, no making a mistaken identification of a sound and being unable to change it.

In fact, if a student has trouble making progress in the program, it is almost always because he or she has not been practicing word growing skills sufficiently, and lazily tries to guess at words in a somewhat random way. Once the student becomes good at word growing, the problem goes away.

Eventually the biggest problem becomes the students' shortages in vocabulary development as they learn to sound out many words whose meanings they don't know. At that point, their decoding skills may actually surpass their other language skills.

This means that a fundamental part of their language experience is learned with a high degree of precision, rather than with the sloppy methodology that is at the bottom of many people's reading experience. By developing a clear sense of the way words in print are put together, they acquire the foundation for the kind of reading that flows effortlessly. What may have been a source of failure and disgrace for students becomes an enjoyable activity they often turn into a game. Sometimes students spontaneously compete with each other to see who can read the most words in sequence without a mistake. Sometimes they invent word games for the class to play. Sometimes they argue earnestly about alternative meanings of particular sentences. Sometimes they act out stories in order to show the elements of structure in narratives. Sometimes they bring problems they face at home into the class discussion to show how they relate to things they are reading about.

The sound signal system of teaching allows us to use a much wider variety of words than are usually taught to beginning readers. Once a group of sound signals has been learned, it's possible to use them to teach long and complicated words, provided that these words are composed of only the sound signals taught. So students who have struggled to sound out the word "ham" might, eight weeks later, be reading with ease words like "concentrate," "development," "significant," "demanding" and "aspect." After a few months of instruction, a typical sentence for sight-reading might be, "A journey of a thousand miles begins with the first step, as the proverb from China says. I intend to take that journey in search of finding out what life is all about."

When students who have never performed in class at all become leaders in the class discussion and demonstrate insight into the problems revealed by the text, teachers are often amazed. They are also amazed when a student runs to the sound signal chart to show how a particular word can be traced through it. When a group of sixth graders was asked to apply for the job of helping a new third grade student for whom no teacher could be found, several of them wrote letters explaining why they thought they should be picked for this job and why they thought the new student could learn to read easily, just as they had. They had quite a bit to say about what fun it is to read.

Why America's Children Can't Think

The Need for Precision

The previous vignettes should demonstrate that precision in the recognition of sound signals need not be learned in a rigid way. Precision is not the same as rigidity. You can get precisely the right notes when playing a musical composition and still play it with great originality of expression.

Respect for precision is one of the qualities most difficult to find in today's workforce. It used to be widespread, and it is in some foreign cultures. People whose lives hang in the balance of a task that must be performed just so have a respect for precision.

I once asked a group of low-paid and poorly treated roofers if they sometimes wished the boss might fall off the roof. They were horrified at the suggestion. Observing safety regulations was such a way of life for them, they could not conceive of violating them out of spite, however annoyed they might be about the way they were treated on the job.

People who are taught that rules may or may not apply don't normally gain that respect—at least, not nearly as much. And often when they must learn to be precise, as happens in learning computer programming, for example, they are more likely to see it as a special case, not applicable in other situations.

So it's important to teach reading in such a way that we know what we are looking at with each word that we read, and so that we have the same respect for the precise spelling of that word that we have for the spelling of our own names. This precision with the spelling of words leads to a respect for greater precision in identifying their meanings and their applicabilities. It means that we are more likely to see the situations around us with a productive awareness of their potentialities than would be the case if we were taught to blur out differences and accept rules that are only randomly applicable.

It may seem strange that a problem that has been so widespread for so long could be solved in such a simple way. Strange, perhaps, but not illogical. A great many problems are like that. Complex solutions will often fail where simple solutions will work like a charm.

The Need for Clarity

Suppose your baby is crying and you try everything to stop the crying. You coo at the baby, you offer candy, you make funny faces, you bounce the baby around, and you exhaust your creative resources in trying to stop the crying.

Then you discover there's a diaper pin poking into the baby's skin. You remove the pin and the crying stops.

In thousands of classrooms, millions of children are having trouble reading because they can't distinguish what the words are. If they're given an unambiguous approach that allows them to read only words whose components they can recognize, they will become expert readers much more quickly. It's possible to get through all the sound signals in one year of reading instruction. Then students will have the decoding skills to read any word in the English language. After that, the only problem is to improve comprehension of concepts that they may not yet have been exposed to. That's an altogether different problem, the kind that good teachers really enjoy grappling with.

As you may gather from this discussion, the issues that surround the teaching of reading are so many and so complex that an encyclopedia could not detail them all. Therefore, in the following thumbnail sketch of some of the larger issues of the problem, I must ask forgiveness for glossing over a great deal, and for attempting to give only a quick picture of aspects that need to be thought about in this arena.

Briefly, those who argue for whole language believe that reading should be taught in the spirit of enjoyment. Children should read real books, real stories, and experience themselves as writers in relation to the reading they do.

This is all well and good, but, in practice, whole language has been found to work for about 40 percent of the population of schoolchildren.[7]

Phonics, on the other hand, works for about 60 percent of them.[8] Advocates of phonics argue that if good word attack skills are not developed early, the process of reading will become chaotic because most of the words will remain unrecognizable.

Still, phonics drills are pretty boring, and produce few of the personal rewards that inspire children to keep reading. It's not much fun to read lists of words like "cat," "hat," "bat," "sat," "rat" and so on. Yet the ability to read depends on easy recognition of the similarity of these words. By the time you've listed all the words that are similar to each other, you've taken the child through a great deal of material that has no meaning except to teach word recognition. How much better and more effective it would be if all these phonics drills were incorporated into an interesting text, after the manner of Dr. Seuss.

Effective reading instruction, I believe, requires a synthesis of the principles of whole language and phonics.

A Controversy That Shouldn't Exist

The fact that this controversy even exists is attributable to the lack of understanding of how people learn and how they read that pervades the industry of teaching reading, much of it the result of profiteering as large publishing companies make commercially motivated deals with statewide school boards. Still, the chaos and lack of coherence in dealing with the problem are not surprising, given the fact that the best and the brightest are—as David Halberstam described them in his book about them—people who, generally speaking, don't really understand how to read. If our leaders do not understand the full scope of what reading involves, why should the leaders of schools understand it either?

This is the problem in public schools all over the country. First of all, the art of teaching reading itself is in a poor state of development. The result is that practically no one teaches children to read in a manner that has the remotest claim to having been tested scientifically. That's why 48 percent of the population is barely literate. That's why politicians on both sides of the aisle keep campaigning for school reform.

Scientific tests reveal clearly that both phonics and whole language are flawed methods of teaching, because they have too high a failure rate. All reading instruction that has any hope of being successful must be based on phonemic. This fact is well documented in educational research, but has seldom made its way into the classroom. Some reading instructors have no idea that there is any difference between phonics and phonemic awareness; but the difference is profound, as I have suggested earlier in my analysis of why spelling rules cannot be effective in teaching people to read.

All this is well and good, and should be fairly easy to resolve. But that leaves the second issue that is seldom, if ever, adequately addressed in reading instruction: How do you create the context for what you read?

9

We're Always Reading
about Ourselves

*What's the point of reading anything that has
nothing to do with us, and how can we make
everything have something to do with us?*

Once you've solved the problem of decoding words on a page easily,
so they flow into your mind without your being aware of reading, the
next problem is to teach yourself how to become involved in the subject
of the text.

There's nothing in the world that doesn't interest someone. Everything
is inherently interesting. But we tend not to be interested in the things we
don't understand, or with which we can't identify. Our brains are built that
way. The "limbic system" in our brain is where all of our feelings are generated. It's also true that that part of the brain is where we access our long-
term memories, and where we make all our most important decisions. It's
impossible to make a rational decision that is not trivial, because all decisions that involve feeling are made by the limbic system. Then, after they've
been made, they're rationalized.[1]

In a sense, the whole point of all the cognitive skills we have is to make
us feel better about things. Some people feel best if they can boss other people around. Some, if they can dive to the bottom of the ocean. Some, if
they're intellectually at the top of the heap. Whatever it is, though, we're
driven on the basis of our feelings. If we're too proud to admit that we want
to be happy, and we spend our lives depriving ourselves of happiness, that's
a feeling, too. It certainly isn't logical.

Why America's Children Can't Think

The above arguments might sound strange, but on the basis of neurology it's impossible to argue otherwise. In *Beyond the Pleasure Principle*, Freud showed that indeed pleasure is not the only feeling that motivates us. He showed that since people don't always commit suicide just because they aren't pleasuring themselves, there's something more deeply motivating in human experience than pleasure. Whatever it is, however, that motivation is a form of feeling, not an intellectual decision.

Many problems arise in school, and in the teaching of reading, because we misguidedly assume that everybody ought to read and know the same things, even if that's impossible.

It's true that there are a good number of ideas that every person who wishes to be thought of as literate should be aware of, but all of them are potentially very interesting and should appeal to anyone who has learned to understand them well. As a teacher I have found that students who understand Shakespeare will develop a great love for that writer. The people who don't like Shakespeare are those who don't understand the meanings of his words.

That's not true of all writers. John Grisham, Isaac Asimov and J. R. R. Tolkein are all very popular writers. It's possible to thoroughly understand the writings of any of these authors and yet not be particularly entranced with their books. They are writers who appeal to a certain sort of reader, but not all readers.

Read to Discover Relationships

It would be possible to learn to read any number of popular writers and find them interesting if, for example, you were doing a study of why they are so popular. Then you would be reading not for the story, but for characteristics of the story, and that's quite a different matter. A case in point is that I do not particularly enjoy the writing of Horatio Alger, Jr., but I find it fascinating to read his books in search of the many different ways he found to create in the minds of his readers a strong motivation to succeed.

Here's the difference: If I am trying to understand a particular book on its own terms, I may not find what it has to say interesting. But if I am reading it to discover its relationship to something else that I do find interesting, the reading experience will be altogether different. So the trick is to find something in myself that will be enriched by something in the book I have before me.

Once I discovered this, I found that nearly all books on nearly all subjects interested me—or at least could conceivably interest me, given a relevant context in which I might read them. This has caused severe problems in my house because there aren't enough bookshelves to hold all the books that interest me.

So the first question to ask yourself before you begin any book is "What's in it for me?" What do you want to know that a particular book might help you find out?

This is a bootstrap operation. At the beginning, you might not be interested in anything.[2] But then, say, you adopt a kitten and you become interested in kittens. Books on taking care of kittens may not interest you because you think you can figure all that out for yourself. But perhaps you'd like to know more about the personality of kittens. What can explain all their different behaviors?

One way to study this is to read about kittens. Another way is to read about other kinds of animals. By studying other animals you can learn how kittens are different.

This process of expanding from one interest out into dozens or hundreds of others has infinite possibilities. Each new interest increases the richness of your life experience, giving you new eyes.

The trouble comes when you've already spent so much time reading books you didn't enjoy that you've adopted the attitude, "No more pencils, no more books, no more teachers' dirty looks."

Many people are alienated from reading by their experiences in school because of unpleasant associations with school itself.

Expose Yourself to Lots of Books

If you are dealing with someone who dislikes reading, ask the person whether it is caused by subtle difficulties in dealing with print of the kind we've considered earlier, or if it is the result of her (or his) not having read enough books that she liked. If it's the former, find a way to make decoding a more successful experience for her, taking into consideration the issues previously discussed.

But if she hasn't read enough books that she likes, then get her a pile of books of all types and allow her no more than five minutes with each of them. Have her read the jacket notes and table of contents, dip into the book at random, and then tear herself away from it after five minutes. You might even want to set a timer for this exercise.

It might take fifty books, but eventually she'll come to one she can't put down. She'll get stuck in it, transfixed by it, and while she may not necessarily read all of it, she'll have an experience she enjoys because she's found something in it that connects with something she thinks is important. It may be that she's had nightmares about being chased by a criminal, so she gloms onto detective stories because they help to appease her fears. Or perhaps she always wanted to do some gardening but never had time, so she finds a book about gardening that makes her want to get out and do it. Whatever it is, she'll have what could be her first experience (or the first one in a long time) of really enjoying reading.[3]

After a while she'll be ready to structure this process more. She'll have discovered that a lot of books have something to say to her. Then she'll want to find ways of broadening her understanding more systematically so she can explore a wider range of subjects in her reading.

The thought process here should dominate our schools and guide the thinking of teachers. In some states, as many as 50 percent of the students are reading below grade level. If these students had been taught the skills of decoding so they could actually make out what the words say, then they'd be ready for the exercise just described.[4]

What Turns Off the Reader

Now let me approach this subject in the opposite way. Let's see what happens that makes people dislike reading. Following are some possibilities:

  1. I have to learn all this stuff for a test, but I don't see how I'm

going to remember it all.

2. This book is boring, but since I've started it, I've got to finish it.
3. I can't figure out what's going on here. I've read fifty pages and nothing has made sense yet.
4. I don't see why on earth I should have to learn about (x).

All these objections boil down to problems with self-esteem. What underlies all these reactions is a sense of personal helplessness, beginning with "I don't understand this," extending on to "This is boring, so I shouldn't have to waste my time with it," and culminating in "Most of what's out there is other people's business."

I suspect that a well-conducted poll of attitudes toward reading would reveal that somewhere in the backgrounds of most people are attitudes like these toward the vast majority of books. True book lovers—people who feel as if everything is potentially their business—are rare.

This seems to be a cultural characteristic of the United States. There are many more readers in Great Britain, even though the population is much smaller. There is also a great deal less violence per capita.

Tolstoy once wrote that "art is the alternative to violence." Extend the word "art" to its widest sense, as in "the art of cooking" or "surgery is an art," and you may have a formula for reducing the violence in our society.

The reader who thinks, "The world is my oyster, from which I can snatch its pearl" is one who can bring to the experience of reading a commitment to the life of the mind. When readers take their problems to the printed page instead of to the streets, it provides a safe outlet. However, the condition needed for this process to work is that there be good readers, capable of submitting their beings to the enrichment of the vast body of knowledge that can be obtained from print. This is not always so easily done, as one can get sidetracked in the backwaters of knowledge and lose the perspective of the whole.[5]

In *Reading with the Heart*, Suzanne Juhasz explains how she reads the great romance novels to try to find the mental environment that ideal parenting should have produced for her.[6] In novels like *Jane Eyre*, the heroine experiences many trials and challenges but, in the end, receives the blessings in life that the ideal parent would have provided. This search for the solution to one's emotional problems motivates a great deal of reading, some of it limited to Harlequin romances, religious books or self-help books.

Seeking help with personal problems is probably the way most of us get started in the development of our intellectual lives. Some of us get stuck recycling the same problem for a lifetime, never making a dent in it, but wearing it like a Purple Heart, displaying our wounds as a badge of honor.

Others come to realize that personal problems can be seen in a larger context, and the more we know about the world in general, the better our chance of going beyond an obsessive focus on past troubles. Developing intellectual skills, we go beyond ourselves into a world that is endlessly fascinating.

Reading instruction should help develop this focus.

Investigating Happiness

In the reading program I developed, I began with the assumption that we would like to relate everything we read to our own experiences. Then I worked out a story line that focuses on how we see our own happiness, how it is related to the happiness of others, and how we can negotiate our differences so as to develop a much deeper satisfaction in life, based on communal feelings and the honing of a personal worldview.

By telling a nonsense story based on this theme, I was able to escape preaching and attempting to impose my views on others. Instead, I created a kind of Rorschach experience that allows readers to find in the text whatever makes sense to them.

Bettelheim and Zelan's *On Learning to Read* explores the ways in which children unconsciously read their own lives into the text, only to be discouraged in this by teachers who correct their "errors." In contrast, a text that can be interpreted a number of different ways, depending on the personal view of the reader, allows children to bring their own lives and perspectives into the discussion without violating the integrity of what they are reading.

There are at least two kinds of symbolism used in literature. One, usually characteristic of the best literature, zeroes in on a particular point of view, attempting to reveal experiences that are precisely defined by the images and symbols used. A simple example of this kind of writing is Aesop's Fables. The morals these stories teach are relatively precise and not open to a variety of interpretations.

The other kind of symbol, much less frequently used, is the "open" symbol. This can be interpreted in many different ways, allowing the reader to play a more extensive role in the interpretation of the story. As a writer in pursuit of literary eminence, I seldom use open symbols because they lack specificity in elucidating a situation or feeling. As a teacher, however, I use them as much as possible. That's because the exercise of finding something in a text specifically meaningful to you is a crucial part of the first stage of finding yourself as a reader.

Because children are so suggestible, it is relatively easy to stamp out the personal spark in their points of view and alienate them from themselves. Many of the adults I know have spent half their lives trying to overcome the effects of well-intentioned socialization that alienated them from their inner drives. Once they have cast aside the demons of their childhoods, many people are ready to take on the world more productively.

Language as Self-Expression

In the broadest sense we cannot become involved with anything unless we connect it somehow to ourselves. In order to trace the development of self-awareness as it is expanded by exploration of the world, much of it through reading, let's look a little more closely at the acquisition of language and how that makes us more self-aware in a way that may prepare for success in reading. A child who gets no response to a cry of hunger doesn't have an early experience of self-confidence. She (or he) may feel that life is unpredictable and controlled by others. The cries turn inward and the child becomes sullen but obedient, since she knows that she is unlikely to get her way.

Nevertheless, as the cries and laughter, which produce noticeably different responses from adults, begin to develop into proto-words like "ma" and "da-da-da-da-da," the child gradually becomes aware that she is naming something.[7]

As the child continues to gesture, she makes sounds that are not entirely random. Sometimes these sounds are happily repeated by the adults around her, and she gets a lot of attention from them. At some point it dawns on her that she is naming things, and she begins to collect names, many of which she initiates herself. In turn, her elders help her to identify these things with names. Some of these interest her and some don't. Gradually she builds up a working vocabulary of maybe twenty-five proto-words and a few actual words to go with them. By this time it is pretty clear that she can use these sounds as instruments to communicate, and sometimes get, what she wants. She begins to perform experiments with the words, putting them together in combinations. A few of these combinations (like "bye-bye") may have come from the language use she has observed, and these have been learned by rote. Many of them are her own experiments. "Car" said in a demanding tone while she points is gradually replaced by expressions like, "You wanna car," in which "you" means, for the time, "I."

Gradually she starts to notice relationships between sentences she creates and sentences created by others, and she adopts more complex sentence patterns. Soon it dawns on her that "you" doesn't mean "I," and she tries, "Give me car."

A grammarian would note that she is using the imperative form of the verb, an indirect object and a direct object. Grammar and syntax have arrived on the scene intuitively. (She never says either of the following sentences: "Give car me" or "Give I car.") Pretty soon she can say, "Baby want car," and soon after, "I want the car."

Nearly everything she says, and nearly every word she uses, is her idea. She has, in effect, reinvented the wheel, creating language all over again with the linguistic tools she has observed, and to a certain extent originated, from her observations of the speech that surrounds her. Her language expresses an inner drive to communicate, which originates from a desire to get or control something out of reach. It is born in frustration, since if every desire were instantly satisfied, there would be no reason to communicate.

Now go back to the primers with sentences like, "Mother said, 'My funny, funny family,'" and see how much of this early experience of creating language is carried over into the structure of the primer.

First of all, nothing in the book is about the particular child. Her use of language began in an attempt to communicate her own inner needs and desires to others. She was seldom interested in describing people she didn't know, and if she did so, it was only to comment on them from her own perspective. Objective comments about life in general were unknown to her.

Thinking about this in relation to my own development, I remember back to December 8, 1941—I was getting close to six years old—and my mother was listening to something on the radio. She felt a need to explain to me what was going on, so she said, "The president is very sad."

This made a big impression on me, because it told me that the president (who was just a picture in the newspaper and a voice on the radio) could have feelings like me. So my first understanding of war came in the form of a simple emotion, which I and a very remote personality could share. War itself was an abstraction. Planes bombing ships somewhere else in the world didn't mean anything at all. But a sad president was a phenomenon I could understand.

A couple of months later I was actually trying to read sentences like "Mother said, 'My funny, funny family.'" I was learning of the experiences of Dick, Jane and Sally. But no one was ever sad or happy. No one was connected to me emotionally. And though the parents and children were white like me, and lived in houses not too different from mine, they did not seem connected to any of the extremely important emotions that motivated my acquisition of language in the first place.

"See Spot run" did not interest me. There was nothing fascinating to me about dogs running. That happened around me all the time. "Be careful, he might bite you" would have been a sentence I would have read with interest. But Spot never threatened to bite anyone. In fact, nothing dramatic ever happened. There was nothing to hold my attention in the comings and goings of those characters.

As I have read more modern primers, I have noted great strides in political correctness in their pages, but no strides at all in creating human dramas that can truly enchant children or other new readers.

Today I know all about Little Red Riding Hood and Winnie the Pooh, who were around in my childhood. I also know a lot about *Teenage Mutant Ninja Turtles,* the situations in *Goosebumps* and *Harry Potter*. But no bright young faces are screaming at me with delight about the stories they've read in their primers. Until the primers are competing in reader interest with the books mentioned above, they'll just be more of the same indigestible pabulum that I was given as a child.

Stilted Reading Experiences

Early experiences of reading usually differ from early experiences of making up and using language in the following ways:

1. The reader's personal feelings are seldom mentioned or appealed to.
2. The words are never originated by the reader, nor can the reader see any place of interest where they might be coming from.
3. There are no coherent patterns in the way words are spelled for the reader to make sense of.
4. The pictures in the book, colorful though they are, do not replicate the reader's world, nor do they invite him or her into another world, different from the reader's but still very interesting, the way all great children's books do.
5. The stories never mention problems of interest to the reader, or those related to the problems the reader has to solve in real life.
6. All of the words used are familiar, but none of them are particularly dramatic or interesting in themselves. There is seldom any reason to wonder what might happen next in any of the stories. No clues are given as to how the spellings of the words might relate to their sounds. The overall impression I have now, looking back on the experience of learning to read, is that I was being talked down to by adults who were certain they knew how my mind worked, but actually didn't have a clue about

what might interest me. Nothing I have seen in the books now used to teach reading, or in the attitudes of those who are learning to read, changes this impression. The best I can say is that many elementary school reading programs now include children's classics or popular books like the ones I've mentioned.

What a Primer Should Be

Following are some things you should look for in a primer:
1. The material should arouse comprehensible feelings that are not particularly comfortable or "safe." If you don't believe me, read or watch *The Wizard of Oz*, *Snow White, Cinderella* or *Teenage Mutant Ninja Turtles*. Throughout the history of children's literature, right up to the present, stories have always dealt with danger, threat, family conflict, frightening demons or witches, and many other things not safe or comfortable, but certainly compelling. The plasticene characters and events used in most children's primers are so far removed from any of this that it's no wonder children so often reject the experience of being taught to read.
2. In the early experience of language, words are generated by situations. I remember when I was just under four and my mother was going to have a baby. I became extremely interested in naming the baby. (I still resent my brother because his name is Michael instead of Goozey—my choice for the name.) On another occasion my parents got me out of bed to listen to Arturo Toscanini conduct a symphony on the radio. I remember this vividly, because there was a lot of interference and voices kept coming into and mixing with the music. The effect fascinated me, generating images I can still remember with excitement.

   The child's world is bursting with new and wonderful experiences. Adults should listen to and take account of these and help the child write them down. The resulting narratives can be turned into books the child has written. Then he or she may look for similar types of narratives in other books.

An infant may use unusual combinations of words to make a small vocabulary fit many different situations. So the words used in a primer should somehow seem to arise from a particular situation and represent an appropriate struggle in a small, but developing vocabulary, used to elaborate a series of incidents that might be described differently with an adult vocabulary. For example, a child might go out in the woods and see the leaves falling off a tree. The wind, to the child, seems to be breaking the tree. The child could describe this in a conversation with the tree, who says to the child, "No, the wind is not breaking me, it is giving me a haircut." Or the child may happen to see a house burning down. "Why did someone put that house in the fireplace?" the child might say. "God needs to burn up old houses so that new ones can be built," the adult might say.

The point here is that too little time has been spent investigating how the child sees the world and how to capture that in words that seem relevant to the kinds of intellectual problems the child is actually trying to solve. We have known something of these for a long time from child psychologist Jean Piaget and others like him, but we have been so concerned to tell children what we think is important, we forget that they can eventually discover that by themselves. The attempt to be natural and "adult" sounding in most primers merely debases the possibilities of language. What these books painfully lack is imagination.

3. It's possible to develop a series of words in such a way that consistency between sound and spelling is observable. Phonics drills consist of such patterns. Yet phonics drills debase language by presenting a boring and irrelevant use of it. Phonics drills should be incorporated into the text in such a way that the child is fascinated by the story while noticing coherent patterns

of sound and spelling relationships that establish consistency before exceptions are introduced. Instead of "The cat hit the hat with a bat that sat terribly flatly on the mat," which doesn't take the imagination anywhere, it's possible to spread these "at" words out more, introduce other patterns mixed in with them, and tell a story that involves the reader. This is what I have done in the stories I have written, which have captured the interest of many young readers. The trick is to get the elements of reading instruction synthesized so they're all working at once without the learner even noticing what's happening. This is not difficult to do, but it has seldom been done.

4. Since pictures seldom come close to what you might imagine in response to the text, primers should not contain pictures. The pictures are too often used as crutches that encourage students to guess at words rather than actually figure out what they are. Most books for adults do not rely on pictures and those that do, use them in artistic and compelling ways, or (as with scientific treatises) to illustrate and amplify material discussed in the text. Once again, when students guess at words, they aren't learning to sound them out. Guessing is fine once the context is so clear that the next word is obvious. That can save time in sounding out a word. But it should never be a substitute for developing the skill in the first place. Children's books with pictures by genuine artists are another matter. In some cases the interpretive genius of a visual artist can amplify the stylistic richness of a good writer. This almost never happens with the slick, glitzy or vacuously cartoonish pictures used in primers. For the most part, these are more like illustrations used in advertising than examples of the art of great illustrators like N. C. Wyeth, W. W. Denslow or E. H. Shepherd.

5. Reading practice, particularly during the early years, should focus on helping readers establish their own mental pictures and share them with each other. Reading a book should be more interesting than seeing the corresponding movie, because

the pictures created in the imagination are more interesting, vivid and distinctively personal.[8] Just as a matter of course, we're all built so we notice unusual things more than usual ones. Therefore we ought to practice reading about unusual things that compel our minds to form images.

6. Most children are caught up in problems of interpreting the world, building relationships with others, establishing some degree of fairness in life, and wondering about questions that have no easy answers. Great children's books deal with such issues. Most primers are so afraid of offending someone that they shy away from mentioning anything interesting, provocative or likely to stimulate class discussion. Bear in mind that, for children, there's no such thing as objective reality—only their own version of it.[9] Any steps toward objective reality are taken as a result of establishing similarities and differences between the reality that you perceive and the different realities that others perceive. You learn to understand that people of different backgrounds have different points of view only if you spend time working through and understanding their perspectives. The younger you are when you do this, the better. School is probably the best place to begin to focus on such matters.

7. There's a reason why children love words like "supercalifrag-ilis-ticexpialidocious." Words are fascinating. They are treasures to be added to your vocabulary. Children should be taught to decipher and use big words, words that are interesting to them, words that may enrich their speaking vocabularies. The sanitized four hundred–word vocabularies in wide use in primers today do not furnish the mind with anything except cheap and outmoded Danish Modern furniture bought second-hand from the Salvation Army.

8. I'm standing in my bedroom. A hippopotamus falls through the ceiling. What happens next? Good stories get your attention with the dramatic and unexpected. "Mother said, 'My funny, funny family'" doesn't do that. "Mother said, 'My fren-

zied, frenzied family'" might. Particularly if father just brought home a dragon that has escaped from its cage and now no one can find where it's hiding in the house. The dragon should be really frightening, though, or the story might not be exciting enough.

Dr. Seuss was great at getting children to see unusual things, except that he did much of the work with his pictures and little with his words. Print a Dr. Seuss book without the pictures and you've lost much of the experience.

Playing New Tunes with Old Characters

It's possible to engage children in something that causes them to interact with the text a good deal more than they usually do when reading the classic stories. Making these familiar stories strange to them in a way that inevitably leads to discussion can provoke the interaction. Following is an example.

Once upon a time there was a Zizzerzazzerzuzz. This creature lived on top of a very high mountain where it was constantly being attacked by hawks. In order to protect itself from the hawks it burrowed under the snow on top of this mountain and built itself a very strange sort of house that the hawks could not break into by any device they could dream up. The creature had done a lot of research to design its house. It had gone to see the Three Little Pigs and it had asked them what kind of a house works best.

The Three Little Pigs lived in a very large building where they sold information about how to build houses. "Don't use straw," said the Pigs. "And don't use sticks."

"What should I use, then?" asked the Zizzerzazzerzuzz.

"Bricks," said the Third Little Pig, who sat behind an enormous desk and wore a three-piece suit with a watch chain visible across his front. He was smoking a large and obnoxious cigar.[10]

"What about snow?" asked the creature.

"Snow is definitely out," said all the Pigs, speaking at once.

"What's wrong with snow?" asked the creature.

"It melts," said the Pigs. "Then you've got no house at all. It doesn't even take a wolf to blow it down."

"Oh, dear," said the creature. "You don't do any research, do you?"

"Research?" said all three Pigs at once. "Of course we do research. We hired a wolf to test all the different kinds of houses we could think of, and we found out that bricks work best."

"Not where I come from," said the creature. "Where I come from there is lots of snow that never melts, and there are no bricks."

"Never mind," said the Pig behind the desk with a large smile on his face, "we can sell you some excellent bricks and thus help you upgrade the quality of your life."

"Not interested," said the creature, and he went back to his mountaintop.

When we mix up the Dr. Suess stories with *The Three Little Pigs*, we are dealing with material that many children are used to hearing in a more or less rote fashion. Children who have not heard these stories, incidentally, could easily be introduced to them before a story like the one above is offered for discussion.

By putting familiar characters into an unfamiliar situation, we create a new kind of experience. Most children tend to be very conservative about their stories and don't want them changed. However, a story like this uses the other stories as a background for something new, something that children can readily accept.

The technique used in this story is called "making the familiar strange." Whenever you do this, you stimulate the mind to think.[11]

A discussion about this story will stir up strong opinions in many children. To start with, there are simple questions they can easily answer from their previous knowledge: Why did the Little Pigs warn the creature against using straw? What was wrong with sticks?

Thinking about a Story

Once questions about content are out of the way, children can start dealing with the central conflict in the story, which is a conflict of point of view. Following are some relevant questions:

As far as the Pigs are concerned, bricks are the only material from which a house should be built. Why do they believe this?

What, in the creature's experience, makes him disagree with them?

What problems might have arisen had the creature tried to build a brick house high up on the mountain?

Why did the creature believe a house made of snow would be perfectly satisfactory?

Why couldn't the creature figure out for himself that he could build a house made of snow, before going to see the Three Little Pigs?

Is it sometimes true that bad advice is helpful, because it makes you think of your own good ideas instead?

Is there some way to decide what kind of house should be built in a particular place? Do houses differ depending on where they are built and who is building them? Do houses used by animals reflect this, as well as houses used by people?

See how much can be spun out of this nonsensical story. In most nonsense there is an undercurrent of sense that helps to make the nonsense fascinating. By probing that undercurrent of sense, we can often notice things about our real-life situations that we might otherwise miss.

So it's possible to write, read, tell and discuss stories that, just because their meanings are not obvious, can provoke interesting discussion and begin teaching the process of critical thinking at a very early age.

The critical thinking is possible because the mind has been asked to manipulate very clear images. We know what the Pigs and the creature look like, what backgrounds they have, and what the houses they are discussing look like. When we think about the answers to the above questions, we must look more closely at these images. Thus the mind gets practice not just in storing and remembering images, but in manipulating them.

The fact that the images in this story are taken from familiar stories and manipulated into a new form helps the children see how this kind of mental manipulation works, and how it is possible to take familiar things and transform them into something new. These skills may not have been much in demand half a century ago, but today they are as essential as any of the basics.

Such an approach would develop an important connection between the type of thinking children normally do on their own and the thinking they are encouraged to do in school.

What Scares Educators

Some parents and educators might ban a story like this from the first grade classroom.[12] The reasons are many. Some groups are opposed to any kind of teaching that encourages imagination. Others react negatively to anything that even suggests the possibility of violence or a world of witches, wizards, talking animals and strange creatures—the common ingredients of most of the classic children's stories. Some have political agendas for the stories that tend to squeeze out of them anything resembling reader appeal. Beyond that, too often educators believe that school must deal with "serious" matters, and that means it cannot stimulate the imagination. An education, too many think, requires you to discipline yourself by learning the kinds of information found in encyclopedias.

There's nothing wrong with encyclopedic knowledge, but if that's all that's in your mind, you are little more than a walking reference book. In any event, what you don't know you can look up in an encyclopedia when you need to know it.

What you do need to have installed with the furniture of your mind is the capacity to bring perspective and context to all situations around you, whether you encounter them in life or in print.

Children have a natural tendency to seek out the context for whatever happens around them. They are always asking about things they have observed. They want explanations for some things their parents can't explain. They have a great deal of scattered knowledge about the world, and they need to order it.

Too many educators, however, assume that children need to have their minds organized by a pre-established curriculum. Because it's necessary to cover the material, there's no time to speculate on philosophical questions—the answers to which you can't look up to make sure you are right.

That's what's so boring about school, and that's why most people's learning is so radically slowed down and often largely extinguished by school experiences.

It's time to reevaluate this approach and to recognize that children think about many of the same things adults think about and can learn to process their ideas about such things in interesting and productive ways. One child who has engaged in the discussion about the houses built by the Three Little Pigs might be inspired to pursue a career in architecture. Another might resolve to take a trip around the world someday and explore how people differ in perspective because of where they live. A third might notice that people are often limited by what they have learned from experiences and might therefore resolve to question, with some frequency, the lessons that experiences seem to teach.

My point is that it's just as important in first grade readers to raise issues that intrigue the mind as it is in books designed for college courses. If we don't begin the experience of reading by intriguing our minds, the interior voice will never be awakened by the print on a page, and we may be in danger of learning to see books as boring and irrelevant.

Our Underestimation of Children

The misperception that underlies the failure to do any of these things is that we assume children know practically nothing and have no worthwhile opinions, so we try to pour ideas, skills and habits into them without investigating what they actually do know, think about and want to learn.

I once heard about a kindergarten teacher who had no idea what the curriculum for kindergarten should be. After all, you don't really have to teach anything in kindergarten because no one does anything serious until first grade. So on the first day of school the teacher asked the children what they wanted to learn about that year. Their answers covered most of the curriculum of the first six years of school, but included all sorts of other things not usually covered in school. What the students were most curious about, however, was how babies are born. So the teacher showed up the second day dressed as a baby and things got off to a rip-roaring start.

The ability to find out and teach what students are interested in is crucial to success in stimulating excitement about learning. Young people have passionate interests. If you teach to those, their minds will awaken. Once, at a Christmas party, a teacher asked my advice about a student she had who wasn't doing anything and wasn't interested in anything.

"There must be something he likes," I said.

She thought for a while and then told me that he liked bowling.

"Then have him write a book for the class about bowling," I said.

A couple of months later she sent me a picture of her student proudly holding before the camera a copy of the book he'd written. That one experience of writing about and sharing a deep interest changed his outlook on all the rest of his school experience.

Over the years I have seen this phenomenon happen to students dozens, if not hundreds, of times. But it seldom happens in schools where the whole point is to stick, robotlike, to a curriculum that often radically underestimates what students of a given age are actually capable of doing or understanding.

I once visited a first grade class in which a movie was shown. The movie, as it happened, was the wrong one. It was intended for the sixth graders and was being shown to the first graders by mistake. At the end of the movie all the students clapped. They thought it was the best one they had seen in class that year.

Curriculum designers seldom talk to children about what they want to learn. What they do instead is invent fictitious notions about what children can and cannot handle and are and are not capable of thinking about.

For example, I was once told, in no uncertain terms, that children cannot develop any kind of moral sense before they reach a certain age. I have observed in my own family, with two different children, that this is wildly untrue. It may be true, as Piaget has observed, that a child thinks a tall glass and a wide glass that will hold the same amount of fluid actually are holding two different amounts of fluid. But then the question is, what do you really mean by "amount"? The child may have a different notion about that from an adult. What matters is that we study children's questions in a way that no serious educator appears to have done as yet and find out what kinds of things their instincts are telling them to investigate. Then we should teach them those things without any further regard for the ridiculous notion of what is and is not age appropriate. No one can say what is age appropriate except in the case of a particular individual. What was age appropriate for Mozart at six is not yet age appropriate for me at ten times that age. It's all a question of where our minds want to go, and no curriculum committee can legislate that.

Deprivation Through Lack of Challenge

While one kind of limit is to keep people from thinking about and doing the things that interest them, another is not challenging them to expand their possible means of expressing themselves and of understanding the expression of others. From the beginning, children can learn what good prose is and begin to get a feel for the qualities of language invoked by good writers. So we need to consider the prosody in which primers should be written.

Good prose and poetry, both, have rhythm. But human beings do not speak in prose, they speak in awkward stops and starts that when literally transcribed are painful to read. Therefore, written language must transcend spoken language. M. Jourdain in Moliere's *Le Bourgeois Gentilhome* was delighted to discover that all his life he had spoken prose.[13] If so, he was the only one who ever did.

First graders need to begin the process of translating prose into the vernacular. Only by considering the meaning of each sentence in turn can they learn to do this. The cadence of prose must be learned gradually, and appreciation of it comes from a subtle transformation of the reader's thinking into the writer's framework. "Whose woods these are I think I know" is a poetic expression that comes out of New England speech. It may fall poorly on the ear of someone from another region unless that reader can see writing as a way of increasing the range of expressive language that can be used to get a point across.

"Oh what a rogue and peasant slave am I" is an expression that no modern American would ever come up with. We do not usually use the word "peasant," and we would be loath even to conceptualize the notion that we might become slaves as a form of self-deprecation. When we call ourselves slaves, we mean that someone else is picking on us, as my mother did when she would do the ironing and declare, "Lincoln freed the slaves, all but one," as if it were my idea that she should iron my underwear. So the latter expression has to be translated in order to be understood, and the ability to make that kind of translation can be developed in first grade.

The reverse transition—from common speech into prose—becomes easier if it is carried out in the form of self-talk. Infants use language that is very basic and describes observed actions in extremely simple terms. Infant self-talk is sometimes called "autistic" in that it resides in its own world without a desire to include anyone else in it. Reading should activate self-talk in the reader's mind.

Part of the problem of learning to read is that beginning readers (even adults) do not spend a lot of time thinking in the third person. Most of their internal sentences begin with an "I": "I am hungry." "I can't stand Betsy." "People are always picking on me." ("I am always being picked on by others.")

So sentences in primers should use a first-person perspective to show the reader how a developing consciousness observes what's going on around it and gradually expands its knowledge of the world. In this manner they can gradually ease the reader into the cadences of prose in Standard English, coming out of the "autistic" proto-English in which the child (or the child in the adult) thinks.

If you write, "See the ball. The ball goes up. Up, up, up goes the ball," I think you must be kidding. My five-year-old intelligence is insulted. But if you write, "I see the ball. It is going up. How can it go up so high? Up, up, up it goes. Will it ever come down?" you've captured my interest. I, too, have sometimes wondered why some things go up and never come down. It seems like you're crawling around inside my mind.

This is a subtle difference, but it's important. No reader ever truly reads anything that is not fundamentally about him or her. Maybe you don't believe that now, but I hope you will by the time you finish this book.

Interlude

Once we know the mechanics of reading, what are we supposed to do about it?

So far this book has been about developmental reading. The assumption among experts tends to be that there's a certain way people are supposed to read, and it's their job to see to it that everyone learns to read that way.

While, to some extent, this attitude is essential to getting the job done, it also tends to sell reading short. There is a great deal more to reading than can be tested by pencil-and-paper exercises. While we do indeed read to acquire information and instruction, there are other equally acceptable ways of acquiring both of these.

Reading offers something else that is unique, however: It offers the opportunity to construct one's own point of view and expand one's mental life.

In part 2, I'll explore this process. T. S. Eliot's remarks about the developing poet in his essay "Tradition and the Individual Talent" provide a thumbnail sketch of what is to follow:

> What is to be insisted upon is that the poet must develop or procure the consciousness of the past and that he should continue to develop this consciousness throughout his career.
>
> What happens is a continual surrender of himself as he is at the moment to something which is more valuable. The progress

of an artist is a continual self-sacrifice, a continual extinction of personality.[1]

We experience the extinction of personality that Eliot speaks of when we lose ourselves in a wider, less limited frame of reference than we've been aware of previously. This is a personal paradigm shift—a fundamentally new way of seeing life.

I suggest that this progression of personality through various transformations need not be confined to poets, but may be undertaken by readers of all kinds, and that reading is perhaps the best way of accomplishing such a transformation.

As you go through life, you can make yourself more valuable by extending the range of your awareness and the number of experiences you have integrated into a meaningful whole, which you would describe as "me." And yet with the rise of modern technology, there are many forces working against this process, as if to make it more difficult for you to become civilized.[2]

Despite all the advances in the media and computers, the old-fashioned book is an instrument of learning that can never be improved upon. Something about holding a book in your hand and indulging in the daydreams an author has constructed for you is unlike any other kind of experience. It is both intensely private and universal at the same time. As you read the works of someone known to millions of other readers, your impressions are uniquely your own. You are at liberty to carry on a conversation with that author that no one has ever had before.

In what follows you'll find some hints about how that conversation might be developed and improved upon.

I am aware as I write this, near the beginning of a new millennium, that I am looking forward into a time when we are in danger of losing something valuable that the majority of people have been able to enjoy for only about five hundred years.

Technology will not improve our lives if, in the process, it takes this from us. But if we practice, teach and encourage the art of reading, we need not fear such a consequence.

I do not believe a computer can ever replace a book. For example, when I write a book on my computer and read it over I find it very different from the experience I have of it after it is printed out and I read it on paper.[3]

It is my hope that, for the next thousand years at least, we shall continue to have books much like the ones we have had and have been civilized by for the past several thousand years. Nothing can replace them.

Part Two

Constructing
the Edifice

*How can those of us who have mastered
the mechanics of reading develop a highly
sophisticated capacity to arrive at our own
thoughtful interpretations of a wide range
of complex texts?*

10

Reading to Promote Thinking

How can we learn to dig ever deeper beneath the surface of a text and thus expand the parameters of our own beings?

Reading need not be just a passive response to a story or line of argument developed by someone else. It can be as active and combative as a good conversation. You can condemn a writer or idolize him, gently correct or enthusiastically endorse him. You can passionately reject what he has to say, or amplify it into a new system of thought that becomes your own.

This process of actively reading to promote your own thinking cannot start too early. So I shall begin this chapter by demonstrating the process of considering closely the meaning of some sentences that a beginner might learn to read:

"I am a ham. Me? A ham? I can ham. I am a ham. Can a ham ham? A ham can ham. Can I can ham? I can can ham."

This is the first paragraph that students are asked to read in my reading program. Before that, the students learn to read a couple of sentences, and they learn what sounds all the letters used above make when they are used in these words. In this way, the process of decoding is easy, and the student can read the paragraph at sight.

This is a far cry from *Fun with Dick and Jane*, and it disturbs some people because it is not written in a way that reflects how people normally think or talk. Indeed, I have found few adults who can read all these words in sequence the first time without making at least one mistake.

Why America's Children Can't Think

What people miss when they complain about the cadence in which this paragraph is written is the fact that the biggest hurdle to overcome when you are learning to read is to recognize that words printed on a page have relatively little relationship to the way anyone actually talks. Rather than try to put off this realization by presenting new readers with something that some adults think is the way words usually occur to them, it's better to confront this dilemma head on. Reading, at least when you first take it on, is no more "natural" than doing a jigsaw puzzle.

When you talk, you effuse language without thinking about it. When you write, on the other hand, you put together words that represent ideas, often at great pains to select them carefully so they will convey precisely what you mean.

Given the care that authors put into what they write, it behooves readers to spend a bit of time reflecting on the meaning of what they are reading, rather than to breeze through it with scant pause for thought.

The sample paragraph I offered above is challenging not in its orthography, but in its various forms of ambiguity. Readers who engage in self-talk about what they are reading have a lot of thinking to do when they encounter a sentence like "I can ham."

To begin with, the paragraph is written from the point of view of the reader. The main character is "I." So it's the reader's job to consider whether his or her experience is accurately represented here.

Let's examine the first sentence: "I am a ham."

In my teacher trainings I ask the person who has read this sentence whether or not he or she actually is a ham. The responses are often quite interesting. Here are two of them.

"No, I am not a piece of meat."

"No, I don't consider myself a ham."

In the first case, the reader may not actually know that "ham" can have more than one meaning. But let's ignore that for a moment and suppose that meat is what I'm talking about. If ham comes from pigs and she's not a pig, that settles the matter. But how can she say that she's not a piece of meat, when the fact is that she is and every moment of her life depends absolutely on that fact? So how is it that she fails to define herself in this most basic way? Is this a way of asserting that what is essential about her is the ineffable mental state that comes and goes so unpredictably and unreliably, while the part of her that is meat remains quite distinctly there, wherever consciousness might be wandering at the moment?

Suddenly we are into some pretty fundamental questions about the nature of being. Is the only thing about me that is valuable also the only thing that no one can be certain, at any given time, is actually there? After all, how can we establish, for certain, the fact that someone else is conscious? It's theoretically possible to look and act as if we're conscious and not be in a conscious state at all.

Suddenly a lot of things that we've always more or less assumed about life, without really thinking about them, are up for grabs.

Now let us progress to the second answer, "I don't consider myself a ham."

"Well, what do you think a ham is?"

"Someone who's always joking around in a ridiculous way?"

"And you never do that?"

"No. Well, not usually. Sometimes. Yes, come to think of it, maybe I am a ham."

My experience with a roomful of public school teachers is nearly always the same. When they first show up, they're very businesslike. They're there to do what they're supposed to do. They wouldn't think of joking around or even smiling.

But since learning really doesn't happen unless it's a lot of fun, it's important to get them to lighten up as quickly as possible, to bring out the "ham" in them.

Fortunately, this is pretty easy. No one decides to spend a career working with children who isn't interested in having a good time occasionally. You just can't get anywhere with children if you're never ready to have fun.

Besides which, I've noticed that any group of human beings anywhere will start to have fun as soon as the possibility exists and they think it's okay to do it. There may be something vaguely evil about having fun, something irresponsible at least, but since it's fun, we're going to do it now and then if we get a decent crack at it.

What this boils down to, in fact, is the basic realization that, at heart, we are all hams. We all want to be running around, wearing funny party hats, singing silly songs, rolling around on the floor, and all of that. After all, that's how we spent the best years of our lives, which were, in most cases, the first five.

Discovering New Dimensions in Who We Are

Let's move on to the next sentence, which consists of a single word and a question mark: "Me?"

"What does that sentence mean?"

"It means that I'm surprised I said I was a ham."

"Why would it surprise you to have said that?"

"Because normally I don't think of myself that way. But now that I've said it, I wonder if it's true."

The operative word here is "normally." "Culturally" would be a better word. For some reason our culture has a great deal invested in keeping us from behaving spontaneously, the way children do, even though the most successful people have a spontaneous streak in them.

We then have to ask why discovering one of the most human things about ourselves should be a surprise. What kind of energy has gone into making us all into such stuffed shirts, and who profits from this?

The answer is clear: No one profits from it, and everyone would be happier if everyone else were more spontaneous. The fact that we go through life mostly frowning, that we struggle to get up in the morning and get through the day and all the rest of it is ridiculous. It should be a simple matter for anyone to put a stop to that sort of thing. The trouble is, it's expected of us to be like that, so most people are.

So that one-word second sentence is a startled awareness that the human species ought to wake up and smell the roses. There's no reason why we can't whistle while we work.

But let's go on. The third sentence is two words and a question mark: "A ham?"

Now why should one echo one's own comment like that? Well, the fact is we're constantly talking about ourselves in ways we don't fully understand. We need some of those ways reflected back to us. Creeping around subserviently, apologizing for our existence is not a good way to live, yet lots of us seem to be doing that much of the time.

Look at it this way. During our lifetime the universe will supply us with a good many resources. These will include tons of what used to be living plants and animals, enough oxygen to meet the needs of a whole city, several thousand beautiful sunsets for us to watch if we're so inclined, and several million other opportunities along those same lines. How can we noncommittally and somewhat unconsciously consume all of that largesse and then tell ourselves we're not really important? If we're not, then why is the universe wasting so much energy on us? And if we really think we are important but are afraid to say so, then we're hypocrites.

It may turn out that basic self-awareness of the most fundamental kind is in rather short supply.

Let's go on: "I can ham." Well, what's the relationship between someone who *is* a ham and someone who *can* ham? If someone is a doctor, can that person doctor? Obviously yes. Well, if someone can drive a car is that person a car driver? Assuming you have a driver's license, do you usually think of yourself that way? So what determines when something you can do somehow defines your being and when it doesn't? Is the distinction arbitrary? Does it require a certain amount of commitment?

I go through life being someone, and now it looks as if I've spent very little time considering who it is that I am being, because as soon as the subject comes up I'm not quite sure how I stand on some of these rather basic issues.

Suppose you were buying a car and the salesman told you he didn't know what it could and couldn't do. He wasn't sure whether or not it should actually be considered a car. He certainly wasn't sure how good it was; but he knew it had a virtually inexhaustible supply of potentially remarkable and indeed mind-boggling qualities, only no one had taken the trouble to figure out what they were, or even what they might be.

Why do we consider it so much more essential to define everything else in the world than we do to define ourselves, or each other?

But let's go on: "I can ham." I'm reading that fourth sentence over again, and it looks different this time. I'm standing in front of a platter of ham preparing it for canning. Well, that's straightforward enough, except that I don't know whether or not that makes me a canner. Maybe I only do it once a year.

If we think of this as a metaphor, it's as if we were saying to the spontaneity in ourselves and others: "Can it!" We're usually trying to keep the lid on things in a desperate attempt to prevent something from happening that might go out of control or be disruptive or that we might not understand.

Walk into almost any classroom and after a while you'll notice that most of the energy being expended is used to keep the lid on things. This chronic condition of classrooms naturally leads to a corresponding chronic condition in workplaces. We're often so busy in the workplace trying to keep things from happening that we give too little attention to whatever it is that we're trying to make happen.

Think of a society that is driving down the highway doing ninety while looking in the rearview mirror. Meanwhile it is devoting 95 percent of its actual attention to trying to prevent anything from going on inside the car that might be slightly disruptive or unpredictable, despite the fact that the car itself is in imminent danger of being destroyed.

But let's go on to the fifth sentence: "I am a ham."

How does this sentence read now, after the above discussion? It may appear to be the same as the first sentence, but surely you realize after all we've been through here that it's no longer possible for it to be even remotely like that first sentence, which we approached in such naive innocence.

Much as I'd like to go further with this, I'll leave the rest to you. You probably get the idea by now.

Developing the Habit of Digging Beneath the Surface

If it's possible to milk this much out of the above nonsense designed for a primer, how much more might be available in almost any work of literature or text that reveals something important about the world?

It's possible for any student to learn to think like this very quickly and go on digging beneath the surface of things for a lifetime. But the threat is enormous, because if everyone did this kind of thinking, society would be transformed. The status quo would quickly become ancient history.

Instead of doing this sort of thing, though, teachers spend much, if not most, of their time doing things that shouldn't have to be done at all.

Nobody knows much about how we learn and, most particularly, about how we learn language. Learning, which is a subdevelopment of consciousness, is still beyond our capacity to understand. That's because the consciousness that perceives the world surrounding it has a hard time understanding how its perceptions occur, since much of perception is not conscious at all. Try pitching a baseball in an important game and, at the same time, being fully aware of what exactly you have to do to make the pitch a good one. Expert behavior and self-conscious awareness of that behavior are almost impossible to maintain at the same time. Taking any form of human behavior into the science lab and analyzing it almost immediately invokes Tennyson's famous line, "We murder to dissect."

For example, it is not usually taught in schools that most learning takes place unconsciously. After all, you learned your native language unconsciously, you learned to walk unconsciously, to relate to people unconsciously, and you're constantly picking up from your friends or from television programs new ways of thinking that you're not even aware you've picked up. If this seemingly obvious phenomenon were well understood, schools would not operate the way they do, they would be organized along different principles. They would trust the process by which people learn most of what they know, and seek to guide them in how to use what they have learned.

That is why so much of what happens in schools does anything but develop intelligence. In fact, it usually puts limits on it. One of the most fundamental ways it does this is by teaching people to read in ways that do not serve them well.

Becoming Conscious of What
We Think and Read

We're constantly bombarded by images. Everywhere we look we see literally thousands of perceptible, discreet objects, almost all of which we ignore. I have driven for miles so lost in thought that I became unconscious of where I was.

So almost all of what we see never reaches our conscious awareness.

Language operates in this same way. We are flooded with words, most of which we don't hear. We can look at words on a page and not see them. It requires a special effort of attention to know what we have seen, heard, read or even spoken.

The best way to increase our conscious awareness of language is to process it visually, since much that is fundamental to language happens in the visual cortex. That is why the first thing we need to do after we hear or see new words is to turn them into images. Failing to do so leads to a reshuffling of vocabulary without reference to meaning.

Consider the following lines from *Romeo and Juliet*:

The gray-eyed morn smiles on the frowning night,
Check'ring the eastern clouds with streaks of light;
And fleckèd darkness like a drunkard reels
From forth day's path and Titan's burning wheels.

Here we gain a visual impression that is almost as rich as that suggested by a fine landscape painting. We can return to this poem and savor the subtleties of its imagery and the resulting pictures the mind can derive from it. The images capture the extreme drama of a dawn in which morning struggles with night to be born. They are as kinesthetic as they are visual, and they suggest a wide range of emotions from the welcoming smile to the frown that greets it, the wild insanity of the drunkard's reel and the harshness of the burning wheels of Titan. Here is a marvelous mixture of balance and imbalance, of gentleness and violence, and of the positive and negative as different aspects of the same experience.

For contrast, consider next the following sentence: "We hold these truths to be self-evident." Here, in an at least equally provocative use of language, the visual components are less obvious, but let's explore how they operate.

Perhaps when you read this sentence you are led to other things you know. You might visualize Thomas Jefferson writing it. You might remember the handwriting in which it was written. Or you might visualize a small group of brave colonists standing up to the British marauders in their stuffy uniforms. You might even imagine that you hear the music of fife and drum.

Paradoxically, then, this sentence does not refer back to itself as much as the previous one does. It takes you out of itself into other associations. To the extent that it does lead you back into itself, it is to formulate a series of questions:

What is a self-evident truth?

If a truth is truly self-evident, why should anyone need to declare it to be so?

If it is not self-evident, why would anyone think that it was?

Is there any way to prove or disprove a self-evident truth?

Questions like these (and there might be thousands of them) take us farther afield from the visual basis of language. Still, they refer back to it subliminally.

Enter, Visual Thinking

For every linguistic impression that we have there is a corresponding subliminal image. Rudolph Arnheim develops this idea in *Visual Thinking.*[1] The imagistic roots of all language are so structured in the brain that we have images we are not conscious of that help us process the meanings of words. Pressed to do so, we can draw these images. They may be incomprehensible squiggles, but they are the brain's way of processing the meanings that lie behind the words.

For example, when I think of a self-evident truth, I imagine Truth looking at itself in a mirror. I'm not certain why I do that, and I never thought of it until I was pressed to come up with a visual image for that idea. I am quite certain, however, that that is the way my brain processes that particular idea.

This takes us to the fundamental structure of reality that is encoded in our brains and expressed through language.

As human beings who have memory and continuity through time, we imagine ourselves to be moving through some sort of a bubble that is the universe as we understand it. This model of the world is always complete and whole. Whatever isn't there does not exist for us. When we add new parts to it, it does not appear to get larger, but rather to be complete and whole as before. This creates the illusion that the world is unchanging, even though we know it is changing.

In one person's model of the universe, Truth may be personified as a being. It might be an angel, or an amorphous spirit that hovers over everything. Other abstract ideas may be personified or objectified in this way as well. That is why allegorical stories come so easily to mind and are so widely enjoyed in all cultures. And thus our minds recreate the universe in our own images. In order to understand a thing, we must be able to see it. In order to see it, we must have an image for it.

Some images may be more kinesthetic than visual. They may be feelings of motion in the body, shifting their positions or shapes like barely visible gray clouds.

As we think, these images, which are more and more closely tied to the words that express them, give rise to a stream of additional words that express these otherwise abstract feelings and ideas.

The images then drop out of awareness as the ideas become so familiar that we can manipulate them mentally without consciously thinking about the images with which we first conceived them.

Our models of the world rest on a foundation, like a building. In the structure of a building you have those things that support everything else and those that seem to go off on their own. We can think of the development of ideas as being like the structure of a building. To the extent that we can translate an abstract argument into a set of visual impressions, we can interpret it more easily and manipulate its elements more freely. The same process occurs as we follow the development of ideas in a text. If we are truly following the argument, we are building a mental structure in this gray, dimly seen visual world that lies behind the words.[2]

Suppose, for example, you read a description of how to build a syllogism. You might see it in the form of a stepladder with possibly some objects, like apples, sitting on the steps. As you manipulate the concepts through the syllogism, you silently feel the motion of the objects on the ladder.

If the model is poorly built, the idea will remain unclear to you. If you go back over it until you have reshaped the model so it works well for you, the idea will suddenly seem clear, perhaps with an "ah-hah" experience.

But it is only when you enter the picture that the words suggest to you that this is possible. Otherwise, the words are simply words. You recognize them. You think you know what they mean individually. But you do not understand their cumulative force.

When the idea is sufficiently familiar so you can return to it whenever you wish, it then becomes possible for you to think of it on your own, and to modify and develop it.

I can stand looking at the dawn, see its combat with the night, and imagine all sorts of things being added to it. I notice, for example, that in *Romeo and Juliet* this scene immediately follows the darkness of the balcony scene. Is the morn the spirit of fulfillment, while the night is the spirit of promise? Does the sunrise seem to promise the union of the lovers who have discovered each other in the night?

As I think about these questions, I can manipulate the picture, bring it into relationship with other pictures, and combine and recombine the pictures. I can manipulate objects in my mind exactly as if they were present in physical form. I can shuffle and manipulate my realities and build my universe in my head any way I want. Ultimately I have total control over it. It is my creation and I can make it manifest anything I desire. Creating my own universe in my imagination has often been shown to be one of the primary ways we strengthen our creativity and ability to achieve success in our real-life activities.[3]

It's important to form a strong relationship between the recognition of words at sight (which paradoxically can be accomplished only by avoiding any form of whole word recognition in instruction) and the auditory and visual-kinesthetic images that may arise from those words. The result is a much greater involvement in the reading experience. Thus the first reading of a book is only the beginning of the relationship with that book. It remains a vital force in the mind, a part of the mental furniture, which can now be used to bring meaning to other things that you read, and to help you interpret your real-life experiences.

Listening to the Author's Voice

In order to develop a full relationship with a book, the voice of the author must come alive in your head as if it were your own voice. The stream of consciousness that goes on in your mind all day long, articulating perhaps forty thousand thoughts each day, must be corralled by the author's voice and become the vehicle by which the words that are observed on the page enter your realm of conscious thought. This stream of self-talk, which need not be fully articulated words but may simply invoke the images that lie behind the words, is the means by which we communicate with ourselves and consciously build our mental structures. This internalized self-talk was first analyzed by Russian psychologist Lev Vygotsky.[4]

Autistically based self-talk observed in very young children, and present in adults mostly when they are upset, runs in self-referential loops. For example, one might spend hours mentally rehearsing a variety of different ways of confronting someone or even violently retaliating against them. This happens because the self-referential loop in the brain, which is processing the feelings and observations that have led to the distress, can't get outside itself in order to open up to new observations or insights.

To give an example, suppose that I have just received a traffic ticket for speeding. Since I will not admit to myself that I have done anything wrong, I experience the fact that the cops are out to get me and that any just cop would have known that I had a good reason for speeding when I did. The cop should know that it is not dangerous when I do it, and that anyway I had lost track of how fast I was going for a moment, but that was okay because I could clearly see that there was no danger in what I was doing.

This line of thought could easily recycle itself for hours. I can interrupt the cycle, however, with other thoughts. I can begin to wonder whether this experience has anything to offer me of a positive nature. Perhaps I have been disturbed enough by the traffic ticket to change my driving habits and thus avoid getting more tickets in the future. I might decide to become more vigilant when I drive, so I will always see the cop before he or she sees me. I might decide to observe the speed limit at all times. I might decide to speed only as a result of being in the flow of traffic so the cop will not single me out from others, all of whom are going at the same speed as I am. I might do any number of other things. What's happening at this point might be called meta-thought. It is thinking about my own thoughts.

Meta-thought occurs when a line of thinking already in process is not acceptable as satisfactory. The ongoing flow of imagery and ideas is interrupted by some other part of the mind that attempts to override a previous direction and move things toward a different conclusion. It can only arise when there is unresolved conflict. By reacting to conflicts we are driven to greater awareness of ourselves and our purposes in life. Otherwise, ongoing experiences are observed placidly and lead only to the most obvious next step. So in the process of taking off in a new, hopefully more satisfying, direction, we have to learn to operate as the editors of our own autistic speech.

It's a lot easier to do this if we are not so upset that our autistic speech overrides every other possible thought or impression we might have. Fortunately we can always expand our thoughts beyond the concerns reflexively consuming our minds. That is when we become the captains of our souls and strive to change the direction we are going to a more favorable one. Often this change of direction may come about as a response to a personal crisis—an accident or illness, for example. At such a time a favorite author may suddenly seem to describe the universe (or some corner of it) in a new and more powerful way. Before the crisis we might not have understood this new way of thinking, but now that we've caught a glimpse of it, the author helps us articulate it in detail.

You'll often find examples of famous people recalling such experiences with reading, like the ones I'm about to describe.

Famous Directional Changes

A paradigm shift often occurs when a writer gets a blinding insight from another writer or from a particular kind of artistic experience. Keats described this sensation in his poem, "On First Looking into Chapman's Homer."

> *Then felt I like some watcher of the skies*
> *When a new planet swims into his ken;*
> *Or like stout Cortez when with eagle eyes*
> *He stared at the Pacific—and all his men*
> *Looked at each other with a wild surmise—*
> *Silent, upon a peak in Darien.*

George Bernard Shaw said that his mind came alive for the first time when he read Karl Marx in the British Museum. He also felt that he understood life better as a result of looking at the paintings and cartoons of Hogarth. Hemingway developed his writing style out of the inspiration he got from Gertrude Stein.

Such love affairs with new possibilities for thinking or feeling can happen at any time in life. Mozart discovered Bach's music rather late in his life, but was terribly excited and profoundly transformed by the experience. Melville, who had published many good sea stories, became able to rise to the heights of *Moby Dick* as a result of reading Shakespeare. For Tolstoy the inspiration to see life as a profound moral struggle came from the influence of a governess who took care of him as a child. T. S. Eliot, in the middle of his life, experienced a Jungian psychoanalysis and developed a deep commitment to Catholicism. I once heard Richard Wilbur say that he became a poet while he was in a foxhole during World War II. George Lucas was able to decide what he wanted to accomplish in life only after a nearly fatal automobile accident.

But these are all examples of people who created works of art. Let's consider for a moment how one might use reading experiences themselves as a take-off point for thinking that leads in a completely new direction.

Probing the Meaning Shared by Two Stories

Consider the following two well-known short stories and the kind of interaction they might cause the mind to play with:

In "To Build a Fire," Jack London writes of a man who has set out on a journey in very cold weather and gradually realizes that if he does not start a fire and warm himself he will freeze to death. The story describes his failed attempt to build the fire and lets the reader experience his gradually developing awareness that he has indeed come to the end of his life.

In "Silent Snow, Secret Snow," by Conrad Aiken, a psychotic little boy gradually builds a defense against the world in which he can hide in total autistic isolation. Each day when the postman comes, it takes longer before the boy can hear his footsteps. The boy imagines a silent, secret snowfall outside that is covering the earth so that the footsteps of those approaching will no longer be audible. The boy finds security in the fact that soon he will not hear the footsteps at all and will thus be entirely protected from any impingement from the outside world.

In these two stories the main characters (in each case, really the only character in the story) come to an end as a result of a misunderstanding of the reality that surrounds them—a misunderstanding that has an element of pride behind it. In the second story both the snow and the death are metaphorical, but the experiences of the two stories are rather similar, since in each case the reader has a perspective on the events that the main character lacks. Thus the reader's interpretation of what is being reported is different from the character's interpretation of it.

The question is, do these two stories, taken together, suggest some element of reality that might be generalized, some truth about human nature that might lead beyond a mere interpretation of a fictional experience?

I have suggested several times that all experience is subjective and there is really no reliable way to establish the nature of an objective world that is supposedly out there.

However, these two stories, taken together, suggest a possible way out of the obvious limitations of taking the lack of a provable objective reality too literally. The characters in these stories fail to observe aspects of their experiences that they would need to notice in order to survive. We notice and we feel that, in their situations, we would behave differently and thus survive. So while there may not be an objective world that can be definitely established, there are some ways of defining our own personal realities that seem to arise from our basic human natures much more than from the accidents of our particular experiences.

No two people survive in exactly the same way, because we all approach the world differently. However there are some common themes to survival that repeatedly emerge from the study of literature, science and the social sciences. By seeing the issues of survival through many different eyes, we deepen the awarenesses we need for our own survival. So as we analyze the characters in these two stories, or the survival situations that are stated or implied in almost anything else we read, we think about our own reactions to them, and this meta-thinking strengthens our own abilities to survive and flourish.

In order to survive and reproduce, we must be able to perceive the world in such a way that the odds of our staying alive are constantly improved by our experiences. Each time we make a mistake that threatens our security, we can learn from it and avoid making the same mistake a second time. That is the value of experience that transcends individual opinion and dictates a tendency for all human beings to behave in the same general ways. When we fail to operate in the interests of our own survival, we behave in a way that seems suspiciously deviant from the behavior we expect in each other.

The question is, why should such a thing ever happen? Why should human beings not be so thoroughly programmed to survive that they would almost never drift into their own death? Are we really forced to make our own individual choice about whether or not we want to go on living? Is this kind of choice a fundamental aspect of life itself?

As the two stories indicate, death may not, under certain conditions, seem threatening. It might feel like the pleasant relief of sleep to someone who has become very tired.

So what would cause one to choose life, and what would cause one not to?

In order to choose life, I must feel the power I have to make an impact on the world so I can create the environment and circumstances that will make me happy, or at least fulfill my purposes as I see them.

The decision to choose death might then come when I have resolved that the effort to achieve and maintain such power is more trouble than it is worth and I am better off welcoming the sweet sleep of death.

One way of seeing our existence in the world is to say that the forces of evolution have created us so that we will reproduce ourselves and continue our species. The forces of evolution, then, have no concern for us as individuals, but only for the species as a whole.

However, if survival is a choice rather than an instinct, that might prove to be a misinterpretation of the evolutionary forces. Perhaps things do not work that way at all. Perhaps the universe is a gift offered to those who care to enjoy it, but the offer is always open to opt out of it. If it is a gift then one ought to be able to find a way to make life enjoyable even if there seem to be barriers to doing so. That would mean that one is meant to discover and develop one's own particular power, and also to help others discover and develop theirs.

Perhaps, indeed, the universe was constructed with this purpose in mind: the opportunity for each individual to enjoy it fully, rather than simply for the proliferation of life in all its possible forms, regardless of the quality of life for anyone in particular. If that were so, we do not construct our lives so that we might live as if it were so. We do not think nearly well enough about how to improve the structure of our own lives. Nor do we think nearly well enough about how to help others go through this same process.

Perhaps the purpose of the human species is to learn to enjoy its planet and there is no point in living otherwise. If so, then the search for a high quality of life for all people should become a universal quest.

This point of view might be held up as a critique of our current culture and tested on the basis of whether or not it could suggest alternative cultures that would better serve the true purposes of humanity. Science fiction tends to develop this kind of thinking. By exploring alternative futures, it helps readers critique the ways we are currently preparing for the future. Scientists, at least half of whom are avid science fiction fans, certainly think so.

But there is a lot more to our culture and our future than technology. Exploring the emotional meanings of life is the subject of much great literature. We can read such works for the story alone, or we can seriously contemplate how they may impact our lives. This latter kind of thinking and reading is all too rare. For many people it must be taught or it will never happen. This is the responsibility of reading teachers.

The Habit of Creating New Possibilities of Thought

Often books can lead to new possibilities for thought and action. You can extend the limits of your thinking by looking at the logical consequences suggested by particular books, stories or news reports. These intellectual exercises are possible in great profusion and show how the mind can create almost anything for itself if it takes the time to meditate upon what it has read in several different contexts.

Occasionally I have conversations that explore the subtle implications of an idea with friends or family members. Whenever we have had such a discussion, there is a feeling afterward that the experience has been very satisfying and the time well spent. No practical results need come from the discussion, but it will have paved the way for more discussions of a similar nature. And once in a while such a series of discussions may lead to a decision to change the course of one's life.

I often find it easier to carry on such discussions with young people than with older ones. The young almost instinctively enjoy the free play of the mind, letting it lead them wherever it will. The old tend to be more cynical and are more likely to have developed ruts in their thinking. People who have discussions like these, however, often lament that there are too few opportunities to have them because they don't have many friends who would want to participate in such a discussion.

I think everyone would want to if the habit was formed early enough. Physicist Richard Feynman tells of how his father engaged in such discussions with him and encouraged him constantly to think about the nature of the universe. This developed in Feynman a habit of mind that never left him and eventually earned him the reputation of being a genius.

By thus training our autistic speech, which forms our stream of consciousness, to interact with our subliminal speech in reading, we can establish a link between the two. We should notice that if a sentence in a book does not provoke the same degree of realism and involvement as our own thoughts do, we need to reread the sentence until it does. Whenever I have instructed students to reread in this way until they can ask all sorts of questions about anything that they read, their ability to think skyrockets. This is what I mean when I say that when we read well, we read about ourselves. We accomplish this by refurbishing the autistic speech of childhood and using it to respond to the material we are reading.

The discipline of using autistic speech in creative and productive ways is seldom taught, but it is quite easy to learn. By directing this stream of autistic speech toward the discovery of greater meaning in experience, we can learn to think better and incidentally have a much better time doing almost everything we do. It is also true that when we read well in this way, we end up expanding who we are.

This might seem a little artificial, but it can, in the end, lead to a transformation of your personality. That will happen as you become more comfortable with the new freedom of thought that reading well brings, as well as greater thoughtfulness about the nature and proper uses of freedom itself.

11

Reading as a
Conscious Process

*How do we know that we're conscious of what we're
reading, and is there any way of controlling the
nature of that consciousness?*

Much of what we do in a day is decided unconsciously. An early window
into this process was provided in W. Grey Walter's *The Living Brain*, which
reported on studies of fighter pilots in World War II who had begun to aim
their weapons at enemy planes before they could consciously see them.[1]
A part of the subconscious mind was involved in this highly technical kind
of response.

Along the same lines, I reported earlier about Russell Baker's experience of integrating all the skills of flying a plane in a single instant. The
blink of an eye divided the time when he couldn't fly at all from the time
when he flew like an expert. So it's not just that the subconscious mind controls the operations and decisions about fine points of distinction among
expert professionals, but also that there comes a point when a new level of
performance spontaneously integrates in a fraction of a second. We may
spend years developing the habits that lead to professional performance and
then suddenly find that those habits have become so much a part of our
beings that we no longer have to think about them.

This phenomenon is found in all types of professional performance.
The figure skater who falters at a crucial moment made a mistake in learning technique months or years before, but (at least on a conscious level)
there is no chance of avoiding the mistake as it actually occurs. The mistake

happens below the level of consciousness, and thus reflects a failure in the learning process that occurred some time in the past.

The brain surgeon must often make split-second decisions because there is literally no time in which to evaluate the situation and decide what to do. Successful performance is possible because the surgeon's mind has stored at a subconscious level at least two different types of maps. One maps out the brain, so the surgeon's fingers know what each part does, just as a typist's fingers know the keyboard. The other maps out activities associated with certain perceived situations that can arise in a damaged or sick brain. These maps are so well established and have so much control over the moment-by-moment behavior of the fingers that the surgeon has little actual thinking to do during the operation—except perhaps to decide on which of several courses of action to take.

What is true of highly competent professionals is also true of artists. The finest artists may plan out a work very carefully, but in the actual creation of it, something beyond the realm of consciousness takes over.

This phenomenon has led some to think that consciousness is nothing but an illusion. We literally have no control over what we do, some argue on the basis of a great many experiments that demonstrate how we perceive ourselves as doing some things a short time after we have actually done them.[2]

This "illusion" of consciousness may cause us to blame ourselves for mistakes we could not possibly have avoided. The tendency to blame may actually make the situation worse. It may persuade the subconscious that mistakes will always occur. Some highly competent professionals have suffered worries of this sort for long periods of time. Sir Laurence Olivier, for example, who was arguably the world's greatest actor in his time, went through years of devastating stage fright almost every time he went onstage. It seemed as if some force in him could never accept the fact that his competence was so well established that it was outside his conscious control.

Actually, actors and other professionals who make blunders also know how to disguise them and recover from them. That's part of the professionalism, and these decisions, too, are made by the subconscious mind.

Doesn't that indicate that those who believe consciousness is merely an illusion are right?

My answer is an emphatic No!

Everything we do has to be learned at some level, and during the learning process, consciousness is necessary. In learning a particular type of skill, for example, you have to know what you must do to improve your performance. Not all of these decisions are conscious. Some very gifted people seem able to observe a new kind of performance once and adopt it immediately afterward. For example, Mozart learned to play the violin by watching someone else play for half an hour.

But for most people the process of learning how to do something well involves intensive conscious thought and analysis. You may unconsciously decide to do the thought and analysis, but most of the time you'll become very conscious of what's involved in doing it.

You may, for example, be able to recall your early struggles to learn to ride a bicycle before it became second nature to you to do so. You may recall struggling to learn a subject that you now feel as if you had invented yourself.

It is here, in the progress toward some goal of excellence, that your consciousness becomes extremely important. That begins with the question of who you are, and, as you remember, this begins with autistic speech in childhood. However, that kind of speech is soon discouraged, so the conscious effort to discover yourself is gradually driven underground as you allow yourself increasingly to be defined by the demands of others. Often the pursuit of self-knowledge has to be reengaged in adulthood after a period of mostly unconscious living.

When this rediscovery of the self begins, books can play an important role in helping the process along. The self seeks a prescription for action, a way of seeing the world that transforms the autistic orientation of early childhood to an expansion into the world and into identity with a society of like-minded thinkers.

It might not be such a bad thing, though, if this self-exploration played a larger role in the educational process. There is no reason why school can't be a place where you begin to find out who you are in a meaningful search guided by books and explored in discussion groups. Even children can have fun with the question, Who am I? But it's seldom asked.

Who am I? Actually that question is impossible to answer. I am a different person every second of my life. While I may be able to make some general statements about my identity, I cannot define my being in detail. If I were able to do so, it would encompass only one moment in my lifetime, and would be inaccurate (and perhaps erroneous) for many of the other moments.[3]

So the question of who you are is continually being asked and answered in new and often thrilling ways.

Building Your Own Character

Think for a moment about how you would describe yourself. Perhaps you see yourself in the various roles you play: a mother, a nursery school teacher, a consumer, a Republican, a Mennonite, a life of the party, a person who loves to water paint when no one is looking, and so on.

A delightful clue to how this process works happened years ago when I called home and my three-year-old daughter Maureen answered the phone. Feeling playful, I asked, "Who is this?"

"Maureen."

"Well, how do you know it's Maureen?"

Without a pause she answered, "Because this is Maureen's shirt and I'm wearing it."

My daughter was sure of who she was because of her clothing. At that early stage of development the physical things that make up our worlds help to define us. Today, looking back on that moment, I can say that already at that young age Maureen had an uncanny sense of fairness and a desire to see it spread around the world. She would not, however, have described herself that way because she had not yet had a chance to discover that everyone else wasn't the same way. What was immediately apparent, however, was that no one else was wearing her clothing.

Indeed physical appearance sometimes seems to be the most definitive statement of personality. What others can instantly see is what defines you, and that's the end of it. No wonder teenagers are so fashion conscious.

Eventually, though, you develop priorities that set you apart from everyone else in the world. That's probably why so many people feel so isolated, because all you need to do is define twenty different qualities that describe you and the chances against your meeting anyone else with all those same priorities are in the billions.

So, given that you're the only one like you in the world, what can you do to make the best of that? It's not easy to search among hundreds or even thousands of potential friends to find the kind of intimate yet multidimensional companionship you'd like, but you can find it with authors, because there are so many authors to choose from. Besides, you can read books about the many different aspects of yourself, one after another. So a given author will take you as far as you'd like to go in one direction, while someone else will take you off for another delightful exploration. And the books that don't take you anywhere you'd like to go can be thrown aside without hurting anyone's feelings—which is not so easy with friends.

Any one of the twenty-odd qualities that make up the dominant features of your character can, by itself, be developed to a high level of excellence. Suppose, for example, you want to be socially popular. There are plenty of books that can help you be more successful at that. You could memorize joke books and *Reader's Digest* short stories from real-life experiences. You could read the newspaper every day so as always to be up on the latest media gossip. You could master the principles of the all-time self-help bestseller, *How to Win Friends and Influence People*, by Dale Carnegie.

Tools like these will eventually integrate with your experience to give even the most cliché-ridden sources a stamp that bears the mark of your personality.

This process boils down to three general steps: input, synthesis and output. In the earlier example of "I am a ham," we saw how the definition of the word "ham" starts the process of arriving at a literal meaning for the sentence. Once that's established, you have to decide whether the statement is true of you. That's where the synthesis happens, for by that process the meaning of the sentence becomes personalized and raises questions about every other aspect of your experience. Finally, once you've decided whether or not you think of yourself as a ham, you'll start shaping your behavior more consciously in relation to that decision. You can go through this three-step process with any sentence in any book. The first question is: "What does this mean?" The second: "What has that to do with me?" And the third: "How does that relationship alter my behavior?"

Once again, everything you read is input. It goes into your brain and is filed somewhere in your memory. It begins to be useful to you, however, when you can see a relationship between what you have read and something that is happening or has happened around you. This is synthesis.

Let's say you've decided to become socially popular, so you read a book of jokes and file these away in memory. Then, one day you find yourself rather unexpectedly at the funeral of a distant friend. Everyone is somber, so you decide to lighten things up and tell a few undertaker jokes. This relaxes everyone like a titanium pillow. The output you have produced in this situation rapidly becomes another kind of input, adding more practical experience to the synthesis. Now you have better information not only about how or how not to be popular, but also about what kinds of social settings invite you to be the center of attention.

Take this simplistic example of one personality trait, multiply it by twenty others, mix them all together, and you have an extraordinarily complex process of continually developing your personality year by year, day by day, and moment by moment.

All of this can happen, of course, without reading, but only reading can take you great distances away from your immediate situation both in time and place, giving you a perspective and wisdom that can't be achieved any other way. Only reading can take you into worlds that never existed but might or should, or are to be avoided. Only reading can give you that private satisfaction of getting advice from the great thinkers of your choice. The basic problem that underlies the comprehension of anything is the problem of getting the world inside to conform, to some degree, to an imagined world outside. Most of us can perfect our skills at doing this far beyond our current levels of achievement. However there's little in our formal schooling that gives us the proper background for developing these skills.

For example, at one time I learned from a sentence in a Latin book that all of the ancient country of Gaul was supposed to be divided into three parts. I remember there was a map in the book, but I don't remember what the map depicted. Revisiting this now, I am curious as to what those three parts were, and I am aware that no one did very much at the time to get me to do anything except substitute English words for Latin ones.

Too much of our schooling goes by this way. It's largely an exercise in substituting one set of words for another. The trouble with substituting words for one another is that it's a round-robin game that can only take you back to where you started. Language cannot survive if it is only self-referential. It has to invoke experiences that are infinitely more complex than the words that describe them. It's also appropriate to allow people to decide what sort of relationship they have with the subject at hand, and how it can impact their lives.

Shopping for Ideas about Yourself

Active, good reading requires working with the material in a book, moving it into imaginary contexts and consequences, and trying it out as a potential expression of your personality. As I read I like to guess what the author is going to say next and see how well I do. If I am wrong, I try to figure out what misled me. This is part of a process of learning to think like the author. As I become increasingly able to do that, I try to think outside of the immediate context, to guess how this particular author would feel about other situations not covered in the text. Then I extend my consideration to things like what life would be like if this author's ideas were consistently applied, what sort of people would like this author's ideas, characters or plot situations best, and what sort would like them least. In other words, I find many different ways to enrich my reading experience by extending it outside the confines of the book.

If you confine your thoughts about what you're reading to the text itself, that's a little like buying clothes you'll never wear. A good book fits you well and you wear it everywhere. That is, you often speak in reference to its ideas and point of view and apply its lessons to the situations you encounter. So in addressing the book you're reading, ask yourself, Do I want to wear these ideas as part of me? Do I want to add them to my intellectual wardrobe?

Looking back now on those three parts into which Gaul was divided, I can supply some tools for investigating them that I didn't have when I first encountered the sentence. For example, I can ask, What kind of mind would begin a book that way? Obviously it was someone who was interested in conquering the world (or at least some part of it) and wanted the reader to know what was available to be conquered. Yet I emerged from my Latin class with very little information about how world conquerors think. I might have known how many soldiers there were in a legion (I forget), and I definitely remember that "to decimate" means to have every tenth soldier stand out from the line and then to kill all those who are out of line. I don't know why that is a good technique for conquering the world, but as I think about it now, I can imagine reasons why some might think that way.

Comprehension, I believe, involves much more than understanding the words, but rather, consciously getting what is in someone else's mind into your own. It helps to do this with suspended disbelief—that is, not worrying about permanently changing yourself by performing this operation. If you did, you'd have to prove that everything in a chosen book is true for you, and it's not necessary to believe in it that much to try it out inside your mind and see how it feels any more than you have to worry about transforming your character by putting on a Halloween costume. In other words, you don't have to believe what the book says, but you want to have an accurate picture of what that is.

The first step, of course, is to have an understanding of what is said in the most literal sense. You need to know, for example, that ten is how many fingers you probably have and not something unrelated to that. However, once you get beyond a certain point, those kinds of issues should be resolved, and if they are not, there should be an easy way of finding out that they're not.[4]

Unfortunately, it's too often true that school learning does not take students much beyond the literal interpretation of texts. Comprehension questions tend to try to establish that they know there are three eggs in the basket and not four, for instance, rather than asking them to speculate about why the eggs are there at all. As a result, people spend a lot of time reading things they don't see any point in reading. Anything can be meaningful if discussed and explored enough so that each student's personal perspective is revealed to the point where the other students know what it is; but I've seldom seen that happen in a schoolroom.

Any book is a source of potential self-knowledge, knowledge of the self you're continuously creating. You are, like everything else, part of a self-organizing system, and as you read you are either organizing yourself further, relaxing into enjoying the contemplation of who you are, or wasting your time. Much of your reading time may be spent reading for pleasure.[5] When you read for pleasure, you rediscover what you already knew to be true.[6] You review your self-knowledge.

For example, if you read a lot of Harlequin romances, you review the self that wants to find the ideal love and believes it is somehow possible, even if you haven't yet achieved it in your own life. You see ever more clearly the disappointed idealist in yourself and the perfect self you could be if you were able to escape from the real world into the more appealing world of the Harlequin romance.

If you read a book about a political scandal, you review your knowledge that you are somehow above all those scoundrels in Washington, who are supposed to be running the government. You revel in their shortcomings and take pride in being so much better than they are, usually because you are morally superior to them. (It's easy, of course, to be morally superior to someone else if you don't have any responsibilities and they do.)

All this is comprehension of a sort, but it's mostly a pastime, not a means of self-discovery or self-creation. However, when you read a book about a new discovery in science, you expand the scientist in yourself. You vicariously become associated with those who made the discovery. And to the extent that you can understand and remember it, it becomes part of the universe you are fascinated to live in.

The fundamental questions that will intensify comprehension go somewhat like this:

1. Who am I in reading this book?
2. How does this book reflect who I am?

    3. How am I, in a positive way, alienated from what's in this book?

    4. How is this book increasing my self-knowledge?

    5. What remains for me to understand in this book?

If all this seems a little too self-referential to be acceptable in a classroom, consider that none of these questions can be satisfactorily answered without understanding what the author is actually saying. If a group of students discussing a book honestly answers questions like those above, they will collectively develop a better understanding of what the author is trying to say than they could without such a discussion.

Sometimes background information can be helpful, and should be thought of as an extension of the content of the book. In the end, however, all that matters is what you think, because if you don't think it, it can't exist for you.

12

Constructing a Personal View

*When and how are we going to stop working so hard
to protect people from ever finding out who they are?*

"I am," the sentence reads, and as I contemplate its meaning, I realize that
I am a unique opportunity for the universe. No one in all of history has ever
been exactly like me or done what I have done. Every observation I make
and every action I take, no matter how trivial, is new for the universe.

This fact is also a revolutionary observation. From the beginning of civilization it has generally been in the interest of governments to keep people
under control. The best way to do this is to convince them of their power-
lessness as individuals. So schools have been designed to teach people to do
what they are told by learning to follow directions and get the same results
everyone else gets. If they do this properly, the schools can mass-produce
successful students who are generally cooperative and employable without
being obnoxious or overly innovative.

The whole point of the old and widely taught approach to teaching
reading was to get everyone who reads a book to come up with the same
evaluation of what the book says. That might be okay if all you're ever
going to read is instruction manuals. It is certainly not okay if you're going
to work in any field that requires imagination or inventive problem solving.

The kind of reading that has been promoted and taught throughout
the educational system for approximately two centuries (and maybe more)
has been the kind that the left brain does. The left brain is logical and

sequential, and deals with language much as the dictionary does. But it lacks the wisdom of the right brain, which attempts to determine the overall drift of an argument and its many implications. We are taught to read almost exclusively with the left brain. That is, we are asked to be concerned with the unfolding of a text step-by-step, but seldom are taken systematically through it paragraph-by-paragraph to translate this unfoldment into a larger meaning in the manner discussed above. So, by excluding most of the insights provided by the right brain, we are too likely to experience reading as a tedious, linear process and too likely to perceive it as a stimulus to the imagination and critical faculties.

Getting Yourself Connected with Text

Assuming that the only successful way to read a book is to read yourself into it, the question "What's in it for me?" is an excellent place to begin. That way the book will be less likely to lose you.

In every book the main character that you're reading about is yourself. If a passage that you read has any meaning for you, it is a personal meaning, which either expands or echoes your own personal experiences or allows you to develop further some aspect of the thought process as unique to you.

This much should be obvious. What does not seem obvious, then, is that the process of crowding your mind with a great deal of information that is not somehow translated into the vernacular of your personality and thought process is largely useless. It is like having additional limbs that you don't use. It is like living in a house with many rooms, only a few of which you ever go into. It is to have a self that includes a huge stock of useless baggage.

Information that has no connection to you is trivial or useless. It is only when information is placed in context that it acquires value. George Bernard Shaw waxed eloquent on this subject in his autobiographical preface to his first novel, *Immaturity*. I have never seen a convincing refutation to any of the arguments below, nor an indication that they aren't essentially true, so I wonder why we have allowed the educational system that inspired these remarks to continue essentially unchanged for so long:

I cannot learn anything that does not interest me. My memory is not indiscriminate: it rejects and selects; and its selections are not academic. I have no competitive instinct; nor do I crave for prizes and distinctions: consequently I have no interest in competitive examinations: if I won, the disappointment of my competitors would distress me instead of gratifying me: if I lost, my self-esteem would suffer. Besides, I have far too great a sense of my own importance to feel that it could be influenced by a degree or a gold medal or what not. There is only one sort of school that would have qualified me for academic success; and that is the sort in which the teachers take care that the pupils shall be either memorizing their lessons continuously, with all the desperate strenuousness that terror can inspire, or else crying with severe physical pain. I was never in a school where the teachers cared enough about me, or about their ostensible profession, or had enough conviction and cruelty, to take any such trouble; so I learnt nothing at school, not even what I could and would have learned if any attempt had been made to interest me. I congratulate myself on this; for I am firmly persuaded that every unnatural activity of the brain is as mischievous as any unnatural activity of the body, and that pressing people to learn things they do not want to know is as unwholesome and disastrous as feeding them on sawdust. Civilization is always wrecked by giving the governing classes what is called secondary education, which produces invincible ignorance and intellectual and moral imbecility as a result of unnatural abuse of the apprehensive faculty. No child would ever learn to walk or dress itself if its hands and feet were kept in irons and allowed to move only when and as its guardians pulled and pushed them.

I somehow knew this when I began, as a boy entering on my teens, to think about such things. I remember saying, in some discussion that arose on the subject of my education, that T.C.D. men were all alike (by which I meant all wrong), and that I did not want to go through college. I was entirely untouched by university idealism. When it reached me later on, I recognized how ignorantly I had spoken in my boyhood; but when I went still further and learnt that this idealism is never realized in our schools and universities, and operates only as a mask and a decoy for our system of impressing and enslaving children and stultifying adults, I concluded that my ignorance had been inspired, and had served me very well. I have not since changed my mind.[1]

The manifesto that Shaw expresses above ought to be emblazoned on a panel in the hall of every school building in a free society. After all, what does freedom mean if not the opportunity to think and express our own thoughts? And yet we are mostly driven, as Shaw describes above, to trivialize our thinking by making it fit in with whatever the intellectual fashions of the day decree.

Recently I sat next to someone at a party who chose to tell me his opinion on a subject that was dominating the news that day. The opinion he expressed was, as I had read in the morning paper, shared by 56 percent of the population. That being the case, I had little interest either in his opinion or the fact that I happened to disagree with it. It seemed to me that the particular issue was one that had merits on both sides, but because it was so widely known and discussed, there was nothing to be said on the subject that had not already been said many times over.

What could my friend have to say that was unique in his experience that might delight or inform me of something new?

I have noticed that at most social events the conversation is mainly a rerun of what has been in the news that day, or else of standard cultural issues that are acted out in neighborhoods. It's as if we are all automatons vying with one another to display the most up-to-date and widely accepted opinions. Strangely enough, this tendency is stronger in faculty rooms than almost anywhere else. Really coming to grips with ideas or an unusual view of events seldom occurs there because people feel it would be inappropriate to express opinions that might be unpopular or offensive.

Few people really know much about each other. Those who do come to grips with challenging ideas are few and far between, and when, on occasion, a really exciting discussion does develop, most of those present seem condemned to sit and listen to it.

That's because the habit of thinking freely and independently is not encouraged in most educational settings. Instead students usually find themselves having to prove that they have the right answers to the right questions and are up on the latest gossip.

This creates the impression that most people are far less intelligent than is actually the case. I have almost always found when I engage someone in a deep discussion, it becomes clear that they can follow the subject with considerable interest. They also can add to it ideas of their own that they have considered for a long time. So it's not a lack of intelligence or information, it's a lack of cultural freedom that's causing the problem. This is a strange set of affairs to have arisen in a supposedly free society. It means that, for the most part, we've never learned that we have not only the right but the responsibility to take our own thinking seriously instead of just frivolously holding on to widely shared opinions.

Jean-Paul Sartre wrote several existentialist dramas and other works to show that all experience begins in subjectivity, that existence precedes essence, and that there is no God.[2] These three ideas were a foundation on which he built his interpretation of life. I personally disagree on the subject of God, but I nevertheless find this construct very useful as a tool for thinking about the nature of human experience; and, as you'll see, the statement "there is no God" doesn't have to be taken literally here.

Let us see how well these three principles describe human experience and what they might have to tell us about how we should relate to our own developing experiences.

Since subjectivity is the only possible way for experience to begin, the meaning of any given experience is entirely up to the person who has it, and cannot be judged by anyone else. This gives the individual radical free will in deciding what meaning is to be found in anything. There is no external criterion upon which ideas of meaning can be based.

If you are the one who decides what all your experiences mean, you are also free to reinterpret them. You shape and accept the reality of your experiences out of your subjective interpretation of what they mean.

These experiences, then, shape the essence of your being. So as you take your place in the world, you are, from your subjective interpretation of it, creating its reality. That is the only reality that can exist for you, since there is no external source of meaning other than your subjective interpretation of it.

To say that there is no God is to say that there is no higher authority that can contradict the nature of the reality in which you find yourself. You are, in other words, the only one who, as far as you are concerned, can create the universe. All there is outside of you is the blind and stupid forces of nature operating through evolutionary accidents that have no meaning at all until that meaning is given to them by the action of your mind. You can, however, make a connection with what you believe to be God. But that is necessarily your connection, not anyone else's, so whatever happens between you and God can't be decided by anyone else.[3]

Consider the Relevance Before Literal Truth

It seems that a small number of people actually operate in the way I have just described. They act as if the reality they have decided to create, on the basis of their subjective interpretation of their own experiences, were the only reality there is. They then proceed on the basis of that internally created reality and make it a powerful force in the world.

Some of them establish new nations. Some of them create businesses. Some of them write political tracts. Some of them create powerful works of art. Some of them build buildings or machines.

And now, stepping back and looking at what we see around us, is there anything that cannot be accounted for by what I've just described? What we see is a huge and complex civilization that has been created by a large number of individuals who brought into being new forms of reality that were never there before they created them.

Apply this observation to yourself as a reader and as a person who learns from what you read and creates reality on the basis of it.

The only interpretation of a book that really makes any difference to you is the one you arrive at after you have considered the book itself along with the reactions of other people to which you choose to respond. What you have, in the end, is uniquely yours, and that is a completely subjective phenomenon.

There are a lot of books out there, but as far as you are concerned, their essence takes form only as you translate them into a part of your reality. You need not read a particular book in order to accomplish this, however. You may merely recognize that it exists because someone else has mentioned it to you. In this case its essence flows, in your mind, from its reputation.

While your interpretations are always open to reconsideration, there is no force anywhere that can decree that you are right or wrong about such things. If you think a particular book or experience means something, then, as far as you are concerned, that is what it means.

As I think about the above three points I can't see any way to refute them. At the same time, I am aware that we seldom teach reading in these terms. We behave as if there were some correct interpretation that students are supposed to get out of what they read, and that it is our job to see to it that they don't get that mixed up with the chaos of their own thinking. Let them learn the interpretations of things that the book says are correct, we self-righteously declare. One result of this is that, for the past four hundred years, nearly everyone has been wrong about almost everything concerning Shakespeare's life, opinions and experiences.[4]

This controlling attitude on the part of schoolteachers is, I think, devastating in its implications for the future of democratic society. It makes the vast majority of students hate important works of literature and turns many off to reading altogether. Furthermore, it shows the most utter disregard for whatever integrity the student's mind might be capable of.

If we don't tell students what to think about Shakespeare, Mark Twain and Thomas Hardy, what are we supposed to do?

Why not simply let them discuss the literature among themselves? Instead of telling them what these great writers have to say, let them express their own opinions on the subjects, but in doing so, ask them questions that bring them back to the text and require them to account for their interpretations.

Students need to learn rules for carrying on discussions. These should include ways of showing respect for one another's ideas, listening carefully to what others are saying, and maintaining consistency in their own points of view, which are always open to revision, but which ought to be based on frames of reference that are clear to them.

There's no reason why students in junior high school can't approach literature in virtually the same way that communities of scholars approach it. That is, to say what they think something means and to demonstrate, to the satisfaction of their peers, the basis on which their opinions are founded.

This is more or less the way I taught literature for twenty-five years, and there never seemed to be anyone who couldn't learn to read better by engaging in such discussions.

The beauty of it was that I never had to decide what anything meant, nor did I have to determine that one person was right and another wrong. All I had to do was make clear the extent to which I could follow the logic that a given student was explaining to me or to someone else.

Suppose a student reacted to the line "to be or not to be" with the following comment:

"I think it's about censorship."

"Why?"

"Well, if something's taboo, doesn't that mean it's censored, or should be censored?"

"Would you read the passage again for me please?"

"To be or not—oh, *to be*, not *taboo*. Oh, well I guess it's not about censorship."

"Thank you."

This kind of thing usually works better if it's one of the students who points out the mistake rather than the teacher who does.

The nastiness lurking behind the scenes here is the most frightful of all the "isms"—adultism. As adults we almost universally assume that what children think and say is cute but basically of no consequence. In taking this almost universally accepted stance, we forget that many of our own most cherished ideas were first experienced and explored very early in life. That should make us aware that the routine and habitual trivializing of what children think, say and ask about is one of the most dangerous practices of our culture because it disempowers the mind at the time when it is growing most rapidly and powerfully.

Whenever people do take a serious interest in what children have to say, listen to them closely, and draw out their thinking in order to discover where it will lead, the impact on the child is profound.[5] Many of the most brilliant people in history have told us of the importance childhood influences had on them.

By not taking childhood thinking seriously we needlessly enchain the young. And a mind, may I remind you, is a terrible thing to waste.

Looking for a Golden Age

Trivializing children's thinking is widespread in our culture, but not in all cultures. In her study of the Yequana Indians of Venezuela in *The Continuum Concept*, Jean Liedloff observed the behavior of parents and children.[6] Throughout the early stages of life, parents would support their children emotionally without limitation. Liedloff found that, as a result, adults in this society lived at a level of contentment with their surroundings that was so profound they would often go to great lengths to do very elementary tasks without any motivation to simplify their activities. They reacted this way because they enjoyed every moment so much that they saw no reason to reorganize anything they were already doing. In this culture life was lived very close to nature and therefore children met only with such dangers as would have been met by human children over the millions of years of their evolution.

In this environment, children's instincts seemed to protect them remarkably well. An infant might play with a sharp knife while sitting on the edge of a precipice, while the mother, moving about nearby, would do nothing to interrupt this activity. The infant seemed quite capable of avoiding danger in this situation.[7]

Because of the remarkable harmony between parents and children and between all the people in the society and their natural environment, only laughter and expressions of happiness seemed to characterize the emotional behavior of the society.

Under the right conditions, and trusting themselves and their children completely, these people lived together with almost no repressive behavior. Of course, since life was so idyllic, there was, as I said, very little motivation to change the behavior of the society as a whole or any of its individual behaviors or traditions. As a result, the same cultural behaviors were probably being handed down for thousands of years. By contrast, people who emerge as leaders in any field are usually reacting to some childhood situation that motivates them to want to change certain cultural conditions that they experienced negatively. If something terrible has happened to you, you can spend your life moping about it, or you can devote your life to trying to eliminate future traumas of the kind that bothered you.

When we talk to children about their experiences, it's important to let them say what's on their minds without attempting to editorialize or to talk them out of feelings they may have. The main attempt should be to understand what they are trying to tell us, and to keep asking until the children are satisfied that we understand whatever it is that's being expressed. Many an idea that was born in early childhood has survived to change the world. Many a question that seems silly or stupid has profound implications behind it.

Sometimes children ask questions that have no known answers, like "How high is the sky?" In such situations it's useful for the child to find out that no one knows the answer, but maybe someday the child will figure it out and tell the world. Children whose thinking is taken seriously this way often grow up to be powerful thinkers.[8]

The bottom line is, childhood experiences can powerfully shape adult thinking and behavior, as the following examples will suggest.

The Source of Shaw's Comic Vision

George Bernard Shaw described a situation that arose when he was a very young child, walking with his father along the bank of a canal. His father, who was drunk at the time, picked him up and swung him several times over the bank, as if he were about to throw the child to his death in the canal. Looking back on the incident, Shaw said that he decided at that moment that nothing and no one could be trusted or taken seriously. This might have been the foundation for a tragic philosophy, but it was also true that his family made the choice to react to his father's alcoholism by laughing at it instead of agonizing over it. This, he argued, became the basis for his belief that all situations could be dramatized in a comic format.[9] Even his drama of *St. Joan* has an ironic tone that avoids emotional distortion. It is as if Shaw, threatened with death at an early age, felt that the rest of his life was on loan so he might as well do whatever he wanted, while worrying about nothing. He never got upset about anything in his life, not even the death of a dear friend. When his friends were gone, he never referred to them again, treating them as if they had never existed. Always, therefore, he dealt with the present situation, applying to it only a logical process and never an emotional one.

Shaw stated in his preface to *St. Joan* that he wrote lines for the characters that expressed not what they said, but what they would have said if they had known what they meant. Another great humorist, Mark Twain, also wrote of St. Joan, but his book lacks the ironic twists Shaw gave her story, and is more a straightforward account. This may have been because Twain, who never became inoculated to the emotion of fear as a child the way Shaw did, could not retain his comic mask under situations that personally threatened him.

Near the end of his life, Twain encountered many terrible personal and professional setbacks. The result was a virtual destruction of his ability to write.[10] Unable to give expression to the tragic side of his life or feelings, he wrote thousands of pages that went nowhere until finally, near the end, he came up with one near masterpiece, *The Mysterious Stranger*. This is a whimsical story of an encounter with the Devil, a much maligned individual, according to Twain. It is as if he finally found the answer at the end of his life: The Devil isn't so bad after all, if only one can get his point of view on things.

Whatever the difference between these two great comic writers, Shaw's vision was more all encompassing and wide-ranging. He posed questions for the modern age in nearly every area of human development, which can provoke productive inquiry, regardless of whether or not one agrees with his answers. In addition to that, he had the largest vocabulary of any writer in the twentieth century, adding about two thousand citations to the *Oxford*

English Dictionary. This was a prodigious record for our time, considering the fact that many writers in their entire careers never even use as many as two thousand different words.

How Newton's Childhood
Distorted His Thinking

Sir Isaac Newton is another example of how early childhood experiences can shape an adult response.[11] Newton was an abused child who grew up with no practice in how to establish his own priorities in relationship to the adults around him. This motivated young Isaac to seek to control everything in his life so completely that he could not even allow the universe to have any mysteries. As a result he introduced into science the notion that nothing needed to be explained, only described. This allowed him to aim for a complete description of the nature of the universe that continued along the direction he set until it fell apart near the beginning of the twentieth century in the face of such concepts as quantum mechanics and the indeterminacy principle.

Newton, by virtue of his studies of optics and gravitation, may well have been the greatest physicist of all time. He was also terribly repressive in his relationships to his fellow scientists, sometimes destroying the careers of people who presumed to look at things from a perspective different from his own. He did severe damage to science by so trivializing its philosophical basis that today many scientists cannot imagine a universe that is not the result of a series of random accidents. The modern view that nothing can be studied unless it can be experienced directly by the senses can be traced to the influence of Newton. Fortunately, increasing numbers of leading scientists are beginning to assert the rather obvious and indisputable fact that modern physics largely deals with phenomena that, even in principle, are not accessible to the senses. In fact, it looks as if our universe is at least as mysterious as wide-eyed mystics have ever suggested or imagined, and probably a great deal more so.

We need to be aware of the extreme importance of very early (usually traumatic) experiences on the later development of thought and character.

Such traumas are intensified by the fact that the child does not, at the time of those experiences, have a sufficiently independent sense of self to elaborate his or her ideas and skills in the face of repression from adults or older siblings. An effectively revolutionary attitude does not mature until adolescence, and by that time it is too late to take charge of the development of one's own behavior, if that behavior is based on a reaction against repression rather than an attempt to elaborate an individual point of view.

It is not difficult to create an educational atmosphere that will benignly allow children to acquire their own personal outlooks on life in a completely positive and socially acceptable way. All that is necessary is that they be listened to and allowed to express what they think, without immediately being told they are wrong or silenced in the interests of their learning the "body of knowledge" to be studied. A relatively small amount of acknowledgment of a child's unique thought process will provide sufficient encouragement for the child to become able to elaborate that process over time. As a result the child will develop enough ego strength to carry him or her through to a mature point of view that is not hopelessly derivative or based on a need to adopt other people's reactions inappropriately.

I know many people who walk around as if they lived in houses with sealed-off rooms. They are terrified to look at some aspects of their past experiences. This is not because they were so terrible, but rather because they have little or no experience in talking about themselves with enough safety to develop the confidence that it is okay to be who they are and to discover as much as they can about that.

A friend was, in childhood, repeatedly raped by an older relative and slapped down by her mother the one time she attempted to report the fact. She is now, rather late in life, learning to look at that experience and derive some positive life energy from it, only because it has finally become safe enough for her to talk about herself. After a very successful life as a business consultant, she is at long last able to realize that she has touched only the tip of the iceberg in discovering who she is.

Revisiting childhood experiences like this can be less traumatic if you know you can tell them to someone you trust who will not judge you negatively because of them. But relatively few who have had such experiences avail themselves of the opportunity that all negative traumas provide—drawing positive energy from realizing that they have lived to tell the tale. The other side of negative trauma can be a strong and positive sense of victory in life; but in order for that to happen, one must become comfortable in reading and interpreting one's own past experiences.

Children Need to Handle the Darker Side of Life

The habit of thoughtfully processing what you're reading, which is the best way to foster an individual point of view, should be taught from the beginning of the time a child is learning to read independently. And it should be taught using materials that recognize the great truth that life is not all rosebuds and chocolate sauce, as the children's classics have always done. When a cyclone takes Dorothy's whole house away from Kansas, it separates her from her parents and places her in a land of strange creatures. Here, rather than be rescued, she must rescue others and, indeed, save many of the citizens of Oz from the tyranny of a wicked witch. In the process, the child learns important lessons about how life's greatest traumas can be faced and mastered. And she has a profound multicultural (and even multispecies) experience.

This is a far cry from Dick, Jane and Sally, who never leave their white middle-class milieu, and whose dog, Spot, has none of the spunk and character of Toto. Modern descendants of the Dick, Jane and Sally that I learned from seem to have acquired no wisdom of experience in their evolution, only a tendency to become even more anonymous and uninteresting. This is, no doubt, because book-adopting committees on school boards are terrified by all sorts of things that do not terrify children at all.[12]

By contrast, I believe that along with decoding the actual words, the child should become accustomed to decoding the always fascinating, and sometimes a little threatening, ideas at hand. Practice at doing so will eventually mean that it seems natural always to translate whatever is on a printed page into one's own personal vernacular and then deal with the given text on the basis of its own merits and consistency.

In his poem "Terence, This is Stupid Stuff," A. E. Houseman compared the habit of taking small amounts of poison in order to build a resistance to it to the habit of reading about traumatic situations so you can build up enough vicarious experience and emotional stamina to deal with them when they happen to you (as inevitably some of them will). Here are a few salient lines from the poem:

> *Therefore, since the world has still*
> *Much good, but much less good than ill,*
> *And while the sun and moon endure*
> *Luck's a chance, but trouble's sure,*
> *I'd face it as a wise man would,*
> *And train for ill and not for good.*

School boards seem to be allergic to anything that might help children know themselves better and face, with some well-forged armor, the challenges that life will inevitably bring to them if it has not already done so. Our current system produces about the results we would have if the medical community were to ban all vaccinations and other preventive medicine. The moral is that if we want to learn to handle the challenges of life we have to practice. As long as children are raised on moral and intellectual pabulum, we can expect that, as adults, they will tend to run for hiding as soon as the going gets a little rough in any aspect of their experiences.

Indeed, even at the most advanced levels, what passes for critical reading today is, too often, merely an attempt to instruct students in a particular set of criteria to be used in analyzing a text. This preordained filter invalidates any particular point of view a student might have that is not in agreement with the premises of that filter. As a result there is a widespread tendency for people who have supposedly become adept at critical thinking to be incapable of dealing with paradigms that do not conform to the ones they have been taught to expect. As a result the story of "The Emperor's New Clothes" is a parable for the rejection of new ideas that are later revealed to have merit. These sorts of repressive filters could be avoided simply by teaching critical thinking without preestablished criteria and by eliciting the criteria themselves through the process of open and thoughtful discussion.

To sum up, then, we say we have a free public educational system to promote responsible citizenship in a free society. Responsible citizenship implies the ability to think for oneself. It isn't remotely enough for a few intellectuals to be doing this, everyone needs to be doing it. That means everyone needs to learn to use books not just to acquire information (though that is important), but also to advance an individual and highly articulate thinking process.

What needs to be learned today is not so much a long list of facts as a series of templates that can facilitate our learning to interpret what we read—in whatever context it might appear.

In the chapters that follow I'll share with you some of the ways I believe this can be accomplished. For twenty-five years in the classroom, I was constantly searching for new and unusual ways to get students to think for themselves and outside of the structures that are too often imposed unthinkingly upon them. It's my hope that teachers who are also doing similar things will recognize themselves in this book not because their methods are the same as mine, but because they are from the same spirit. And those who can afford to increase the thinking challenges they present to their students (whether first graders or graduate students) will find here some practical methods that they can adapt to their own needs and uses.

After all, if the world is ever to become a safe place for children and small animals, we're all going to have to learn how to make it that way.

13

Finding Ourselves in a Book

How can we learn to connect up the universe of our perceptions?

One of the most powerful literary experiences I ever had occurred in the following way:

As a senior in college I had been introduced to the ideas of George Bernard Shaw by my theater professor and had fallen in love with them. My love affair with Shaw was my first great intellectual breakthrough. For a time I felt as if Shaw's ideas about the Life Force, a sort of pantheistic pseudo-religion, explained the world better than anything else I had read.

Meanwhile, I was having a terrible experience in a course in modern poetry in which we had been assigned to read T. S. Eliot's *The Wasteland* and write a paper on it. It was evident to me that this poem was nothing except pseudo-intellectual mumbo jumbo that might possibly mean everything, but certainly could not mean anything in particular. I felt so strongly about this that I persuaded myself the college was morally corrupt in wasting my time with such nonsense.

So I decided to rebel. I decided I would do something so desperate that the entire English department, along with the dean, would be forced to their knees in submission to my superior wisdom in spotting the absence of clothing on the emperor.

I resolved on a hunger strike.

I took with me into my room my copy of *The Wasteland* and several commentaries that purported to explain it, sat down in my chair, and vowed that I would not arise again (except to go to the bathroom) until I fully understood the poem. Since the poem, in my mind, would be impossible to understand, I would remain in the chair for days and then weeks. Campus police would come by and try to force me out of the chair and back to class, but I would resist, declaring stoically that I had dedicated myself to doing what I had been told, however impossible that might be.

I actually did stay in the chair eight hours, by which time I thoroughly understood the poem, and it has been my favorite poem ever since.

Using One Writer to Understand Another

You would have to search a long time to find any two twentieth-century writers who were less alike than Shaw and the inscrutable Mr. Eliot. Where Shaw was flamboyant and rhetorically clear about all his ideas, Eliot was enigmatic. Where Shaw delighted in taunting religiosity in all its forms, Eliot affirmed that art and religion could very easily be one and the same. Where Shaw was one of the greatest advocates of the idea of progress of all time, Eliot saw little future for the idea of progress, and as for time, well, that was, according to him, present, past and future all at once.

All this might have been just food for thought had not the same drama teacher, who had inspired in me such a great love for Shaw, happened to mention that he thought Shaw and Eliot both wrote from a spiritual point of view.

Since I had found my spiritual center through empathy with Shaw's endlessly fascinating prose on the subject of the Life Force, I was moved to see how that empathy might fit with Eliot as a dramatist. Through the spectacles of a Shavian, I read *Murder in the Cathedral* (the story of the assassination of Thomas à Becket), found its spiritual center, and suddenly felt a strong identification with all that Eliot was doing in his poetry. The irreverent socialist and the dogmatic ultraconservative lost their distinctiveness from one another. The Life Force that motivated Shaw's Superman seemed to me to emanate from the "still point at the center of the turning world" that inspired Thomas à Becket to elect martyrdom in preference to compromise of his dogmatic values at the hands of a betraying king.

In a white heat of inspiration I wrote a piece called "The Spiritual Center in Eliot's Plays" and sent it to *Harper's,* which found it extremely interesting, but said it wasn't for them, and suggested a more academic journal instead. So I sent it to the *Kenyon Review*, where it was accepted for publication by John Crowe Ransome, who felt I had expressed an original and compelling interpretation of Eliot's plays.[1]

I, who had never managed to eke out an A on an English paper in college, succeeded in publishing something that came from a connection between a passion I had already established and an analogous interpretation of that same passion in another context. The experience proved to me the truth of evolution: Everything in the universe is analogous to everything else, since all of it has metamorphosed out of the same primal dust. The question is never whether or not there is an analogy, but rather how metamorphologically far off you have to take the analogy to find its counterpart in what may, at first, seem alien. Analogical thinking of this kind has long been known to be one of the primary roots of creativity.[2]

Making Meaningful Connections

Sometimes we are bombarded by information that has no meaningful context. I have discovered this bombardment to be most frustrating in airports and on airplanes. Those are almost the only places I go where I have no control over what I am forced to listen to. As I sit in the airport waiting for a plane that may be several hours late, I have to listen to a barrage of messages over loudspeakers, none of which apply to me.

Then one day I discovered how to develop an emotional connection with some of those annoying messages.

Shortly before a plane lands, the stewardess usually announces the connecting gates for anywhere from a dozen to thirty or forty different cities. This annoying litany is repeated at the end of every flight, and there will always be a maximum of one bit of information in the whole list that is relevant to me.

One day, though, I noticed that almost all the cities on the list were places I had visited. So I settled back, closed my eyes, and as each city was announced, I attempted to summon up a memory of actually being there. The result was a delightful guided imagery trip around the country, or perhaps, the world.

It's almost always possible to find some way to make irrelevant bits of information both personal and meaningful. You can do this best, however, if you have an overall picture of the world of which you are a part and a place in it in which to put everything that comes to light that might be useful to you.

For example, I find it interesting that the total weight of all the ants in the world is greater than the collective weight of the humans, animals and other insects all taken together. Inasmuch as anthills produce a gas that destroys the ozone layer in the outer atmosphere, I meditate on the fact that this natural phenomenon may be as threatening to the environment as all of human civilization.

As I think about this rather surprising phenomenon of the great plurality of ants in our tiny world and their effect upon it, I'm drawn to notice other facts about them. An ant brain contains only nine hundred neurons, while a human brain has about thirty billion. So, taken one by one, ants are almost unbelievably stupid. But I've heard it said that an ant colony may be more like a single organism than a collection of individual creatures—the ants as individuals are more like cells in the body than like separate beings. So perhaps an ant hill is a creature that doesn't bind itself together, but leaks out all over the place.

Does that great plurality of ants, then, I wonder, have a kind of collective consciousness that, taken altogether, might actually be smarter than some larger animals with a great many more neurons at their disposal? How would we recognize whether or not that is true? How might we find out? These speculations don't seem boring or trivial to me.

What I do know is that the little exercise I have just engaged in is possible with anything. Just take something that is of little interest to you initially, learn a few facts about it, and play with the implications of those facts until you come up with a relationship among them that interests you.

Every time you do this, you have brought order into the universe of your mind, which is the outward extension of yourself, through imagination, into the surrounding world. However impractical or useless such mind games might seem at first, they keep you alert to everything that is going on, looking for patterns and constructible meanings. Out of those meanings some new aspect of yourself may eventually coalesce.

Richard Feynman told the story of how he was in a cafeteria one day and someone threw a Frisbee across the room. As he watched the vibrational patterns of the object moving through the air, he got the first glimmer of an idea that would become a major scientific breakthrough.

As you observe what's going on around you, or read of others' experiences, you have endless opportunities to construct new portions of yourself. Out of the whole will come some pieces that may acquire significance long after you have first stowed them in your memory.

Connections may be casual at first; but then, perhaps, a crisis will occur in your life. As you attempt to respond to the crisis, something you have observed will surface and you will use it to solve the problem. Out of that solution your sense of yourself as a person who can make a valuable contribution to understanding the world may be born.

It is often said that chance favors the prepared mind, so the trick is to prepare the mind through mental exercise so chance can have the opportunity to come along and work its magic.

The difficulty with this kind of mental play is that it can produce a lot of things going on in your mind that seem to have no relationship to one another. Let's take another step in designing the game and see how one might connect ants with something else of importance.

What Can Ants Tell Us about Economics?

As I think about the ants in their anthills, I wonder whether this ant society is capable of generating poverty. Could there come a time when there are more ants than are needed to run the anthill and some of them have to be cast aside as useless to the community?

It doesn't seem likely, but if it doesn't happen, what mechanism in ant societies keeps all the members active in just the right relationship to the society as a whole? Is there some force among ants that makes their society work more harmoniously than human societies have worked? If so, could that force be discovered, and might there be an analogous force that could be developed in human societies?

Suddenly the idle speculation about ants becomes transformed into a more directed thought process that might lead to a real breakthrough in understanding human society. I don't know that it will, but I now find that, for the first time, two disparate parts of my thinking are connected so that a small amount of investigation might reveal the connection either to be useful or a blind alley. Were I now to study ant societies, I would be looking for something specific that would motivate my study and make it more interesting.

While I still have to evaluate this particular insight, I have had many experiences in the past of just such connections proving fruitful in the search for a solution to some problem.

The challenge, therefore, is to integrate the knowledge that does not feel like a part of you with that which does. In so doing it isn't that you acquire either new knowledge or a new part of yourself, but that you open up aspects of yourself that have not previously been used. I mentioned earlier that I only recently became aware of or concerned about the following:

1. What "cigarette" really means. (Chapter 3)
2. A metaphor based on the color of amber. (Chapter 3)
3. What three parts Gaul is divided into. (Chapter 11)

Here were bits of my personality that had never become connected, as if my self were scattered about in little pieces, waiting to come together. Most of us have unintegrated bits of self lying all over the place, just as our houses contain many things that we do not use and often haven't looked at for years, and our address books contain the names of people with whom we are out of touch.

That doesn't mean that these ideas, possessions and former friends have nothing to do with us, it means that we have a working relationship with ourselves that is less fulfilled than it could be, just as we probably own many pieces of technology that can do all sorts of things we've never considered learning to make use of. One of the things you'll discover from a close reading of Shakespeare is that he probably never learned anything or had an experience of any kind that did not make its way into his writing somewhere or other.

The enormous vocabulary Shakespeare used (much of which he invented himself) is paralleled by the incredible amount of largely accurate information he had accumulated in many different fields of knowledge. His writings include hundreds of legal references, not one of which is inaccurate. He tells us about the flora and fauna of his time with amazing versatility. His knowledge of history was that of a great historian.[3] He had read virtually every classical piece of writing that existed (many of them not yet translated into English). He knew sports, medicine and court protocol and could distinguish between the way different people use words with blazing insight. His observation of human behavior is probably the best that any writer has been capable of.

Shakespeare was a writer who defined himself in terms of everything he ever learned. He does not appear to have acquired any piece of information for which he did not have some use. But this was not mere accumulation, for it all blended together to create a body of work that has impressed nearly all readers who have ever read deeply into it with the sense that he was writing about them personally, and about their lives. That is why he wrote, "not of an age but for all time," and that is why he has been able to tell us more about ourselves than anyone else ever has.

I have little reason to be interested in cigarettes or cigars because I don't smoke and don't particularly care whether others smoke or not, so long as I don't have to inhale their fumes secondhand or attend their funerals. Nevertheless I am interested in language, so it is exciting to discover a relationship between these two words I have never noticed before. I also care about social issues, so it interests me how other people deal with the issue of smoking as a matter of corporate policy, personal freedom and medical responsibility. All of those issues interest me greatly.

Amber interests me because I know that many fossils are preserved in ancient amber, as the film *Jurassic Park* dramatically brought to my attention; and I know that we can learn about our own past and about what the world before us was like from the study of fossils. So the connection between the amber that contains fossilized insects and the color of a field of grain enriches my appreciation of the great tapestry of nature, and I think of that now whenever I look out over a beautiful midwestern landscape.

Bringing Caesar Up-to-Date

The changes wrought by Caesar's *Gallic Wars* and the impact those changes have on my life today fascinate me, and I also wonder what motivated those changes. What was it that moved humanity from the level of the Greek city-state or the tiny tribes of wandering Jews and Philistines to the hugeness of the Roman Empire, and what did all that have to do with the parallel history of the Chinese, who had much earlier learned the art of ruling huge populations successfully? Today we are living in a world that must learn to govern itself as a whole and take care of itself ecologically, if it wants to survive. I care about the issues of the balance of world government and personal freedom. I know that, two thousand years ago, Julius Caesar built the most modern civilization that England was to have for a subsequent fifteen hundred years. I know that in order to rule his great empire he had to have a body of law quite different from that of the Hebraic law, and in many ways downright ruthless. I know that that body of law was, more than five hundred years after his death, finally codified by Justininan, and that that is the ancestor of the legal system we live under today. All of these issues seem very current to me as I think about my own time, my personal freedom, and even what I am allowed or not allowed to write about in this paragraph.

I have just put myself through an intellectual exercise that anyone can perform. We all know things that we have never connected to anything else. But it is always possible to do that in retrospect. The more we connect the things we know, the more we actualize our ability to understand our own experiences and to deal with our environment safely, honorably, morally and (I hope) prosperously. When we have gathered information, we can make use of it at the time, or we can put it away and pull it out for examination later. The self is always creating more of itself, and it can do that with longitude as well as latitude. Many of the things I learned nearly half a century ago are more interesting to me today than they ever were before. That's because the wisdom that can come only from experience grows organically and can be fostered by reflection on how everything that has happened in life can connect.

A prominent lawyer once told me that he would never hire a graduate from Harvard Law School if he had a very high grade point average, but he would hire one whose grade point average was at a medium level. He believed that the top graduates had become something like tape recorders of information and, in the process, had acquired little understanding of how that information might be used in natural situations. Practicing lawyers, of course, need to know not just the law, but how it may be applied in many different contexts. The ability to do so means that they have absorbed this knowledge so deeply that it has become a facet of their personalities.[4] Reading, then, is an opportunity for personality growth and integration. We read not just to discover who we are but, much more profoundly, to create who we are.

14

How Teachers Can Help

How are book whisperers like horse whisperers?

Young readers need to be taught the kind of morphological thinking that proceeds through analogies, seeing in one thing the spirit that has been identified earlier in some other thing.

The teacher's challenge is to help students open portals to any subject by building analogies to the students' strong personal interests. These will be different in each individual case. So in order to be a good teacher, one has to be an original thinker who is capable of learning something new from each student and helping that student create a new set of possibilities. If a teacher can do this for even a handful of students, he (or she) will have impacted the world beyond his wildest dreams. To accomplish this, he has to crawl around inside the student's mind, find where the interest is, and then build the metaphors. The next step is to teach the student to do this for herself or himself, to teach her how to identify or develop a strong personal interest and make analogies between how it works (say it's taking care of horses) and how something else works (say it's taking care of a car).

Then the teacher can go on to other analogies: How does the president take care of the United States the way one takes care of a horse? How is reading like riding a horse? How would Robinson Crusoe take care of a horse? One can teach any student to think in analogies based on personal interests, and if done right, the student will love the process.

Now let's learn a little Shakespeare this way:

But look! the morn in russet mantel clad
Walks o'er the dew of yon high eastward hill.

Pretend you are riding your horse early in the morning and you stop for a moment, gazing out over the horizon. What do these lines suggest that you might see? Are there any sounds you might hear at that moment? Can you imagine hearing the feet of the morning as it walks on the dew? Can you listen well enough to hear that sound, or is it drowned out by the much louder sound of the horse breathing? How does the horse feel about the dawn? Do horses appreciate the beauties of nature perhaps more than we do? Why or why not? Suppose the morning was expressed as a horse. How might the poet have used this metaphor?

Enriching the Content

What is the being that is walking over the dew in Shakespeare's line? In *Hamlet*, from which this line comes, some characters have just learned that the ghost of a king who has recently died is trying to tell them something. You know about taking care of horses. Do you think a horse might ever be trying to tell people something? Is there a best way of treating horses? Would that be anything like the best way of treating people? Or ghosts? If there were a play about a man whose father has been killed by the man that has married his mother, he might be pretty upset, wouldn't you think? Have you ever seen a horse that is upset because something bad has happened to it? How do you try to calm such a horse? What do you think a man who is upset by what has happened to his father and his mother might need to calm him down?

Thus self-referential thinking can gradually be shifted to cross-referential thinking. The process is a little like the way a horse whisperer can communicate with a horse by first speaking its language and then getting it to speak the whisperer's own language. It turns out, of course, that the art of teaching horses successfully is identical to the art of teaching people. Horses require the same degree of understanding, tenderness, patience and certainty that people do.

When teachers successfully transmit the art of reading, then each of us may become our own teacher. We have to learn to whisper to ourselves, find our own inner languages, and then, with gentle patience, bring those inner languages into communication with the language of a book's author. Each of us can figure out how to do this even if the book is about chemistry or differential equations. We just have to find our own inner chemistry or differential equations.[1] You'd be amazed to discover how much of both of these are going on inside of you. There's the chemistry of love and the fact that it causes you to be equal to someone else, but in a differential way. Most people never get quite enough of that kind of thinking.

Common Interests in a Classroom

The trouble with most teachers is that they either understand their subject well or they don't. If they don't, obviously they are at a loss as to how to teach, but if they do, that may also lead to a disadvantage in teaching the students.

The things that I understand really well seem easy to me. Therefore, it's hard for me to imagine why everyone else doesn't understand them, too. I'm likely to decide that if people don't understand my subject it's because (a) they are stupid, (b) they are lazy, or (c) they just don't want to.

The actual fact is that nearly all students can understand nearly anything if it is presented in a way that relates to their preexisting interests and already established concepts.

So no matter what it is I am about to teach, it's my job to get into the state of mind of my students and relate what I am going to teach them to things they already know about and are interested in. If I do this well enough, I can whip up white-hot enthusiasm for any subject. If I don't do it, I end up just talking to myself.

When I decided to teach *Hamlet* in such a way that all my students would not only be able to understand it, but would also fall in love with it, what I had to do was find something in the play that would connect with something that was bound to be a major issue in their lives.

I soon discovered that the best place to start teaching that play is the place that T. S. Eliot dismissed as the worst scene in it. This is the Reynaldo scene, in which Polonius hires Reynaldo to go off to Paris and spy on his son. *Hamlet* opens with the following two lines:

BERNARDO: Who's there?
FRANCISCO: Nay, answer me. Stand and unfold yourself.

Later in the Reynaldo scene, Polonius wants to know who his son really is. He wants him unfolded to his view. So he hires Reynaldo to spy on him. Ironically, Polonius thereby tells us a great deal about who he really is—nothing but a spying busybody.

I found the Reynaldo scene a great place to start discussion of the play because all my students had a strong opinion about what was going on there. "Do you think that parents should be spying on their children?" I asked.

"Of course not!"

"But what if they're using drugs and the parents wish to protect them from hurting themselves?"

At that point the discussion really began to take off. Of course ghosts are very dramatic and all that, and people poisoning and stabbing each other can get our attention—or could before television made such activities as commonplace as commercials. The real question, though, is, what does all that have to do with parents spying on their children? which is what a great deal of *Hamlet* is about. Not entirely, however, because what the play is also about is the importance of spying on one's parents. Most of us don't spend a whole lot of time doing that. We get exercised about what our parents know (or think they know) about us; but I have, after teaching thousands of high school students, never met one in that age group who had the slightest interest in knowing what was really going on with his or her parents. In the students' opinion, it was nearly always true that their parents were getting in the way of many things they wanted to do, usually because the parents weren't very bright or had too many outmoded ideas. Why they might have those ideas and how they got to be that way was seldom of any interest. If it ever became of interest, incidentally, that usually turned out to be very helpful to the student to know.

Teaching *Hamlet* to seniors in high school, then, is an excellent opportunity for teachers to get students to think about how people in their own age group might approach the elder generation by trying to find out what is really going on in their minds.

The Art of Being a Revolutionary

Since almost everyone is, at about the age of eighteen, something of a revolutionary, it might be useful for eighteen year olds to explore what other eighteen year olds have rebelled against in other places and at other times. This could stimulate a strong interest in history, for example, or sociology, or even the history of art. Teenagers rebelling against their parents are very similar to the Colonists rebelling against King George. Teachers could watch the latest fad developing among high school students and then take them back to the Roaring Twenties—the age of the flappers, the recovery from the fatigue of war, and the headlong race toward the stock market crash. It's all there, happening all over again right in that high school classroom.

Or if they like, they could compare the latest fad to the spread of Byronism throughout Europe as an outburst of rebellion against classical art forms. They could even go all the way back to Euripides, who dared say what the Athenians didn't want to hear and got himself exiled. Or later, in a somewhat more ribald context, to Ovid, who also got himself exiled for having perhaps too much fun at the expense of too many cherished idols of the culture. It's all right there, happening over and over again, but if it doesn't get mentioned, no one will notice it.

The loss of a sense of tradition, history, knowledge of how the world works and all the rest that is complained of so loudly in criticisms of schools stems from the fact that reading is not taught as a way of accessing and critiquing one's own personal experiences and then finding echoes of them in the universal panoply of history. Students are almost never taught to engage in the fascinating enterprise of placing their own experiences on the stage of world developments in all fields of knowledge.

A teenager will get a lot more interested in the theory of relativity if you tell him or her that Einstein wasn't very good at math, couldn't get a job as a university professor, and later, after he began to get famous, attended a meeting of an anti-Einstein society and cheered on their detailed denigration of his theory of relativity.[2]

Instead, *Hamlet*, like almost everything else, is nearly always taught as something "out there." It's taught as an excuse for vocabulary development, or a chance to give lectures on the Elizabethan theater, or an opportunity for discussing how themes are expressed by poets, or how characters are developed in good writing, or what have you, none of which has anything much to do with what high school seniors are actually thinking about.

Now if our school experiences are entirely based on learning that what we read in books has little or nothing to do with our actual mental processes, then comprehension for us will, at best, be an exercise in how to pass multiple-choice tests, which is what schools seem to be, for the most part, really interested in.

I've already gone to some lengths to make the point that comprehension begins when the still, small voice inside of us begins to carry on a conversation with the still, small voice inside of any given book. The question, then, is how to find those voices. For each of us, of course, the still, small voice inside the book is unique to each of us as a reader. So if we can identify what inner impulse is seeking clarification and/or knowledge and find a book that will speak precisely to that need, we're in for a compelling reading experience every time. That's particularly true of *Hamlet*, of which Coleridge said, "There's a little of Hamlet in me, if I may say so." In some sense a book (any book) is a little like a Rorschach test. It has the potential to reveal to us who we really are, at least in relation to the subject matter in the book.

To sum up: In order to read a book successfully, we first have to find our languages in it. Once we have done that, we can begin to let ourselves learn the language of the book. Every reading teacher should be primarily dedicated to helping each student do this first, by finding the student's own most meaningful language and then by showing the student how to translate that into the language of the book's author. The process is fascinating, emotionally moving and deeply intellectual.

Making It Fun

Of course, we're still left with the rebellious teenager, whose only interest in life is hanging out with friends at the mall.

So what happens, I ask them, when you hang out with friends? Who are you trying to impress? How do you do that? Suddenly we've got another situation and set of prerogatives that can eventually be elaborated in the direction of a love for reading.

I decided to teach my reluctant science students about cosmology by treating the whole universe as a sex scandal. In a dialogue between a reluctant student and a persistent teacher, which I called "Dr. Einstein Meets Dr. Seuss," I had the professor awaken the student who had been sleeping in class endlessly, dreaming about sex, by explaining that the only way one can really understand what goes on inside the atom is to realize that the whole thing is completely sexual.

By this progression I took the student reader far afield into the mysteries of relativity, the twin paradox, how the Big Bang occurred, and various and sundry other things. My reluctant science students rose to the occasion splendidly. Some, who had never had more than a passing interest in anything that wasn't overtly sexual, read the book over four or five times to make sure they really understood the arcane structure of the universe.

There shouldn't be anyone who is forever immune to the whispering that comes from good books. It's just a matter of cracking the code that's unique and different in every student. We might call that book whispering, acknowledging the fact that every life is a book waiting to be written. If we're going to write the books of our lives, though, we have to learn how they fit in with the books of other people's lives. Otherwise nobody (including us) will be interested in the books that are in there hoping to get written. Experienced readers may be in even greater need of being taught how to do this. Certainly the people who run our civilization have given us every indication that they need this—as Shaw so eloquently saved me from having to point out. More about that later.

15

Getting the
Beginning Straight

*What's the quickest possible route through a sea
of unfamiliar complexities?*

The place to get started with reading comprehension is at the beginning
of a book. You have to learn the vocabulary and way of thinking peculiar
to the individual who is writing it. Once you're clear about these, you can
move rather easily through the rest of the book, because you'll understand
the special words and concerns of the author.

I once found myself in the position of having to teach six high school
students how to act a play by Swedish dramatist Strindberg in three weeks.
This particular play, *Easter*, deals with profound conflicts between the
sexes, which are only nascent in adolescent experience, but are far better
discussed and thought about than ignored and stumbled on later in life,
when it is too late to recoup the losses.

In any event, the material was rather foreign to the students' experience, so I began by spending three hours of rehearsal time on the first six
lines in the play. We read those lines over and over, examining every par-
ticle of motivation that might lie behind them. In the process, characters
began to emerge, and the students understood what they were going to
be doing in that play. After that we could move through the rest of the
play rather quickly and it all made sense.

It's like that with any book that might prove difficult. You invest most
of your energy in the beginning, and the rest will fall into place. If you're

a teacher, you need to find out what everyone in the class, individually, thinks the first paragraph is about.

As a teacher I was sometimes arrogant enough to think I knew and the students didn't. Therefore it behooved me to tell them what things meant.

Gradually I became aware that this was almost never true. What I could do was spin out a story about what the words might mean and then ask my students whether or not they agreed with my story. Usually they'd nod their heads with a blank stare, but then one student would question something in the text and I'd throw the question back to the others, and pretty soon we'd find ourselves discussing why the author chose those words and why everyone in the class could possibly have a different impression of the meanings involved.

Let me give a simple example by returning to the opening lines of *Hamlet*:

Who's there?
Nay, answer me. Stand and unfold yourself.

Topics for discussion might be: Why would you want to know who was there? Describe the conditions under which this question would arise. What does the question mean? When do you find yourself wondering who is coming toward you? When you see someone you know, do you ever wonder who that person is? Why or why not? Why would a person choose to return the question rather than answer it? What's the probable relationship between these two people? How do they feel about each other? What does that say about the environment in which they live? What's the difference between the question, Who's there? and the command, Stand and unfold yourself? Is there any kind of power play going on? What does it mean to "unfold yourself"? Have you ever unfolded yourself to anyone? Are there different ways of unfolding yourself? Why would anyone want someone else to unfold himself or herself? What would society be like if everyone could easily unfold himself to everyone else?

This is just the beginning of a series of questions that might arise about these two opening lines in the play, but already perhaps you can see how a good deal of the thematic material is likely to unfold itself in the discussion that will ensue when these questions are asked. It's a good thing when you read a book to, as soon as possible, try to anticipate everything that's coming later in the text. Then you'll either turn out to be right, in which case you could have saved yourself the trouble of reading the book, or you'll modify your impressions continually as you go.

I began this book by saying that when you read, you are reading yourself. The paradox, of course, is that the self you are reading is the very self you are creating by the process of reading. But you can create that new self, or continue the unfolding development of your self, only by starting somewhere that you can recognize and by going not too fast into uncharted territory.

Fun and Games in Paradise

Milton's *Paradise Lost* has a reputation for being the longest, most boring poem in the English language. Well, if you give a quick overview of it, it isn't so boring, with all those devils at the beginning lying around in the fumes of hell and gradually getting up and building the great palace of Pandemonium. Then comes the part about the Angel warning Adam that he'll get in trouble if he eats the Fruit of the Tree of Knowledge. Adam is completely forewarned, but Eve is nevertheless seduced by the Serpent, who has a very good argument against God's rather arbitrary withholding of the delights of that tree. So Eve eats, all is lost, and Adam, rather than turn his back on her, does the heroic thing, eats it too, and both get booted out of Paradise.

There's a lot here to make you wonder, particularly because the Puritan beliefs that underlie the poem hold that all is destined from the very beginning anyway, so there's not much you can do about it.

I found that teenagers quickly became aroused about many of the issues that arise from this story. It wasn't long before they found it a good deal more interesting than the television soap operas they had been watching, primarily because it dealt with issues of right and wrong that they were wrestling with in their inevitable conflicts with their parents. So the whole thing came down to what happens to them if they don't do what their fathers tell them and just how okay are the consequences of that? The issue about destiny and free will keeps most people going on discussions that last well into the night.

The trouble with the poem, however, is that if you want to know what it has to say, you have to be able to read it, and it's impossible to do that unless you're good at diagramming sentences, because otherwise there's no way to keep track of how a sentence that goes on for half a page, with phrase in linking phrase in endless periphrasis, will in the end sort itself out.

So I always spent the first week just diagramming the first sentence in the poem, the first half of which is a remarkably ingenious noun phrase of direct address. Believe it or not, while it is boring to diagram the kinds of sentences that show up in grammar books, it's not boring to diagram that one. It's like doing a huge jigsaw puzzle. When you take it apart and look at what language can do when it's allowed to pull out all the stops on its syntactical, grammatical and structurally linguistic possibilities, it's a drama all its own, kind of the way Beethoven's *Fifth* comes across when Peter Schickele sportscasts it.

Once you've spent a week doing that, you get the hang of how Milton's prosody works. Then you find you can not only read but understand it and you're pretty proud of yourself, particularly if it wasn't so long ago that the *Babysitter Books* were about all the challenge you could take.

In activities and discussions like this, I usually found that a student would become able, somewhere along the way, to hear his or her own voice coming through and connecting with the larger voice of the poet that was speaking from an age long gone.

Milton's worst qualities served my purposes as well as his best. For example, he was absolutely committed to the notion that women are biologically, morally and in every other respect inferior to men. He made the best possible case for that position, given what he knew at the time. It's great to watch students, who know that isn't true, trying to come to terms with it in a writer who is impressing them in many other ways. They're forced to love him and hate him at the same time, and that's always a great deal more interesting than blind idolatry, a sport in which teenagers tend to overindulge.

16

Appreciating Writing Style

*What did Oscar Wilde really mean when he said,
"In matters of grave importance, style not sincerity,
is the vital thing"?*

When I first started my own school I was, like many teachers who are sympathetic to the values of their students, eager to strip away as many of the old school rules as possible. For this reason I did not react negatively to the bad language my students were prone to. After all, adults that know each other well use such language routinely, so why shouldn't young people as well?

However it soon became apparent that so-called bad language is actually a crutch. If every time you feel an emotion, no matter what it is, you can use the same small group of four-letter words to respond to it (which in teenage circles is regarded as cool behavior), your mind is seldom stretched by the problem of finding more precise terms in which to express yourself. It's like trying to paint a picture with only two colors.

So one day I announced to the students that bad language was, from that time on, prohibited on school grounds because it was damaging their brains. I said that the point was not to prevent them from being spontaneous and expressing their feelings. Quite the opposite. It was to get them out of the ruts into which they had fallen, in which the feelings of one person were indistinguishable from those of another, and the emotions aroused by one situation could not be distinguished from those aroused by another. There were no shadings of emotion in the group, no insights that led to penetrating distinctions among feelings and perceptions.

The quality of life, I explained, is largely a function of the quality of feelings one is able to have about it, and these tend not to be articulated fully until they can somehow be expressed, usually at first by language, although later this expression may take the form of art.

So I encouraged people to censor their own language and replace the obvious expressions with more subtle ones. In order to do this, I encouraged them to read and discuss more literature, especially poetry, so they could learn to think like poets; for I have found that, in the discussion of poetry, one of the most important things that happens is the discovery of new possibilities for expressing one's feelings precisely.

Throughout the history of civilization there have been golden moments when it was possible to say something in an incomparable way—a way in which it could never be said again. It was precisely at those times when language reached its greatest heights of expressiveness. Think of some of the psalms in the Bible, for example: "The Lord is my shepherd, I shall not want."

The author of this psalm knew of the special relationship between real shepherds and their sheep. He knew of the patience the shepherd shows, as he guards the flock all night long, protecting them from the attack of wild animals. In the same way, he says, he is protected by his Lord. All of his needs will somehow be met.

Never again would the occasion arise to express this particular thought more concisely and beautifully than it is expressed here. Notice how in two clauses the entire point of the psalm is captured. First there is the statement of relationship. It is immediately followed by the consequence of that relationship. Whenever we want to reexperience the feelings of being protected throughout life in that very patient way, we can return to this psalm. Nothing else on this subject is quite so eloquent.

Centuries later, the Greek playwright Sophocles told the story of Oedipus, who, learning of his fate, tries to run away from it and only runs headlong into it. Having killed a stranger at the place where three roads meet, he moves on to find the land where the king has died, and becomes the new king. Years later, he seeks the man who killed the previous king, only to find that it is he himself who did the deed, and that the king whom he killed was his own father. In the moment when he learns the truth of this, Oedipus realizes and finally accepts the enormity of his fate: He has sought to outwit the destiny the gods had in mind for him, only to find out that such a destiny cannot be eluded.

No work of literature can ever express this compelling theme with such tautly inevitable power as it is expressed here. Reading or seeing the play, we relive the fate of Oedipus, knowing what will happen to him, and watching in amazement the manner in which fate coils itself around this proud man and forces him to realize his mortal limitations. "We must know our true capacity," the author seems to be telling us, "and not seek to step beyond it."

The state of being described by the Twenty-third Psalm suggests passive acceptance of one's lot. *Oedipus Rex* tells the story of one who rebels against his lot only to be caught in the trap he has, in effect, set for himself. Each literary experience is, in its own way, stark, economical and precise. Each tells of a condition of life that is possible for anyone to experience.

If the Psalm assures us of the patient caring of a benevolent God for the one who follows him as a servant, the play shows us what it is like to pit ourselves against overwhelming forces and lose as, under the circumstances, we must.

The above are two great works of literature that express opposite types of experience, each with unique and unforgettable power. We cannot know all of life through the Psalm alone or through Oedipus alone, but as we contemplate their extremes, we sense the vast reach of human experience possible for us.

Growing up in the neighborhood, hanging out in the mall, working our way through school with our own little social group, we live in an unbelievably narrow and delimited world. There is little opportunity to reach out beyond this circumscribed life and feel what it might be like to live a vastly different life.

Great literature is a primary means by which we can vicariously supplement the meager experiences of our little lives by reaching out to a much vaster realm of possibility for experience, sensation and emotion.

If all the student knows of these works, and hundreds of others like them, is what can be stated about them objectively, then there seems little point in reading them. For example, what is the "valley of the shadow of death"? This is an example of a phrase whose meaning is unknowable unless you give it your own meaning. If you cannot remember a time when you despaired so deeply that you felt death's shadow upon you, you cannot know the consolation that comes from God of which the author speaks. No amount of discussion of this phrase that doesn't take you inside yourself will increase your understanding or cause you to value what you have read.

Similarly, if you've ever set a trap for yourself and walked right into it, you can understand the dilemma of Oedipus, but if you haven't and can't imagine doing it, the play may be lost on you.

Consider the following line from *Hamlet* in relation to the above two works of literature: "Oh God, I could be bounded in a nutshell and count myself a king of infinite space, were it not that I have bad dreams."

One might think of the bounded life of the shepherd who has his own Shepherd as so satisfying in its total reliance on the support of the Lord that it amounts to being a king of infinite space. In contrast, Oedipus, who wanders far and wide and actually becomes a king, realizes, to the ultimate extent, his own worst dreams.

We have worked through two symbolically represented aspects of life, as represented in two works of literature, and imagined how we might identify with each. The line from *Hamlet* pulls them together into a single experience, placing the one against the other in a statement about alternate and opposing life experiences.

If you have understood and accepted all this, you have greatly expanded the life experience of which you are now capable. A rich metaphorical way of thinking has begun to open itself to you, and as you encounter each new work of literature, you are able to add something new to that reservoir of imagined experiences that provide metaphors you can apply to the situations in your own life, so that everything you encounter has a rich resonance of possible meanings.

These meanings are embedded in our imaginations through the words that express them, and the more beautiful their music, the more powerfully they will stick in the memory.

With that in mind, let's give some thought to the word "music," in which so many of the metaphors that profoundly move us are expressed.

The Music and Emotion of Language

On a visit to Denmark, I noticed an astonishing phenomenon. Whenever I heard someone talking but was not close enough to distinguish the words, I was convinced I was hearing English. Only after I had paid close attention did I realize that the voice I was listening to was speaking Danish. This taught me that the cadence of Danish speech is remarkably similar to that of English. Cadence is the rhythmic sequence, or flow, of sounds in language. It may characterize the language as a whole, be used to distinguish among dialects, identify the characteristic style of a particular writer, or even be used to make a poetic point all by itself. Consider the following by Robert Frost:

> *The old dog barks backwards without getting up.*
> *I can remember when he was a pup.*

You hear the slow-moving sounds associated with the old dog in the first line and the bounciness of the puppy in the second line.

So when I heard Danish and thought it was English, I was responding to the cadence of English as it usually sounds to me: a slightly European version of the language, not quite Oxfordian English, but certainly not Southern drawl either. The two languages are, of course, related, as the Danes (or Danskers, as they call themselves) were rulers in parts of England prior to the Norman conquest in 1066.

The melody of the voice in speaking a language and the way it is phrased are important aspects of linguistic structure, and the human species is sensitively attuned to these musical qualities in language. Recent research has revealed how much more important phrasing is than had previously been thought.

Traditional theories of language comprehension have held that adults employ prosodic cues only to flesh out a sentence's meaning after they have deciphered its grammatical structure. For instance, rising pitch toward the end of an utterance signals a question, whereas falling pitch indicates a statement. New studies, however, place prosodic cues at the core of understanding the grammatical structure of speech. Pauses, inflections, emphases and so on aid our understanding of word meanings.

The new research emphasizes the importance of the musical values in language. It's not what is said that is important so much as the *way* it is said. And it is not the way it is said so much as the melodies that are carried inside it. You hear the old dog's bones creak in that first line, and you can almost see the puppy cavorting in the second.

Language as the Expression of Feeling

One of the problems that has arisen in the modern age is the debasing of the sounds of language. We have become so pragmatic that we see no reason to emphasize language use except as it points to precise and often technical meanings. But language is not only important as a vehicle for getting information across; it is also a means of expressing feeling. We humans usually value feeling more than information because it lies deeper in our brains and motivates everything we do.

The student who is forced to focus on grammatical structures gets little hint of the feeling quality in the language, of how musical it is. But without it he or she would scarcely be motivated to learn to speak. The cooings and burblings of a baby seek similar responses, and the speech of adults contains those responses deeply buried in it. Take away all the referential meaning, all the baggage of the workaday world, and we have something like "Jabberwocky":

> 'Twas brilig and the slithy toves
> Did gyre and gimble in the wabe.
> All mimsy were the borogoves
> And the momraths outgrabe.

I have performed the complete poem as a dramatic entertainment many times and had others perform it as well. Even though there is scarcely a word in it that has a dictionary definition, the story of the poem comes through clearly. We know what's happening, why it's happening, and how everyone feels about it.

It's this musical quality in language that carries so much more weight than we might imagine, which we tend to lose sight of in academic circles.

Musical Values

Now to put all this in a somewhat different perspective, try listening to some instrumental music that has no words associated with it in your mind. Listen for the characteristics of music that resemble characteristics of the speaking voice.

What constitutes a phrase? How do phrases in music comment on, respond to, and develop one another?

Then ask yourself to what extent our interest in and love for music derive from the language function in our brains. Consider the fact that animals have no response to music at all (except when it suddenly becomes very loud). Do music and speech arise, to some extent, from the same impulse in human experience? Perhaps you have, from time to time, listened to poetry beautifully recited in a language you do not understand and marveled at how much was communicated in the sounds of the words without any direct access to their meanings.

It's true that we seldom place much emphasis on listening to the spoken word in a foreign language, but we do listen to opera and art songs in the languages in which they were originally written far more often than in translation. This is because a composer, in setting a text, responds to the musical values of the actual words used and extends these in the musical setting. When the text is changed through translation, the music does not sound the same, and the emotion does not feel the same. The prosody of Italian or German sounds different from the prosody of English, so a Mozart opera in English sounds a little bit off because the melody of the music and the melody of the words no longer match perfectly. Consider this, for example:

"Già la mensa è preparata" ("Now the table is set") can be sung to these words: "Now it's time to have my dinner." In the Italian version, the emphasis falls in the middle of the sentence (*"mensa"*) whereas in the English version that matches the meter, the emphasis falls at the end ("dinner"). But the music emphasizes "time" more than "dinner," which almost becomes an afterthought. So the music, when married to English, speaks it continually with the wrong accent.

I mention this in the context of music, because it makes it clearer what we're dealing with here. If your native dialect is not Standard English, then what you read always seems to have the accents in the wrong places, and the nuances are uncomfortable for you. That condition will continue until you have learned to read in English as a language slightly foreign, but completely comprehensible, to you. Then you will have made yourself somewhat bilingual. This is one of the major reasons why so many more minority children have reading problems than those whose native dialect is very close to Standard English. The problem goes much further, though, because as our reading continues, we increasingly read things that are not written in the currently fashionable form of Standard English.

How the Brain Hears Spoken Sound

The French psychologist Alfred Tomatis discovered that we go through a developmental process in our hearing. By about the age of one and a half, we have reached the point where we no longer hear linguistic sounds that are not part of our native language. We have mentally "set" the accent in which we shall speak from that point on. Other sounds, which don't fit our native dialect, go unheard. This creates problems in comprehension, because sound distinctions necessary to convey information may go unheard, and the information may be lost.

So the inner ear needs to develop as we learn to read in dialects not our own. This problem arises when we learn to read Elizabethan literature. The linguistic expressions of the time are different enough from ours that we have to learn some of the aspects of a new language to be able to comprehend them fully. It helps to listen to professional actors reading the words until the nuances of expression they convey have become familiar enough to enter our mental prosody. Then the music of the words can play in our minds so beautifully that we can imagine writing Elizabethan poetry ourselves.

It also helps if we listen to music while simultaneously listening to actors speak. This lowers the filtering mechanism of our language perception and allows us to hear linguistic sounds that otherwise wouldn't register. That's because the ear responds to music through the entire frequency range, but responds to language only in selected preset frequencies. For this reason reading teachers have often noticed that if music is playing while their students attempt to read, their reading improves faster than it does without it. This is not just because the music increases the frequency response of the ear, it is also because as we read to music, we are invited almost subliminally to try to match the phrasing of the words to that of the music. Gradually this will increase our sensitivity to the possible ways in which words can be grouped, which in turn will increase our sensitivity to different literary styles. The fine-tuning of our ears will make us sensitive to many subtle musical values in the developing sound of vowels and consonants differently grouped.

Why Word Music May Triumph over Ideas in the Best Writing

Probably 90 percent of what people love about Shakespeare is in his word music, of which he is the grand master. At least, that's what Shaw thought was true of Shakespeare, for as far as he was concerned, Shakespeare didn't have a fresh idea in his head—and, in fact, while you'll find the plays loaded with immortal quotations, you won't find many new ideas among them:

> The two *Richards, King John,* and the last act of *Romeo and Juliet,* depend wholly on the beauty of their music. There is no deep significance, no great subtlety and variety in their numbers; but for splendor of sound, magic of romantic illusion, majesty of emphasis, ardor, elation, reverberation of haunting echoes, and every poet-

ic quality that can waken the heart-stir and the imaginative fire of early manhood, they stand above all recorded music. These things cannot be spectated…: they must be heard. It is not enough to see *Richard III*: you should be able to whistle it.[1]

So, consider the following lines:

The quality of mercy is not strained.
All the world's a stage.
To be or not to be, that is the question.
If music be the food of love, play on.
My only love sprung from my only hate.

You might be able to write an essay on any of these topics, but the ideas in it would be your own, not Shakespeare's. He gave us the word music, the power of the language. He taught us how to feel. He almost never made us think. On those occasions when he seems to be doing that, he's usually borrowing ideas from someone else.

This is not to denigrate Shakespeare, it's to challenge the supremacy of ideas. Ideas are far less important to us than feelings, which are a great deal more important than most people will admit. Almost no one ever does anything just because it's a good idea, but people live and die on the basis of their feelings.

Strange, then, that we seem to think that reading is all about getting ideas and that it has so little to do with feeling. That seems to be because we have come to believe things about language and language comprehension that are not true, and these untruths have motivated our teaching.

Emotion Versus Ideas in Language

Emotions cannot be planned, they must flow spontaneously. Language is predominantly a means of expressing emotion and only secondarily of expressing ideas. Those who have been most successful at getting their ideas across have given them an emotional context and means of expression. Why else were the rhetorical devices learned by orators in the nineteenth century so manipulative of the feelings of listeners? Perhaps the best-known example of this manipulation of emotions to persuade is Mark Antony's speech in *Julius Caesar*. In the very process of declaring himself objective and unemotional, Antony whips his audience up to a white heat of fury.

One of my primary objections to textbooks is that most of them have no word music, feeling or emotion anywhere in them. This robs their subject matter of much of its charm. Removing the icing from the cake or the sizzle from the steak only increases the challenge of learning, quite unnecessarily, because the subject becomes both dry and apparently much more difficult than it really is.

Recently, for example, I helped a student struggle through the following sentence in a math book: "Care must be taken in performing operations to attend to the absolute value of the numbers." There is no reason that sentence couldn't have been written like this: "While you're working on a problem, you'll want to be careful to take into account the difference between a number when it is all by itself and the same number when it has a plus or a minus sign in front of it." The original sentence gratuitously introduces the passive voice so as not to bring the student into the picture at all. Students want to know that the author of a textbook is right there along with them, not some bodiless voice coming from an indeterminate place. This sort of disregard for the plight of the student that pervades nearly all textbooks may be responsible for more high school dropouts than the drug culture. In fact, it may be one of the drug culture's best friends.

Bulgarian researcher Georgi Lozanov's work on the methodology of education firmly established the fact that people learn anything, no matter what it is, much faster and better if they are fully involved emotionally than if they are not.[2] So to eliminate affective elements from the classroom is to invite pedagogical disaster. And much of the emotional element I'm concerned with is to be found in the tone of writing used by the authors of textbooks. You can tell they're writing for the boards that decide which textbooks will be adopted this year, and not for the students who will be using them.

Why America's Children Can't Think

Below I've devoted some attention to a single line from *Hamlet*: "Something is rotten in the State of Denmark." I was inspired to pick this line because early in my teaching I found it misquoted in a series of sentences presented to students in a grammar book. At the time I was struck by the way the line lost much of its punch and flavor when rewritten thus: "There is something rotten in the State of Denmark."

This simple change from the original brought home to me how precise are the musical values of poetry and why it is so often said that poetry is what disappears in translation.

What is true of poetry is equally true of prose: "It was the best of times, it was the worst of times." "It is a far, far better thing that I go to do than I have ever done before."

The timing, rhythm and sound of lines are a large part of what makes them stick in the memory, a large part of their emotional content.

And indeed it is not surprising that this should be so, for the way that we phrase our words in intimate or dramatic interactions with others carries more of our message than the intellectual content of the words. According to an analysis carried out by experts in neuro-linguistic programming, the way we communicate in speech is 7 percent through the actual words that we use, 35 percent through tone of voice, and the rest through body language.

The musical values of prose and poetry are the representation in print of tone of voice. There's a gap of unimaginable proportions between the following two ways of saying approximately the same thing:

Had we but world enough and time,
This coyness, lady, were no crime.

As opposed to: "Hey, baby, get with the program here."

Again, the literal content of the message almost disappears compared to the effect of the way it is said. The content is the intellectual part, while the tone conveys the emotions. In most cases, the emotions carry the day.

The bulk of the emphasis in teaching writing is on spelling (an entirely supererogatory concern in English until about three hundred years ago). In addition, we are taught to use words in the ways that are considered standard for our time. This, of course, ignores the emotional values of the message conveyed.

One of my problems in teaching English teachers is that many of them seem to forget about how the great literature they're teaching reflects the way that language sounded in the mouths of the actual people that the great writers knew. Characters in Shakespeare, Dickens and Hemingway speak the way that the people these writers knew actually spoke. Or at any rate, the speech they wrote was derived from the speech they had heard, much as a portrait artist derives the appearance of a subject from the look of the subject himself. When you listen to an actor playing Falstaff, you know that Shakespeare knew exactly how the fat, ridiculous old man he was both observing and creating had to breathe in order to get his words out.[3]

Speech Versus Prose

When students attempt to write the speech that is in their heads the way they hear it, they are too often criticized for doing so, even in situations in which it is appropriate.

Teachers insist that correctness must precede creativity, but actually it is the other way around. Children speak creatively long before they adapt their speech to reflect more accurately the sounds they hear spoken by others. As for correctness, all notions of what that is are in flux. If students are trained to listen, and to mimic what they hear, and to read and imitate what they have read, they will learn the essence of correctness without becoming so pedantically immune to the feelings language is meant to convey that their self-expression is stifled.

In the process, they will learn that spoken speech that is written down word-for-word becomes unreadable. All the things we do with tone of voice, phrasing, emphasis and most other forms of expression disappear when our remarks are reduced to print.

The art of writing requires us to put all that back in. Descriptions of facial expressions and gestures or a hint of the emotion behind a remark can supply some of it. Most of it, though, comes from an editing of the words of speech into a new form that distills the emotions behind the words.

Why America's Children Can't Think

You and I can get away with the same old three little words when we tell our true love how we feel, but that won't do for the lover on the stage or in a novel, who must do something to make up for the lack of flesh and blood on the printed page. He must observe that his lady "doth teach the torches to burn bright," or she must ask him to doff his name and take all herself in exchange for it. It takes that sort of imaginative interpolation of the things that real people are never clever enough to say to replace all the richness of feeling that even the most dull-witted lover can convey with the tritest words in the exact right setting and circumstances. Hollywood understands this well and seldom attempts in its scripts to avoid the clichés of love, trusting the actors to give the script the flesh and blood that will redeem it. But when a work of literature must stand on its own, the lovers must become characters who have never lived and never could live, but are indeed archetypes for what we all wish we could be. This is the job that literature is meant to perform for us.

Young writers must be allowed to discover such things for themselves. Through experimentation and examination of each other's writings, they will gradually stumble upon their particular way of replacing, in the written word, all the richness that is squeezed out of it by having to be written instead of spoken.

Thus the art of writing can begin. Students should be allowed to write creatively, but to gradually come under the spell and influence of writers they love until they can absorb some of their styles and learn to write from them.

If we were to transcribe the actual words spoken between lovers discovering they are in love, leaving out all the stuff that's there on the scene but can't be observed in the transcription of words alone, we might get something like this:

ANDY: Excuse me, uh (sound of bell ringing)—oh shit, there's . . .

SALLY: Oh, hi, Andy I didn't see you there. Just a minute. Yeah, Suze call me. Sure. Sorry, Andy, I dropped my . . .

ANDY: Yeah, say, I was . . .

SALLY: Anyway, sorry.

ANDY: Yeah, well, okay, I guess.

SALLY: Sure, see ya.

ANDY: I was wondering . . .

SALLY: Oh, you wanted to say?

ANDY: I was (cough, cough) only wondering. (Bell rings)

SALLY: That's the . . .

ANDY: I don't, you know, have a class.

SALLY: Neither, uh, uh, do I.

ANDY: That's uh, that's uh, that's funny.

SALLY: What's, uh, funny?

ANDY: That you don't—we both don't . . .

SALLY: It's kind of like—sort of you know like fate, isn't it?

ANDY: Fate?

SALLY: Oh, well, I suppose.

ANDY: Oh, you mean, like, well, destiny, or whatever. Listen, Sally, I was wondering, could I call you sometime?

SALLY: Geez, Andy. Do you mean it? I thought you were, you know . . .

ANDY: Naw, we broke up last night.

SALLY: Uh, well, I don't . . .

ANDY: It's okay, I just thought I'd ask.

SALLY: No, I mean . . .

ANDY: If you're not free . . .

This sort of transcription is interminable, unreadable and leaves out everything that's important about the conversation: feeling, character, intention. Besides, it's dreadfully particular and mundane with little appeal to universal values. It has to be translated into prose to have any power. Fortunately our library shelves are crowded with great writers' interpretations of just this kind of boy-meets-girl situation. Studying and absorbing good prose expand our own expressive capacities as speakers and writers.

How Writers Find Their Own Styles

Benjamin Franklin reported on how he formed his style by copying long passages from Joseph Addison. T. S. Eliot observed that writers go through a stylistic evolution by falling in love with the style of one writer after another and imitating each until their own styles eventually emerge from the collage. The way in which a young person should learn to write is by reading well enough to be able to distinguish a favorite writer from others by the cadence, prosody, style of phrasing or more general style of the writing (which even includes specialized vocabulary). When they have become sensitive enough to such values, they will learn to write that way, too.

Following are some things to look for in noticing stylistic qualities:

- Does the writer prefer fancy words or simple ones? Shakespeare was almost allergic to using any word in a way that it had ever been used before. He was constantly inventing new ways of using words, and often even invented new words. About a thousand of the words we use today were originally used by Shakespeare. Robert Frost, on the other hand, conscientiously avoided saying anything, no matter how complex, in words that wouldn't likely show up in the mouth of a New England farmer. Consider the highfalutin vocabulary of Algernon Swinburne, who often used words for their musical effects without much regard for their meanings.
- How long are the sentences the writer likes to use? Hemingway single-handedly reduced the average length of the sentence in the modern novel by at least half a dozen words. Milton and Melville were two writers that reveled in long sentences.
- Is the writing routinely grammatical or conscientiously ungrammatical?
- What kinds of references does the writer typically use? Are they literary? Do they refer to pop culture? Does the writer like to go into long descriptions of meals? Do sports metaphors hang heavily about the page?
- How are phrases used? Are they mostly avoided, or do they pile

up one after another in a huge collage of competing possibilities for what's most important in the sentence? Are there phrases within phrases? Clauses within phrases within clauses?
- Do you find the writer's personality looming large in the text or hidden somewhere behind an anonymous mask?
- Do you feel the writer is sincere, or thinks sincerity is merely a way of being sentimental?
- What kinds of settings does the writer prefer? In some books people always seem to be surrounded by burned out buildings and trash heaps. In others, they're cavorting in the fields with Arcadian shepherds.
- How does the writer deal with stereotypes and social classes?
- Does the writer seem to be trying to prove a point most of the time or merely observing experiences noncommittally?
- Does the writer want to be thought well of, or is he or she perhaps taunting the reader by trying to appear dissipated and horrible?
- How much irony and paradox does the writer use?
- Does the writer like to play word games?
- How distinctively from one another do characters emerge from the writing?
- Does the writer move among a variety of different styles easily?

"Style is the way a man takes himself," Robert Frost once said, using the old sexist expression of a New England farmer, but speaking to the point nevertheless.

Why Style Is Important to Everyone

Each of us should develop an individual style, for unless we do, we are not in pursuit of our inner being, we are compromising with life, settling for the life of a composite of others' half-wished desires for us without the executive intervention of our own decision-making ethos. I have sat with many friends as they worked through the process of casting off the chains of inhibitions acquired somewhat randomly in childhood that have kept them walking a fine line between moral turpitude (as they saw it) and the suicide of the impulse to express oneself spontaneously.

Robert Frost wrote brilliantly of this force that is "most us" in his poem, "West Running Brook":

> *It is this backward motion toward the source,*
> *Against the stream, that most we see ourselves in,*
> *The tribute of the current to the source.*
> *It is from this in nature we are from.*
> *It is most us.*

Once the imagination has been given free reign, the old irrational enchaining principles have been discarded, and the spirit can breathe freely, a personal style of expression will be born and will continue to evolve throughout life. Then everything that one reads will take on new meaning, for the world will begin to unfurl itself in a new way, its global issues unfolding in all their grandeur, perhaps for the first time. And because one is now able to be more secure in one's own mind, one is free to contemplate the differences between oneself and the minds of others. It is not so much for the way other writers are like me that I admire them. It is their differences from me. Often the ones I enjoy reading the most are those I disagree with most strenuously because, with them, there's the possibility of reconciling what appear to be opposites into a great synthesis that transforms the author's ideas and my own into something above and beyond the possibilities of their polarized positions. This is one of the most splendid possibilities for thought that comes from reading with the suspension of disbelief. For while I read a writer, I see the world through her (or his) eyes. She and I are one, and she is informing me of the exact truth as she sees it. When I awaken from the dream and realize how very different my truths are, I struggle to reconcile the differences and am led to insights that would not otherwise be possible. For the essential nature of experience is paradoxical. In the act of living we move daily toward death, and in the act of dying we discover life. All experience is laced with that refusal to be one thing or the other, containing yin and yang so deeply as part of itself that it is like the neutron that combines proton and electron into one and the same.

The key to learning to write and express ourselves well is thus to learn to read with great love for the experience of reading in and of itself. Much of that experience comes from recognizing the stylistic differences among writers that capture, through the anticipated sounds of words when read aloud, the subtle nuances with which we are capable of expressing ourselves, which are often more important than the content of what we have to say. James Merrill, a writing teacher of mine in college (now a famous poet), used to say that the ones who become good writers are not so much those who have something to say as those who love to play with words. And certainly it is true that no one ever loved playing with words more devoutly than Shakespeare.

Finding Your Own Style

In finding your own style, you must become sensitive to your peculiar emotional patterns, which in their full complexity have a character different from that of anyone else. By learning to hear the sound combinations that characterize you, you can let the words you write sing your own particular song, which is like that of no other.[4]

If style is the way you take yourself, then if you are to expand who you are, you must increase the potential richness of your style. All great writers have unique and recognizable styles, just as great artists in other media do. Learning to recognize the style of a writer is the first step. Learning to replicate it is the second. In adolescence I quickly learned that if I spent a little time reading Dickens (or better yet, listening to Charles Laughton read him to me), I would start to write like Dickens. Learning to write in the style of other writers will increase the possibilities of your own style. It will also increase your sensitivity to the varied styles in which the world's great literature has been written. Therefore it is useful to teach reading in such a way that students can learn to mimic the styles of their favorite authors. Discussions of what makes one style different from another are fascinating, and should be part of reading instruction, even in the early stages.

You can get at this by having students read a sentence and then paraphrase it in several different ways, commenting on how the effect of the sentence changes with each new paraphrase:

> Something is rotten in the state of Denmark.
> There is something rotten in the state of Denmark.
> Things aren't right here in our neck of the woods, old buddy.
> It gives me the heebie-jeebies, what's going on around here.
> A crime has been committed and everyone is uneasy about it.

It should be obvious that the first of these lines was written by a nobleman used to thinking of his country as an extension of his own ego. Like a frontal attack to the spirit, the basic rhythm of the iambic pentameter line is contrapuntally violated in the first beat:

> Some*thing* is *rot*ten *in* the *state* of *Den*mark. (wrong)
> *Some*thing is *rot*ten in the *state* of *Den*mark. (right)

This indefinable *something* disrupts the order of the state as it does the rhythm of the line. The stench is everywhere, but no one knows what it is. Because the word "something" doesn't fall easily into the pattern of the line, the word seems to rise up like a corpse from the grave and demand attention, the way the ghost has done in the preceding action in this opening scene of *Hamlet*.

These qualities disappear in the paraphrases, which bring the wonder and fear of the humble servants of the state down to the level of ordinary people who are not sure why sometimes things disturb the normalcy[5] of the universe.

As we learn more about the range of styles possible in self-expression, we shall acquire more tools for elaborating the ways in which we are able to "take ourselves."

17

Building Mental Models

If we wouldn't unscrew something without a screwdriver, then why read a book without first identifying the author's tools of perception?

A personal view, for all its value, is not particularly useful if it cannot be applied successfully to the world that it presumes to describe. The challenge your own perspective brings with it is that you must establish communication with others so you can do many things with them and know what to expect. It's miraculous that there are billions of people with whom you could instantly establish social contact on many levels so well that if you were stranded on an island with any one of them, the two of you could work out survival strategies together. Such complex social interactions require us to share a myth of objectivity. We pretend that there is a world out there on which we all agree.

One way to do this is to build concepts that are shared. These concepts describe things that don't actually exist in the real world—things we cannot see, hear, taste, smell or touch. Things like love, loyalty, respect, economics, philosophy, religion, the rules for sports, commerce, fair play and so on. These shared and agreed on concepts become the basis for culture. Human beings are the only creatures we know of who can create a large number of unseen things like those mentioned above and treat them as if they actually existed.

So we live together in our imaginary world that is solely the product of our shared mental powers. Most of the educational process is devoted to sharing these creations of our collective consciousness.

These conceptual structures are conveyed through mental models. Mental models are metaphors that help us think about the things in the world we cannot see, like atoms and corporations. They are part of the vast architecture for thinking that arises in the human morphogenetic fields through an adjunct to our visual systems. They represent the infinitely varied parts of that imaginary world and explain how it works.[1]

Here are some examples of what I mean. Consider the following word list and reflect on what you do when you encounter one of these words:

Democracy

Conflict

Revolution

Paradigm

Mental illness

World peace

Ecology

Science

Ridicule

Population explosion

Assuming you understand each of these concepts, you should be able to summon to mind several different pictures associated with it, and also be aware that you have organized these various impressions into a working model of the particular concept. For example your concept of "revolution" might include an impression of something spinning around, a few cameos of people being executed, a scene on a college campus with police or soldiers moving in, and perhaps some Fourth of July fireworks. Coming out of all this is an impression that one regime or set of rules and regulations is violently replaced by another and that, after a period of great upheaval, things simmer down and the new order gradually takes over.

You don't have to invoke all this every time you read the word "revolution." It's filed in your memory, and you have a feeling of recognition of the word without having to remind yourself each time of what it consists.

Every thinking person has acquired thousands of such mental models, somewhat amorphously defined, but nevertheless a memory engram that can be accessed whenever the concept needs to be discussed or probed further. We know that we know these things without knowing how we know them or feeling we have to account for that knowing in detail.

Without such a mental model behind it, a word like any of those above would merely be a barrier to understanding.

Consider the following:

Upon exposure to ultraviolet light for a time period of about thirty seconds, a small sample of the human blood will contriolate.

In the above sentence, I have made up the word "contriolate" to represent a process that, as yet, has no scientifically established models to support it. But if I tell you that the word "contriolation" identifies a biochemical process that may happen in human and animal blood when it is briefly exposed to full spectrum sunlight or ultraviolet light in selected frequencies, then you can make sense of the above sentence.

The Architecture of Ideas in a Thought Process

In the example just given, I have modeled the scaffolding of ideas that writers have to build in order to inform their readers of new ideas or sets of ideas they may wish to explain. Unless the reader takes the trouble to replicate this intellectual scaffolding so as to mentally install the models required, it is impossible to follow the logic that it supports.[2]

Every subject of study is based on such constructs. Without them, you cannot understand anything that has been written about that subject. With them, you can follow and participate in the arguments as they develop in that field of knowledge.

So if you're planning to read a book, you will soon discover that you either do or do not have the mental models requisite to understanding it. If you don't have them, you can easily install them. All you need to do is identify the concepts the writer is referring to that you do not yet understand, and then do what is needed to understand those concepts by building mental models that explain them. You may have to go through this process several times with each new concept until the new models become part of your intellectual vocabulary. Then you will be able to make rapid progress in your newly chosen field of study.

It is just this kind of mental model construction that has led to progress in all fields of knowledge. For example, when Niels Bohr proposed that electrons might go around their nuclei the way the planets go around the sun, he created a mental model that is today ubiquitous but outdated. Drawings of atoms nearly always show those electrons in orbit, though their orbits do not resemble the edges of discs, like those of the planets, or the rings of Saturn.

It wasn't long after the Bohr atom was proposed that problems with it began to surface, and the model of planetlike objects circulating around larger objects had to be replaced with largely mathematical constructs suggesting that the so-called orbits of electrons are more like probability clouds (whatever those might be). In other words, an electron is more like your chances of being in a traffic accident in the next year than it is like a tennis ball.

This, too, is a mental model, albeit a puzzling one. The point is that we cannot think without images, and we can't get far in a book without having these images in place.[3]

Anything, of course, may become an image. For example, *2 + 2 = 4* is an example of symbols of abstract concepts that have taken on lives of their own as images. You do not need to visualize two bowling pins plus two more bowling pins, or anything else like that, to get to the answer. The numbers alone will do it for you, because you have become so used to the rules according to which the numbers operate that you can manipulate them in your head well enough to be quite comfortable if someone asks you what *2 + 3* is.[4]

As the mathematical symbols pile up, however, you may become far less comfortable, assuming that you haven't learned all the mathematical language involved. If you know how sines and cosines behave, then you can deal with them in your head as well, much in the way you might imagine a horse leaving the barn before the door is closed. So images can be symbols that are not concrete things, but behave according to predictable rules you are comfortable with, the way you are comfortable with horses and barns.

We store the whole universe (insofar as we are familiar with it) inside our heads and can manipulate it at will. It's just as easy to imagine a collision between two galaxies as it is to imagine one between two automobiles. All you have to have is a set of images that operate in predictable ways and you can freely think about them. Building mental models whose components you understand allows you to predict relationships that might develop within and among them.

Computers can do the same thing, and that's what makes them virtually an extension of the human mind. Computers are designed to make calculations that humans can't make, and to make them at warp speed. So computers can simulate all kinds of interactions far too complicated for the human mind to deal with unaided. But they can't do anything at all unless their programmers have developed mental models that can dictate how the simulations will approach the problems that are set for them. Armed with the right toolboxes full of mental models, we can plan our futures, build new businesses, invent scientific breakthroughs, write great poems, and rob banks so successfully the FBI will never find us. The existence of mental models means that there can be few limitations placed on the capacity of the human mind.

Why, then, has the construction of mental models never been the business of education? I have spent a good deal of time with telecommunications experts whose job it is to train other experts in their own fields in areas of knowledge that have been newly developed or are being more widely applied. In order to increase the effectiveness of teaching and efficiency of learning in these classes, I helped the instructors and course designers find suitable metaphors to describe what they were trying to teach. A particular communications system might resemble an airport, a supermarket or a railway switching system. The question was always, "What, in metaphorical terms, is really going on here?"

How Symbols Lose Their Freshness

One of the things I've discovered about symbols as images is that once you've adopted them as a result of learning the symbolic languages involved, it becomes very difficult for you to imagine what it's like for people not to know this symbolic language. That's why math professors are always writing long equations on the board instead of acting out the way a truck speeds up while accelerating on the freeway in order to get across the notion of a function in calculus.

When I deal with people who think in numbers, I have to spend a long time getting them to translate their thought patterns into commonplace models that anyone can understand. Once we've accomplished that, it becomes relatively simple to teach the core structure of the subject so quickly and so well that the meanings of the symbols that express that subject become quickly apparent to those who have to learn them, and the learning can take place very quickly as a result.

Let me give a quick example of how this works and why it is important. One of the simplest formulas in computer programming is $x = x + 1$.

The trouble with this formula is that it's terminally confusing to anyone who knows something about algebra and nothing about computer programming. This formula has only one possible solution as an algebraic equation, and that's a nonsense solution. It works only in cases where x is infinity. Since all infinities amount to the same thing, no matter how much larger one might be than another, the definition of infinity has become that it is a condition that always allows you to add one to the largest number you can think of. So as you increase the size of an infinity, it remains the same. There is no way the human mind can fully grasp this paradox, so all we can do is talk about it and go on, which doesn't help at all in understanding an algebraic formula.

Other than in the surrealistic case I have just discussed, there is no value for x that will make it equal $x + 1$. There is nothing other than infinity to which you can add one more and have exactly the same thing that you started with.

One may logically ask, therefore, why such a formula ever got written. Unfortunately, however, this logical question is seldom formulated in most people's minds, so when you try to teach them what this formula means, they immediately hit a brick wall, smash all their trust in you, and tune out everything else you have to say. It's the same reaction you would get if you said, "This little bottle of soapy water contains a substance that will cure you of any known (or unknown) illness, and you can have it today at the special marked down price of five thousand dollars." When you say things like that, people walk away from you. This kind of reaction occurs in people's minds a lot more often than you might think, since different people have different mental models for explaining the world and, to the extent that the mental models don't match, whatever is being communicated is not understood in the sense in which it was intended. The reason that the formula in question works in computer programming logic is that the expression "=" doesn't mean the same thing in computer logic as it means in algebra. In algebra it means "is the same as," whereas in computer logic (at least in this case) it means, "is replaced by" or "is transformed into."

Here's how it is actually used: Your goal is to teach a computer how to count from one to ten and above. You don't want to do this by rote, however; you want to give the computer a general notion of what's involved so you can change the kind of counting it does. Sometimes you want it to count by ones, sometimes by twos, and so forth. So $x = x + 1$ equals the English statement, "The number I am going to write next is the same as the previous number I wrote, with one added to it."

Once this is established, it's possible to write $x = x + 2$, or $x = x + 398$, and the computer will know exactly what you mean. In the latter case, it will produce the following column of figures:

1
399
797
1195
and so on.

It's not easy for most people to string out a column of figures that satisfies this formula at the rate of about a billion new numbers per millisecond, but computers can do that easily.

In many cases, the barrier to understanding in a particular field of knowledge may be as simple as the above source of confusion illustrates. Because a particular, very basic aspect of the subject has been misunderstood, the student has no idea where the subject is going, and can't proceed at all. This happens because a stimulus-response relationship to the symbolism used is so strong that any attempt to change it is overridden by habit. It's like trying to teach someone to stop at a green light and go at a red light. The person might be willing, but the body will not respond.

Misconceptions That Destroy Thinking

Misinformation acquired at an early stage of one's developing knowledge can create serious problems for people who are trying to develop skills or understanding later in life. Very often these confusions are never identified and therefore cannot be corrected. I have found, however, that when I am confronted with someone who supposedly has a learning problem, I can usually find an experience that lies at the root of it. Then it's sometimes possible to clear up the learning problem in a short time.

Unfortunately, though, if some particular aspect of a problem is misunderstood and never corrected, the student will be permanently unable to proceed with the reasoning process in question. This would not happen if teachers taught their students using mental models. A mental model allows them to elaborate their ideas about that subject rather quickly, in a number of different directions, and to come to conclusions that have some degree of accuracy and relevance.

Perhaps the reason teachers teach facts rather than mental models is that, about a thousand years ago, well before the invention of the printing press, facts were extremely hard to come by. So professors did the necessary job of reporting to their students the contents of books that the students could not read for themselves because the books were not available to them. Even today many teachers do the same thing, despite the fact that computers, which are rapidly making available to students all the information on record anywhere in the world, are quickly replacing books.

The result is that teachers assign term papers in which students are supposed to write about information they have looked up somewhere and have put into a new format. This is a comparatively useless activity, and therefore students have a propensity to get prefabricated term papers off the Internet. It's pretty difficult for the teachers to determine that these papers are not original, because they can't possibly check out everything on the Internet. It would be far more useful for teachers to propose original problems for the students to solve. The teacher could then help the students evolve in class the mental models that might be relevant to solving these problems. The students would then have to work out the means of solving them, using the mental models developed in class. They would, of course, report their solutions in well-written papers in which grammar, spelling and all sorts of other fine points of communication would be important, and their results could then be graded by teachers who would know that the students had had to do their own original work because the Internet could not supply them with papers that would meet all the criteria developed in the class discussion.

This, however, would require teachers not only to change their teaching methods, but also to think in new and original ways. Since some teachers don't relish doing that, they'd rather try to think of new and more powerful ways to catch students who are cheating by lifting or buying term papers off the Internet, or perhaps just let the whole thing ride until they can conveniently retire and forget about it.

The thing that's interesting to me in all of this is how much easier it is to build a logical system and follow it through to all sorts of conclusions if you use mental models to do it. Over time the mental models may turn out to be defective and need correction, but you won't discover that unless you're in the habit of using them in the first place.

18

Reason and Emotion

How can we learn to stop wading though a mire of other people's unprovable assumptions? And how can we cast out our own?

The development of mental models is a useful way to increase our mastery over the logical processes in our thinking. While it is clear from the history of philosophy as well as the philosophy of history that the human species, taken as a whole, does not operate rationally, we have long prided ourselves on our ability to do that.

Of course we cannot, because in order to do so, we would have to establish some outside authority or set of standards, independent of the beliefs, ideas or prejudices of any particular individual or group, against which logical analysis could be measured.

While there are many useful tools for logical analysis, the most logical people in the world will inevitably disagree from time to time on points that seem as if they ought to be open to objective analysis. This system works very well when it works. The trouble is, however, as I shall show in this chapter, that institutionalized emotional distress, which leads to power, control, censorship and financial manipulation in the interests of small special interest groups, too often keeps this system from working. In many cases it doesn't work, even despite the best intentions in the world. In some cases, though, the intentions are anything but good. Meanwhile, the general public has assimilated, as if it were true, an enormous amount of nonsense that will not stand up under careful critical examination. If we were to eliminate even a small fraction of this nonsense, contemporary conditions of living for the vast majority of people could be improved mightily. Not only are limits placed on our prosperity, they are also placed on our health, our access to justice, and our basic intellectual integrity. These limits are not legitimate, and those who are committed to democratic government in a free society need to be eternally vigilant against them. Instead we are a lazy people who accept, without skepticism, many things that should arouse our ire and determination to replace the incompetence and corruption in high places with something more favorable to the interests of those who wish to lead good and thoughtful lives unimpeded by the illegitimate connivings of those who have supposedly won the public trust.

The difficulty, of course, is in establishing what can be accepted as objectively true. Bias, emotional prejudice, cultural perspective and even miscommunication at the most basic level all corrupt what is generally assumed to be a body of objective knowledge of a generally scientific nature. At present, most people would assert that there is a developing body of scientific knowledge that has come closer than anything else ever has to a kind of universal logical acceptance. After all, we have (sort of) probed the farthest reaches of space and time. We have not only observed the microscopic, we have built whole kingdoms of technology within that realm. We have discovered enormous wonders in realms never dreamt of. Despite all this, however, our scientific community has not yet figured out how to be completely logical, and has certainly not proved itself as objective as it would like to think it is.

First of all, every step in the development of the body of scientific knowledge was hotly disputed along the way. When, over time, a particular point of view won out, it was often accepted by a large number of thinkers, but seldom by all of them. Often the very virulence of attacks on new ideas has weakened the possibility of critiquing the real flaws in them once the attacks have been overcome.[1] Furthermore, ideas that have seemed to be unassailable for long periods of time have later been called into question and sometimes even abandoned.

We, in what we think of as modern (or even postmodern) times, tend to believe that we have more answers than any people who have preceded us.

Nevertheless there are plenty of examples of groups who have entertained views quite unlike ours that seem, to some at least, to be more rational than the current views.[2]

The trouble is that, lacking any objective means of measuring logic or establishing realities that may be held as universally true, we continue to be susceptible to the influence of unnoticed assumptions in our thinking that will not hold up under logical analysis.

The greatest enemy of logical thinking is the human brain itself. It was never intended for logic, it was intended for survival. Its structure is so designed that when we are emotionally threatened, we drop all pretense of logic and adopt behaviors that are likely to support survival under primitive conditions (not necessarily those that prevail today). Unfortunately, many of us were so severely threatened in childhood that we carry throughout life an underlying fear for our survival that prevents us from being logical in certain situations, or when dealing with certain ideas.[3]

Furthermore, a whole culture can develop a sense of being threatened in some area so that nearly all those who live in it are swept away by the same irrational behaviors, convinced, meanwhile, that their view of life and their own safety is completely rational and necessary. When cultures other than our own behave this way, we condemn them. When our own does, we respond with patriotic fervor.[4]

Emotions, then, are the ever-present enemy of rational thinking; but their operation, as I am about to suggest, is most difficult to counteract at the very times when it is most important that it be counteracted. That's because the human brain is organized so that decisions originate at the seat of emotion, which is in the limbic system, or mid-brain.

As complex animals, we have survival needs that we must respond to or die. Emotions that are triggered within us, often with very little warning, are time-honored mechanisms, traceable back millions of years. Their function is to help us by providing feedback about whether a situation is good or bad for us, whether we like it or not. The information coming in from our senses is neutral until it has been interpreted for us by the emotional-processing mechanisms in our bodies and brains. Thus emotions provide information to our decision-making processes.

Why America's Children Can't Think

It's interesting, too, that if we try to proceed in a purely logical manner (sticking entirely to left-brain thinking), we often become trapped in unconvincing ratiocination. However, when we allow the more global instincts imbedded in the right brain to enter the picture, we can often rescue the situation by redirecting our thinking into a more productive approach to the problem.

Historically, one of the most interesting, if tragic, examples of unresolved emotions dictating every word a man said is in the career of Senator Joseph R. McCarthy, who eventually brought about his own political demise by attacking the U.S. Army with accusations that were so unfounded in fact as to render him virtually insane in the eyes of the television audience that was watching the proceedings.

This and countless other examples should demonstrate that when survival is perceived to be at stake, everything else becomes trivial by comparison. Therefore, emotions tend to dominate and take precedence over less intense and dramatic thoughts, and these emotions, if they are inappropriate to the situation in which they arise, may ironically bring about our downfall.

This happens because of the rigidity with which our more primitive emotional mechanisms have developed. Our evolution over millions of years has assured that when we are attacked, we must respond with full force and fury, without thought or compromise, drawing on abnormally large stores of energy to repel the attacks against us, and thereby, hopefully, to survive. Creatures that did not respond this way would soon be eliminated from the gene pool.

So the emotional responses we have are relatively rigid and difficult to modify. They may have been designed for a different kind of world than the one we live in now, but they still operate, still command attention and still, from time to time, cause us to do, with great conviction, things we may be heartily sorry for later.

Using magnetic resonance imaging (MRI), scientists have shown that these emotional responses shut down areas of the brain that are associated with logical thought and evaluation. Thus we find it impossible to think properly while we are aroused by them.

All this is preparation for addressing what I find to be a severe cultural malady: Because we do not know how to think and act on the broad national scale without arousing widespread negative emotions in the process, we allow ourselves to drift into many counterproductive situations. By failing to harmonize our intended actions with the appropriate visions of success that will come out of them, we often engage in programs and policies that lead nowhere or may have disastrous consequences.

First of all, we have often decided to do what we do not from rational considerations, but from emotional ones. The decisions are made first on the basis of feelings, and then rationalized afterward. This makes it difficult to be logical, since one often wants to believe things that would collapse under logical scrutiny if one did not go out of one's way to prop up the logic with arguments of questionable relevance.

All of us are victims of this developmental process in the organization of the brain. None of us can really think without the influence of emotion. We can only pretend that we are doing so.

It's far better, then, to recognize the fact that our logic is a prisoner of our feelings, but that we can best get beyond this dilemma by the most careful examination of the logic we do convey with our words. In this way, we avoid the possible corruption of our logic by half-hidden emotional content that we have not allowed ourselves to recognize. Those who are really honest intellectually will take steps to free themselves from the emotionally based prejudices that underlie their thinking so that a more balanced and intellectually honest view may be forthcoming.

For example, in the current debate over evolution, it is clear that both sides are heavily influenced by their emotional commitments. Those who feel that current scientific knowledge threatens their cherished religious beliefs make no bones about glossing over or dismissing ideas that have been scientifically grounded for nearly a century. On the other side of the coin, there are many scientists who seem to have a personal axe to grind in "proving" that God is a myth.

In fact (as many prominent scientists have often asserted), there has never been any real scientific evidence that seriously calls into question the "God hypothesis." The rational approach to this question, one that is easy enough to pursue, would be to see how the idea of God and the idea of natural selection can be reconciled in a way that takes into account all the facts that have been universally accepted by the scientific community and all the fundamental descriptions of God that are shared by the world's great religions. Those who have taken such an approach have not found it particularly difficult to reconcile the two.

This is but one of dozens of examples I could give of how we can sidestep our tendency to be led astray in the most erudite intellectual circles by emotional conflicts that remain unresolved. Rather than fall into this trap, it's better to realize that emotions are always involved but that the careful use of language that analyzes both emotion and logic can move our thinking into a more rational process. Language, if moved in the direction of its more rational function, free of the emotions residing in the limbic system, invokes vision.

Vision applied to such a notion as the domino theory that rationalized the Vietnam War, for instance, would have examined whether the simple mechanical action of dominoes could ever be successfully applied to such complex entities as countries. Such questioning might well have led to other ways of handling the Vietnam problem. Had such thinking occurred among the top decision makers, the flawed logic behind the Vietnam War would have been revealed for what it was. Then a new, more rational policy would have been designed to replace it.[5]

One could take almost any event in history and show that much of the thinking behind it was flawed in a similar way. Building the vision behind the policy and testing it out in real situations to see whether or not it actually made sense could have eliminated the flaws. Instead, national policies are usually based on widespread emotional distress and seldom have any rational structure underpinning them.

Such dilemmas are the result of a failure in thought processes, and ultimately in the proper functioning of language itself. For language, if properly used, invokes the kind of vision that is designed to compare observations in the outside world with internal images. If what we are experiencing is what we have predicted, we know we are on the right track. If it is not, then it's time to see what needs to be done to get the results we're after.[6]

The following vignette from a Harvard faculty meeting illustrates the fact that, even among the best and the brightest, language is mostly used haphazardly. Physicist Richard Feynman once asked his fellow professors, "What does the term we have been discussing actually mean?"

"That's obvious," replied a faculty member.

"Then tell me," said Feynman.

The man gave a definition that another immediately objected to. It soon devolved that no two people in the room agreed on the definition, and the discussion fell apart completely.

Much of the foundation on which our civilization operates is like this. I have already discussed how the bizarre and erroneous notion expressed in the domino theory kept the Vietnam War going for many years before the United States finally resolved the whole thing with unilateral withdrawal from the conflict. In other words, we admitted that we had lost the Vietnam War and never should have gotten into it in the first place. It took about a decade of public protest in which the majority of the population made it clear to their leaders that they opposed the war before the futility of it finally sunk in. A few years later we established a healthy trade relationship with the Vietnamese. Their communist government did not infiltrate neighboring nations and bring about the fall of additional governments. What happened in Vietnam resembled the American Revolution in that it was an internal struggle among a people who wanted to find the form of government that suited their needs best.

None of the things we were afraid would happen if we abandoned the Vietnamese people actually happened. Unfortunately, though, we pretty thoroughly destroyed public faith in the government of the United States, with the result that the majority of the population of this country is now unmotivated to vote in any election.

Similarly, we founded the Cold War on a misinterpretation of Kruschev's famous remark, "We will bury you." We allowed ourselves to be persuaded that he was threatening a nuclear holocaust, instead of realizing and admitting that he actually meant, "We will outproduce you." When the Soviets finally realized that their system would not allow them to outproduce the Americans, their government fell apart.

These examples illustrate the extent to which civilization usually bases much of what it does on outmoded assumptions—assumptions that a well-conducted discussion among intelligent people might quickly reveal and do away with.

The Problem of the Intellectual Fallacy

Entrenched assumptions remain embedded in a culture when those who are in a position to lead fail to examine the roots of their thinking. That prevents them from realizing that it may either be fundamentally flawed from the beginning or, perhaps, based on assumptions rendered irrelevant by changes in the situation or environment. Inevitably and unfortunately, even though ideas that flow from erroneous assumptions may be well reasoned, supported by intensive research, and brilliantly imaginative, they nevertheless move things in wrong directions. Such errors will become avoidable only when people in leadership positions are able to commit themselves to facing well-reasoned and thoughtful challenges, no matter how fundamental and global they may be. What is lacking in contemporary society is a proper forum for dialogue between opposed citizens that is less confrontive than it is a search for mutually agreed upon synergy.

I realize that such a process is difficult to create in the current state of the media, which thrives on placing people in the most confrontive situations that can be dreamed up. Television talk shows all too often get higher ratings when they pit intelligent people against one another in the mood to destroy each other's arguments.[7]

The solution, I believe, is the kind of thinking that children should learn from the beginning, in their classes in school. It is the thinking that triumphs in the Shakespearean sonnet—and indeed in the entire collection of works generally attributed to William Shakespeare. Collectively, they compose a giant poem about the process of synthesizing the hugely ambiguous array of conflicting points of view that is endemic to human experience.

German philosopher Georg Hegel saw the dialectic as the source of constant movement in history, life and the universe. In our own time, however, it has all too often led to the continuous expectation that one of the two opposing lines of argument will eventually triumph over the other—without compromise or synthesis. Indeed a rallying cry of the entire century, and not just the Civil Rights Movement, seems to have been "We shall overcome."

The trouble is, when you overcome, you lose, because almost invariably those you have conquered subtly continue the fight and end by undermining you. In any event the advantages that might be gleaned from the conflict are lost because when two opposing points of view clash, it is difficult to preserve the best of the losing argument—and to discard the faults of the winning one. How much better to let your opponents guide you to a new level of awareness that synthesizes your best ideas with theirs and leads to the possibility of creative breakthroughs. Of course, this is possible only when both sides in the conflict are honestly pursuing a vision of reality they believe in, rather than merely trying to manipulate the situation for political purposes.

Because of the tendency to overcome rather than learn from, many fields of knowledge are infested with beliefs that should never have survived critical analysis. They endure only as part of the intellectual dictatorship of the dominant belief system. The price to the individual who contests this belief system is almost invariably a loss of credibility.

But even when a synthesis is attempted, it is too often compromised. The concept of consensus, so widely viewed as the key to resolution, is, in effect, merely domination by majority opinion.

From my Quaker friend, the late Barry Morley, who was an expert on the subject, I learned about the possibility of arriving at true synthesis through achieving what the Quakers call the "sense of the meeting." This leads to an assurance that no member's conscience or inner truth will be violated by the group.[8]

Democracy moves slowly and sense of the meeting even more slowly. Thus in life as well as in *Hamlet*, "the native hue of resolution is sicklied o'er with the pale cast of thought." On the other hand, when the most extreme and heartfelt positions have been fully honored, a true synthesis emerges, and the result may be a relatively rapid transformation of the entire situation and a new level of cultural awareness.

I have come to believe that any problem may be solved, provided those trying to solve it are willing to walk in the shoes of extremists on both sides of the issue, so that they may determine the full extent of the required synthesis. For even the ugliest positions may conceal unfulfilled positive values. The rankest racist may, at the root, be struggling for recognition and understanding—as occasional remarkable conversions sometimes suggest.

Unfortunately in the angry climate of an overly litigious, blaming and vindictive culture, there are many problems that don't get solved because too many people derive more energy and excitement from fanning the fires of conflict than from the possibility of resolution. On the practical level, if you are hired to solve a problem and the problem goes away, you are out of a job. On the spiritual level, you are out of a cause. In the Elizabethan Age, self-righteous honor felt itself betrayed by compromise, apology or a new perspective. Old allegiances required a fight to the finish "and damn'd be him that first cries 'hold, enough!'" to use Macbeth's words." The drama of righteous indignation may sometimes be a lot more fun than creative thinking. Most of us enjoy having a valid excuse for public temper tantrums. That's one reason, in my opinion, that so many problems outlive those who try to solve them.

It's also why, I believe, throughout the history of civilization there has been a widespread tendency to read without interpretation and without question. This is the kind of reading that is too common. It is encouraged in school by teaching to satisfy tests that have multiple-choice questions. It is a product of control patterns that seek to manipulate without understanding. It leads people to believe erroneously that there is a body of knowledge presided over by experts who know everything, while the general public knows nothing.

You'll notice, if you read a lot of history, that much of the time in the past the majority of leaders in virtually all fields had ideas that were delusional and would never be entertained in today's cultural environment.

This was also true of the majority of the common people. People fought wars over issues that were absurdly nonsensical—just as they do today, if they could only see it. They got themselves into trouble for reasons that today seem patently ridiculous. They habitually refused to listen to the best new ideas when they first appeared, and often scorned the greatest art when it was first exhibited. They allowed thousands to die of diseases for which perfectly good cures or preventatives had been discovered. They considered themselves to be decent, moral individuals who could preach and dictate to others, even though they owned slaves who were often treated worse than their farm animals. Whatever they believed was true or was not true mostly doesn't jibe with what we believe today.

One wonders, in the course of studying history, how the human species ever kept going with so much delusional thinking and bad behavior to impair its progress. Unfortunately, we are largely blind to the fact that we are still operating much in the same way today. The issues are different, but the behavior is almost identical. No one is exempt from criticism in this context. Delusion is everywhere, and is as widely shared by the intellectual elite as by the superstitious poor.

I hope that you who have read this book will subsequently become able to take some of the most cherished intellectual notions of our time and retire them from your own personal delusion factories. Some of these delusions are shared by people who don't know how to think very well and don't claim that they do, though they sometimes behave as if they had received all their wisdom directly from God, who has commanded them to impart it to all who will listen. Other delusions are shared by many of our most prominent intellectuals.

Indeed, even at the most advanced levels, what passes for critical reading today is, in the majority of cases, not critical reading at all. It is an attempt to instruct students in a particular set of criteria believed to be valuable in analyzing a text. What it fails to do is raise questions about the assumptions that may underlie the discipline within which the standards of critical thinking are operational.

Copernicus disproved the theory that the sun goes around the earth and thereby overthrew the mental model of epicycles in planetary motions. He had the good sense to publish his proof only on his deathbed so no one could torture or execute him for his heresies.

Today we have much need for thinkers like him. We need minds capable of upsetting the apple cart in any number of theories that are founded on delusory assumptions. Most modern theories of diseases blindly ignore the mental processes that tell the body whether and how much to respond to infecting organisms. Most modern theories of economics assume a market-place that responds to supply and demand in a more rational way than any marketplace ever has.

We have schools that teach teachers methods that have never worked in the classroom and never will.

In nearly every field of study, widely accepted assumptions that have never been proved act as filters, which invalidate any particular point of view a person might have that is not in agreement with the basic premises of that filter. As a result, there is a widespread tendency for large numbers of people who have supposedly become adept at critical thinking to be inca-pable of dealing with paradigms that do not conform to the ones they have been taught to believe in. The story "The Emperor's New Clothes" is a para-ble for intellectual activity that tends to produce consensus in the rejection of new ideas later revealed to have merit. Repressive filters that seriously impede the advancement of knowledge in nearly all fields of study could be avoided by teaching critical thinking without the preestablished criteria used now. Most of these have the effect of inoculating the student's mind against viruses of thought that could undermine whole fields of knowledge, which stand on ground that is too often little better than quicksand.[9]

How to Achieve Critical Thinking

The way to achieve such thinking is to ask students in any class what assumptions about the world seem to underlie the field of study under examination in that class.

These should be listed as the students think of them, and completely without comment. The students should then be assigned to go out and look for more examples of assumptions on which their field of study rests.

When an extensive list has been compiled, without censoring even the most bizarre ideas that have been suggested, the students should be given copies of it. The list should remain ever present in the discussion from then on, so that the assumptions on which all arguments are based are kept under continual scrutiny.

Rest assured that no field of study that is founded on valid assumptions can be overthrown in this way. Skeptics may produce false criticism based on their own assumptions, but the habit of questioning assumptions, if it is firmly established, will ricochet back on such arguments.

That way, in engaging with the material under study, the students will be more likely to detect flaws in its logic, which experts in the field may have ignored. Knowledge of these flaws will help them strengthen their intellectual discipline and advance their field of knowledge through continual correction and readjustment, so that the worst fallacies are gradually eliminated.

Such things cannot happen, however, as long as teachers feel their survival is threatened every time a class discussion moves outside the limits of their knowledge, control and censorship.

Until a significant percentage of the world's people learn to think like investigative reporters, questioning everything and challenging all assumptions, we shall continue to accept standards of performance, from those who assert leadership in nearly every field, that fall far below the level that public trust in such people should require.

Making Language Precise

In 1963, I developed a course designed to arouse my students to pay closer attention to what was going on around them and the various ways it could be interpreted. Over a period of about a decade, I used it in a number of different schools in which I taught. I called it the "composition course."

Whenever I began teaching the course, the initial reaction to it by most of my students was a short period of fascination, followed by a much longer period of outraged contempt for what I was supposedly doing to their minds.

After about a month of this contempt, which often bordered on rage, and usually led to a student or two rushing from the room and slamming the door, the class attitude would begin to change. One by one the students would discover that what I was really doing was giving them access to their minds and freeing them from the chains of secondhand thinking, which they had adopted longer ago than they could remember.

Why America's Children Can't Think

Briefly, here is how the course was organized: The first composition was based on a trick that is fairly widely used in teaching. I gave my students a very simple drawing to describe so that, from their description, I could make another drawing on the board just like it. This happened to be a line drawing of a house. When the compositions had been written, I would ask my students to read them one by one. As each composition was read, I would follow the instructions in the particular sentences.

For example, the first sentence might have read, "Draw a line in the middle of your paper." There were a number of reactions I could have to such a sentence. First of all, it was impossible to follow the instruction correctly, since the precise middle of a piece of paper (assuming that it can be located at all, which in most cases it cannot) would be identified by a point, not a line. However, leaving that problem aside, I would find the approximate middle of my writing surface and would draw a vertical line.

It turned out, of course, that the student wanted the line to be horizontal, but had not said so. I also might make the line a non-straight line, such as a wavy line, thus revealing another aspect of the directions that had not been sufficiently specified.

This little exercise is an interesting challenge at first, because it quickly demonstrates how inaccurate our use of language usually is. In fact, it is not possible to come up with any statement that can be proved to be true except on the basis that it is either "self-evident" or (what amounts to the same thing) based on assumptions that themselves cannot be proved.

This extremely frustrating aspect of thought and language has been mathematically proven for some years by virtue of Gödel's theorem, which argues that no system can be used to prove itself true. The consequences of Gödel's theorem are unfortunate indeed, for because of it, it is possible to prove mathematically that a particular sphere is actually twice or half (or some other multiple) of its actual size. This either means that the entire basis of mathematical reasoning is wrong or (more probably) that the universe is not at all as we perceive it, but rather an illusion based on mysterious forces that the human mind is not yet capable of comprehending.

All that aside, however, my course progressed by making my students gradually aware that they were accustomed to using language in an extremely sloppy and imprecise manner, which leads, in human communication, to an inordinate number of misunderstandings. This is largely because the assumptions that underlie any particular statement are so many and so complex that getting them all in hand and accounted for is a simply impossible task.

Why Attempt the Impossible?

So what's the point of attempting the impossible? One of my students, at the dawn of awareness of what I was getting at, once put it this way: "When my mother asked me what we were doing in English class, I couldn't explain it. But I was aware that I was doing a far better job of trying to explain it than I would have been able to if I hadn't had this course."

The point is that it will always be impossible to say exactly what you mean, but the extent to which you are able to get some part of your meaning into someone else's mind is a measure of how effective you are at doing whatever you do in life. This applies to such diverse behaviors as parenting, scientific researching, writing poetry and building fences. It is a universal problem in human affairs, and it is central as a concern in language arts.

How remarkable, then, that it is universally ignored by virtually all the language arts teachers I have ever seen in action. All, that is, except me.

My composition course began with the problems of a student I encountered in 1963 who, in the tenth grade, could diagram any sentence, but could not read or write any sentence accurately. Thinking that this student needed a great deal of writing practice, I set up a series of tutoring sessions with a fellow teacher, asking my colleague to get young George simply to describe things around the room.

My colleague, whose name was Hunter, came back to me after a couple of sessions with the observation that George "could not tell the difference between what a thing is and what it does." In other words, he did not understand the difference between saying that a swimming pool is a rectangular hole in the ground and saying that it is a good place to swim. I gave this problem some consideration and decided that this is a fundamental distinction in human thought. I later found out that it is so fundamental that it is handled by two different parts of the brain. This accounts for the fact that an aphasic, or someone unable to correctly use and comprehend words, may not be able to name an umbrella, but may be able to say instead, "It's the thing that keeps the rain off of you."

The Subject-Verb Dichotomy

The distinction is a general one between the subject and verb (or predicate) in a sentence, between objects and processes, or between matter and energy. In human development it is a distinction between *who I am* and *what I do*. One of the biggest problems in psychology is to get people beyond the notion of *I am what I do*. If I am what I do, then if I fail at what I do, I have failed as a person. If I am a person who incidentally does certain kinds of things, then I can correct my mistakes without feeling that I am a failure in life because of them.

Not being clear about this distinction makes many people so defensive about everything that their minds snap shut and they become incapable of learning anything new. Two opera composers, Samuel Barber and Arrigo Boito, both wrote first operas that were miracles of successful operatic writing. Unfortunately, both of them were so sensitive to the criticism that they shortly received from critics that they spent the rest of their lives trying to get a second opera into final shape, and neither succeeded.[10]

In contrast, Guiseppi Verdi, whose second opera was treated with a scorn and rancor unique in the pages of musical history, and which came immediately after his wife and child had died unexpectedly, was enough of a curmudgeon not to take the criticism overly seriously, and went on to be the most successful opera composer that ever lived—so successful, in fact, that the Italians symbolically credited him with the unification of Italy (partly because his name was an abbreviation for "Victor Emmanuel Re di Italia").

The point is that the best and the brightest are as human as the rest of us, and the inability to reject criticism and move on because one has not been sufficiently inoculated against the scorn of the narrow-minded and unvisionary is a very high price to pay for the lack of a little of the right kind of schooling. Often people who have allowed others to impose limitations on them make terrifying attempts to impose their limitations of thought and action on others, who have no interest in being so horrendously restricted.

Given all this, I designed my composition course on two fundamental distinctions: The first was between what a thing *is* and what it *does*, and the second was between subject and object. I led my students through a series of exercises in which they were asked to define what they saw on a piece of paper, in terms of what it looked like. They were asked to be precise in the same way a scientist is precise in describing something like a new allergen or galaxy.

Once my students had become sufficiently aware of the problems in doing this, I then led them to the question of defining what it is that a particular thing might be expected to do, or how it might be expected to behave.

The climax of the first part of the course was that I made a deal with my students that anyone who could successfully define a circle (based on the picture I made of one, which I gave to the class) would receive an automatic A in my course for the entire year. Motivation was extremely high, but no one ever succeeded in this feat. And, in fact, I never had to shoot down any of the definitions that were presented to me (at least not after a few initial examples that set the tone for the rest of the class to tear into any definition that was proposed). The students themselves found the flaws in each other's thinking so well that I could have sat in the back of the room and just watched, had I wanted to.

Of course, geometry books were the first things that went out the window in this process, to the great consternation of my colleagues who were trying to teach geometry. If a circle is a set of all points that surround a given point at a specified distance, then it would be impossible to draw one, since a point cannot be visible if it is to retain its identity as a geometrical point, because it is infinitely divisible. In fact, any point that can be drawn is so thick compared to the tiniest fraction of itself that it is, in fact, infinitely large (in the same sense in which an inch can be subdivided to infinity, so that one of the infinity of infinities is the infinity of points that subdivide an inch).[11]

Of course, mathematics and physics part company at this juncture, since space is known to be too "bubbly" to be infinitely divisible, at least with any integrity. But mathematics does not describe space, it only describes itself. It is what we call a "self-referential process." So is the human mind. That being so, there is no way you can ever draw a circle. But since we call drawings of circles "circles," then we cannot have a fully acceptable definition of a circle that leaves out the possibility of seeing one on a piece of paper, or somewhere else, such as in the middle of downtown traffic (at least if you're in the United States and not in England).

Nearly everyone I throw this kind of reasoning at becomes extremely frustrated with it, and ends up declaring me insane; but the fact is, such reasoning is inescapable, because if we are to hope to understand the world and our experiences in it, we are held to the standard of meaning what we say, and my students, in the process of attempting to define a circle, were forever (in the judgment of their own classmates) incapable of saying what they meant, or, as it turned out, even knowing what they meant. Paradoxically it's that very realization that makes us struggle hard to become as precise as we can in our language use.[12]

Moving on to the issue of "what a thing does," we might examine a line drawing of a gun and ask what it does. Immediately we are into one of the most heated debates in the history of law and order. One question is, do guns murder people, or do people murder people? An equally strong argument can be made either way, and no one has come up with any means of convincing everyone else that either position can be used to drive out the other.

Without going into great detail here, I can say that the question of what is happening in any given situation is infinitely debatable. A great deal of the controversy in the world (much of it extremely destructive, as it often involves or leads to war) is based on disagreements of this sort. Such disagreements are just as pervasive in the private confines of an intimate relationship as they are on the floor of the United Nations. One person's misunderstanding of what another is doing can just as well break up a marriage as lead to the formation of a marriage that never should be entered into in the first place. These issues are in no way trivial. It is just that, by universal consensus, they are almost always ignored as general philosophical principles and entered into only as particular cases. Of course by the time they have become particular cases, the damage has already been done.

We're Stuck in Our Nervous Systems

Let's move on to the next part of the course (which, in fact, I never developed or taught): the difference between the objective and the subjective.

It quickly turns out that there is no difference and that everything is really subjective, because there is no way we can escape the prison of our nervous systems. But to the extent that we are trying to be objective, we are talking about things that are presumed to be observed in the same way. To the extent that we are trying to be subjective, we are in the realm of poetry, where we are trying to discover some objective correlative that will convey our unique view of an experience, more or less accurately, to someone else.

The fact that this is, to some degree, possible is demonstrated by the observation that nearly everyone seems to understand what sky-blue pink is, even though the spectrum makes it impossible that there could be any such thing. So we live in a world of language that is doomed to a degree of approximation that is endlessly frustrating, produces most of the human misery in the world, but which might, if a serious attempt were made to understand these kinds of issues, lead to a cultural point of view that would greatly enhance human communication and problem solving. I have to say at this point that it usually seems to me (and I don't think I am alone in this) that whenever a group of experts is put together to solve a problem, the results are little better than might be expected if the same problem were given to a group of zoo animals to solve.

This is true, of course, only if the experts have not established some prior relationship, which would require them to have spent a great deal of time learning to understand each other and the problems they are dealing with. A string quartet, for example, is a group of experts trying to solve a problem. Those intimately acquainted with string quartet players know that most of them become frustrated with each other because they never arrive at complete agreement about how a particular piece should be played (unless the piece is a trivial one) and therefore are forced to compromise on much more than they wish to. Nevertheless their results are usually satisfactory to their audiences.

Similarly, a group of scientists working together in a research lab may occasionally perform miracles. Teams of experts working with each other to produce something of value include many of the people who lived and worked together in fifth-century Athens. Add to them a number of scientists and artists who helped each other create the Renaissance. More recently, there have been the physicists who gathered earlier in this century at the Niels Bohr Institute, where they did little except talk to each other and write on blackboards. There have also been groups of artists of various sorts, such as the French composers who called themselves "Les Six." We also have, in our own time, examples of "skunk works," where people become intellectually intimate with one another in the pursuit of a solution to some business or industrial challenge and often achieve a great deal at a comparatively minuscule cost.

One thing seems certain. You cannot make any particularly good contribution to an enterprise unless you have learned how to be faithful to your own experience and are not just interested in trying to stay out of trouble by aping the thoughts and feelings of whoever may be in control at the moment. The best way to become the kind of successful person who can negate the failures of large numbers of committees is to learn to read in such a way that you habitually translate everything you read into your own vernacular and test it out for yourself.

The Problem of Who Determines
What Is Accepted as True

This plea for understanding, which assumes that readers should decide for themselves what is true—based on the logic of the argument presented—is, in the present cultural atmosphere, a voice crying in the wilderness. Our society worships experts, many of whom, when outside their narrow spheres of awareness and cumulative prejudice, become wildly incompetent. We cannot hope to have reasonable behavior from the best and the brightest among us until we have learned to judge for ourselves what we read and not blindly believe all of it just because it has appeared in print. This means that we have to get very good at assuming that any statement, no matter what it is and particularly how sacrosanct it is, might be wrong, and then apply whatever tests we can generate from our intellectual equipment to trying to determine its degree of truth or falsehood. Everything ever written, let alone published, is someone's opinion. Many of these opinions represent honest attempts to tell the truth about something. But truth, as should be obvious, is extraordinarily illusive.

So in order to avoid having our minds polluted with a great deal of highfalutin nonsense, we need to develop the kind of healthy skepticism that is not activated only by unpopular ideas, but also by those that may be extremely popular and in very wide usage. Go back a hundred years, and we find that almost everything that was then popularly believed is now demonstrated to be largely untrue. The same will be true thirty years from now, if we are to survive as a species.

The trouble is that a great many essentially cowardly people, once they have an emotional stake in something, would rather die than change their minds, for fear that they will be suddenly rendered incompetent in their own fields of expertise and will never recover any ability to proceed competently. This is as true of the myths of the intelligentsia as it is of those of the cultists. Everyone's brain works the same way in that respect. In both groups, and, indeed, in all human communities, codependency in the area of delusory thinking is quick to develop. Corporate management shares the delusion that workers are mostly irresponsible and lazy. Workers share the delusion that corporate management is out to get them. These delusions become so deeply etched in the thinking of the people who have them that they eventually tend to produce the reality that was previously only imagined. Scientists often have to die before radical new theories can be accepted.

Delusion is everywhere and no one escapes from it. Those who claim to be skeptical are seldom skeptical in any real sense. They are only skeptical about things they don't agree with.

Those who rely on faith often refuse to follow the inevitable logic that their faith leads to. Declaring that they love their neighbors, they seek to wipe out those of their neighbors who do not think the way they do.

The trouble with all this is that it retards progress to a ridiculous degree at a time when we are committed to progress and must proceed with it intelligently or risk simply destroying ourselves. So it's time to work out a method of eliminating delusory thinking wherever and whenever it pops up. We must move thought processes out of the limbic system, where they are rendered impervious to logic, eliminating sacred cows and subjecting all our ideas to the test of experience and debate in as wide a context as we can manage.

In other words, we need to make our inner images of the world conform much more powerfully to the kinds of experiences we would like to have in the future. That way, we won't endlessly find ourselves digging holes that we will only fall into and try to explain away, as if falling into the hole had been the object all along.

For that reason, every individual should be taught from the beginning to bring his or her personal experience to bear on the comparative truth and logical excellence of any argument that arises. It should be irrelevant whether or not the received wisdom of the time approves of that point of view or method of inquiry on the subject. This means teaching people to listen to each other and critique each other's ideas respectfully and without judging the quality of the person by the quality of thinking demonstrated at any particular moment.

Only those who are willing to make big fools of themselves are capable of developing an individual point of view that has some hope of making a contribution to the world's knowledge. The pages of history are full of the stories of people like Einstein, Robert Goddard,[13] Emily Dickinson and hundreds of others who were ignored or spurned for long periods of time before their ideas, works of art or general contributions were acknowledged and accepted on a large scale. Many did not live to see the fruits of their successful achievements. As a result, the world's knowledge, while awesome in its quantity at present, is largely poverty stricken in its quality and useful application. That's why our entire society currently finds itself in jeopardy. Or hadn't you heard?[14]

19

Discussing Books
with Others

*How can we teach groups to discover the excitement
of sharing their different perspectives about what
they read as continual inspiration for each other's
intellectual growth?*

One inescapable fact about the world is that it has a tendency to generate
an almost infinite variety of points of view, coming from many different,
often incompatible, cultures. All this cannot hope to be sorted out unless
every citizen develops the capacity to understand a wide variety of points
of view on the one hand, and to have an informed opinion about them on
the other. A society that encourages such multiplicity of points of view will
inevitably have to deal with a great deal of nonsense, but the nonsense will
be far less abrasive if it is always in the position of having to deal with
sense, which inevitably arises to combat it. In our time, far too much nonsense goes unnoticed and is never combated by those who ought to know
better. If we routinely teach children to read in a way that profoundly disempowers them (as we do now), we can expect that the loudest voices of
different cultural groups who emerge will always get considerably more air-
time than they deserve. Anyone who argues that one race is biologically
inferior to another ought to get shouted down, not for being "politically
incorrect," but because the evidence that they are wrong is uppermost in the
minds of most thoughtful citizens. By contrast, if someone were to argue
that different races and/or cultures might have something to learn from one
another, this should not automatically be confused with biological nonsense. There is nothing to be gained by trying to argue that all cultures are

exactly the same, because obviously they are not. We can easily become just as prejudiced in the argument of supposedly good causes as we are in the argument of bad ones.

Prejudices cannot survive in a dialogue among thinking people because they get ripped apart the same way hungry dogs rip apart meat that is thrown to them. However, enjoyable as it may be to rip apart bad ideas, it is best to step back from this metaphor and reconsider. Most of the world's greatest ideas started out as bad ideas according to the scions of wisdom of their day. So it makes sense when ripping apart bad ideas that everyone should have time to complete whatever thoughts are relevant, and the shouting contests that show up so often at town meetings and on talk shows should be verboten. The rules for functioning as a thinking society may be observed most readily in documents like Platonic dialogues, in which an argument is examined and unfolded carefully by two people, one of whom is always in a position to dispute the other.

Group Discussions That Really Work

Fairly large numbers of people can effectively participate in discussions similar to the Platonic dialogues, provided there is an agreement always to stick to the point. I have found an effective method for doing this, which seems to increase the rationality of large groups of people arguing about something that is worth arguing about. It is the job of the facilitator of such a discussion to do two things: One is to clarify any point of established fact that might be unclear. For example, if someone were to casually mention that two and two is three, the facilitator would point out that if the established view that it equals four is to be overridden, the person who has argued that it equals three will have to show why that might be so in such a manner that the point becomes worthy of serious debate. This, in some cases, might have to be postponed to a later time, merely in order to keep the argument from becoming so diffuse that it cannot proceed. The other function of the facilitator is to write (or have written) on the board the names of people who wish to speak. These people are then called on in the order in which they raised their hands.

The result is that no one speaks who hasn't had several minutes to think over what he or she wants to say and how it relates to the discussion at hand. This assures that every comment has far more thoughtfulness behind it than it would if it were allowed to interrupt the discussion at the moment it happens to surface in the mind of the speaker. Under these conditions, a reasonable group of people can progress very well toward coming up with ideas and plans of action that can be extremely productive. Let me say more, then, about what I think "a reasonable group of people" is.

In the last chapter, I discussed my composition course as an exercise in trying to make acceptable statements about some fairly simple objects and situations. An intelligent person who participates in a discussion lasting over several weeks that is unable to arrive at a definition of a circle that is logically acceptable to everyone present has a gut level awareness that there is more to most situations than meets the eye.

My last experience in teaching this course was with two tenth grade classes at Sidwell Friends School in 1972. My students were certainly above average, and some of them were also rather hot-headed. They were also, in general, a little more passive than other students I was used to, because they came from good families that did not easily tolerate too much random bad behavior. The result was what, to many teachers in other schools, might sound like science fiction: If I gave an assignment, everyone did it.

Experiencing Macbeth *in a New Way*

Having spent about three months teaching what I have identified as the "composition course," I moved on to the study of Shakespeare. I gave my students copies of *Macbeth* and asked them to read it on their own. I then read to them in class and discussed with them two scholarly essays about the play. One was "The Unity of Action in Macbeth," by Francis Fergusson.[1] This essay argues that *Macbeth* as a whole can be understood as a metaphorical development of a single infinitive phrase. Fergusson supplied the phrase, but, as you will shortly see, that part was not particularly important.

The second essay, called "The Naked Babe and the Cloak of Manliness," by Cleanth Brooks, discusses the thematic imagery of *Macbeth* and shows that all the themes are interwoven in an organic way.[2] I then told the class that their assignment was to select an infinitive phrase that might describe the action of *Macbeth*, and write a paper arguing why the whole play might be understood in terms of that particular phrase.

Several of my colleagues contended that such an assignment was inappropriate because it was impossible for tenth graders to do. Some of them thought that no one should ever think for himself about anything until he or she has absorbed the entire body of knowledge prescribed by people like Seymour Hirsch. I replied to that with the observation that anyone who has had no practice in thinking until the entire prescribed furniture of the mind had been assimilated would never be able to think at all, and I believe that historical analysis shows that to be true.

Anyway, having made the assignment clear, I rested my case and had no further agenda for the class except to be a resource. So each day, at the beginning of the class, I would say, "Are there any questions?" Immediately most of the hands in the room would go up. I would call on people one by one, and either answer their questions if they were easily answerable ones (such as what a particular line might mean) or throw the question back to the class if it were more philosophical. There followed, in each of those days, one of the most interesting and deeply analytical discussions I have ever witnessed. The students went to the heart of the play, exposed numerous themes, actions and metaphoric structures in it, argued about them, always with respect for one another and with the acknowledgment that no two people in the room were even permitted to have exactly the same idea about what was going on in the play. All the papers came in on time. The shortest (out of thirty) was six handwritten pages, and the longest was thirty-two typewritten pages. When I had collected the papers, I asked, "How many enjoyed doing this assignment?"

Every hand went up in both classes. I contend that it was the months spent previously on the composition course that enabled these students to probe the inner meanings of Shakespeare so deeply and with so much respect for dissident points of view. They had learned that no one can really be sure about anything, but there are degrees of clarity possible in the arts of observation and exposition. As a result, they had sharpened their intellectual swords to the point where they could engage in debate about a comparatively arcane set of subjects in a friendly and respectful way.

Respect among Opponents

By the time we reach school age, we already have a large vocabulary of mental models with which to perceive the world; we reach a point where we can increase that vocabulary primarily by sharing our perceptions with our peers. So one of the most important functions of schools is to bring people of a similar age and reasonably similar cultural background together so they can share their experiences with each other in order to learn how to refine these and give them meaning.

We cannot do this, though, unless we respect one another. It is, therefore, necessary to teach young people not just how to respect their elders (which is all that is attempted now) but also how to respect each other.

This can be accomplished in several ways. One is simply to have them, from time to time, describe to one another what it is they admire in each other. Over the years, as I have worked with this process, I have noticed that everyone can learn to do this rather quickly, even though it runs counter to the dominant culture, which is based more on put-downs than on expressing support and admiration. Because of this cultural phenomenon, students must be taught how to override the tendency to think in put-downs and to express instead what they find likable in one another. There is always something, however simplistic it may be at first. Simply noticing that someone looks nice, is wearing one's favorite color, or has a pleasant smile, is enough to get things started.

The next step is to teach students how to work in teams so they each contribute something to the whole. Thus they can learn, through practice with each other's work habits, to respect whatever it is that another person can most effectively contribute to a group project.

Why America's Children Can't Think

The "Think and Listen"

A third step toward developing respect is to introduce the Think and Listen activity, which simply involves one person listening in silence for a stated period of time while the other thinks, either silently or aloud. Permitting silent thinking, as well as thinking aloud, takes the pressure off and means that someone who is too shy to talk or doesn't have anything to say at the moment need not feel under pressure to speak his or her thoughts.

During the Think and Listen, people give each other positive nonverbal cues; but they should not actually say anything during the other person's time, nor should they comment later on whatever it was their confidante said. The speaker, meanwhile, should be careful to avoid saying anything that sounds like an attack on the listener, either as an individual or as a member of a group.

When a class has mastered the technique of the Think and Listen, a change has been accomplished in the culture of that particular classroom. There is a much deeper level of respect and sensitivity, as trust begins to emerge palpably into the atmosphere.

Occasionally the trust will be broken. It's important for the class to understand from the beginning that this is inevitable in groups because people have different standards of behavior and therefore sometimes misunderstand each other. Broken trust is difficult to repair, but the exercise of learning to do this is essential for being able to develop ongoing and long-term relationships in life. It is, in fact, the most important thing we have to learn about dealing with each other.

Groups that have taken the three steps just described will be able to participate in discussions with one another at a much higher level than was formerly possible. Additionally, groups that master the art of discussion tend to develop respect for each other from that alone. So if both approaches are developed in tandem, the results can be far better and more productive than otherwise.

The Think and Listen, frequently used, trains people to search for and develop their own opinions. These will almost always be rudimentary at first, but anyone who has learned how to have an opinion will tend to develop the ability to a higher level of sophistication rather quickly.

Learning how to develop and express opinions early in life is a valuable tool for intellectual growth, as we tend to remember things that fit into the structure of our opinions far better than things that don't. We're attracted to the things we like and repelled by those we don't, and those are the things we understand and remember best. The rest makes little difference to us, and that's as it should be. We were designed to respond to the things that attract us emotionally, not the things that have no perceptible relationship to us. So the formation of opinions about things and experiences is essential, because it supplies the emotional element that gives them personal meaning.

On the other hand, if we're going to be opinionated (which is a good thing when balanced with the ability to hear others' opinions), we should also become adept at accounting for our opinions, which means that we should be willing to change them when we find they are founded on insufficient fact or experience.

People who develop comfort and security in expressing their opinions are more likely to become able to change them as new information makes that appropriate. This can be learned very effectively in class discussion, as students practice being both firm and flexible in expressing opinions and developing them until they become new ideas.

Eventually the process of articulating and restructuring opinions and ideas will begin, in a student's mind, to extend beyond the issues immediately at hand, seeking to integrate other opinions the student may have formed. In the process, members of a class will come to know each other well and become increasingly able to describe each other's points of view.

Those who have had little experience in hearing about and dealing with a variety of points of view are more easily threatened when they hear an opinion with which they don't agree. The wellsprings of prejudice found in certain groups or geographical areas are largely the result of too little experience with discussion about and exposure to a variety of alternative ways of looking at things.

I have found that having students discuss challenging texts that arouse strong emotional reactions is a valuable tool for developing flexibility in thinking and point of view. It is well to discover that a person who is sounding off about something in, what seems like, a bigoted way may relatively easily change to a more flexible view if treated with respect instead of scorn and rejection. By reducing the atmosphere of threat in discussion, we make it safer to let go of opinions that do not survive careful examination.

Ironically, it is through discussing with my friends those matters I consider important that I discover myself. Until I know how I am different from them, I do not know what it is that distinguishes me from the rest of humanity. By discovering how my friends and I can differ on some matters and actually agree to disagree about them, I come to a better sense of what makes me unique; and I also discover how to use that uniqueness to influence others for the benefit of the common good.

Finding Common Ground

How far apart can we take our opinions in a discussion, finding the joy of knowing our differences, while realizing we can come back together after having explored the great gulf between us?

I remember a powerful moment in a workshop I was leading when a self-made man shared with the class his laissez-faire economic philosophy. After all, he had made his way in the world, so why couldn't everyone? Why shouldn't all be forced to fend for themselves as best they could?

He finished this statement of his personal philosophy all aglow with his own eloquence. He had, he was certain, captured the imagination of everyone in the room.

In the silence that greeted his conclusion, one of the participants was clenching her fists. Finally she spoke.

"It was all I could do to keep myself from jumping out of my chair and punching you in the nose," she said.

He appeared rather startled, and wanted to know why.

"I was brought up in a communist family," she said. "I heard a great deal about the misery and injustice in the world. People do the best they can, but the vast majority of them have no possibility of enjoying the fruits of their labor in the way you have."

In that moment, I could see in a flash how deeply those two people felt about a common concern. Beneath the specifics of what they were saying was a shared feeling about the importance of making the world work for everyone. They had conflicting ideas about how this should be accomplished, but they wanted essentially the same thing.

As the workshop progressed, these two spent more and more time together. Each was challenging and learning from the other. It was the very intensity of their original antipathy that bound them together in what may have grown into a very special kind of friendship.

Throughout history, people have generally tried to surround themselves with others who were as like them as possible. They have shied away from disagreement, expressed differences of opinion, possible conflicts that could lead to anger, or other difficult emotions. The ideal has been conformity, to be just like everyone else, so as to be accepted, never to have to risk rejection because of what one thinks.

This is what we need to get past. We need to teach each other to be secure enough in our opinions that we are willing to expose ourselves to the antipathy of opposites. Then, when the sparks are flying, we can begin to learn from each other what essential truths lie behind the controversy. We can discover ourselves more deeply through the many encounters that are possible with strangers. These strangers, while leading a very different life, can peer through the window into ours for a moment and get something from it. Meanwhile we can peer out at their experiences and see possibilities that exist for them that we can never know about, unless we choose to live those experiences through their eyes.

20

Writing Our Thoughts for Others

How can we dip (perhaps for the first time) into deep wellsprings of inspiration to discover the poetry that lies dormant within us?

I have never seen a more powerful moment on the screen than one that occurs in a movie that was never made. In 1937, Alexander Korda set out to make a film extravaganza based on Robert Graves's historical novel, *I Claudius*. The filming was plagued with a series of problems and setbacks. Ultimately its leading lady, Merle Oberon, was in an automobile accident that injured her face and the film project was abandoned.

According to reliable sources at the time, most of the problems on the set came from Charles Laughton, who played Claudius. Day after day, Laughton showed up for filming and wept about the fact that he couldn't find his character. The filmmakers scurried through the script, looking for scenes that he felt he could do and those scenes were filmed.

Laughton's struggles to find his character may have inspired the brilliance of his acting in the scene in which he portrays Claudius discovering his own power. Claudius was born with a pronounced limp and a terrible stammer. This made people think he was a fool, and he turned his handicap into a ruse that probably saved his life. His more illustrious relatives were killed before they reached the throne in various attempts to seize and control the power of Rome. Since he was the last remaining survivor of this dynasty, Claudius eventually found himself ruling as emperor.

At that point, after waiting all his life, he summoned up the resources of his magnificent intellect to persuade the Senate to support him in his policies of reform.

What happens on the screen in the 1937 film is a picture of a man finding his voice for the very first time. As he transmogrifies himself from a broken cripple to a magnificent world leader, Laughton as Claudius gathers gigantic forces from deep inside himself, gradually focusing his darting gaze, controlling his twitching body, and framing his words into such elegance that they defeat his stammer.

Awakening the Sleeping Giant of Personal Creativity

I mention this astonishing performance of Claudius because I believe it is symbolic of the sleeping giant within each of us. As I argued in the last chapter, a personal view is composed by measuring our own experiences against those of others. This involves continually questioning according to a set of criteria we ourselves can develop by testing others' observations in terms of our own experiences. The result inevitably leads to strong personal opinions that are well informed and have a critical backbone so they are not just jumbled emotional impressions.

Too many people, unfortunately, never reach this point in thinking for themselves. They have been so inhibited by insensitive reactions to their attempts to express themselves that the inner voice that asks so many questions in childhood gradually becomes silenced. The result is that, in adulthood, it becomes necessary to find a way to awaken their personal sleeping giants.

For many years in my work as an educator, I have performed what almost amounts to an educational parlor trick. In an exercise called Poetry and Relaxation, I tell the participants at my seminars that they are about to let their pencils write a poem. Poetry is a creative task many believe is beyond them and this exercise allows them a chance to discover how much of their creativity is untapped. In order to counter their lack of confidence, I put on some classical music and tell the group that I'll count backward from ten to one to take them to the place where the poetry is. They are free to close their eyes and let their minds wander if they wish, or to respond in whatever way seems appropriate to them.

After counting down, I invite them on an imagined journey, in which I present a number of guided images designed to make the mind more receptive to physical sensations and a sense of the body's motion through space.

I conclude with the suggestion that when they feel ready, the participants may let their pencils write their poems. Allowing the pencil to do the work removes any resistance or inhibition the writer may have. I wait quietly as, one by one, the participants work on their creations. I have told them that once the pencil has completed the poem, they may revise it if they wish, and that when it is finished, they should bring it up to me so I can read it to the group. I assure them that all of the poems will be read anonymously, so they will not need to reveal which poem they wrote, unless they wish to do so.

It usually takes forty-five minutes to an hour before I have collected all the poems. I then read them to the group, after reviewing them quietly, to a background of classical music. I do my best to bring out the poetry in each one, so the words will be given the eloquence they deserve. After all, it is usually true that poetry readings are delivered eloquently. I shall never forget the sound of Robert Frost's voice as he read his own words, "Provide, provide," so they sounded like a magnificent organ intoning a chord in a Bach chorale prelude.

When I have completed the poetry reading, the group is stunned. Some are in tears. Participants look around the room, wondering where all this poetic genius has come from. All the others there are just ordinary people like themselves. Who let all the poets into the room?

In hushed tones, they comment on the experience. Almost invariably, someone says that the collection of poems we have heard should be published. They marvel at the deep feelings they have heard expressed and the variety of images and approaches that were used.

The people who have had this experience are not usually the sort who like to write poetry. For many of them it is a first try. They are usually a collection of schoolteachers, government workers or line workers in a factory. And yet, uniformly, with every group I have worked with, much the same kind of eloquence emerges.

Why America's Children Can't Think

The Emergence of Eloquence

What do I mean by eloquence? Consider a poem like this:

> *It is a beautiful spring day.*
> *My heart sings.*
> *Never in my life have I been so happy.*

The beauty in such a poem is not the actual words, which are reminiscent of millions, if not billions, of such verses expressing happiness. It is the feeling that lies behind the poem, together with the desire to express that sentiment in words. That is one of the most intense experiences anyone can have.

Imagine getting from that to this:

> *But soft! What light through yonder window breaks?*
> *It is the East, and Juliet is the sun.*

Or this:

> *Oh, she doth teach the torches to burn bright.*

In the first poem above, there is only one metaphor: "My heart sings," and this has been used so often that it is a cliché. The writer is indicating feelings that are fresh and vivid, but he does not use figurative language to define them precisely. For the moment, the feelings themselves occur in the context of writing for the very first time, and that is enough.

The next time, that poet may write something like this:

> *The spring day sings to me*
> *And my heart answers*
> *In a beautiful duet.*

And later, perhaps, something like this will emerge,

Lilacs perfume their melody as
My heart provides the beat.
Together we orchestrate the morning.

This progression, from reporting feelings to conveying them through figurative language, is quite natural when people listen closely to what's happening inside themselves and find words to convey that message to someone else.

The Way We Learn to Write

The trouble with the way we learn to write is that at almost no time are we invited to do what I have just described. Yet each of us stands ready to deliver our own kind of primitive but genuine eloquence the first time it is called forth.

It's true that the expressions in my poetry examples are impossible if one does not know how to get words onto paper at all. So a considerable amount of practice with spelling, punctuation, grammar and the rules for writing a paragraph is necessary in everyone's education.

It's also true that, at some point, every writer depends on the thoughtful and critical analysis of what he or she has produced in order to improve it. This may very well consist of indications of spelling and grammar mistakes, together with red-pencilled comments in the margin questioning certain points.

But the sum total of what most people experience in school while learning to write is like studying cookbooks for years without ever once sitting down to a delicious meal.

Through the sleight of hand of Poetry and Relaxation, I've taken a group of starving refugees from culinary purgatory on their first trip to a fast-food joint. To such people, fast food will seem a great deal better in that first exploration than gourmet meals seem to experienced palates.

How easy it is to touch into the heart of self-expression, and how seldom it is ever done!

So the vast majority of us have to go through life never knowing what it's like to commit a revelation of personal feelings to paper when we have thoughts or feelings important enough to convey to someone else.

In addition, while millions of us have written unpublishable books, screenplays and what have you, very few of us ever get a chance to spin out our imaginations in a way that enables us to discover how to become delightful companions to ourselves.

We are fortunate or unfortunate, as the case may be, in the company we keep with ourselves. Some of us enjoy it a great deal, because what passes through our minds is endlessly fascinating. Others seek to escape their own company by surrounding themselves in crowds of superficiality, engaged in rather vacuous activities.

I think that the difference between these two types of people is caused by the failure of some brains to integrate their right and left sides. In the writing of poetry, the right brain sources the feelings, and the left brain sorts them out into well-ordered, polished verses. This integration of the self heals the personality, for it makes it possible to assess experience both intellectually and artistically. The examination of life that thus takes place may seem like the reason for living.

Consequently, writing is a two-step process. The first step is to get ideas on paper in any form in which they emerge. This is channeled through the right brain. The second is to shape the raw material of the first draft into a polished piece of writing. The left brain labors with this. Therefore the art of writing is a whole-brained experience.

Perhaps the goal of exercises like Poetry and Relaxation is to teach people how to be their own best friends and dearest companions. If they can achieve this, what they have to offer their friends and the rest of the world will surely be enhanced as well. But the main thing is, thoughts flowing through the brain at the rate of forty thousand per day will be turned into delightful conversations, endlessly churning up and enhancing new ideas.

Consider Emily Dickinson, seemingly one of the most isolated people who ever lived, who was actually one of the least isolated. She alone was constantly in the company of Emily Dickinson. Imagine what it would have been like to have such a companion to talk to! If you read her letters and not just her poems, you see that indeed virtually every sentence that flowed from her pen was a priceless gem. How delightful to be able to bask in the company of such gems, heard for the first time, day after day and year after year!

I have found that those who have had only a few exposures to Poetry and Relaxation often move on to find a unique writing voice. What they've always wanted to tell the world comes out with the kind of increasing eloquence that I'm convinced is the result of a self-organizing process in the brain.

In other words, writing skills develop as a result of the linguistic abilities genetically programmed into our brains. I believe these skills improve only as they are used in the service of what we want to say that stems from the inner conscious mind. It does not come from an attempt to please others or to become rich and famous. All it takes is a combination of practice, a continuing determination to communicate what's really on our minds, and the observation of the tricks of the trade that other writers use.

For most people, it would seem that inhibition comes from years of viewing writing as fodder for the degrading comments of teachers and other critics. Poetry and Relaxation is one technique I've used to banish writer's block altogether. What I do, anyone can do. I play a recording of my favorite music and tell myself that the idea I want to write will come to me. I always count backward from ten to one to put myself into a relaxed state of mind, and then simply trust the process. Over and over it has given me what I needed. Each time it does, I play with it and then let go of it, so it can return later in a more developed form. After a relatively short time, I feel I have something that I can write effectively.

A Creature Great and Small

There's an additional problem for the writer, though, that I think needs addressing. Writing is also a two-step balancing act that depends both on a macrocosm and a microcosm of the material to be written. Often it's difficult for people to handle both of these at once.

In the old days when most people wrote, they actually rewrote stories and legends that had been told from time immemorial. Then the idea of plagiarism was invented. As a result, we now assume that each story we have to tell must be new, as must each idea we want to develop.

Since information circulates today more than it has in past centuries, finding new ideas is not an impossible demand, but it does mean that a writer must be clear on the overall structure of his or her work before developing it in detail. In *The Everyday Genius*, I dealt with this problem extensively, suggesting Mind Mapping as a way of arriving at the overall structure.

Another technique for filling in structure is Expand-a-Story, which consists of eight sentences that shape the skeletal form of a story. You can easily write one by taking a well-known tale like "Little Red Riding Hood" and compressing it into eight well-chosen sentences that tell the essentials of the story. After you have done this, fill in the spaces with detail to include setting, character development, dialogue and unusual plot twists.

The fact that you know where you're going with your story will liberate your imagination and allow you to do things that you never expected you could do. In other words, Expand-a-Story is a well-structured glass into which you can pour the juices of your inspiration.

After you've given a half hour of practice to several different stories, you'll have limbered up your imagination enough to focus on a more serious effort—a longer story that you intend to polish.

The combination of Poetry and Relaxation and the Expand-a-Story has helped many people convince themselves that they really are writers, and some have gone on to publish their works as a result.

Find a Support Group

Many people find that the support of another writer can further their own writing. If that's what you'd like to try, find yourself a writing partner, or perhaps a writer's group. It's important that all of you are compatible with each other, but not that you want to write the same type of work. Each of you will serve as a mirror for the others. In doing so, you'll offer responses, positive criticism and editorial comment as needed. Most of all, you'll affirm what's good in the writing you're hearing or reading. It's very effective to listen as an author reads a new piece of work, so as to hear the intention behind it as it emerges in the author's voice. On the other hand, it's much easier to offer editorial advice if you have a text in front of you.

As people practice supporting each other in their writing, the quality of work produced by the members of the group improves at a remarkable pace. That's partly because when you're writing by yourself, it's often impossible to tell how your writing will strike someone else.

For my own part, when I start writing a book, I often find that a single comment from an editor will be sufficiently enlightening to make momentous changes in how I approach the task.

All of us writers are in the same boat, in that we can't be sure when we're good and when we're not. It takes at least one other person to provide the perspective for accurate judgment.

Be careful, though, because what one person thinks is good, another may think is terrible, and vice versa. I've had people give me negative feedback on my work, and I've rejected it because I wasn't convinced that the other person's judgment was correct. Only when a critic points to something in my writing that I have overlooked but immediately recognize as significant, do I feel confident that the criticism is a good one. And that is not an absolute either. I've had one or two knockdown drag-out disagreements with editors, only to be grateful later that I'd lost the argument and that their excellent skills had prevailed.

Finally, it seems that much of what you write should be inspired by what you read. That's why I've included in a book about reading the discussion of writing in this chapter and the two that follow.

The Great Conversation

The inevitable result of the Great Conversation that I referred to in the beginning of this book is that reading should, and does, lead to writing. When we have read about something thoughtfully, it serves us well to record our ideas on the subject.

When I read, I like to check footnotes to see where the ideas I am reading about originated. The history of the development of ideas is the history of the human mind articulating itself.

There is room for all of us in that Great Conversation. The moment we set pen to paper to express our views of what we have read, or express our views of something new, while influenced by the style, thought or general character of our reading, we are participating in that conversation.

So it behooves us to fill blank pages with our thoughts, lest they some-day be gone from our memories. Never has that been better said than in Shakespeare's Sonnet 77:

> *Thy glass will show thee how thy beauties wear,*
> *Thy dial how thy precious minutes waste.*
> *The vacant leaves thy mind's imprint will bear,*
> *And of this book this learning mayst thou taste.*
> *The wrinkles which thy glass will truly show*
> *Of mouthèd graves will give thee memory.*
> *Thou by thy dial's shady stealth mayst know*
> *Time's thievish progress to eternity.*
> *Look, what thy memory cannot contain*
> *Commit to these waste blanks, and thou shalt find*
> *Those children nursed, delivered from thy brain,*
> *To take a new acquaintance of thy mind.*
> > *These offices, so oft as thou wilt look,*
> > *Shall profit thee and much enrich thy book.*

21

Writing as Integration of Experience

What are the simplest and most time-honored methods of coming to terms, at a number of different levels of understanding, with a text or a subject we are planning to write about?

In Gilbert and Sullivan's Iolanthe, the entire conflict arises from a law that exists in Fairyland: If a fairy marries a mortal, she must die. The problem is that all the fairies have fallen in love with all the members of the House of Peers, who return their love. To resolve this conflict, the Lord Chancellor, an expert on legal draftsmanship, comes up with the following inspiration: "The insertion of a single word will do it. Let it stand that every fairy must die who does *not* marry a mortal, and there you are, out of your difficulty at once."

This exercise in topsy-turvy legislation illustrates a very important principle in writing—the creation of a denouement. We look for a writer to fit things together for us into a pattern that makes sense. By integrating otherwise disparate elements of experience, the writer enables us to make new connections, to see things in a new way, and thus to find a new view of reality that somehow enhances and defines the meaning of an otherwise chaotic situation or experience. It would be nice, of course, if every problem could be resolved as neatly and easily as the Lord Chancellor resolves the one above. But lots of good literary work would be lost to the world if life were too simple and problems too easily resolved.

In the previous chapter, I gave you some tools to get your creative juices flowing so you can write more easily about whatever is on your mind. In this chapter, I'll explore how writing can join forces with reading as a tool for integrating experiences or disparate information so as to resolve conflicts or solve problems.

After all, life is based on discovering patterns that help us to integrate the disparate forces we come up against. Generally speaking, we enjoy life most when we're doing a good job of resolving such conflicts. This can take many different forms: succeeding in sports, repairing a relationship, building a house, or helping someone else to solve a problem.

By combining good writing with good reading, we can integrate old patterns into new relationships and create something fresh that resolves previously conflicting elements of experience. This results from deeply considering the meaning of experiences we've previously had—including reading experiences.

Interpreting Reality

In chapter 10, I dealt with the issue of learning to read with a probing mind. In this chapter, I'd like to take those arguments a step further and put them in a broader perspective, with a more formal structure. The goal is to combine reading and writing and build a complex relation between them.

To illustrate, consider the process of reading interwoven with writing that arises when many different books or other sources are brought together to answer questions or to interpret vague or hidden meanings. Bear in mind that no book or document ever presents a complete reality directly. I mention this because the impression is often created in classrooms that the textbook is the be-all, end-all of knowledge in a particular subject and must be memorized as if it were the final, unshakable truth.

In fact, textbooks can only represent the point of view and perspective of a particular moment in time. The body of knowledge in every field is growing at such an astonishing pace that more than half of what we learn in high school is outmoded, and thus untrue, by the time we graduate from college, although it's impossible to anticipate which information this will be. To complicate matters, some textbooks have recently been shown to contain factual errors.

So the best any writer can do is to offer an *interpretation* of reality. That means that other interpretations are always possible. The more we learn to read beyond content and toward interpretation, the more our lives and perceptions of the world will be enriched by our reading. This, in turn, will affect our writing as well as the topics about which we are compelled to write.

Useful Tools for Interpretation

A useful tool for thinking about this issue is a method often used to interpret the first five books of the Bible, called the Torah. Hebrew scholars carry this method to thirteen levels that seek ever-deeper understanding, but the first four levels are the most commonly understood and used. These are, in their Hebrew terms, *p'shat*, *remez*, *d'rash* and *sohd*.

P'shat comes first, because it determines the basic meaning and structure of the written word. In other words, the sentence "The dog ran down the street" doesn't mean "The *god* ran down the street." You have to get the images and the information right, before you can go on to understanding meaning.

This may sound ridiculously simple, but it isn't. Sometimes the "literal meaning," as most people refer to it, cannot be established. The Delphic Oracle, for example, was famous for statements that could be interpreted more than one way. The whole action of *Oedipus Rex* centers on the fact that in flying from his destiny, Oedipus flies into its arms, for when he kills the man "at the place where three roads meet," he does not recognize that this man is his father.

Two more recent examples: Like Christopher Marlowe's *The Jew of Malta*, Shakespeare's *The Merchant of Venice* is often interpreted as a blatantly anti-Semitic play. However, that opinion is not shared by *The Jewish Encyclopedia* or by a mock trial once set up and presided over by Supreme Court Justice Ruth Bader Ginsberg. Their point of view, which has also been that of many theatrical producers for more than a century, is that the play condemns anti-Semitism by showing its main character, Shylock, to be a complex and suffering human being.

Arsenic and Old Lace is one of the great hits in Broadway theater history. It's generally regarded as one of the funniest plays ever written. However, the author, Joseph Kesselring, intended it to be a serious play and was heartbroken when audiences laughed at it.

In the next chapter, I'll show that *p'shat*, the simple or basic text, can be a much more complicated part of the analysis process than anyone would think at first.

Remez comes next. It's the search for hints, suggestions and symbolism lying behind the basic meaning. The sentence "The dog ran down the street" leaves open whether, for example, the dog was chasing something, being chased, running to greet someone, or just having a good time. There is not yet enough context for this sentence to establish its implications. One might, however, interpret the image itself metaphorically, as a symbol of assertion of power, or aggression, as when Henry V cries out, "let slip the dogs of war."

D'rash provides the commentary. For example, in the Torah there are a great many situations that are not fully described and therefore can be argued about for an eternity. In fact, some of them *are* argued about in a seemingly endless progression of commentaries. One might say, for example, that the image "the dog ran down the street" conveys the release of natural or even bestial forces or impulses. Since in most cities there are now ordinances requiring that dogs be on leashes, the unleashed dog suggests an irresponsible and uncivilized release of a creature that threatens to disturb the peace, with the implication that the social order might be breaking down or under attack.

Or one might interpret the image in the opposite way: The dog is experiencing and happily expressing the joy of freedom.

In just this way, commentaries may arrive at many different conclusions. This is the Great Conversation at work, for because life is inherently ambiguous, many possible perspectives on a situation deserve to be aired, debated and tried on for size.

Sohd is the secret, or hidden, meaning. It may never be revealed because, perhaps, it cannot be known. Yet it will inevitably be the subject of speculation.

What is the relationship between the dog running down the street and the human civilization that surrounds it? Over the centuries, dogs have evolved into a relationship with humans that provides them with protection. Who is in charge of this relationship? Often it seems that the humans are the caretakers of the dogs—their servants, perhaps. Unlike the horse, often pressed into service requiring hard labor, the dog is usually allowed to do as it likes, and when it does perform a service, this usually grows out of its own instincts and desires. It may defend the house from intruders by barking, but it does not have to be trained to do this, and it does not do it under compulsion. Or the dog may perform a service to the hunter by returning game. But again, it is the dog's instinct, desire and, in some cases, choice to provide this service. So we have here a paradox. Human beings must labor to survive, but dogs are given a free ride by owners who feed them, groom them, house them and love them. In addition, cruelty to animals often excites more horror in the general public than cruelty to people. So is it the human that has tamed the dog, or the dog that has tamed the human?

I've given these examples of how a single sentence might lead to all four kinds of analysis in order to show that anything is susceptible to this analysis.

Writing to Read, Reading to Write

It's important to choose a writing subject carefully, since a life's work may conceivably evolve from it. As a writer I frequently struggle with the infinite variety of subjects one might write about. Each of us writes best when exploring something we find important or attractive. In our writing, we search for material that will draw out the best in us. We write to guide our reading, and then read to inform our writing. The two processes are inextricably linked.

In my own search for subjects, I have sometimes found it impossible to say why something is important enough as a subject for me to write about. Obviously there are many things that are important to me that I have no desire to write about, such as my family and friends. That's because I desire to relate to them, not to observe them. As long as the relationship is satisfactory and rewarding, there is no drive to investigate it further in writing.

The things I am compelled to write about come from my need to probe for a deeper understanding—usually at all four levels previously described.

The search to understand is usually motivated by the presence of controversy. For example, there is no controversy about the fact that life exists. That is obvious to everyone. We ourselves are alive, which is sufficient evidence that life exists.

But there is a great deal of controversy about *how life first came into existence*. From the beginning of social discourse, people have probed this question in every conceivable way. Who are we? Why are we here? These are questions everyone wants answers for.

Such questions are much too broad, however. The controversy must be more specific. Does Darwinian evolution explain everything there is to know on that subject? For some it does; and *if* it does, then the controversy centers on particular aspects of evolution, such as the relationship between DNA, mutation and the characteristics of the environment.

But if the Darwinian model does not seem adequate, how and in what respects should it be modified? That is a question of great controversy. Some, who believe that God created the universe, try to modify it by eliminating it altogether. Others search for ways to show how Darwin's model, somewhat modified, is the means of creation that God uses. Still others deny that Darwin and God can be discussed in relationship to one another. Any resolution of such an intellectual conflict that would be capable of satisfying intelligent people would require years of careful study of the relevant issues.

Perhaps the answers lie instead in the meaning of the fossil record, which in recent times has revealed a strange phenomenon called *punctuated equilibrium* (which means that organisms sometimes evolve rapidly, but mostly they barely evolve at all). Endless controversies are to be found in sorting out such questions.

What I Like to Write About

I prefer subjects with which I have some experience and a great deal of interested involvement. The subjects that I like to read and write about become clearer to me when I can identify controversies that arise from them. Often I pursue both sides of an issue with great interest. For example, physics has developed two main theories over the last century: relativity and quantum mechanics. These two theories do not seem to describe the same kind of universe and are, so far, incompatible with one another, even though both of them have been experimentally verified.

Knowing how and why they are in conflict helps me to see their outlines and central issues more clearly. I then feel caught up in an internal discussion about how the conflicts might eventually be resolved. Therefore, reading about them fascinates me as a good mystery thriller would. In reading a book on such a subject, I am eager to see how well it will succeed in its ability to move a particular theory into a more comprehensible relationship.

Recognizing that a case has been made for both theories, even though they may seem contradictory to one another, I try to put together the case for each and understand it as fully as possible. After achieving a basic understanding, I elaborate it with subtleties and details. As I deepen my understanding, I will eventually become able to conceptualize how they might fit together to tell a coherent story.

In the process, I come up with my own theories and try them out on friends who have a deeper comprehension of the subject. I figure out how my argument might arouse objections in someone else, so I can work out a means of defending it against those objections.

In the end, I hope to achieve a synthesis of all the different elements I have discovered.

I have approached several different fields of knowledge in this way, as if solving a jigsaw puzzle. The more actively I become involved in the controversies that underlie a subject, the more excited I become about it. That's because the controversy brings out the deeper issues that underlie each point of view and enhance one's overall understanding of the subject.

For example, I am extremely fond of classical music. My enjoyment is greatly enhanced by reading probing reviews of different recordings of a given work. It is not uncommon to find that one critic will praise a work or a performance as having the highest value, while another will dismiss it altogether as not worth listening to.

Why America's Children Can't Think

When I have identified a controversy such as this, I find that the way I listen to a recording is enhanced. That's because I compare my own feelings with those expressed by the critics who disagree. That way I can decide which side I'm on, or whether I have a different opinion of the performance from either of them.

I don't think many people approach controversy in this way. Perhaps that's because we're taught to look for simple answers and ignore the opposite points of view.

However, my experiences in teaching suggest that most people really enjoy exploring things deeply in a spirit of controversy, and only need to be encouraged to do so and given tools that are comfortable for them to use.

Who Was Shakespeare?

Of all the subjects I've investigated, the one that has fascinated me the most has been the Shakespeare authorship controversy. Because I love the writings of this author so much, I want to know all I can about who he was and why he wrote as he did. This, as it turns out, is no easy matter, since there is considerable dispute on this subject, which has lasted for more than two hundred years.

In exploring the issues involved, I've run into considerable opposition. Some people try to dismiss the authorship question as unimportant because "after all, they're the greatest plays ever written, so what does it matter who wrote them?"

The best answer that I've found to that objection comes from *The Art of Literary Research,* by Richard D. Altick:[1]

Almost every literary work is attended by a host of outside circumstances that, once we express and explore them, suffuse it with additional meaning. It is the product of an individual human being's imagination and intellect; therefore, we must know all we can about the author. Sainte-Beuve's critical axiom, *tel abre, tel fruit,* is a bland oversimplification, to be sure, but the fact remains that behind the book is a man or woman whose character and experience of life cannot be overlooked in any effort to establish what the book really says. A book is also the product of an age; it represents someone talking to his contemporaries, and only incidentally to us. In addition to biographical inquiry, therefore, we must try to find out precisely how the intellectual, social, and cultural atmosphere of its epoch, and most especially current standards of taste affected its form and its content.

In the next chapter, I'll tell how I grappled with the questions about Shakespeare until I had discovered an interpretation of the facts that matched the creator with his creation and, in the process, deepened my appreciation for Shakespeare's works.

22

Looking for Mr. Shakespeare

How far can we penetrate the secrets of history by descending into a maelstrom of hidden ambiguities?

Cyrano de Bergerac *is one of the* most popular romantic comedies ever written. It tells the story of Cyrano, who loves Roxanne, but can express his love to her only through letters he ghostwrites for her suitor, the handsome but uninspired Christian.

Few who see this wonderful play realize that a real-life story of a similar nature lurks in the background of dramatic history, waiting to be revealed in its full dramatic force. For the greatest of all the playwrights was, like Cyrano, forced to address his beloved audiences through the personality of another man, who has overshadowed his memory for four centuries. And yet, like Cyrano, this playwright chose to hide his face and personality behind the more appealing mask of an alter ego, to appear as if he came from among the masses, not from the feared English nobility.

In this chapter, I shall relate my own most intense reading experience, which centers around this compelling story. It also happens to have been my most intense writing experience. It has occupied my thoughts obsessively for more than a decade and has helped me plumb the depths of the mechanics of writing. The mystery of how writing is born in the human brain is perhaps the greatest puzzle ever to surface in the world's cultures. What better way to probe that question, then, than to ask why the greatest writer in all of history wrote the way he did?

Why America's Children Can't Think

Who Shakespeare Was Not, and Who He Was

The man who wrote *Hamlet* and many other works was not a native of Stratford who came to London to seek his fortune while tossing off transcendent masterpieces of dramatic art in exchange for a playwright's meager income, and without a thought of their preservation for the future.

He was instead one of the most prestigious noblemen of his time who, because of a very difficult and somewhat antisocial personality, was a tremendous problem for the English monarchy.

This man, Edward de Vere, the seventeenth earl of Oxford, was forced, for very compelling reasons, to conceal his identity as a writer, literally on pain of death. In the process he wrote plays that seemed to support the establishment point of view of his time. For reasons I'll come to later, he was paid to do so, but was required to hire a commoner to represent himself as the author of these works—a man who, as it turned out, would have to sustain that role for several decades.

Because of an overwhelming frustration with the society of his time and the noble rank into which he was born, the earl of Oxford struck out against the dominant values of the Elizabethan court that surrounded him, but did so in such a subtle way that the queen and her courtiers never became aware that he was doing it. The enormous suffering and tragic degradation he experienced caused him to bury within his writings a plea for an understanding of human nature and of values much deeper than anyone could understand and appreciate in his own time.

In a nutshell, this is why those carefully crafted and exhaustively revised works have proved to be endlessly fascinating and deeply meaningful to readers and theatergoers ever since.

A Reading Romance

From the time I was in high school, I have been fascinated by Shakespeare: the ebb and flow of his language, the metaphors and symbolism, and the range of human emotions in a dramatic art as emotionally comprehensive as humanity itself. For a long time I had trouble understanding his lines, as nearly everyone does. At first I thought that was because they were written so long ago, but that's not the reason. Shakespeare's lines are difficult because, like an artist sculpting a statue of clay, he molded language into more original patterns than any other writer ever has. He seemed constitutionally incapable of writing a simple line like "the sun rises." Instead, he wrote:

> But look, the morn in russet mantle clad
> Walks o'er the dew of yon high eastward hill.

Poetic outbursts like that tend to make people say, "Why couldn't he just say it in English?" The reason he couldn't, of course, was that he was driven, as the best poets usually are, to find a unique and wonderful way of expressing every thought, as if it were to be displayed like a rare jewel or cultivated flower.

When he needed a word that didn't exist, Shakespeare simply made it up, the way the earliest humans made stone tools. He used words not only for their functionality, but also for their beauty and imagery.

After many struggles to understand Shakespeare's writing, I found my road paved toward an easier access to his meanings by means of a comic book. This was a version of *Macbeth,* approved by the Folger Library, which contained the entire, uncut text of the play. A picture of the action accompanied every line, which made it much easier to understand than the original script.

Once I understood it, the effect of this play was so powerful that I have never been able to stop thinking about Shakespeare. What struck me the most was that all of the events in the play seemed to be tied together by a complex web of poetic expression that made the reader wonder about and question every single thing that happened.

The play isn't just about a man who kills a king and then suffers the consequences. It is about the many states of feeling such an action calls forth. If you read the lines of Macbeth, who is a character very few people would want to compare themselves to, you find yourself feeling like him, taking his anger, frustration and passion for power into yourself. You can understand what it feels like to be a villain who regrets every step he takes into villainy, but somehow cannot help himself from doing what he himself despises.

The Plot Thickens

As my love for Shakespeare grew, I became involved with productions of his plays, and later came to teach him, year after year, to my students. Gradually I began to notice a peculiar feeling about him.

I could not account for this feeling, but over time I came across a few well-informed people who also felt it. Together we wondered why this man, as he has come down to us in history, is so completely unrelated to the writings he produced. There is not one thing that is known about Shakespeare's life that translates into the way he penned his masterpieces.

In junior high school, along with the usual pabulum students are fed about the "life" of Shakespeare, I first heard about the idea that Bacon had written Shakespeare's plays. Also it was then that I heard that that was nonsense, since after all, the styles of the two writers were completely different, and besides, how could one man have had time to write all those works? I ignored the strange feeling I had about the authorship at the time, but remembered the puzzle. Why was there a theory that someone else had written Shakespeare's plays, but no comparable theory about any other writer or artist in all of history? Why Shakespeare and only Shakespeare? What made the writer (as he was discussed in class) and his works so disparate in contrast to one another?

There were no answers since everyone I encountered insisted that those who thought someone else had written Shakespeare's works were simply insane fools, hungry for publicity.

Then, in January 1959, one of my students brought in an article in a law journal written by its editor, Richard Bentley.[1] This piece argued that every legal reference in any Shakespeare play was correct to its finest detail. Since many legal situations referred to in Shakespeare would have been understood only by legal experts, the article concluded that the author of the plays had to have attended law school. Indeed, argued the author, a great many lawyers had come to this conclusion, including (at present) several supreme court justices.

Over two hundred years ago, when the idea of Shakespeare's expertise in the law was first suggested, the only lawyer who was also a writer that popped into anyone's head was Sir Francis Bacon. But in 1920, a British schoolmaster made a list of characteristics he thought the author of the plays must have had and set out to find someone who personified some of those traits. This man turned out to be Edward de Vere, the seventeenth earl of Oxford, whose personality, education and style were a perfect match for the man behind the mask described by those who had tried to reconcile the life of the man from Stratford with the plays attached to his name. One of the first champions of this new theory was Sigmund Freud, who felt that the psychological situations dramatized in the plays (particularly in *Hamlet*) reflected the biographical facts of Lord Oxford's life very closely.

I was so excited when I read this article that I immediately decided to apply for a Fulbright Scholarship to go to England, study the life of Oxford, and write a play about him. I contacted one of my favorite professors at Amherst, asking for a recommendation. My professor wrote back that he was happy to recommend me, but also warned that this theory had already been proved incorrect. At first I thought he was narrow-minded but quickly changed my mind when I learned that Lord Oxford had died in 1604, many years before several of the plays were written.

When I read that, I closed the book on the Oxford theory for the next thirty-one years.

Stalked by a Theory

Relentlessly, the Oxford theory continued to shadow me. Every time anything was written about it, even in journals that I didn't normally read, the article would happen to come to my attention.

Strangest of all was an event that took place at American University in 1987. I was driving around in Washington, D.C., and happened to hear on the radio a mock trial of Lord Oxford, presided over by three supreme court justices. I didn't catch the whole thing, but I did hear what Justice Stevens had to say in conclusion: The problem with Lord Oxford as author was that he was *too intelligent* to make the mistakes that had been found in the Shakespeare plays.

It would be several years before I found out that the "mistakes" he referred to weren't really mistakes at all, and that, realizing this fact, Justice Stevens had changed his mind and become convinced that Lord Oxford had written the plays. But neither he nor I knew that at the time.

The trial, it turned out, was a tribute to the case presented by James Boyle, whose argument for Shakespeare was better than any other I have ever seen. However, Peter Jaszi, who argued the case for Oxford, was woefully unprepared and made very few of the points he could have made.

A few years earlier, I had had as a student in one of my English classes Nissa Ogburn, the daughter of Charlton Ogburn, the most highly respected and thorough proponent of the Oxford theory. I listened politely whenever Nissa asserted that the earl of Oxford had really written the plays. But as her teacher, I felt I knew better than to encourage her "misguided nonsense." And, indeed, at the time I thought I was right, for her father had not yet written his landmark book, *The Mysterious William Shakespeare*, which is now the bible of the Oxfordians. There were still some very large holes in the case for Oxford, which in any event had to be pieced together from the writings of a great many different writers, none of whom were gifted with the ability to make a point with any particular clarity or readability.

Still, the theory was so energetically and persistently argued, that I began to wonder why it wouldn't go away. Surely if it had been proven wrong (as so many said), intelligent people would laugh it off and stop paying any attention to it at all. And yet three supreme court justices had taken the time and trouble to hear the arguments.

A couple of years after the mock trial at American University, I had heard so much more about the Oxford theory that I began to think perhaps Oxford and Shakespeare had collaborated on the plays, and that if they had, that would explain a lot of the mysteries surrounding them. So I started writing a novel about what such a collaboration might have been like.

Meeting a Renaissance Man

At a reunion of some former students from my class of 1960, I started talking with Peter Kreeger, who asked me what I was writing about. I mentioned my novel and its thesis.

"That's completely wrong," he said. "Shakespeare was illiterate."

"How do you know that?" I asked.

"My father is an expert on the subject. Why don't you come to my house some night and let him tell you what he knows?"

That was how I met David Lloyd Kreeger, who came as close to being a true Renaissance man as anyone I have ever met. A graduate of Harvard Law School and founder of the Government Employees Insurance Company (GEICO), Kreeger was a noted art collector and music lover, a violinist whose skills were sufficient for him to play duets with the great cellist Pablo Casals, as well as with some noted string quartets at his private parties.

But the greatest of Kreeger's loves (besides his wife, Carmen, and their children) was Shakespeare. Kreeger was certain that Oxford was the author of the plays.

Since I knew that couldn't be the case, I began the evening's conversation with what I felt were unanswerable questions.

"How could Oxford have written the plays when he died in 1604 and *The Tempest* was written in 1611?"

At this, Kreeger picked up a copy of the variorum edition of *The Tempest* and reeled off the following dates, which have been suggested by various scholars for the writing of that play: 1596, 1602, 1603, 1604, 1609, 1610, 1611, 1613 and 1614. "That's hardly," he said, "a consensus. Those who think it was written after 1604 are influenced by the publication in October 1610 of [Sylvester] Jourdain's narrative of the wreck on July 25, 1609, of Sir George Somers in the Bermudas during his voyage to Virginia. However, this narrative was classified by the government secret service, and there is virtually no chance that a commoner like Shakespeare could have read it or been influenced by it."

I was rather bowled over by Kreeger's scholarship and by the cavalier way he demolished the chief objection that had kept me away from the Oxford theory for thirty-one years.

"And did you know that this whole ruckus is confined to the shipwreck scene and its aftermath in the opening scenes of the play (though the ship isn't actually wrecked)? The rest of the play doesn't enter into the issue of Jourdain's narrative at all. Besides that, if the play was performed five years before Jourdain wrote his narrative, he could have been influenced by some of its lines in writing his report, rather than the other way around. In fact, that's a far more likely explanation."

"So this whole thing is about a shipwreck that's not even in the play?" I gasped in amazement.

Kreeger nodded, then went on. "The real issue isn't what Shakespeare may or may not have read that's somewhat like what he wrote. He was surely resourceful enough to make up the material in question for himself. But when there is a provable source for the play (which the Jourdain description definitely is not), that's the best way to date it. In such a case, it must have been written after its source was written. And of course, it must have been written before its first printed edition appeared. That's about all you have to go on in trying to date most Shakespeare plays; and, indeed, virtually all of the dates are heavily disputed by scholars with varying opinions. It's convenient, though, if you want the Oxford theory to go away, to tell people that we know for sure that certain plays were written after his death, when in fact there's no proof of that at all."[2]

"Is there any definite source for *The Tempest*?" I asked. "Anything that everyone can agree about?"

"The author used material in it from a translation of Montaigne made by John Florio that was published in 1603, though it was available in manuscript before then."

"So there's no proof at all that *The Tempest* had to have been written later than that?" I asked.

"None," he said. "And anyway, there were a number of shipwrecks well before that date that actually bore a stronger resemblance to the situation in the play than Somers's misfortune."

Kreeger went on to say that a great deal more interesting than any sort of shipwreck was that Oxford was a cousin four times over to Bartholomew Gosnold, the explorer who named Martha's Vineyard after his daughter. Ariel describes the yellow sands of Martha's Vineyard in his song, and Caliban, the song's hero, is an American Indian. Indeed, there's nothing at all in the play to suggest that it has anything to do with Bermuda, and of course voyages to the colonies were very much in vogue at that time.

Furthermore, in 1589, Gosnold built on his estate in Otley, England, one of three Elizabethan age playhouses that still stand. Otley is in Sussex County, near where Oxford grew up. It's widely thought that both the earl of Oxford and the earl of Southampton participated in play productions there, and that *Hamlet* may well have first seen the light of a performance in that playhouse.[3]

As I listened to Kreeger, all the objections to the Oxford theory that I had accumulated quickly bit the dust. I told Kreeger that my wife and I planned to write a novel on the subject, and we hoped to have it ready in a year.

"Will you have time?" he thoughtfully asked, showing far more understanding of the situation than we did. Then he went on, "There's only one book you need to read. It's the best resource, and it's eight hundred pages long," and he told me about Ogburn's book.

It turned out that I would have to read more than a hundred books before I felt I understood the subject I had so naively decided to investigate. But this one was a good place to start.

Before I finished Ogburn's tome, I had read it four times, and parts of it more than a dozen times. It is one of the most densely packed treatises on anything I have ever read, so crammed with information that keeping it all straight is virtually impossible on a single reading.

Shortly after I began reading the book, I had a chance to meet Ogburn in person. He was one of the nicest men I have ever met, and extremely interested in my educational consulting program. Meanwhile, I was convinced that he was one of the most remarkable literary historians ever to publish. His book had completely changed my picture not just of the Shakespeare plays, but of the entire Elizabethan age.

Why America's Children Can't Think

The Life and Times of the Real Shakespeare

Lord Oxford was born in 1550, and was one of the most precocious youngsters in history. By the age of five, he was riding horseback great distances to be tutored by the finest minds of his time. At the age of nine, he entered Cambridge University and received his master's degree at fourteen. An anonymously printed translation of the Narcissus episode from Ovid's *Metamorphoses* that appeared when he was ten is thought to be his first published work. By the age of sixteen, he had translated the entire work, though the published version was attributed to his uncle, Arthur Golding, since the boy's noble rank forbade his own name being ascribed to any published work.

There's also remarkably compelling evidence that, in 1562, Lord Oxford generated the English translation of a French translation of an Italian poem called *Romeus and Juliet*, which was later to be the source of *Romeo and Juliet*. Almost all Oxfordians (including a number of noted scholars) agree on this.

Reading *Romeus and Juliet*, I sense in it a precocious twelve year old at work. For one thing, like most boys his age, he's allergic to the idea of romantic love and writes of the irresponsibility of the villainous Friar and Nurse, who encourage the lovers in their poisonous passion.

Furthermore, the young man had good reason to be disillusioned with love because his father had just died and his mother had been remarried to a man distinctly inferior to his father. All the emotions recorded in *Hamlet* find their roots in this situation—a tragic turn of events for Oxford, which occurred when he was twelve years old.

But there's a great deal more of *Hamlet* in Lord Oxford's life. In the event of his father's death, he had been contracted to go to London to live with the queen's secretary, Sir William Cecil, who virtually ruled England side by side with the queen. Cecil's style of expression and general demeanor are exactly like those of Polonius.

Cecil's son, Thomas, received practically the same farewell advice that Polonius gives Laertes. Like Laertes, Thomas went to study in Paris, and Cecil, like Polonius, hired spies to report on his behavior.

The most tragic figure on the stage of Oxford's life was Anne Cecil, six years his junior and shy, sweet and modest. When she reached Juliet's age, she married Lord Oxford. Her character resembles Ophelia so precisely that the relationship sends chills up my spine every time I think of it. This was such a deeply tormented marriage for both husband and wife that I strongly suspect the author's depiction of Ophelia's madness was learned from direct observation of his wife's behavior.

A Wedding Play

In 1571, Lord Oxford married Anne at the most important social event in London that year. In celebration, he staged a little play, a custom popular for wedding entertainment. What was not so much the custom was that the groom was the author.

The play concerns a Mr. and Mrs. Page and their daughter, Anne. Mr. Page wants Anne to marry Slender, while Mrs. Page wants her to marry Dr. Caius. Anne herself wants to marry Fenton. The trouble with Fenton, however, is that his rank is too high for her father's taste (a problem unique in the history of literature), and he is guilty of reckless behavior with lewd companions (though at no time in the play do we see him associating with such companions).

The real-life story behind the wedding is that a year before Anne married Lord Oxford, she had been betrothed to the earl of Leicester's nephew, Philip Sidney, who was a rather effeminate teenager. Sidney decided that he didn't want to marry Anne, so the marriage was called off, but in the meantime there were complex agreements about her dowry, and the amounts of money and servants Sidney would bring to the marriage. All these are faithfully and accurately recorded in the play, where Slender's uncle, Justice Shallow, dwells on them exactly the way the earl of Leicester did in negotiating for his nephew.

Meanwhile, Anne's mother had been opposed to marriage with either suitor. She wanted her daughter to marry someone intellectual, like a professor. The real Dr. Caius was Oxford's professor of medicine at Cambridge.

Why America's Children Can't Think

Sir William's objection to Anne's marriage to Lord Oxford, who was also his ward, was that his rank was too high and that he spent a lot of time hanging around with "lewd companions," the way Prince Hal does in the *Henry IV* plays. The problem with Oxford's rank was that his inheritance was not sufficient to support the spending his high rank required of him. Cecil knew this would seriously interfere with his ability to support his wife—and throughout the marriage that proved to be true.

In addition to Mr. and Mrs. Page and their daughter, there is a brief stint onstage for Anne's younger brother, Robert Cecil, who was eight years old at the time and had been crippled by an accident in his infancy. As he moved across the stage in the part of the Page, the audience of socialites had the opportunity to scrutinize the deformed body that, for the rest of his life, Robert would hide from prying eyes as much as possible. Young Robert grew up to succeed his father as the right-hand man both to Queen Elizabeth and King James. But throughout her life, the Queen referred to him as her "dwarf," an epithet that is glancingly applied to him in the play. "Dwarf" meant "midget," and Robert's physical deformity made him walk with the slow deliberation of an adult, which made him look like a midget, to the mirthful delight of the audience in attendance.

In the above details, the exact events of the courtship and wedding are preserved. They remind us that Lord Oxford was the reckless nobleman who was indeed "out of Anne's star."[4] This fact and all the other details add nothing to the entertainment value of the play, but clearly show that Oxford was determined to advertise his extreme dislike for the occasion before the assembled guests. He had been forced to marry Anne by the queen herself, but he was not in love with her.

Shakespeare's plays are noted for their delicious and rapturous love poetry, but if you read *The Merry Wives of Windsor*[5] a dozen times (as I have done, because I have produced the play), you won't find a line in it that even faintly suggests romance.

The play, as we have it today, existed in at least two versions, the first of which has been lost. It was about an hour long and contained no mention of Falstaff, the beloved "wool-sack round old knight," or his companions (other than the brief reference noted above, though even in the present version, Fenton never associates with Falstaff or his friends). The second, written decades later, simply revised the original to include the scenes and characters associated with Falstaff. The style throughout is completely consistent, and no one has ever suggested that more than one person wrote this play. Yet William Shakespeare of Stratford was seven years old and lived a great distance from Westminster at the time when the wedding took place. He could not have known the details of it (including the exact sums of money—several of them—mentioned in a contract for a wedding between Philip Sidney and Anne Cecil that was supposed to have taken place in 1570 but didn't). And even if Shakespeare could have known these things, he would have had no reason to put them in the play, as they contribute nothing to it, except as a series of private jokes of the kind that show up in skits written for such an occasion even today.

J. T. Looney, who wrote the original book revealing that Oxford was Shakespeare, discovered the connection between the play and the wedding and wrote about it in a separate article after his book was published.

Other Events in Oxford's Life

So far I have taken you briefly through Oxford's life up to the age of twenty-one, when he was married and wrote the wedding play, which still exists today.

From that time, in 1571, until 1586, Oxford wrote a great deal, achieved great glory, and suffered terrible hardships. Nearly all of the important events that transpired in his life, and most of the people he interacted with, showed up in his writings, some of which were as autobiographical as Eugene O'Neill's *Long Day's Journey into Night*. Here are a few examples:

- His affair with Queen Elizabeth, described in *Venus and Adonis*, eventually produced the changeling boy referred to in *A Midsummer Night's Dream*. This was the earl of Southampton, the son he could never acknowledge, to whom Lord Oxford poured out his love in the Sonnets.
- Oxford staged a mock robbery at Gad's Hill in 1573. This was treated at length in his second extant play, *The Famous Victories*

of Henry Fifth. It was retained in the historical trilogy that followed more than twenty years later. This play, by the way, also existed in two versions, only one of which has survived. The second of these versions served to bring William Shakespeare into Lord Oxford's life, as I shall argue shortly.

- There is compelling evidence that *Macbeth* was written in protest against the execution of Mary Queen of Scots. Oxford's cousin, the duke of Norfolk, had years earlier been part of a plot to free Mary, and was executed for it—the first time the queen put anyone to death. Oxford opposed this execution, but his pleas in defense of his cousin failed. This drama was more or less repeated more than fifteen years later, bringing even deeper suffering to Oxford, and inspiring a play about the murder of a royal guest. Oxfordian scholar Ruth Loyd Miller has shown that certain documents, available only to the inner circle of the Elizabethan court, influenced the writing of this play, which also derived from Oxford's participation in the campaign in Scotland in 1569.

- In 1576, Oxford threw his wife out of his home for five years, believing that she was unfaithful to him. In 1581, he took her back, no longer believing that this was true. Seven of his plays, including *Othello, The Winter's Tale, Much Ado About Nothing* and *Cymbeline* draw heavily on this experience.

- In *King Lear*, the fact that Lear's hundred followers are taken away from him by his two daughters brings on the old king's madness. The Oxford family tradition was to travel about with a show of more than a hundred followers. When Oxford rode into London at age twelve, he had 140 retainers and followers with him. No other family at the time attached so much importance to this particular mark of noble birth.

- Lord Oxford became embroiled in rivalries during his days at the queen's court. Many of his rivals are caricatured in *Twelfth Night*, in which Malvolio is based on Christopher Hatton and Sir Andrew Aguecheek on Philip Sidney. It is amusing to read a letter of Sidney's that is so similar to the challenge to a duel written by Aguecheek in the play that it scarcely seems that Sidney was being caricatured.

- Lord Oxford's imprisonment in the Tower of London for adultery led immediately to much of the imagery and atmosphere in *Richard III*, and retrospectively to the thoughts of Cardinal Wolsey in *Henry VIII*. Most of those who were sentenced to the Tower found it more like a hotel than a prison, but the queen's jealousy over Oxford's affair with one of her maids of honor was so great that Oxford experienced the Tower at its worst.

These examples are mere tidbits in a rich lode of information that fills nearly a thousand pages in Eva Turner Clark's seldom-read book, *Hidden Allusions in Shakespeare's Plays,* masterfully brought up-to-date by Ruth Loyd Miller.[6] A companion book of almost equal length is William Plumer Fowler's *Shakespeare Revealed in Oxford's Letters*, which exhaustively compares the language in thirty-seven letters that Oxford wrote to family and friends to that to be found in the Shakespeare plays.[7]

Stylistic DNA

In reading through Oxford's correspondence myself, I stumbled across the rare word "disfurnish," which means "divest." Oxford uses this word once in his letters, but also a variant, "defurnish," which does not appear in the *Oxford English Dictionary*, and thus was never used in any major work of literature. The word "disfurnish" is used in three Shakespeare plays and very rarely elsewhere. However, it also appears in *The Spanish Tragedy*, now widely thought to be an early Shakespeare play of about the time of *Titus Andronicus*.[8] Another rare (and therefore likely Shakespearean) word I stumbled across in that same play is "filed," as in the line from *Macbeth*, "for Banquo's issue have I filed my mind," where it means "defiled." However, all the editions of *The Spanish Tragedy* I have seen misspell this word as "filled," even though it clearly has the same meaning as it does in *Macbeth*.

As you can see, there's a great deal of very impressive research on this subject, but a great deal more that remains to be done. Once the fact that

Oxford wrote these plays has been universally accepted (and this should happen very soon), the floodgates will be open for a whole new onslaught of research on Shakespeare.[9]

But is there any absolute documentary proof that William Shakespeare did not write the works attributed to him?

As I see it, the most powerful evidence comes from Charles Hamilton, who in reality set out to prove the opposite. Hamilton, who was an amateur Shakespearean scholar and a highly esteemed forensic graphologist, examined Shakespeare's will and found that he had written it himself, in his own hand. In addition, the same handwriting was found in a bill of sale that the fifteen-year-old Shakespeare drew up for a piece of his father's property. The same handwriting appears in the following: (1) a letter signed by the earl of Southampton, (2) annotations on the pages of several books, and (3) the manuscripts of three Elizabethan plays.

Then doesn't the evidence for Oxford fall to the ground in the face of the fact that William Shakespeare is thus proved to have been literate both in writing and in the law, and to have been the author of the plays whose manuscripts we have in his handwriting?

Astoundingly, the answer to this question is a resounding no. Two of the Elizabethan plays, *The Book of Sir Thomas More* and *Edmund Ironside*, are unquestionably Shakespearean plays. The first has been familiar to Shakespeare scholars for a long time, and "Hand D" in this collage of a manuscript was long thought (correctly, as it turns out) to be in William Shakespeare's hand.

Edmund Ironside, on the other hand, was thought to have been written nearly a century later. Now, however, the impeccable scholarship of Eric Sams shows that it is an authentic Shakespeare play, written just before *Titus Andronicus*. These two plays have in common many examples of physical mutilation, and reflect Oxford's stint as a commander in the wars near Antwerp. (Antwerp means "hand throwing" and reflects the custom at that time of chopping off the hand of an unidentified foreigner and throwing it into the nearby river.) In that respect the two plays are similar, but in a very significant way they are *not* similar, and to that point I shall return shortly.

The third play in Shakespeare's handwriting is the one that gives away the store. This is a fairly well known anonymous play entitled *The Second Maiden's Tragedy*. Charles Hamilton renamed it *Cardenio*, suggesting it was the long lost play by John Fletcher and William Shakespeare that scholars had been searching for and speculating about for over three hundred years. *Cardenio* was supposed to have been based on *Don Quixote*, and indeed the two plots of *The Second Maiden's Tragedy* are based on two subplots in *Don Quixote*, and in the adaptation their stories are considerably improved.

There's no chance that this play, which is known for certain to have been written in 1612, was by Oxford. When Oxford died, *Don Quixote* had not yet been published.

But William Shakespeare didn't write it either. In fact, it bears so little resemblance to Shakespeare's writing that out of twenty-four scholars who attempted to guess who might be the author, only one suggested that Shakespeare could have had anything to do with it. Fourteen of these scholars selected Thomas Middleton as the author, and the others all picked playwrights whose style is relatively similar to Middleton's.

If you compare Middleton's best play, *Women Beware Women*, with *The Second Maiden's Tragedy*, all sorts of similarities will leap out at you.

Middleton was a very good playwright. In fact, T. S. Eliot praised him as second only to Shakespeare. But he was extremely unlike Shakespeare.

Removing All Shadow of Doubt

If there's any further doubt about Shakespeare's authorship of *The Second Maiden's Tragedy*, it's worth reading scholar Anne Lancashire's comments on the changes made in the manuscript by the copyist. In her view, some of these reveal that the scribe didn't really understand the subtleties of the work he was copying, and in any case, none of the alterations are improvements.

Beyond that, if any one of the three manuscripts contained a single example of the playwright improving a line as he worked, as all playwrights of the time did, there would be reason to think that the author was writing an original manuscript. Since there isn't one example of this in all three plays, the only conclusion that can be drawn is that, for some reason,

William Shakespeare was a scribe who took credit for the authorship of the plays he copied.

But what was the most popular playwright of his time doing copying out the manuscript of someone else's play? As I see it, there's only one logical explanation for this peculiar fact.

William Shakespeare made a career of copying Oxford's manuscripts and delivering them to the theater companies, representing them as his own. In fact, he was specifically hired and commanded to do just this by Oxford.

Undoubtedly, when Lord Oxford died suddenly and unexpectedly in 1604, he left behind manuscripts of plays that had not yet been copied and sold for theatrical performance. Shakespeare would have copied these and released them gradually for a few years after Lord Oxford's death.

And indeed, when the supply was gone, the only thing to do was buy a manuscript from a working playwright, copy it as his own, and sell it for a higher price than he paid for it. Since he was the most popular dramatist of the time, he could no doubt have made a decent profit this way.

He probably would not have attempted this scheme more than once, however, as the Elizabethans were highly sensitive to writing styles and must have wondered what had happened to their beloved Shakespeare. That's probably why the man from Stratford threw in the towel and went home at that point.

The Story Behind the Story

In this very sketchy account of the facts of the authorship as it has gradually emerged over the years, the entire effort has been to arrive at a literal description of what happened. But we have learned nothing about the *significance* of what happened. All that I've presented so far, complex as it is, comes under the heading of *p'shat* (determining the basic meaning and structure of the written word). Specifically, what does the word "Shakespeare" mean when denoting the author of a play? The answer I have given is that it means "Edward de Vere."

But what hints, suggestions and symbols lie behind all this? What's the *remez*?

In a matter as complex as this, where four hundred years ago a great effort was made to keep us from knowing a great many things, the explanation for what I have reported must be obtained by looking at the hints that were left behind, clues as to what happened.

Two Plays with a Difference

Let me return to the comparison between *Edmund Ironside* and *Titus Andronicus*, for in their difference lies an important clue to what actually happened.

Edmund Ironside is an historically accurate play that looks as if it were intended to be the first in a long line of history plays, chronicling events over a period of five hundred years. It is set just before the time of William the Conqueror, and like *Henry IV, Part One*, it ends without being resolved, clearly implying a second part to the play. But there is no second part.

In *Edmund Ironside*, we see something happening that will never happen again in a Shakespeare play. It contains a scene that ridicules a cardinal in a highly sacrilegious way. Because of this scene, England's licensor of plays at the time forbade its performance.

So imagine that the playwright had decided to write a long series of plays that told the story of English history from the very beginning down to the author's own time. Imagine his high hopes as he set out on this project, writing the first of an intended cycle of two or three dozen plays. And imagine that right at the start, the project was nipped in the bud, and he was told that he had overstepped the bounds of decency. At that point he stopped, reconsidered his project, and began to approach it differently.

But why would he have planned such a thing in the first place?

Today we are very much aware that when a nation is violently attacked, its citizens will rise up in anger and put all their energies into destroying the attackers as quickly and thoroughly as possible. But prior to the violent attack, there may be little or no willingness to build the defenses necessary to prevent such an attack in the first place.

Now imagine that you are a ruler of a great nation and you know that your chief enemy is secretly planning such an attack. In 1586, Queen

Elizabeth knew that the Spanish were building a powerful armada that would seek to destroy England. The English fleet, meanwhile, had fallen into serious disrepair.

The thing to do was raise enough taxes to finance a fleet capable of defeating the one the Spanish were building. This would require "great impress of shipwrights,"[10] and it would also require much higher taxes. In fact, the taxes would have to be doubled and then tripled before the problem was solved.

But the queen could not raise taxes without the approval of the House of Commons. And she would never obtain that approval unless the English could be raised to a patriotic fervor in support of the defense of their beloved country.

England had been torn by civil strife for more than a hundred years prior to 1485, when the queen's grandfather ascended the throne. Since the death of her father, the conflict between Protestants and Catholics had torn the country apart even further. But for some years, advertising herself as "a prince of peace," the queen had brought about a sense of security that most people had enjoyed long enough to become complacent. Besides, there had been no foreign invasion of England for 520 years.

Thus the queen desperately needed propaganda that would arouse the people from their false sense of security sufficiently to enable her to get the consent of the commoners to double the tax base. Since the majority were illiterate, the best form of propaganda was in the popular theater; but the theater, under attack by the Puritans at that time, was not thriving as much as it might have been. The queen needed a series of plays that would demonstrate to her people the horrible, disunifying effect of such civil brawls. These plays also needed to show how terrible things could get when citizens took the law into their own hands.

The effect of such plays should be (and was) to create in the population a strong desire for a unified government that could protect their interests against both civil strife and foreign invasion. Meanwhile, there had been a small number of really good history plays, which had seemed to arouse in their audiences a sense of patriotism that was otherwise lacking.

So the queen planned a grand project. She would deluge the commoners with history plays and revenge tragedies that would clearly demonstrate the horror and chaos that resulted when the power of the central government was weakened, challenged or ignored.

The problem was, however, that, far and away, the best plays came from the pen of someone close to the throne, who had been identified in the public mind as one of her most glorious courtiers. If this man were to head up the playwriting effort that would inspire the increase of patriotism, the commoners would be likely to realize that they were being manipulated by propaganda. But if a commoner wrote the plays, there would be no reason for them to think this. Or at least, so the queen must have reasoned.

Her solution was to pay her best author to write and inspire others to write the history plays that would do the job. So on June 29, 1586, the queen bestowed on Oxford an income of £1,000 a year, whose purpose was to be kept secret and was never to be audited. In other words, Oxford was now a member of the secret service, and his job was to write history plays under the stipulation that he would hire someone to represent himself as author so no one would suspect that Oxford had written them.[11]

One reason that the queen knew that Lord Oxford could carry out such a project magnificently was that, in 1574, he had presented her with the best history play ever written at that time, *The Famous Victories of Henry Fifth*. For this new task, Oxford thus had the idea that the plays he wrote needed to be scholarly. He himself was a consummate scholar, familiar with virtually all the classical literature known in his time, much of it still untranslated from Greek, Latin, Italian and French—all languages he could read fluently. He was also quite well versed in history.

However, since he had first written *The Famous Victories,* a great deal of new historical work had been published, so Oxford felt he needed to update the play. He was also aware that he had written the play rather casually, so he needed to review the history he had read twelve or more years earlier. This, however, would be complicated, because the works on which it was based were very long and complex. These were Edward Hall's *The Union of the Two Noble and Illustrious Families of Lancaster and York*, published in 1550, and Sir Thomas Elyot's *The Book Named the Governor* (1531). The first of these would have taken him a great deal of effort to read through a second time. So he appears to have hired William Shakespeare, not only as a scribe who would take the credit for writing these plays (since Oxford's authorship had to be kept secret), but also as a secretary who could save him the trouble of rereading the book by annotating it for him.

The annotations Shakespeare provided were very thorough, and would have sufficed the author to make any corrections of historical fact that were needed. But as you read through them, evidence accumulates that the annotator has none of the qualities one would expect in any writing known to be by William Shakespeare. Allan Keen and Roger Lubbock, who have written a book on the subject, summarize their impressions with:

> These are not the kind of illuminating comments and comparisons that a subsequent reader is glad to find in a margin; nor are they of the infuriating 'what bosh!' type; they are more methodical than that. They are not all simple cross-headings, pointers left to the information available in the book. They are not even the casual nota-benes of a man intent on his own erudition—the selection of that striking detail, the exact total of Richard's fortune, would be of no value to him: nor, on the other hand, does the interest in Richard's character suggest a compiler of statistics.[12]

Later, the authors conclude their observations with, "Certainly we do not find, in these marginal scribbles, any sign of the flashing imagination, the sinewy style, 'the evident pulse of a powerful mind,' that we look for in every sentence that Shakespeare wrote."[13]

The evidence that Oxford was pressed for time in revising his play, but trying very hard to make it as historically accurate as possible, is in the fact that the first half of the play uses material from the more recent historians Stowe and Holingshed. However, throughout the second half, which is actually more abundant in historical subject matter, there is no further influence derived from these sources.

Clearly, the updated version of *The Famous Victories* was put into production as quickly as possible, and before the process of its revision could be finished. Then Oxford turned to the next project, the hastily written, but historically accurate *Edmund Ironside*. This time he had Shakespeare make a summary of William Lambarde's *Archaionomia*, a book about pre-Norman law.

But, as I've said, this play was a disaster. Perhaps that caused Oxford to ask the queen how important to her it was that his plays be historically accurate. "Not at all," she must have said, "I wish only that they depict the horrors of war and disloyalty to the monarchy, as well as the destructiveness of taking the law into your own hands without the guidance of a strong government."

In response, she received *Titus Andronicus* and *The Spanish Tragedy*, historical fantasies that had nothing to do with real events. But they both concentrated on bloody horrors and gave the illusion of being historical, even though they were not.

That's probably why we have no further annotations by William Shakespeare that seem to have usefulness as historical research on which a play might be based. Furthermore, the four plays I've mentioned are all, more or less, in the form in which Oxford laid them aside before 1590. Most of the plays that came after that have been heavily revised, sometimes over more than one decade. These later plays show none of the haste that you find in the ones we've considered so far, but rather a deep commitment to achieving the highest level of poetic excellence.

In this analysis of how the first history plays came to be written and the particular conditions of secrecy under which Oxford had to work after 1586, as well as how the relationship between him and Shakespeare was begun, I've been specifically looking for the significance hidden behind a group of historical documents that, taken all together, provide an explanation consistent with all that is otherwise known historically.

There's still something missing, however. We are at a relatively low level of significance in this story, for though we now know more about what happened, we still do not have an answer to the question, why does it matter? In other words, we haven't considered how these events, if they happened in this way, affected the development of the literary art that grew out of this situation and that continues to be so greatly admired.

Why America's Children Can't Think

Commentary on a Life

It's time for the *d'rash*—the commentary.

One thing that has always struck me about the Shakespeare plays is their complete lack of understanding of both commoners and children. All the commoners are clowns, though some of the clowns are philosophers. But there's no hint of awareness in Shakespeare of the problems of the common person, or what might motivate such people. And, as for the children in the plays, all of them are miniature adults.

This is easy enough to explain, since Lord Oxford was neither a commoner nor able to enjoy a carefree and playful childhood. Few members of the nobility were.

That said, no writer, with the possible exception of Dante, ever displayed such a profound understanding of human character and values from one end of the spectrum to the other. So what can account for this?

Apart from the obvious answer implied by the mysterious quality of genius, the evolution of style in the plays—from the ordinariness of *The Merry Wives of Windsor* to the sublimity of the great tragedies, and even of *The Two Noble Kinsmen* and *The Winter's Tale*—argues that an enormous amount of growth occurred over this man's lifetime.

In fact, one of the problems inherent in putting Oxford forward as the author of the plays has been that the writing with his name on it is so inferior in quality, even though it is stylistically indistinguishable from the writing attributed to Shakespeare. Not surprisingly, it was all written many years earlier than the well-known plays and poems.

Most of what was published in the *Complete Works* was heavily revised and mulled over for more than a decade. Indeed Oxford is thought to have written early drafts of nearly all his plays by about 1589. This meant that he spent fifteen years revising them without adding more than a couple of entirely new ones. Furthermore, during most of those years, he had little else to do.

Even so, early works like *Titus Andronicus* and *Henry VI, Part One*, brilliant dramas though they are, pale to insignificance compared with *Hamlet* and *Lear*. Oxford's learning curve, even after he had hit his stride, was surely one of the steepest ever recorded.

The central fact in Oxford's life, apart from the personal tragedies he suffered, was that he was prohibited from the public presentation of anything in which any reader could identify him as the author. This was even true of the Sonnets, which were not intended for publication, but rather for the contemplation of the people they were addressed to—primarily his unacknowledged son, Southampton.

Significantly, he is the only Elizabethan writer who ever used the phrase "I am that I am," which is God's declaration to Moses in the Geneva Bible. He used it twice, once in a letter to his father-in-law, and once in one of the Sonnets. He also used the inversion of it, "I am not what I am" once in the speech of his villain, Iago, and again (in a slightly altered version) in the speech of another villain, Don John. And it is used comically by Viola in *Twelfth Night*.

The paradox was that throughout Oxford's life, he knew that his writing would be read by a great many people, possibly for hundreds of years into the future, and that practically no one reading his words would ever know who he was. Thus he was seldom motivated to write in order to please, impress or persuade, or in order to win fame and fortune. In the end, his only reason for writing was to satisfy his own profound need for self-expression.

This put him in the odd position of writing essentially to himself, while at the same time to all of humanity. So it is not surprising that he should lift his self-definition from the mouth of God, for he came as close as any writer ever has to the position of God as he communicated his thoughts, images and experiences.

There were a number of different kinds of influences in his writing. On the one hand, he had read very widely and was inspired by the greatest of all the writers who preceded him. He sought to be universal.

On the other hand, he sought to escape the peculiar kind of isolation he felt as a misfit at the pinnacle of society. This is the kind of isolation many in his noble position felt. Such people tend to believe that a great deal is expected of them, but they don't know what it is, because they have no specific role definition or apparent purpose in life.

Why America's Children Can't Think

Lord Oxford was a failure as a soldier and as a politician, the only two jobs his position in life qualified him for. As a nobleman, he could not seriously pursue any other sort of career—including writing. So, in an odd way, he had nothing going for him—his world was totally unsatisfactory. Because he had nothing to do, he was left to contemplate the unsatisfactoriness of the world he knew—or to create a new one.

An Author ahead of His Time

One of the typical attitudes of Elizabethans was an astonishing lack of respect for the simple things in life combined with the simple beauties of existence. Too much was hyperbolic, excessively ornate, fawningly hypocritical, and geared toward world domination. Life was chaotic, unpredictable, dangerous and too often thoughtless. It was also cheap—so cheap that while there was an ever-present obsession with death (memento mori), there was also an ease and familiarity with it. It was ubiquitous, and too often appeared in its most terrifying and painful guises.

Many have said that it was Shakespeare who taught us how to feel about life, and to identify many of the values that are important today. "Shakespeare" was an animal rights activist and an ecologist four hundred years before his time. He represented women with a deep respect for their intelligence and an awesome awareness of their point of view. An aristocrat in training, by birth and by nature, he often implied (but could not openly argue for) the values of a rational society, ruled by consent and social contract.

This was perhaps easier for him to imagine than it would have been for a commoner, because people in his class were used to being consulted in affairs of state, and their opinions had to be taken into account by the ruling powers in much the same way as elected officials today must consider the desires of their constituents. One might say, in fact, that life at the top was highly democratic, and if you were a member of the social elite, it would scarcely occur to you what life would be like for those who weren't in your social sphere.

There is barely a moment in any of his plays when the characters do not react to the situation with total believability, and from the heart of their characters. They routinely say things so well that no one since has been able to say them better. In *Bartlett's Familiar Quotations*, Shakespeare is cited twice as often as the Bible.

I believe Oxford's vision and creativity were honed by his isolation at the top level of his society. His confrontation with a world that could offer him no meaningful rewards, either because he had already been born with them or because they were forever beyond his reach, was obviously painful. The only thing he could do was explore every possible aspect of his own character—projected onto the characters that he wrote about—and every possible feeling he had ever had. As such, he became a microcosm of humanity. Since this was the only way for him to make life meaningful, he pursued this outlet for his emotions with an unequalled intensity and integrity of expression.

The character of the Stratfordian Shakespeare, as he has come down to us through the ages, is almost exactly the opposite of the character of the author. Having no one to please except himself, and finding himself impossible to please, Lord Oxford struggled throughout the second half of his life to find the most perfect expression of every possible feeling that his fertile imagination and gift for the invention of words and expressions could come up with.

The Final Plea

The summation of Oxford's anguish and his message to the world is hinted at in Hamlet's farewell:

Report me and my cause aright
To the unsatisfied . . .
Oh God, Horatio, what a wounded name,
Things standing thus unknown, shall I leave behind me!
If thou didst ever hold me in thy heart,
Absent thee from felicity a while,
And in this harsh world draw thy breath in pain
To tell my story.

And what is Hamlet's story? It is about the consequences of being trapped at the very pinnacle of power by a world gone astray at the hands of those whose words conceal their thoughts, and whose minds cannot guess the depths of life's potential meaning. It is the combined story of everything the collected works have to tell us, for all of it is implied in the autobiographical characterization of Hamlet.

In real life, it was a veiled plea from Lord Oxford to his favorite cousin, Captain Horatio Vere, that he might make his name known as the author of all that he had created—a plea destined to remain unsatisfied until our own time.

In the gross and scope of all that he had to say, he defined the notion of personal integrity—a notion foreign to his father-in-law, from whom he must first have heard these words falsely uttered:

To thine own self be true.
For it must follow, as the night the day,
Thou canst not then be false to any man.

We live life not so that we can achieve glory or acquire great fortune. We live it simply and solely so that we can experience the feelings that will define for us what life is. Neither glory nor wealth is of any value if it doesn't provide an *experience* of value. In contrast, a life that acquires nothing may be of the most tremendous worth if, at the end of it, we have explored with integrity the possibilities of feeling.

Thinking Makes It So

A Gandhi or a Mother Teresa does not shy away from the tragedies of life, but faces them squarely and head on. Such a person is guided, moment by moment, by an inner sense of what is right, and that is more important than life itself. Such a person is always aware of being surrounded by what is *not* right and can see the full range of human character, in all its possibilities of both ugliness and beauty. Such a person seeks to enhance the

320

beauty and leave behind the ugliness.

When you come to the end of the bloodbath that climaxes a Shakespearean tragedy, you are not depressed, but uplifted. That's because the author has given you eyes and ears to see and hear what such a person might be predisposed to see and hear. He has shown you experientially why there's "nothing good or bad but thinking makes it so." The author has shown what it takes to get to the heart of feeling: the moment-by-moment response to the precise qualities of experience that enable a soul to fully comprehend and respond to earth-shattering dramatic events.

I believe "Shakespeare's" underlying sense of the meaning of life can be found in the ambiguities that fill the plays, which resemble the way nature presents us with ambiguities that run as deep as the core of the universe.

At virtually every moment in every Shakespearean work, someone asks, "Is this moment of my experience a reality or an illusion?" This question literally permeates the *Complete Works*, impacting virtually every line in every play or poem—not excluding the more recently discovered works.

Just to prove this point, I have opened my *Shakespeare* at random and selected this line from *Troilus and Cressida*:

BOY: Sir, my lord would instantly speak with you.

This is the messenger from Troilus speaking to Pandarus. Literally, the line means that Troilus wants Pandarus to come to him right away so he can tell him something. Since we never witness the conversation that presumably follows, we don't find out what Troilus wants to say to Pandarus, so the line only serves to get Pandarus offstage so that Troilus's lover, Cressida, can deliver a soliloquy. Therefore, this is as unpromising a line as I could have chosen to make my point. In fact, it is even a flaw in the playwriting, since it leads nowhere in the developing action.

And yet, based on what we know of the characters, it contains a humorous irony of character. Pandarus is very similar to Polonius in *Hamlet*, and like him is based on the character of Lord Oxford's father-in-law, Lord Burghley. He is a busybody who frequently uses more words than he needs to make his point.

The boy might have said only, "Sir, my lord would speak with you." But "instantly," if properly acted, is good for a laugh. Thus the boy might have delivered the line: "Sir, my lord would—*instantly*—speak with you." With the right inflection, this would draw attention to the fact that speaking with Pandarus "instantly" about anything would be almost impossible, since Pandarus interrupts, drones on and on, and throws in so many irrelevant comments that it is almost impossible to say anything to him in a short time. One way to stage it would be to have Pandarus move as if to speak after the word "would" and to have the boy raise his voice on "instantly," as if to cut him off. In that case, the audience would see Pandarus's pomposity as revealed through the eyes of a humble messenger. And, as nearly always happens in Shakespearean plays, the two characters are engaged in different perceptions of reality, each regarding the other's reality as an illusion.

Try it yourself. Flip through a Shakespeare play and see how every scene exemplifies this perceptual dichotomy.

We have seen that a throwaway line given to a messenger has the potential to develop and draw attention to character. It accomplishes this by the addition of a single word. In performance, it can be delivered to call attention to a fundamental irony about the character to whom it is addressed.

This constant probing of the secrets that lie hidden in ambiguity is essential to discovering a meaning that must always remain secret. At any given moment, the observer, and only the observer, defines what is being observed.

That is the revelation of quantum physics, first revealed more than four centuries ago by the man who until now has been known as William Shakespeare.

23

Constructing a
Worldview

Since no one else is in charge of the world,
why not us?

The German word for worldview is *zeitgeist*. It sounds a good deal more respectable termed that way, since in this age of specialization most people aren't expected to have worldviews, while this foreign expression with its philosophical and literary heritage is time-honored enough to pass muster.

In chapters 19 and 20, I discussed the issue of finding the inner voice that expresses in each of us what is most characteristic of our view of our experiences. This does not necessarily, however, lead directly to any particular worldview, because it is primarily a reactive way of approaching a discussion. It is a series of direct responses to whatever happens to come along. A worldview cannot be constructed this way. It results only from bringing oneself into contact with the worldviews of others, taken as a whole, much as I have demonstrated for the subject of Shakespeare in the previous chapter.

This means paying close attention to major works of literature, philosophy, science and history, works that provide coherent expressions of what the world is and how it operates. The job of absorbing any particular worldview involves putting yourself very deeply in contact with the mind of someone else, being all the while aware that what you are doing is like a conversation or, better yet, a serious dialogue. As you grow in understanding of what the other person has, over a lifetime, decided is true, you form your own opinion about that person's success in describing the world. Few of us today would be tempted to see the world exactly as Shakespeare saw it. But by following through the web of paradoxes that underlie a work of art as profound as *Macbeth* or *Hamlet*, we can put ourselves in a position to begin asking questions about it. One such question might be, To what extent does the world as I see it match what I seem to be looking at through Shakespeare's eyes in this particular work? If you've never given a whole lot of attention to anything except *Macbeth*, for example, that particular work may convince you, at least for a while, that it is a true picture of the world. Though of course you'll be looking at it selectively through your own philosophical filters.

I remember, incidentally, a discussion about *Macbeth* during which I heard a retired army officer say that he thought it was a study of the military mind. In my superior way, armed with mountains of Shakespearean scholarship, I quietly noted to myself, "This guy is completely out of it." I had to live a few decades in order to discover that, in his perspective of the world, he was quite correct.

If you continue the process of comparing your developing worldview with those of outstanding individuals who have devoted tremendous energy to the construction of theirs, you will find that your worldview begins to take on a quality of its own. It will be a quality that cannot be fully explained by reference to all the influences that have brought it about.

Toward a Well-Integrated Philosophy

There is no reason why every thoughtful person should not have an opportunity to develop a worldview that is complete and coherent and is not submissive in an abjectly obeisant way to the "superior" worldviews of others. Your experience is your own. It is unique, and no one else has had the opportunity to have it. Therefore you have a right to formulate it and put it forward. You do not, however, do yourself any favors by lying about it (even to yourself), or trying to maintain it uncritically in the face of reasonable opposition that finds fault with its consistency. Rather, the opposition, if doing its job correctly, should point out flaws that you can correct so as to strengthen your point of view even further. We need a great many more people who have well-formed worldviews and can argue them with integrity if we are ever to straighten out the mess that the world is presently in. It takes an enormous vacuum of informed opinion to allow bad ideas to carry the electorate and continue to move civilization away from its highest achievement and in the direction of further ignorance. A thinking society would not behave that way.

One of those who, in relatively recent times, developed and articulated his worldview rather consistently over a lifetime was George Bernard Shaw. Few writers have been as explicit about their beliefs as he was. From Marx and Engels, he absorbed socialism. From Nietzsche and Wagner, he absorbed the idea of the Superman, the intellectually superior individual who carries society forward toward some higher level of development. From Schopenhauer and Larmarck, he absorbed the idea of a Life Force that struggles to direct all of life toward a higher potential. From Ibsen, he absorbed the idea that a playwright may point out social flaws and be a force that leads in the direction of a more perfect society.

He seldom strayed from these central ideas, which gave shape and intellectual power both to his plays and the prefaces of philosophical speculation that the plays allowed him to write. He never held back his perceptions of anything. As a critic of music and theater he usually revealed himself more than the performance he was reviewing.

You are struck, when reading almost anything by Shaw, that you are in the presence of a distinctly literate mind that is always on the verge of an ironic chuckle about even the most serious of subjects. The clarity and articulateness of his worldview, whether or not you agree with any of it, lures you into wanting to agree and going with him wherever he chooses to take you.

Shaw began life as a reclusive, ultra-shy person who gradually came out of his shell to speak with authority about almost everything. Earlier I intimated that his reaction to his schooling made a great deal of sense and may have protected him from the kind of wishy-washiness one tends to develop if one tries too hard to please or at least appease others at the expense of one's own perceptions.

If you can read with a mind that is at once receptive and skeptical, you should find eventually that the exercise of bumping heads with everyone you read leads you to take a position on any subject without being inflexible. A good way to develop this skill is to decide what you think is right and hold to it as long as you can, while being honest about relinquishing any position that does not stand up under careful examination.

As a good reader, you become, in a sense, the author's thoughts. It's like trying on another person's brain in order to see what it feels like to think and believe in a certain way and know certain things. Then when you step out of that other brain and return to your own, you find you have taken some of it with you. A bit of the way of thinking and means of articulation in what you have read will have rubbed off on you.

You can't know everything, and you can't be right all the time. You'll get farther, though, if you behave as if you could, while never forgetting that you can't.

The important thing is to take the uniqueness of your experience and make the most of it. Redefine what you have learned about life by continuously examining it through the eyes of those whose works you read. But keep the whole structure of your view intact as you do so, asserting it strongly from the latest point you have developed in your perspective.

If you do this well, the world will always seem whole and complete to you. In the words of the late Victorian poet Matthew Arnold, you'll be able to "see life steadily and see it whole."

Whenever we look at anything, we see it through the prism of our entire life experience so far. Learn to speak what you see as fully and accurately as possible whenever you feel moved to express yourself. Then frequently, throughout your life, read some new work of great power and allow it to enhance what you can see. The world will grow bigger and more detailed for you, but it will still seem complete, just as it did before.

Shaw had perhaps half a dozen ideas that he returned to repeatedly in his writing. These major ideas, the mental models that meant the most to him, were elaborated with many offshoots, or sub-ideas, that made it possible for him to write an enormous amount about each of them without repeating himself.

You can have a similar experience if you decide what ideas are most important to you, and read in order to elaborate and subdivide them so you continue to enrich your worldview constantly throughout your life. Looking at your experiences through a well-constructed prism fashioned from your own worldview will fulfill the purposes of your unique brain, which is the only one that will ever be able to look at things and know them from the particular perspective that only you can know them.

There is no one who can say precisely and in all cases how an individual should behave. Therefore that individual must, in the end, decide for himself or herself. The only way to decide one's behavior is to develop the habit of mind that seeks to create truth out of the marriage between whatever wisdom one can acquire from others and the conclusions drawn from one's own experience. If we proceed through life this way, we will not fall short in solving practical problems. We will be able to achieve our goals, make all the money we need, and provide for our families. But we will meet our larger responsibilities by being good citizens of our communities, our countries and the earth. We will not stand aside and look away in the presence of injustice. We will not blindly seek gratification when that is inappropriate. We will habitually consider the nature of experience, create some new truth from our perceptions of it, and proceed accordingly. Only if all of us proceed in this way can we have an informed citizenry and an effectively democratic society.

Democracy may be the least efficient form of government, but it is also the only acceptable one. This means that all of us are stuck with the obligation and necessity of thinking for ourselves. Therefore we should make our schools centers for acquiring the tools for doing so as effectively as possible. This is much more important than acquiring any particular body of knowledge, though it cannot be accomplished at all without acquiring a great deal of knowledge.

The world's knowledge is forever changing and is widely accessible, but the quality of an original mind must be sought rather a long time before it is found. Everything depends, therefore, on how, from the beginning, we teach children to read so that they can easily recognize all the words they will see and know how to reflect productively and in thoughtful conversation with others about everything they mean.

Afterword

How do the ideas in this book fit into the
perspective of larger educational issues?

I

My editor asked me to include in the Preface some commentary on the history of education, traditional and otherwise, mostly in the twentieth century. "Even though this book is not an essay on the history of educational reform," he advised, "you should be clear on where you perceive it stands in relation to past thinkers, and why we need a new direction."

A worthy idea, for while the book I set out to write was about reading, it was not necessarily a commentary on contemporary education, but rather a guide for the enrichment of individual reading experiences and how this might be learned in educational settings. Nevertheless, I believe such a commentary provides good grounding for the book, because if we all knew how to read well, most of the current crisis in education would simply disappear, since good readers are quite capable of educating and thinking for themselves.

Additional comments about the current educational crisis seem to stray somewhat from the main theme of this book, and while I touched on this issue throughout the text, I have decided to handle my good editor's suggestion mostly in this Afterword. I have also decided that my next few books will consider the history of health, education and welfare, and what this history has wrought, both good and bad, for our contemporary culture. Specifically, I shall take up the issue that as many as ten trillion taxpayer and consumer dollars may have been wasted as a result of ignoring solutions to these three public concerns, which have existed, in some cases, for well over half a century. So serious is this problem that our next presidential election may well be decided on this issue. Therefore, you might consider this Afterword a preview of coming attractions.[1]

I wholeheartedly believe that it is possible to cultivate excellence in all of the skills educated people need, and not leave anyone behind. There is no reason for any member of our society to be academically impotent, uncreative, unmotivated, unachieving or insensitive to the needs of others, all qualities essential for citizens of a healthy, safe and prosperous society. A complete education that nourishes the multitude of human intelligences would cultivate these qualities across the board in everyone.

Unfortunately, at present, that is very far from the case. In spite of the wealth of information immediately available that would enable educational systems to attain these goals, the bizarre and inexplicable inability of many administrators to recognize the value of these ideas is impoverishing too many students and exhausting too many qualified teachers.

To remedy this, educators must identify any problems within their schools and recognize that faults or flaws can be repaired by some relatively easy and remarkable fixes. I know this is possible because I have built my career on it.

The problem is that, even today, practically no one is looking for solutions. Among professional educators, there seems to be little desire to put the needs of students first on their list of priorities. Instead, the political intrigue of the workplace causes most professionals to be more concerned with their retirement funds and fearful of suggesting any improvements to their schools, lest it cost them their jobs. This is unfortunate, since good teachers are far more essential to the development and maintenance of a viable society than are lawyers or corporate CEOs. Teachers should be nurtured while they do their important work, but as everyone knows, this is very far from the case.

The most important reason that schools don't work well is essentially the same reason the health care system in our country has fallen into serious trouble. In a penetrating essay, Michael Porter, the great expert on the worldwide competitive forces at work in a capitalistic economy, points out that health care has ceased to work efficiently because of the third-party intervention of HMOs and insurance companies. Corporations have taken over paying medical bills and have thus removed patients from the one-on-one quality control practiced by doctors that completes the circuit of their transactions. Corporations far more concerned with healthy profits than healthy patients corrupt the delivery of a doctor's services. One example of this phenomenon is that prescribed medicines or therapies are denied and countermanded by third parties as either unnecessary or cost prohibitive. The myriad adjustments in quality, customer satisfaction and cost reduction that businesses must make when directly appealing to, attracting and retaining customers do not happen under such a system, and most assuredly, they don't happen in the field of education either.

Consider for a moment that in our culture, we are constantly tempted by the delights of shopping. We are able to choose from thousands of colorful and useful options, and most stores and on-line businesses cater to us at every point in the purchasing process, fawning over us to get us to buy something. This kind of range in what is offered, and sensitivity to the needs and desires of who it is offered to, is almost completely lacking in the field of education. The opportunity to learn something is seldom presented to students as either appealing or useful, nor do they have the opportunity to exercise buying power in learning to make wise life choices. Instead, schools toss out dusty, shoddy and outdated merchandise that seems unpalatable and useless to most students, since it is not presented in step and in context with their present-day or future realities. This merchandise may be dressed up in expensive and glitzy packages that line the pockets of publishers, but it is shoddy and out-of-date nonetheless.

Compare this experience with the saying that "the customer is always right" and think of the average eighth grader in an American public school. She (or he) is assumed, by most educators, to be quite a bit lower than the angels and not entirely distinguishable from a wild animal. She is required to endure a typical school day that no thoughtful adult, however resilient, could stand for more than a couple of hours at the outside. At a time when the whole point of life is to discover her identity, the student is asked to sit down, shut up, ignore personal threats to her safety, walk through a metal detector, pay attention, and do asinine assignments that appear completely irrelevant, even to most of the teachers. No wonder the natural rebellion sparked by gonadal changes quickly causes teens to succumb to the allure of drugs, alcohol, sex and violence. And no wonder that the passivity induced by flashy television programs has so revised the structure of many brains that they cannot understand the simplest cause-and-effect relationships. Meanwhile, flirting with danger and testing limits are what adolescents need to do in an uncertain world. They don't like squirming in uncomfortable chairs, listening to teachers complain redundantly about their collective unruliness.

During my nearly half-century career as an educator, I taught hundreds of adolescents and know that when you get them involved with issues that are important to them, they behave with wisdom and maturity. But the process of arousing their interest in a project by connecting it with the thoughts and experiences that are natural to them requires sensitivity to their perspective on life. You can read more about this in the Appendix, where I demonstrate, through a sample of an interaction with a single student, how successful learning can be keyed to specific intellectual needs as well as passions.

As the quote by George Bernard Shaw in chapter 12 illustrates, there is no learning without passion. I have found that principle to hold true for everyone, perhaps because it is endemic in nature. When we heed the passion that most enlivens a student (especially the passionate struggle of the ego for survival in an ever-changing social environment), we can help her (or him) develop contextual extensions of her individual world picture in a holographic context. This then motivates her to probe more deeply into ever-widening areas of knowledge and skill development, much in the way an amoeba incorporates into its body those things it encounters that will enhance its growth.

All true learning is language learning, in that all subjects share unique vocabularies, grammar and syntax, and emotional, logical and persuasive qualities. Therefore, all subjects can be learned the way language is learned by infants and young children—as a means of self-expression and exploration. To learn a subject and attain full mastery and personal ownership of it, one must walk around in it, taste it, touch it, laugh about it, cry about it, and do all the things little children do when they are exploring the unfamiliar world into which they were born. This provides the spontaneous structure of self-organization that is part and parcel of learning. It is both imperative and paramount because it naturally arises from the operation of the human brain, the primary organ of learning.

Horrifyingly, the same people who understand that the heart pumps blood and that lungs process oxygen fail to understand that the brain and the central nervous system process our senses, and that learning is meant to titillate and stimulate neuronal growth, thus enhancing human performance.[2]

If the body houses the mind, it is important to remember that the mind also houses the body. The holographic structure of DNA that embeds the same information in every cell of the body is a metaphor for how learning affects civilization. In other words, as I pointed out in chapter 3, it is important for everyone to internalize maps of knowledge and navigate them well in order for each person to manage some small part of the mechanism of our rapidly changing society. Traditional education does not satisfy the need for building this kind of societal- and self-preservation when it considers some students winners and others losers, some excellent and others essentially worthless. Throwing away potentially productive minds will do nothing to heal the problems of our troubled planet.

It was almost by accident that I discovered how crucial a role teachers play in meeting this need. In 1958, when I first began teaching in a private high school and served as chairman of the English department, I had never had an education course. With a few remarkable but brief exceptions, I felt that nothing any teacher had done for me had worked very well. Consequently, I had little idea of what to do, although I had many ideas about what *not* to do.

Given that there was no one else available to instruct me, I turned to my students for guidance. As a result of doing so, I developed an intense personal radar to hone in on their reactions and determine whether a particular lesson took flight like a rocket or crashed to the ground like a spent cannonball. I quickly discovered that my students made no secret of their boredom or their excitement. Like a salesman hawking my goods, I decided to aim for excitement and simulate the effort of a business luring the attention of customers to get them to buy my intellectual wares so as to ensure their satisfaction and continued patronage. I knew that there were other influences competing for their intellectual wallets. Before long, I heard that many of my students spent four or five hours a night on assigned homework, not because it was difficult, but because they were fascinated by it and couldn't bring themselves to stop working at it any sooner than that. People who are involved in trying to complete a creative task, or solve an intellectual problem that really has them in its grip, hate to be parted from the process before it is completed. They never cheated, if only because they couldn't. Each assignment was based on their own personal relationships to each subject. One girl confessed that she studied in the basement next to a loud radio so that her parents wouldn't discover that she was actually doing schoolwork and start to expect too much from her.

In my career, I've noticed that most teachers feel too well prepared when they enter the classroom. Consequently, their overconfidence leads them to *think* they know what their students will say or do. It doesn't occur to them to ask for feedback, since their students don't have a master's or a Ph.D. in education that certifies that they know anything about learning. This is a grievous mistake.

We all come into the world without instruction manuals. Therefore, as infants, our daily tasks require us to solve problems continually. We spend approximately the first five years of life as our own full-time curriculum developers, designing and carrying out our learning projects, hopefully to the applause of delighted parents, grandparents and others. But then, small and somewhat intimidated, we go to school and are confronted by tall professionals, strangers who supposedly know more about us than we do. We are made to stop doing all the things that were so effective at teaching us the finer points of language learning, relationship building, and operating the complex machinery that causes our bodies to move about in the world.

Instead we sit still and batten down our insides with our learning, held hostage to the pace set by others, while we expectantly wait for something fascinating to happen. For many of us, it never does. This may, at one time, have been a fruitful way to condition factory workers to survive a lifetime of boredom, but it isn't useful anymore. About 1965, after something like ten thousand years of technological development, there were enough machines in the world to assume the tasks of slavery previously assigned to a majority of the world's population. As a result, boring, repetitious jobs requiring automatons, not minds, began to shrink in number.

Meanwhile, in the last half century, even though there has been a great deal of research on how learning works in the brain, little of it has been applied in actual classroom use and only sporadically in a few isolated settings. The pedagogical results of that research are desperately needed now because as the listless, slave-like behavior formerly required from factory workers disappears, it is being replaced at an ever more rapid rate by challenges in dealing with technology that require a highly intelligent degree of variable responsiveness. The lowest level jobs that were formerly available in the United States are being exported to third world countries. Therefore we now need a new kind of education, designed to provide us with well-developed technological, social and economic skills. We needed it yesterday.

Fortunately yesterday's failures can be healed today as adult education repairs the massive amounts of damage done to much of the population by the educational and social failure of the previous generation. It is therefore not true, as so many have despaired, that "we need to give up on a whole generation."

Nevertheless the current failures of schools continue to be an enormous tragedy because the uncertainties of life are proliferating so rapidly around us that most young adults are unprepared for the world in which they must live. The profound acceleration of change necessitates an entirely new educational system, which does not strap children down and force them to avoid the management of their own thinking, relegating them as adults to the trash heap of unemployment in the wake of economic downturns and corporate downsizing. Despite the hyperactive, dyslexic future today's young people have to deal with, our children are still taught as if our culture were mired in the industrial revolution.

No mammal on Earth fails to teach its children basic survival skills. But I believe that if twentieth-century American schools were given a report card for fostering learning skills in our nation's children, they would flunk as miserably as their poorest students. No amount of "extra credit" on the part of our society can redeem our children or reprieve their futures unless efforts are made now to incorporate brain-compatible learning into our schools. For just as modern medicine thrives on a wealth of detailed biological information, so modern education should be exploring an equally rich lode of neurological information.

To encourage learning, the classroom at every stage of educational development—all the way from preschool to graduate school—must become a playroom. Geniuses have long been recognized as having child-like minds that play with ideas and technologies and make connections among what, at first glance, appear to be random thoughts, structures and relationships. Genius itself is thought to be random, the result of a healthy dip in the gene pool. But contrary to popular belief, genius can and is nurtured through play, whether it is in a high school physics class, a production of *Hamlet* or a philosophy seminar.[3] While most educators are afraid of toying with ideas and are stuck in textbooks, lectures and drills, the better part of learning is beyond the fringe of rote routines.

I didn't fully understand this concept of infantilization until I encountered it in the work of Bulgarian researcher Georgi Lozanov in 1972. Lozanov was able to teach adults to become independent in a foreign language in twelve weeks, with three hours of instruction per day and no homework. His classes were so much fun that his students were convinced they weren't learning anything, until they found themselves mysteriously to have acquired independence in the language they had studied. By carefully observing how children learn language in the nursery, Lozanov was able to build the same processes into adult learning, thereby exploding the myth that we become less teachable as we grow older.

I ran into this same phenomenon on a trip to Cambridge, Massachusetts, in 1965. There, I talked to William J. J. Gordon about his work in Synectics, a process being used in industry to speed up the rate of creative inventiveness, so that industrial problems that usually took six months to a year to solve could be overcome in only a few hours. Also, Clark Apt of Apt Associates told me about how his company was using "serious games" to teach important concepts. The common element in both of these programs was intellectual play.

This excitement about toying with ideas didn't seem to appeal to most educators, however. Isn't it true, I asked some of our nation's leading professionals, that the developmental processes of early childhood can be maintained throughout life, so that with the right kinds of very subtle stimulation, the mind can learn to become engaged in continuous improvement that doesn't just add knowledge, but adds new tools for processing thought? Researchers like Jerome Kagan told me that this could not be true—at least not in the way I imagined it. Others, like T. G. R. Bower, seemed fascinated with the possibility, but couldn't tell me where to find research to support the idea. Still, after that trip, I became convinced it was possible to create schools many times more effective than anything seen before, simply by allowing students to play with ideas in carefully designed and highly structured ways.

Looking back on this seminal journey from the perspective of several decades, I've become convinced that the most virulent myths in education are the notion of a fixed, inherited IQ, and that genius is some sort of genetic mutation. What irks me the most is that the "Shakespeare" myth described in chapter 22 is the most likely source of the idea that genius is not, and cannot be, a product of good teaching and learning. I believe more passionately than I believe anything else that genius can be taught to anyone, but that the transformation of the tools of teaching required to accomplish this is as great as the difference between the Bronze Age and the atomic age.

II

Over the years, I have thought about the work of many of the educational reformers of the twentieth century. I believe that most of the benefits of their work came from the assumption of the distinction between children and adults that impacted how elementary school was taught, which may have started with Froebel's invention of the Kindergarten back in the eighteenth century. A number of subsequent researchers established the great importance of play in human development, some of them arguing that it should be extended to adulthood. Meanwhile, Swiss psychologist Jean Piaget noted developmental stages in the evolution of thinking skills, so that early instruction became better suited than ever before to the needs of young children. Prior to the work of these thinkers, children had generally been seen and treated as miniature adults, as they still are in some parts of the world today.

But the evolution of this body of work is incomplete, since we have not yet recognized that the real challenge is to see adults as grown-up children, with similar emotional and psychological needs. All the elements of play that were important in childhood continue to be important in adulthood, and for the same reasons. Only when we are playing, laughing, singing and generally "carrying on" can we relax our perceptual barriers and become sensitive to important new truths previously unknown and undiscovered. Our culture is entirely too grimly serious about being adult, as it once was about being a child.

I have consistently found, when working with adults, that introducing elements of play activity into the classroom—whether physics, telecommunications or calculus—makes it possible to speed up the learning to a degree that must be experienced to be believed.

Since we do not "grow out" of childhood, we can enhance its influence by toying with ideas that heighten the imagination and stimulate learning.

It has been apparent in my work with corporations and other "adult" organizations that the culture of high school has simply been transferred to them. All the oppressive neglect of creativity in the resulting corporate culture has wrought a superficial ineptitude that is completely unnecessary, and one of the main reasons that Murphy's Law applies so widely.

This fundamental misunderstanding of how human beings mature is compounded by insensitivity to the subtleties that have recently been discovered in the functioning of human nature that when properly developed, lead to genius, and when underdeveloped, lead to incompetent and frustrating behavior.

This is why I think that John Holt, A. S. Neill and the many others who created the educational revolution in the 1960s were only scratching the surface when it came to the role of play in education and how teachers should interact with students to achieve positive learning goals. Throughout the century, the debate over education as a means of producing the responsible citizenry needed to make democracy work waxed and waned. The question of whether or not all students could be brought to the level of achievement defined by the elitist educational standards of the Ivy League was widely debated. In recent years these arguments have been reinvoked by many passionate critics, longing for a return to the good old days of a recognized body of knowledge, who have argued from a doom-and-gloom perspective that educational standards are far too low and are damaging the great tradition of Western thought.

Meanwhile, there were mainstream attempts to change things, like the progressive movement promulgated by John Dewey, followed much later by Jonathan Kozol's sledgehammer books that validly condemn inner-city schools as de facto prisons. On the sidelines, there have been many reformers like Rudolf Steiner, Maria Montessori, Kurt Hahn and A. S. Neill who have never been mainstreamed. Their awareness that all children learn differently provided a chorus of voices crying in the wilderness.

Then there were those who wanted us to be concerned with higher standards in education, which meant to them that we should read the great works of literature and be up on the so-called body of knowledge. Their contributions are significant and valuable, but also somewhat one-sided. Mortimer Adler's *Syntopicon*, designed to accompany his *Great Books of the Western World*, provided a valuable educational tool, which has been almost completely ignored. Allan Bloom berated us in *The Closing of the American Mind* about how the universities departed, in the 1960s, from their presumed commitment to teach the essentials of Western intellectual thought.[4] Certainly a nodding acquaintance with most of that material is essential to understanding how we got where we are. There should be no doubt that it needs to be part of the shared intellectual background on which the evaluation of our next step into the future should be founded. Still, that's only part of what needs to be learned, because such knowledge, by itself, doesn't really help manage information that is proliferating at warp speed.

A much more believable critic, because he came from a recognized level of acknowledged success within the system, was John Gatto. Twice recognized as Teacher of the Year, once for New York City and the second time for New York State, Gatto hurled what is probably the most effective invective against the public school system that any writer has ever penned. His collection of essays, *Dumbing Us Down*, should be carefully studied and pondered by every thinking person, for it gets at the heart of the socio-logical price we pay for the herd mentality we are developing in today's educational system.[5]

On a more positive note, there's an impulse to cheer for the Children's Aid Society and the Coalition for Community Schools, who, in recent years of partnership, have done much impressive work to improve the milieu of selected public schools. Their work focuses on building a community infra-structure to provide the school itself with much-needed social, sociological and psychological support, so that students will be better able to deal with what they learn in school. They also promote programs like cooperative learning and theme-based learning, which, properly handled, can produce very good results. A closer look at their "best programs," however, usually invites the kind of critical analysis Diane McGuinness brings to many of the innovative early reading programs, whose results often fall far short of what is possible, needed and to be hoped for.

Still, this kind of community effort, paired with a really aggressive pro-motion of truly brain-compatible learning might, in the long run, solve a great many learning problems nationwide.[6]

Taken overall, though, whatever the educational reformers of the twen-tieth century did or did not accomplish, very little of their work became standardized, perhaps because it was not supported by the kind of scientif-ic experimentation and research that might have given it real clout instead of mere idealism. As a result, we are now in the middle of an ongoing edu-cational crisis that remains stolidly impregnable, impervious to the many billions of dollars that are poured down the drain in misguided attempts to fix it. We should by now have learned from experience that we can't just throw money at a problem, we have to throw tested ideas at it as well, and we also have to have the means of helping the institutions we're trying to change get the results they want. There are few, if any, examples in the history of bureaucracy where this approach has worked very well. So it may be that the solutions will have to come from the private sector, which they will do only when a very strong market is established for the tools to build high-quality educational experiences.

Meanwhile, the folly of current educational thought has one foot in virulent anti-intellectualism and the other in nineteenth-century ideas about what constitutes a liberal education. This latter is ossified in the Harvard traditions that give rise to the quip "You can always tell a Harvard man, but you can't tell him much."

Because of particular assumptions and attitudes that remove abstractions from their various contextual associations, the spirit of Harvard University can still be described fairly accurately with the words used by Henry Adams in 1858:

> Free from meannesses, jealousies, intrigues, enthusiasms, and passions, not exceptionally quick; not consciously skeptical; singularly indifferent to display, artifice, florid expression, but not hostile to it when it amused them; distrustful of themselves, but little disposed to trust anyone else; with not much humor of their own, but full of readiness to enjoy the humor of others; negative to a degree that in the long run became positive and triumphant. Not harsh in manners or judgment, rather liberal and open-minded, they were still as a body the most formidable critics one would care to meet in a long life exposed to criticism.

Most people would class a great intellectual icon like Alfred North Whitehead as somehow firmly in the Harvard camp of elitism in thinking, but the two are actually poles apart. Whitehead believed there was no value in learning anything that could not be meaningfully applied or related to something else. Harvard, on the other hand, upheld that learning has value purely for its own sake and is corrupted by demands for relevance or practical application. That's the kind of ivory tower prejudice that has caused education endless problems. It probably began with Aristotle, who made it seem that elitists engaged in learning for its own sake, whereas slaves and plebeians had to deal with practical things beneath the dignity of the elite. This prejudice is still alive and well today.

An interdependent global civilization can't afford such intellectual compartmentalization. The free play of the intellect is absolutely essential to the acceptance of revolutionary new concepts, but so is the search for practical application.

Our stagnation as a society comes from reacting and not *pro*acting to the needs of our schools. We're not rejecting what doesn't work so that we can replace it with what does. For example, programs for teaching even the least interested sixth grader to enjoy learning calculus are available, at least in theory. Morris Kline, among many other mathematicians, has argued that today's teaching methods in math are centuries out-of-date. The result is that 94 percent of those who are taught to manipulate numbers retain little from their years in the classroom. We could easily accomplish great reforms if we weren't so determined to remain stuck with programs that don't work, rather than admit that our whole approach to status quo education is completely skewed. This lockstep behavior prevents us from achieving the kind of success that our students deserve and that our future demands.

If you want a compelling overview of twentieth-century education, you can't do much better than read Martin Mayer's *The Schools*.[7] Little of what Mayer said decades ago is out-of-date today, and that's the problem— almost everything that was wrong with education then is still wrong now. Things have only gotten worse.

Mayer points out that public schools were designed to do three things: to teach students to show up for work on time, follow instructions without questioning them, and avoid rocking the boat. In some work situations, these are essential tools that still must be rigorously taught to those who have not internalized a work ethic. It is true that without these skills, it's practically impossible to find or hold a job; but unfortunately, our times demand more. Today's economy is no longer the industrial or information age, but rather an "ethereal age," groping for new kinds of relationships. It is in jeopardy because so few people fully qualify for the most demanding and essential jobs in the present economy. The Internet has speeded up the development of virtually everything, and unless one can think simultaneously in terms of precise details, problem solving and global relationships, progress comes to a dead halt and forward motion backfires.

Education as we have it today has not greatly changed from what it was in the Middle Ages. Back then, those who had access to books were needed to tell those who didn't have access precisely what the books said, thus giving birth to the lecture method. Such droning should have died after Gutenburg's printing press made books accessible to everyone, thereby making literacy potentially universal, but it didn't.

When books are readily available, people need to be taught to read them and process their information and not be lectured to about what they say. For example, math teachers tend to *tell* students what they should discover, instead of encouraging them to solve their own problems—not exactly the best bang for the buck in terms of storing information in the long-term memory.

Still, an educational system in which teachers and students are cocreators of their curriculum wouldn't entirely solve the problem, unless learning differences were taken into consideration. Only when we address all of the different learning styles equally will all students be assured of success.

The best overall vision I have seen for a better educational system comes from Harvard economist David McClelland, in an essay originally published in the Fall 1961 issue of *Daedalus*. In it, McClelland laments the choice America has made to send "the best boys" to "the best schools" and feed intellectual pabulum to everyone else. Here are a few quotations from that article:

> The core of the problem lies in the definition of excellence implicit in our current nation-wide attempts to recognize and encourage talent. Ability means, for the purposes of these tests, academic excellence, skill in taking examinations, in following instructions and finding solutions to problems set by others. . . .

Why America's Children Can't Think

A single standard of success is being promoted, which, in Riesman's telling phrase, tends to homogenize our cultural value system. . . .

Ours is a male-oriented society. It is so male-oriented that the women, particularly the better educated ones, have felt unhappy about not being able to achieve great success in terms of such standards. . . .

The institution must avoid admitting students solely in terms of one type of excellence, namely, academic promise or performance. That is, if our new model provides for a variety of types of excellence encouraged in a variety of excellent ways, then one type of excellence must be prevented from becoming a monopoly and placing a strong restraint on "trade." Academic excellence has very nearly reached a monopoly position, despite the protests of admissions officers that they are still operating in terms of "other criteria." They are fighting a losing battle. The logic is inexorable. Students with the highest predicted grade-point averages are increasingly the ones admitted to any school or college.[8]

While this last comment indicates a situation far more inflexible than it has become in the intervening years, it remains true that academic excellence is assumed to be preferable to other forms of educational excellence, and is attainable by the very few. I believe that the balance McClelland advocates could become a mainstay of education in general, and would make academic excellence achievable by everyone at a level that exceeds the standards set for the best students today. This can be done, but it will require a major commitment from educators to bring it about. McClelland advocates that if we are to have an educational system that cultivates desirable traits, it will cultivate all of the following on an equal basis: academic excellence, achievement motivation, curiosity and humane qualities like "sensitivity to other human beings, compassion, richness and variety of imaginative life, or a lifelong concern for a particular scientific problem, whether one is paid to work on it or not."

He also considers the fact that such qualities can, in theory, be measured, though he is less sanguine about teaching them directly. I believe that
they can all be taught, though in most cases only by experiential processes
that allow people to discover them for themselves.

The virtue of McClelland's vision stems partly from the fact that he is
one of very few educators who have been able to show a continuum
between educational theory, practice and results in actual changes in behavior. His course in developing achievement motivation has been taught to
business leaders in third world villages with powerful economic consequences. In contrast, Douglas Heath measured, some years ago, the relationship between academic success in school and success in later life and
found that there was no connection at all. At about the same time, the
Coleman report found that the best predictor of academic success in the
long run was whether or not Dad read the *New York Times*. And the then
National Institute of Education (later to be the Department of Education)
did a study that showed that people who were identified as highly successful
in the world had in common only the fact that in their childhoods or youths
some individual had taken a strong personal interest in their educations.

By contrast, McClelland was able to show that economic booms and
busts could be correlated with the children's books that were popular at the
time the business leaders were young. If they read books like *The Little
Engine That Could,* which is filled with achievement-motivation imagery,
there was an economic boom. If, on the other hand, they read books like
Tootle, which preaches a self-imprisoning message of "stay on the tracks no
mater what," there was an economic bust.

This is an indirect route to specifying the kind of vision or mission that
a national educational system should have. It should believe in the possibility of high achievement for all, and strive to create classroom conditions
that make excellence the natural by-product of students' love for their
school experiences. It will take a great influx of new thinking and practice
to bring this about, however.

Thus while I have a great deal of admiration for most of those who pro-
voked the various educational reforms in the last 150 years, I do not regard

any of them as having contributed much of importance to the educational theory that is needed today. In fact, while I was living in Washington, D.C., in 1987, I made a trip to the library of the Department of Education to see what was in their card catalog. There, I looked up all my favorite authors on the subject of education and found fewer than 20 percent of them listed there.

So what are the reforms that are needed now?

To answer that question, start by reading *Building a Better Race*, by Wendy Kline, which addresses the basic measuring techniques and implied values underlying contemporary education and shows how they are based on assumptions all too closely related to what Hitler propounded in *Mein Kampf*. IQ tests, for example, were formulated as a means of selecting out the least intelligent women, who needed to be sterilized so they wouldn't clutter up the population with their offspring. And although Kline doesn't say this in her book, Hitler's most significant inspiration came from American psychologist Madison Grant, who believed there was a close correlation between income level and IQ This idea died out after 1929, when a lot of people who had been rich suddenly became poor without affecting their scores on IQ tests.

It is true that a large part of what we call intelligence is inherited. Any intelligence, however, can be developed to a high degree of sophistication if it is allowed to realize its own potential in a harmonized body-mind system together with a receptive environment. Hideo Suzuki's success in teaching randomly selected children to be concert violinists showed educators how it is possible to design courses of instruction that bring all people, regardless of their innate intelligence, to a level of skill, knowledge and creative insight that comes close to the best that humans have been able to demonstrate. Those who use a similar kind of insight to aim at such standards generally succeed, regardless of which intellectual or physical achievements they seek to inculcate in their students. The shame is that only the tiniest, most infinitesimal fraction of teachers even contemplate such a possibility, and fewer still are allowed to develop the tools that will successfully accomplish this mission.

This is, at least partly, because contemporary education has done nothing to free itself from the assumption that some people are better than others and that when children don't learn anything in school that's basically because they're either stupid or unmotivated. In other words, it's the teacher's responsibility to present a well-selected body of knowledge and the student's responsibility to learn it uncritically. Those who can't or won't are shunted into the backwaters of the economy, where they become the human detritus for the welfare system. Welfare itself is organized to be so unmotivating as to provide de facto evidence that we do need to clean up the human race, because everything about the system militates against being able to bring out the best in people.

In virtually unknown contrast to this myth of an inherent intellectual hierarchy, Israeli psychologist Reuven Feuerstein demonstrated that IQ is almost entirely malleable. He was able to increase the IQ of a young man from 50 to 150 by teaching perception skills that provided the basis for organizing ideas. And though his work is among the most important contributions ever made to our knowledge of human potential, it has been virtually ignored by the educational system at large, and has played no part in the incredibly expensive efforts that have been made to improve education—most of them completely unsuccessful.

Others besides Feuerstein should have been enshrined long ago in the educators' hall of fame. Add Georgi Lozanov, whom I mentioned earlier. Using Lozanov's principles, I was able to teach hundreds of public school teachers and corporate trainers how to achieve results consistent with Lozanov's claims in virtually every subject area with virtually all age groups and cultural backgrounds. The results had a profound effect on school achievement scores in Chicago, Kalamazoo and several districts in upstate New York. The New York State Department of Education validated the program I taught for use in elementary schools.

However, the most exciting work that will influence the future of education has yet to be applied in any consistent, scientific or thorough manner. This is the work of neurologists, cyberneticists, optometrists, audiologists and complexity experts that can be applied to the assimilation of knowledge to produce a revolution in teaching and learning that goes beyond the wildest imaginings of today's experts.

The human brain is a system that operates sometimes linearly, sometimes holographically, and sometimes through a complexity of neural networks. It is also a complex self-organizing system that over time can learn to achieve ever higher levels of complexity in any area that it contemplates.

Understanding how to integrate and use a combination of refined perceptual training, feedback loops, neural networks and various discoveries made by cyberneticists and information theorists provides great hope for the future. This is not to turn people into intellectual robots. Quite the contrary, the secret to better behavior is proper harmonization of the nervous system with the biological system as a whole. By enabling people to refine and interpret their experiences, we can help them develop memories and contextual values that make for intellectual excellence. We can also help them learn to pose and solve problems of their own invention, which is the best way to cultivate achievement excellence. We can help them see multitudinous connections between seemingly isolated phenomena and choose the most fertile relationships, thus accelerating their creativity. And we can help them perceive themselves in relation to their whole community so they can become more sensitive, nurturing and understanding toward others, and can effectively improve their families and communities.

It is my hope that we shall soon have research centers in many universities that scientifically explore how to develop better learning systems so that virtually everyone can reach the educational level of people like da Vinci, Einstein and Leon Sullivan. Meanwhile, I would suggest, if you are interested in such things, to investigate some of the works and thinkers described below:

In *The Organization of Behavior*, Donald Hebb of Magill University mapped out neural networks in a way that clarifies the structure and complex behavior of the brain as it confronts new information. He described learning pyramids that organize how we think, and argued that the best way to improve thinking is to go to the lowest level on the relevant learning pyramid and build in new skills. These automatically cascade upward and affect the highest levels of thinking.

In *Vision, Its Development in Infant and Child*, Arnold Gesell of the Yale Child Development Center described the developmental changes of learning to see, and made it clear how poor reading and poor thinking result when vision is developmentally impaired. I know from my own experience that we can solve developmental problems with visual training even later in life. Unfortunately, the AMA in Gesell's time forced his book off the market because it didn't agree with his analysis of vision (though it does now). The book is, however, still available from the American Optometric Association.

In *The Evolution of Human Nature,* Judson Herrick explored the biological processes that develop eventually into learning, establishing some powerful concepts that show how the mind and body interact with one another in the learning process.

Here are some other researchers whose work is worth investigating:

Marian Diamond has explored the reorganization that takes place at the neurological level whenever something new is learned, and how to stimulate the brain with enriched environments so as to enhance the learning process.

Stuart Kauffman's work on complexity offers many clues to understanding the operation of self-organizing systems like the brain.

Roger Sperry discovered the complex relationship between the right and left brains that is important to the processes of learning and thinking. It's particularly important to honor the role of the right brain in directing the efforts of the left, which, being extremely linear, can often spend a great deal of time and effort accomplishing practically nothing.

Paul MacLean formulated the concept of the "triune brain," which shows the interaction between its "higher" and "lower" functions that inevitably affects the learning process. He discovered the reason why learning without an emotional component is likely to be forgotten, along the lines of the Ebbinghaus curve, while learning that is rooted in passion enhances itself over time.[9]

Karl Pribram opened the door on the holographic model of the brain and explained theoretically why a highly complex but completely clear presentation of material is nearly always easier to deal with on first exposure to a new subject than one that is too simple. This, of course, is counterintuitive, but one example of the power of this concept is that when I explain to algebra teachers how to teach the last problem in their textbooks on the first day of class, they can greatly improve the rate and success with which their students learn algebra.

Howard Gardner's work on the multiple intelligences is already being used by many teachers as a guide to course development in all subjects.

Alfred Tomatis believed that the ear grows the brain and stimulates neuronal activity. He developed very effective systems using music to help do just that.

On a somewhat different note, I recommend reading Rousseau's *Emile*, a book that gets right what today's educators often get wrong. Rousseau was one of the originators of a movement to establish a universal educational system. Many of his ideas were unduly idealistic, but in his novel he showed a keen feeling for the kind of learning hierarchy that works best for the development of young minds.

Equally enlightening and potentially applicable to contemporary society is "On Dream Theory in Malaya," by Kilton Stewart in *Altered States of Consciousness*.[10] This article depicts the means by which the Senoi people were supposedly able to maintain, for hundreds of years, a society free of crime, social conflict and stress, largely by daily analysis of their dreams.

Another book that is useful in provoking thought about the contemporary situation is *Beyond Civilization*, by Daniel Quinn, which argues that we can band together in a tribal sense, pooling our individual talents to create results that cannot be achieved either alone or in a corporate society.

The list goes on and on. When, in the future, these thinkers (and their colleagues) are brought into the mainstream of education, we will enter a new era in the evolution of human intelligence, unlike anything ever seen before.

Meanwhile, I hope I have given some evidence that the current crisis in education can't be solved by tightening the screws on schools to enforce "excellence" as manifested by scores on standardized tests. That approach is roughly equivalent to trying to make a flower grow faster by pulling on it.

In the hope of inspiring a better model, I am supplying in the Appendix an example of an interaction between teacher and student that utilizes the abilities of the latter to help determine what line of inquiry will lead to an individual student's progress.

Appendix

The following is a sample of a Socratic dialogue between myself and Korinne, a fourteen-year-old student whose mother, Dawn, withdrew her from the local middle school because she was convinced that it was squelching her mind. Korinne's hobby is training horses, and she hopes to become a professional writer or a crime scene investigator. Her writing skills are already very strongly in evidence.

Dawn, who had decided to homeschool Korinne, came to me with a project for her daughter based on the passing of the 2002 Olympic torch for the opening of the winter games. She had videotaped media coverage as the torch was carried through our city of South Bend, Indiana, and thought it would be good for Korinne to teach her younger sister's class about the history of the Olympics, with the help of the television footage. This was because Korinne had studied Greek history in school and knew something about it.

At first, Korinne was not enthusiastic about the project. But since it is my belief that anything can be made fascinating if you find a way to connect it to your central interests, it was my task as a consultant to help Korinne discover a connection between that project and her life goals.

I started by asking her what she knew about Greek civilization.

Korinne said that since she had studied it so long ago, nothing came to mind. I asked her if she knew that in an ancient town about the size of South Bend, over a period of about a hundred years, a small handful of people dreamed up nearly all the ideas that our Western civilization has been thinking about ever since. With growing interest, Korinne said no, and that this was news to her. It became obvious to me that whatever she'd been taught about the Greeks didn't seem relevant to what was important about them as a civilization, and certainly not to her as a person.

I asked her if she knew who Socrates was. She said she'd heard the name but couldn't place it, and didn't know what Socrates had done. Initiating our dialogue in order to provoke her thinking, I told her that he had been a stone cutter who had walked around the streets of Athens talking to people.

She wondered what was so great about that, and I replied that because of several conversations with Socrates some twenty-five hundred years ago, the groundwork for almost all of Western philosophy was mapped out. This mysterious lead-in caught her interest. Wanting to explain more about Socrates, I asked her to tell me about something she thought was important.

"The Japanese attack on the United States in World War II," she responded.

I asked her why the Japanese had attacked, and she said she didn't know. I asked her why they might have wanted to attack us, and she came up with a working hypothesis that the Japanese didn't like the Americans because they weren't like the Japanese, and so they wanted to obliterate them.

At this point, with no attempt to accept or correct her responses, I asked her if there was anyone she didn't like, and without naming names, she came up with someone who was very snobbish and insensitive. I asked her if she wanted to get rid of that person and she said no, that she only wanted to change her behavior. But if her behavior couldn't be changed, I asked, wouldn't you want to get rid of her? After a great deal of hesitation on her part, I suggested to Korinne that we had gotten to the root of prejudice.

She started to talk at great length about human character and why people don't get along, and after a while I stopped her and asked who was doing most of the talking. She said she was. I pointed out that because I had asked her questions, she needed to think in order to answer them. In doing so, she was teaching herself new ideas. She said she really liked that.

"That's what Socrates did in his conversations with the youth of Athens," I told her. "He talked to people and got them to think for themselves."

In order to demonstrate this further, I started reading her the *Euthyphro*. In the beginning, Euthyphro, one of Socrates' disciples, is concerned that his teacher is accused of criminal behavior and can't understand why. Socrates' explanation is interesting because he doesn't seem the least bit angry with his accuser. Instead, he praises him.

"So here," I pointed out, "we see that Socrates is willing to tolerate the existence of someone very unlike him, the same person who wants to execute him. In other words, Socrates, unlike most people, had room in his heart for everyone, even those seeking his destruction. Perhaps it would be possible for you to do that, too."

Next, I read Korinne the part where Socrates is accused of inventing new gods. I asked her to name a moral principle that she believed was absolutely correct, and she replied by saying that Jesus said people should be humble.

"In that case," I said, "suppose I told you, that in my opinion, humility is the greatest of sins." Korinne took great exception to that. I went on to explain that most people think being humble means having low self-esteem. "If God created everyone with wonderful gifts, and you don't value them or yourself, then in a way, you're devaluing God, and to me, that's a sin," I said.

Korinne said she followed that, but was still disturbed that I seemed to be criticizing Jesus.

"What Jesus meant was not that you should devalue yourself, but that you should acknowledge that your gifts come from God. Therefore, you are obligated to use them in the service of God and not for your own glorification. A person can feel good about her efforts and take pride in her work, especially because God made that possible. Certainly we didn't make ourselves able to see and hear and think and communicate with others. You are able to do those things because they came from God."

What I had illustrated was how an idea that seems crystal clear at first sight can actually be interpreted in several different ways. Only by considering other possible interpretations can we learn to think.

I read on in the *Euthyphro* to show that as his conversation with Socrates continued, Euthyphro was doing most of the talking. Socrates asked him questions that would get him to form his own thoughts.

Once that pattern was established, Korinne and I could discuss why Socratic thinking is important. It began to appear that the Greeks had the distinction of inventing an atmosphere where one could try on ideas that would enable one to see interesting new possibilities.

"So you can see why the Greeks would have put Socrates to death. 'Inventing new gods' meant that he was challenging the accepted beliefs of his time and 'corrupting youth' was the government's way of accusing him of spreading a new philosophic freedom. This is the freedom of speech that we protect in the First Amendment of the Constitution." I went on to consider with her how important it is that we never allow our society to fall into a ruthless contempt for ideas that challenge the "unalterable truth" of the status quo. If a challenge is nonsense, it will be dismissed, but if it has value, it may eventually lead to a better future. In either case, it makes no sense to kill off the exploration of ideas in a totally free and uncensored manner, so long as there is no danger to human rights. The same is true in allowing all sorts of ideas to emerge in the Socratic teaching method.

What did any of this have to do with the Olympics? When I asked her how she felt about the project her mother had suggested, Korinne said she would enjoy explaining things to the fourth graders, but that she thought it would be boring to research the Olympics.

"If it's boring, then it's not research," I said. "If you're not trying to answer a burning question that you really want to answer, then your research isn't worth doing."

Korinne still had to see what might be worthwhile about a lesson on the Olympics.

I had bought Korinne the two volumes of the *Great Books of the Western World,* called the *Syntopicon,* for a Christmas present.

"If you want to be a successful writer," I said, "you're going to need to fall in love with ideas, like the 102 ideas in this book. There's nothing more fun than an idea that fascinates you, so let's see if we can discover the most important one you can think of."

This idea emerged as we talked about the Olympics as an invention of the Greeks. In the Olympics, I reminded her, people from all over the world compete in various athletic events to see who is the very best. Perfection of skill is important.

"When you watch the Olympics, you're looking at the very best that anyone has been able to achieve in a particular sport."

Instantly, Korinne came alive. Perfection was very important to her because she wanted to be the best at exhibiting her horse.

"Ah, then you're interested in quality, but why? Why does it matter how well you show your horse?"

Korinne launched into an interesting lecture about the history of training horses and observed that when they are trained well, they are very beautiful. It became evident that beauty and quality were closely connected in her mind.

"The trouble is, in this narrow field, only one person can be the best at any given time, out of thousands of people who are also trying to be the best," I said. "But in the field of writing, it's possible for anyone to be the best at a certain kind of writing, because there are so many different styles. No one will ever write a Robert Frost poem better than Robert Frost, or a Mark Twain story better than Mark Twain. So you can literally become the best writer if you choose your own distinct style or voice."

We were on to something. The notion of quality was very important to Korinne. I told her that it might take her an entire lifetime to read all the essays in the *Syntopicon*, but that getting into the first one, about quality, was key. By looking at what others had to say on the subject, I said, she could more thoughtfully define her own ideas.

I pointed out that it is rare for most people to think about quality. Most live in messy, ill-furnished houses, have jobs they don't like, and content themselves with things that are second- or third-rate. This is very different when one has a personal mission to live a life of quality.

Now Korinne could think about the Olympics as a way of creating a healthy body to house a healthy mind and as a public festival designed to reveal the highest capacity that humans can reach.

By this time, Korinne's project literally had taken on Olympic proportions. It made sense to her because the idea of quality registered for her in a new way, in light of her interest in horses.

Socratic dialogues like this one work just as effectively in the classroom as they do in one's living room, or, as history has proven, on the streets of Athens.

Notes

Preface

1 Since the early sixties, there has been a general lowering of standards in this respect. In *Crucial Issues in Education*, first published in 1955, Henry Ehlers and Gordon C. Lee invoke a spirit of profound inquiry that should be at the core of education in their preface to the third edition (1964): "Should not the reader be encouraged to subject every paragraph, every sentence, to critical examination? Should he not constantly inquire: 'Is this true? Is this sound? Is this adequate? Is this practical?' Even if the reader holds a nondemocratic outlook (according to the criteria set forth in some selections), is not this one of his 'rights' in a liberal society? If democracy means shared thinking, is not the person who fails to think rather than the one who differs from the majority, the least democratic in his basic attitude?" (p. iii). Their 1955 prologue on the spirit of inquiry states that liberal education should "stimulate in each person a compelling urge to explore the unknown and to exercise to a fuller degree the vast possibilities of the mind." (New York: Holt, Rinehart and Winston, 1964). Today official policies as reflected in the legislation that governs teaching and testing leave little room for idealism of this kind, and the term "liberal," whether applied to politics or education, has become tainted. Ironically, in this conservative atmosphere the chances of educating the infrastructure needed for a successful capitalistic society are severely compromised.

2 See *Dickens as an Educator* by James L. Hughes (New York: Haskell House Publishers, 1971). This book, first published in 1900, is based on a thorough examination of Dickens's works and shows him to have been one of the most important educational reformers of the nineteenth century. Many of his recommendations for universal

educational practice have still not been mainstreamed.

3 William Butler Yeats, in his poem "The Second Coming."

4 I have based this estimate on Moore's law, which states that the amount of computing power you can buy for a given amount of money doubles every eighteen months. So if you set the available computer power in 1950 at one and double it every eighteen months, you arrive at a billion shortly after the turn of the century. This does not actually tell us about the available knowledge, however, for several reasons. One is that when computing power doubles, available knowledge increases by an unknown (and probably uncomputable) rate that much more than doubles. For example, when computing power doubles, you can solve a given problem on your computer in half the time. So if that problem once took you a week to solve, now you can do it in milliseconds. But that doesn't take into account the fact that there are a great many problems that previously couldn't be solved at all, which now can be solved easily. It also doesn't take into account the increased distribution of computing power. As more people start using computers to create knowledge, the available knowledge goes up at an even faster rate. Also, some strange situations have already arisen because of this widespread availability of computer power. Let's look at one of these: A patient has an unusual disease. The patient can go on the Internet and learn everything that is known (and publicly shared) about that disease and the various cures available for it. The patient can now go to the doctor and instruct the doctor on what to do to cure the otherwise incurable disease. This is actually happening with increasing frequency, and it means that any given patient can know more about a particular medical subject than the doctor can, since the patient needs to know only about that one illness, and the doctor needs to know about a great many illnesses. This means that the doctor of the future will probably face only patients who are better informed about their illnesses than he or she is. Suddenly the professionals turn into amateurs and the amateurs into professionals. One can only guess what consternation and soul searching this will cause on top of all the other problems the health care system is now trying to juggle.

5 Even as I write, the South Philadelphia Community Investment Program is making plans to track on its website, on both a daily and cumulative basis, the voting track records of all the representatives for which the voters can vote. An adjacent chat room will invite discussion among the voters of the implications of these votes for their interests. Hopefully this will set a national trend in which all voters will participate.

6 We must never forget, however, that this was, even then, the exception rather than the rule. There was plenty of intellectual vacuum at the top, as we are reminded of by books like *With Enough Shovels,* by Robert Scheer (New York: Vintage, 1983). This remarkable book recounts widely held views, in high places, that America could survive an all-out nuclear war without much damage, provided we all had the presence of mind to dig holes in our backyards deep enough to hide in as soon as the sirens went off.

7 The story of this shameful degradation of book publishing is very well told in André

Schiffrin, *The Business of Books: How the International Conglomerates Took Over Publishing and Changed the Way We Read* (New York: Verso, 2000). This indicates a decline in the general thoughtfulness of the reading public, caused by a combination of too much television and too little early exposure to books.

8 This complexity is ever increasing, ever more thoughtful and thought provoking. Recent research in complexity theory shows that the universe has this in common with the human brain (as described by D. O. Hebb in *The Organization of Behavior* [New York: John Wiley, 1949]).

9 In private interviews with key people at the Department of Education and the National Education Association (NEA), I have uncovered a profound disagreement with this view. For example, Dr. Barbara Kapinus, senior consultant to the NEA, specializing in reading instruction, is deeply concerned at the lack of depth in reading that will develop in many classrooms as a result of "teaching to the tests" now mandated by government legislation that trivializes and fragments the spirit of education that was long at the root of our national traditions.

Part One
Chapter 1

1 This point is nicely taken up by Leonard Bernstein in his "Norton Lectures" on music given at Harvard. Bernstein takes off from Chomsky's deep structuring of imbedded assumptions about context in ordinary conversation to show how a similar deep structuring occurs in music.

2 For more on this subject, see chapter 6.

3 The next step in this process, which will be carried out by computers, is brilliantly explicated in *The Age of Spiritual Machines*, by Ray Kurzweil (New York: Viking, 1999). Kurzweil shows how computers will eventually surpass, first, individual human intelligence, and ultimately that of the entire species. Of course, without the accumulated wisdom of thousands of years stored in books, this would never have become possible. For another valuable perspective on this issue, see *Cybergrace*, by Jennifer Cobb (New York: Crown, 1998).

4 A thought-provoking discussion of this issue may be found in Daniel Quinn, *Beyond Civilization* (New York: Harmony Books, 1999).

5 As of this writing, the overproduction of overnight millionaires has been cut back considerably. However, there is no theoretical reason why it cannot be reconstituted once investors have learned to think more or less in the manner prescribed in this book.

6 These and several other useful statistics further clarifying the problem may be found in *Why Our Children Can't Read*, by Diane McGuinness (New York: The Free Press, 1997), 10.

7 One source of this statistic is an article, "Research-Based Reading Instruction: The Right Way," by Bill Honig, published in *The School Administrator* (September 1997) and

condensed in *Education Digest* (December 1997). However, I have found that every school administrator I have talked to has been perplexed by the fact that there seems to be no really effective way to help children of third grade level and above to improve their reading skills if they are seriously behind.

8 The best introduction to this subject is *The Theatre of the Absurd*, by Martin Esslin (New York: Anchor Books, 1961).

9 Bruno Bettelheim and Karen Zelan, *On Learning to Read: The Child's Fascination with Meaning* (New York: Vintage Books, 1981).

10 Since human beings affect their environment millions of times more than any other species, and since the environment includes other human beings, each of us has an enormous effect just by virtue of being alive. We must choose, therefore, to act either conscientiously and with informed understanding on behalf of the good, or thoughtlessly on behalf of the bad. Neutrality of effect is impossible. When we learn in school that we are insignificant, we are therefore learning to act thoughtlessly on behalf of the bad.

11 These statistics were developed and promoted by experts in neuro-linguistic programming, a process of modeling out the way effective people use verbal and nonverbal language to communicate.

12 Euclid was one of the world's finest dramatists, for the manipulations he worked out in order to prove certain relationships are both fascinating and breathtaking. Euclid is literature, but most geometry books are merely collections of recipes.

13 Marian Diamond's research at U.C. Berkeley has shown that even the adult brain is very plastic and able to change and develop new skills. While neurons are, for the most part, once lost, gone forever, dendrites and glial cells (which carry nutrients up the axon) can increase very quickly under the influence of intellectual and kinesthetic stimulation. Improving reading skills, therefore, is one of the most powerful ways of literally growing the brain. Children who do not learn to read inevitably have less complex brains than those who do. However, illiterate adults who learn to read may experience profound growth rates in their effective intelligence, provided the development of reading skills is accompanied by appropriate stimulation of the kinesthetic and vestibular centers in the brain. I am planning to write a book on developmental visual education that will explain how and why this works and will provide simple tools for accomplishing it.

14 One example is the Indiana Academy, which makes distance learning available to high school students everywhere. Only about one out of every 150 students who live in Indiana will choose to apply to its onsite program, and only about half of them will be accepted. So what's needed is a well-developed set of educational tools that would increase the probable enrollment in such schools by a factor of 300.

Chapter 2

1 From the point of view of modern physics, the reverse is true. At its roots, matter is composed of something more like thoughts than things. Furthermore, in a practical sense, we are as likely to get hurt by running up against a legal or corporate abstraction as by running into a brick wall.

2 To balance the picture a little, it's well to reflect on the rich oral traditions handed down through some tight-knit communities, in which people who may or may not be literate hand down stories and songs that may go back more than a thousand years. Indeed, perhaps the only real downside of print is that it has eliminated so much of the world's former tendency to keep such oral traditions alive.

3 Another factor that brought about the decline in reading was that the populations of public schools were increasing as they took responsibility for educating a larger percentage of the population. A recent book by Diane Ravitch (*Left Back: A Century of Failed School Reforms*, Simon and Schuster, 2000) argues that our educational system has spent the last hundred years pushing aside academic standards as a result, primarily, of progressive education. Nicholas Lemann's review of this book in *The New Yorker* (September 25, 2000, p. 89) points out that in 1900 only 16 percent of the population graduated from high school and the attempt to graduate what is now 90 percent of the population (those who attend public schools) required a watering down of the curriculum, since not everyone could learn well enough to meet the previous academic standards. This situation could be resolved if we were to change the methods of teaching so that everyone who attends public school is able to learn well enough to meet the academic standards of 1900 (or equivalent, but more relevant, standards). The tools needed to do this have been available for some time but they are so much at odds with traditional educational practices that they are very seldom used. Were they to be taught in all schools of education and used in all schools, then more than 90 percent of the population could graduate from high school and also meet very high academic standards. In this conflict, Ravitch represents the ultraconservative and Lemann's observation, the position of the ultraradical. Both sides of the argument are essential in order to construct a synthesis, which is highly doable, but which will not happen as long as radicals and conservatives continue to be unable to learn from one another. Currently, West Virginia's National Learning Foundation is putting together a program of powerful new methods of teaching that have never been mainstreamed. Preliminary results of the methods being brought together make it clear that this eclectic approach should be sufficient to solve the problem once it is mainstreamed throughout the public schools.

4 Forcing children to attempt reading before their eyes are developmentally ready and their minds capable of visualizing the meanings of words is an extremely severe form of child abuse. It is absolutely essential that young children have eye examinations that establish their readiness to read before they are subjected to reading instruction. Yet as

Why America's Children Can't Think

I write, there is legislation proposed in Virginia to abolish reading readiness tests on the grounds that they are unnecessary. This is almost as serious as abolishing polio vaccinations would be.

5 This theme is developed more fully in McGuinness, *Why Our Children Can't Read.*

6 The conflict between proponents of phonics and whole language instruction has recent become politicized, but in reality it has been playing out in one form or another for nearly a century.

This conflict would disappear if reading instruction experts understood that reading is both a right-brain and a left-brain process. The right brain performs the functions that are emphasized in whole language instruction, while the left brain performs those that are emphasized in phonics instruction. No one can learn to read well who cannot integrate both of these functions into reading, but individual readers inevitably differ in the way they do this.

Throughout the nineteenth century, reading and spelling were assumed to be a matter of making the kinds of distinctions that are made in phonics instruction, and most students learned to read pretty well. By the early 1930s, the notion of "whole word recognition" had become widespread, and some children were taught to recognize words by their shapes rather than by a system of decoding the letters of which they were composed. Since some learners pick up the spelling code merely through exposure to printed text, many people will learn to read no matter how you teach them. It is widely agreed, however, that more people learn to read when they are exposed to some form of phonics instruction than when they are exposed only to whole word recognition or whole language instruction.

The main objection to phonics instruction is that it uses boring drills and emphasizes decoding words at the expense of understanding them. Apologists for phonics argue that if you can decode words, you are then in a position to understand what they mean. This is sometimes true, but not always. Apologists for whole language argue that since we learn to speak spontaneously simply by being exposed to conversation, we should also learn to read spontaneously, by being exposed to literature. This idea is generally not supported by research.

The high incidence of poor reading and "dyslexia" that is found in our current school population and the large amounts of adult illiteracy make it clear that, whatever else is true, the problem has not been resolved. In 1955, Rudolph Flesch published *Why Johnny Can't Read*, using a great deal of very good research to argue in favor of phonics instruction. Had the world sat up and recognized the truth of what Flesch was saying at the time, our current dilemma in teaching reading might well be much less than it is. But, though the book was a bestseller, it made little impact on actual reading instruction in public schools. So little, in fact, that Flesch followed it in 1981 with another, better-researched book called *Why Johnny* Still *Can't Read*. Again the book was widely read and discussed, but little change was made in reading instruction in schools on a national scale.

In 1988–89 the pages of *Phi Delta Kappan* carried a lengthy debate between Jeanne S. Chall, who argued the case for phonics, and Marie Carbo, who argued it for whole language. Both writers bolstered their arguments with mountains of research, and each faulted the research of the other. Still, there was no appreciable effect on reading instruction.

The most recent entry into the sweepstakes of explaining the problem is Diane McGuinness's *Why Our Children Can't Read*, which takes the position that by using phonemic instruction, all children can be taught to read in a relatively short time. Like nearly all of those who insist that decoding words is the key to learning to read, McGuinness has very little to say in her book about the complex process of developing reading comprehension. Her evaluation of the reading program developed by her son and daughter-in-law is extremely favorable, but her statistics seem to have been based not on how well the program has worked in public school classrooms, but rather how well it has worked when the experts who developed it use it in their own work with children, which is a very different thing.

Despite the excellence of this book, which represents another milestone in the literature of reading instruction, it leaves much to be desired in presenting a level view of all the different issues that impact this complex field, and makes very little reference to the neurological research that is now contributing so much to our understanding of how people learn, or fail to learn, to read and of what can be done about it in terms of developing learning programs that are compatible with brains that learn differently from the norm.

We still must accept the fact that there are many mysteries about learning to read, but it is time to also act on the belief, which is one of the highlights of McGuinness's book, that virtually everyone can be taught to read to a high level of proficiency. Nevertheless, more and more evidence has developed that it is not phonics (which is phunduhmentilly konfyousing) but phonemic awareness (which makes a wider range of distinctions among sounds, particularly in vowels) that is key to understanding how words are put together. Most research that has looked closely at how people develop fluency in reading has shown that some process of learning the "code" is essential, even though for many learners this may happen spontaneously.

It is not necessarily true, however, that phonemic awareness is the complete answer. Albert M. Galaburda, a Harvard neuroscientist, cites the following case: "Right now we're studying a woman who is a phonological genius. She can decode auditorially at a fast rate in seven languages. She just can't read. The distinctions we make about the visual and auditory brain are somewhat arbitrary." (*The Scientific American* [August 1995]: 15).

Throughout this controversy, no one that I know of has introduced the notion of teaching in a systematic and linear manner the various spellings, or sound signals, that may encode each of the phonemes. Now that I have done this, I believe that I have discovered the code that learners need to master if they are to learn to read successfully. Once they have mastered the code, they can do all the things to enhance their reading experiences that whole language advocates rightly think they should be doing. They can, in fact, do these things from the beginning of their exposure to reading, if a controlled vocabulary is used to prevent the code from ever becoming too confusing to the reader.

7   Some children actually do learn to read this way, and it is almost certain that all of them would if the proper techniques of preparing for reading were used for those who are not yet ready. Indeed, Dr. Steven Ingersoll uses such techniques in three schools in Michigan and has been able to achieve 100 percent performance at grade level in both reading and math among formerly at-risk students. Meanwhile, the problem remains that once children have begun to deal with print and fail to recognize whole words with relative ease, some degree of instruction in phonemic awareness becomes essential.

8   The Talmudic studies that are a fundamental part of Jewish education often teach the skills I have in mind. That may be why, throughout recent history, the Jews have made important contributions to civilization highly disproportionate to their numbers.

9   Adults have fewer dendritic connections in their brains than children. This is evidence that schooling actively "dumbs us down."

10   Much in what I have to say has been founded on the arguments and research in Halberstam's book, which shows the incredible incompetence of many leaders of our society as they deal with the problems that tend to define our options for the future. See David Halberstam, *The Best and the Brightest* (New York: Modern Library, 2001).

Chapter 3

1   *The Rise of the Virtual State*, by Richard Rosecrance (New York: Basic Books, 1999), shows how land is now less valuable than "human capital," which means the ability of a population to think and act logically and creatively.

2   Acknowledging this phenomenon, Arthur Eddington once said of his fellow physicists that they are like fishermen whose nets catch only fish of a certain size, and that they then declare there are no smaller fish in the sea than those they have caught.

3   That's the calculation of Stephen Pinker in his book *The Language Instinct: How the Mind Creates Language* (New York: William Morrow, 1994), 149–50. (Incidentally, lexical units are all the different forms in which we use words, i.e., "say," "saying," "said," etc.) Pinker underestimates by half the number of words used by Shakespeare. He says 15,000, but Marvin Spevak, editor of the *Harvard Concordance of Shakespeare*, found 29,066 and John Willinsky, author of *Empire of Words*, says there are 33,305 citations of Shakespeare in the 1987 edition of the *Oxford English Dictionary*, and that 1,904 of the words Shakespeare used originated with him. These citations are based on standard works and do not include plays such as *Edmund Ironside* or *Edward III*, which now must be added to them, each weighing in with about 300 additional words. Meanwhile, there are probably about ten other plays waiting to be added to the Shakespeare canon, which will further raise the ante. So Pinker's underestimate of Shakespeare's vocabulary may

suggest that he has underestimated the average person's as well.

4 15,877, according to John Willinsky.

5 That's because casual social discourse (which seeks a lowest common denominator of vocabulary) is much more limited in its word choice than literary expression. In most cases, if you use highfalutin words, you're regarded with suspicion.

6 William James, in his *Principles of Psychology*, develops this theme in a compelling way.

7 Neurologically, as well as logically, the only way we can know anything is through our own subjective lenses. Physical science has, for nearly a century, accepted this limit on the possibilities of knowing, but journalism still clings to the myth of objectivity.

8 I admit to being a bit high-handed here. A substantial number of physicists would disagree with this statement. However, since in my novel *The Butterfly Dreams* (written with Syril Kline) I asserted that the existence of God is mathematically proven, I may as well provide here a reader's guide for investigating this notion a bit. One of the last great bastions for the defense of a universe of chance that doesn't know about us, let alone care about us, is Stephen Jay Gould. His ideas on this subject are brilliantly explicated and made short work of in Robert Wright, "The Accidental Creationist," *The New Yorker* (December 13, 1999): 56–65. Wright shows that much of Gould's reasoning is out-of-date and does not take into account some of the fundamental structures of Darwinian evolution that are accepted by other researchers. As a result, he makes evolution seem so improbable that it is as likely that God created the world in seven days as that anything happened the way Gould describes it. Wright correctly indicates that the case for Darwin is stronger than Gould makes it, and also considerably less antireligious. Along the way, Wright dismisses as a darling of the creationists Michael Denton's *Evolution: A Theory in Crisis* (Bethesda, MD: Adler & Adler, 1985). Nowhere, however, does Denton mention God. He simply points out that microbiologists cannot articulate any mechanism that could possibly account for the origin of life. He also points out that there are a great many discontinuities in evolution that, from an engineering point of view, cannot be filled in. You can't, for example, go from scales to feathers by a series of steps, because there's no viable in-between state. This is the kind of argument that must be taken into account if one is to have a coherent theory of evolution. A number of evolutionists have tried to get around this problem by giving it the name "punctuated equilibrium," as if naming it would explain it, which it obviously doesn't. Thus, nothing gets said about what the solution might be, only that there is a problem. Paul Davies in *The Fifth Miracle: The Search for the Origin and Meaning of Life* takes the argument to a much larger context. His point is that if life originated once in the universe, then it could have happened by accident, but if it originated more than once, then it had to be part of a universal plan. Life, in other words, had to be designed from the beginning. This reasoning, if correct, would end all notions of a universe of chance and replace it with a universe of conscious mind. A single piece of evidence (perhaps coming from the Mars probe) that life exists somewhere outside of Earth, and was not spread through contam-

ination, would establish Davies' position once and for all. None of this, however, gets at the mechanism the creative process might have taken. Some useful clues may come from studying the work of scientists like Harold Saxton Burr of Yale Medical School and plant physiologist Rupert Sheldrake. More recently the Mere Creation Symposium of 1996 has surfaced a book of scientific papers by leading physicists, biochemists and philosophers, who make a case that is close to airtight that intelligent design is indispensable in accounting for all the known facets of the universe. A typical quote (from a paper by biochemist Michael Behe) is: "So what difference does intelligent design theory make to the way we practice science? I believe it is this: a scientist no longer has to go to enormous lengths to shoehorn complex, interactive systems into a naturalistic scenario. When experiment and calculation reasonably exclude chance and law, then we should conclude, without going through metaphysical paroxysms, that a feature was designed. We should remain open to the possibility that further analysis will show our conclusion was wrong, but we should not be timid about reaching a conclusion of design and building on it." William A. Dembski, ed. *Mere Creation: Science, Faith and Intelligent Design* (Downers Grove, IL: InterVarsity Press, 1998), 194.

Chapter 4

1 A good source of further information on this subject is Pinker, *The Language Instinct*.
2 Less exact and dogmatic on this subject than some others have been, Stephen Pinker provides an excellent discussion of the parameters of this situation in *The Language Instinct*, 276–83.
3 Ibid., 32–39.
4 Such a view can be constructed from the work of biologists like Christian de Duve and students of complexity theory like Stewart Kaufman.
5 This point emerged strongly from research on language acquisition in children that formed the subject of one of the programs in the "Nova" series.

Chapter 5

1 Light wave particles interacting with your retina stimulate electrical pulses in your optic nerve that are sent to disparate parts of your brain and eventually are gathered together for interpretation.
2 Neutrinos are among the tiniest particles in the universe—their mass only one–ten millionth that of an electron. In other words, if you were a neutrino, an electron would seem nearly as large to you as the United States. Thousands of them pass through your body every second, but they don't know you're there, and you don't know they're there. To a neutrino one piece of an atom in your body would seem to be an enormous distance from another piece of the same atom. The chances are almost nonexistent that it would

collide with anything while passing through what, to it, would seem to be an enormously empty space. Yet neutrinos are among the most important particles in the universe, accounting for perhaps 10 percent of dark matter, or as much of the mass of the universe as all the visible stars put together. cover more distance in the winter (when the earth tilts away from the sun in the northern hemisphere) than they do in the summer (when it tilts toward it). When the sun's rays are spread out they offer the earth less heat per square inch than when they are concentrated. That effect makes possible differences of more than forty degrees centigrade between summer and winter. It's very easy to create a visual impression of how this works. Less than three minutes of instruction of the right kind would make it possible for any student to understand this cause of seasonal change so well that it would never become confused or forgotten. This is one example of why memorizing easily forgotten facts is so far inferior to the practice of understanding the underlying principles of how things are organized. Incidentally, the reason we learn plane geometry, which is virtually useless, instead of solid geometry, which is very useful and actually easier to learn, is that when the mathematics curriculum was set well over two thousand years ago, the priests who determined the order of study wished to suppress the idea that was then becoming common among intellectuals that the earth was round. They wanted to preserve the notion that it was flat.

3　The unfortunate experiences that led to this were originally observed in Germany as an outcome of World War II by von Senden. They have since been noted and discussed by many neuropsychologists, notably Kurt Goldstein and Oliver Sacks.

4　That's because when they learned to read, their auditory systems were fully functional but their visual systems were not yet adequately developed for reading. The result is subvocalization while reading, a difficult habit to overcome.

5　The vast majority of Harvard seniors think the elliptical orbit of the earth around the sun is the cause of the difference between summer and winter. Such a mistaken impression would never be possible if teachers were in the habit of getting students to learn and discuss not what is supposed to be true, but why it is supposed to be true. For example, the difference in distance from the sun between winter (when it is closest to the sun) and summer (when it is farthest away) would account for much less than one centigrade degree in temperature. But because of the tilt of the earth on its axis, light rays have to and profound change in our perception of the world since Newton." According to this view, almost universally accepted in physics, an electron is somewhere inside a probability wave that collapses when a scientist measures it. Until this happens, it cannot be said to be localized anywhere. It's even true that a measuring apparatus (such as an automatic camera connected to an electron microscope) does not collapse the wave until some scientist mentally perceives the event. Only then is the collapsing of the probability wave a real phenomenon, which means that the electron could be said to exist in some particular place. No one can really understand this, but if you'd like to know more about it, a book that might help is *The Atom in the History of Human Thought*, by Bernard

Why America's Children Can't Think

Pullman (New York: Oxford University Press, 1998), 277–ff.

6 Once while demonstrating the revolution of Mercury around the sun, I was criticized by a teacher who said I had Mercury going in the wrong direction. This is a "Northist" assumption. If the Australians had been the ones to make pictures of the solar system (as well as world maps), my model would have been correct.

7 This development in physics is so bizarre that it has been called "the most dramatic and profound change in our perception of the world since Newton." According to this view, almost universally accepted in physics, an electron somewhere inside a probability wave that collapses when a scientist measures it. Until this happens, it cannot be said to be localized anywhere. It's even true that a measuring apparatus (such as an automatic camera connected to an electron microscope) does not collapse the wave until some scientist mentally perceives the event. Only then is the collapsing of the probability wave a real phenomenon, which means that the electron could be said to exist in some particular place. No one can really understand this, but if you'd like to know more about it, a book that might help is *The Atom in the History of Human Thought*, by Bernard Pullman (New York: Oxford University Press, 1998) 227–ff.

8 Visualization requires making the movie in your mind so it has continuity, consistency and specificity.

Chapter 6

1 Visually mature students may never need to sound out words at all, so the following discussion applies to readers who were unfortunately taught to read before they were visually mature.

2 See Marian Diamond, Ph.D., and Janet Hopson, *Magic Trees of the Mind* (New York: Dutton, 1998).

3 Russell Baker, *Growing Up* (New York: Congdon and Weed, 1982), 218–21.

4 An intriguing fact about dyslexia is that some cases of it have been effectively treated with drugs that cure motion sickness. It's also true that some dyslexia can be improved by spinning a child around in a swivel chair in a way that produces dizziness. In both cases the inner ear, which is responsible for maintaining balance, is involved.

The loss of balance, or motion sickness, produces nausea, so there's a direct connection between the way the eyes interpret visual phenomena to produce balance and the way the viscera work in digesting food. Another way of producing nausea is to use lenses to produce optical illusions that are visually impossible.

What these facts collectively suggest is that reading print when you're feeling unsure of the basic spellings along the way is a little like walking on uneven terrain, and the eventual effect is something a little like motion sickness.

If the automatic responses to all the most commonly encountered words are resolved to the point where the words register automatically, and without any ambiguity, the effect is like learning to walk on what was uneven terrain in such a manner that it feels like walking evenly. A road full of potholes has been repaved, and the stride of the eyes across the page becomes regular and comfortable. So the motion sickness goes away and what has been called "dyslexia" simply disappears.

5 This is usually necessary only with words you have never encountered before—as in the sample made-up word I used earlier.

Chapter 7

1 See Marilyn Jager Adams, *Beginning to Read: Thinking and Learning about Print* (Cambridge: The MIT Press, 1994). This well-researched book includes evidence that even highly skilled adults perceive almost every letter in every word they read. If complete evidence in favor of phonics and phonemic instruction is needed, it is certainly to be found in this book.

2 McGuinness, *Why Our Children Can't Read*. The wealth of evidence about the harmfulness of guessing that McGuinness presents should give pause to any teacher who encourages this process in youngsters.

3 Whole word recognition develops naturally with experience and will happen automatically when the reader is ready. Trying to speed it up by encouraging guessing is harmful. It isn't harmful, though, to play word search games that encourage the recognition of words at sight.

Chapter 8

1 John Willinsky, *Empire of Words: The Reign of the OED* (Princeton: Princeton University Press, 1994).

2 This problem is very well explained in Eleanor Wilson Orr, *Twice as Less: Black English and the Performance of Black Students in Math and Science* (New York: Norton, 1987).

3 H. W. Fowler, *A Dictionary of Modern English Usage* (New York: Oxford University Press, 1991).

4 I seriously considered rewriting this sentence, since I am involved in a mathematics educational project that proposes to start first graders off with the study of calculus. The reason this can work is that calculus can be used to describe children's everyday experiences, whereas quadratic equations require one to learn several levels of abstractions before they can be properly understood.

5 Diane McGuinness is equally scornful of rules like these.

6 The solution to this problem is that there are ways of teaching reading (including the one on which this book is based) that never invoke such confusion and the problems that go with it. However, there are a great many skills that must be developed before reading can be learned effectively. Dr. Don Helms, whose program is called ACHIEVE, has

substantially raised the IQs of all the students he has worked with using a program that teaches these basic skills. They provide a background of experience that makes it possible to catch up in reading, mathematics and other academic subjects. Intellectual training of this type should become a staple of all elementary education, and can even be used in adult education. In fact, when Helms demonstrated his method to me, it was clear to me that I myself could learn a great deal from it. Perhaps there is no one who could not achieve significant benefits from this program, since it teaches an array of skills that are almost always learned unconsciously if at all, and also since it is unlikely that anyone would learn all of them to the level of proficiency that Helms demands. When I asked him what the limits of IQ improvement would be, he told me that that is unknown, since programs like his are never sustained for more than a year, and there is currently no evidence that anyone ever reaches a plateau in IQ development as a result of such a program.

7   See McGuinness, *Why Our Children Can't Read.*

8   Ibid.

Chapter 9

1   Most recent books on the human brain can clarify this point. The emotions that are associated with our goals in life, such as family values, are generated in the midbrain, or limbic system. This part of the brain has no access to language or rational thought. And yet all decisions that involve our sense of who we are have to be generated in this part of the brain, because they are deeply rooted in our emotional values. So while it's true that you can make decisions about things like which direction to turn to go north as a result of rational analysis, you can't decide on a purely rational basis whether to take a particular job or pursue a friendship with a particular person.

2   I've worked with students who seem not to be interested in anything. This is because boredom and fear are closely related. If you're afraid of school and afraid of most of the other things that happen in your life, you can seem not to be interested in anything because fear is an alienating experience. To be interested in something, you must find a way of relating to it yourself. The teacher's task in this case is to find something the student has a relationship with and to develop further interests through that connection.

3   I've had quite a few experiences like this with students. In a surprising number of cases, no one had ever previously tried to help them discover what they were interested in.

4   *Hooked on Books* is an excellent manual for operating classrooms on this basis. (See Daniel Fader in the bibliography.)

5   I've met a number of people who can't seem to get beyond one very restricted field of interest. For example, I once met a woman who felt that Notre Dame coach Knute Rockne had never been adequately appreciated. Virtually all of her energy was devoted to learning more about him and inflicting what she knew on everyone who would listen.

6   Suzanne Juhasz, *Reading from the Heart* (New York: Viking, 1994).

7   Recently there have been experiments directed toward building up communication with children well before verbal language begins to develop. Early reports show that these attempts seem to produce healthier, happier and more intelligent children. A book on this subject that interested parents should investigate is Linda P. Acredolo and Susan Goodwyn, with Douglas Abrams, *Baby Signs: How to Talk with Your Baby Before Your Baby Can Talk* (Chicago: Contemporary Books, 2002).

8   During the filming of *Harry Potter and the Sorcerer's Stone*, the author was continuously on the set, making sure that the film followed the book exactly. Many who had loved the book and then saw the film really appreciated the faithfulness of the film in bringing to life what they had imagined while reading the book. This is, however, a rare phenomenon.

9   That's universally true of adults, too, of course, but it's not considered polite to mention that, so I won't.

10 This won't make children think that smoking is cool, but it might provoke a class discussion about lung cancer. I'm driven to write this endnote by exposure to teachers who seem to think that everything that enters their classrooms must be free of the kind of real world corruption that their students have spent hours watching on television the night before. If you encounter it only on television and never in the classroom, how can you possibly hope to evaluate it intelligently?

11 A number of elaborations of old stories into new forms have been very successful. For example, the movie *Hook*, which revisits the story of Peter Pan as an adult, has been very popular.

12 When elementary school teachers started reading *Harry Potter* to their students in the classroom as a way of getting them interested in books, this stirred up a storm of protest around the country that made the front pages. Some parents are terrified that if their children learn to think for themselves, they will start questioning parental sacred cows. This, of course, will happen anyway without the help of schoolteachers—unless the children have no access to TV or children from other cultures or backgrounds. As for me, I've been publicly described as an instrument of the devil. This is not only a blasphemous degradation of the serious religious beliefs held by most Americans, it also pointlessly glorifies me and others like me who have a rather narrowly defined interest in decreasing the rampant illiteracy that festers in the schools. If I really had demonic powers, I'd be using them to exploit the stock market, not public schools in rural and inner city areas where the devil, if he is abroad, is already far too successful to need any help from me.

13 A good translation (titled *The Bungler*) has been made by Richard Wilbur and is available from The Dramatists Play Service (2000).

Why America's Children Can't Think

Interlude

1 T. S. Eliot, *Selected Essays* (New York: Harcourt Brace, 1950), 6–7.
2 For example, the notion of being "civilized" used to imply the thought habits of the dominant Anglo-American culture. Today, with the awareness of the importance of multiculturalism, it implies familiarity with many different cultures and an informed ability to relate to them on their terms. This vastly extends the need for empathy and philosophical flexibility. At the other end of the continuum is the pull of modern technology toward an isolating form of specialization in one tiny area of expertise, with little awareness of how it interfaces with even related areas of expertise. Meanwhile, at the center, we have seen the almost universal adoption by the media of the standards of yellow journalism. This means the average person now is exposed to far fewer examples of what used to be called "civilized" behavior. Almost totally lost in this modern melee is the notion that "the unexamined life is not worth living," which used to be regarded as fundamental.
3 Of course the replacement of paper books with e-books that successfully simulate them is a likely future development and is to be welcomed if it retains all the advantages of printed books.

Part Two
Chapter 10

1 Rudolph Arnheim, *Visual Thinking* (Berkeley, CA: University of California Press, 1969).
2 This approach to teaching and learning is still very rare, but has a sound scientific basis. See Donald O. Hebb, *The Organization of Behavior* (New York: Wiley, 1949), which examines how the brain functions using neural networks. Hebb's research shows that the brain functions are hierarchical—in other words that you have to learn some things in order to learn other things. If you take a particular higher order thinking skill, you can trace it back to its roots in very early experiences. If you want to improve that skill, you can either spend a long time unsuccessfully trying to develop it without a proper neurological foundation, or you can improve the neurological foundation and it will develop almost spontaneously, or with relatively little additional learning experience.

For example, if it is difficult for you to understand mathematics equations, that could be because you have never developed a properly fine-tuned sense of balance. It might be that you could practice walking on a balance board and as a result you would be better able to understand how the equal sign works in a mathematical equation.

Some hierarchical functions of the brain exist within the language structure itself. For example, general conceptual notions may be developed before particular instances of them can be interpreted. An example of this is research that showed that students learned to think in general terms much better after they were taught to interpret the morals in Aesop's Fables. The notions of behavioral cause and effect taught somewhat "nonsensically" in these fables help to explain many everyday occurrences that cannot be easily interpreted until the general conceptual structure is in place.

This notion of teaching generalities that arise early in the brain network hierarchy, or "learning pyramid," in order to bring about a good general understanding later is extremely uncommon in teaching but, when used properly, can greatly accelerate the rate of learning.

Incidentally, Hebb's work went largely unnoticed from shortly after it was published until the last few years. The academic prejudice against the notion that complex ideas are based on simpler ones was so strong that it affected the way research on artificial intelligence was conducted. As a result, about twenty years' worth of effort was wasted in building robots that couldn't learn to walk over rough terrain. More recently the conceptual structure of neural networks is more widely used by researchers in artificial intelligence, but it is still not developed to a level of very much sophistication, and is generally not linked to other models of brain activity that interact with it.

3   Popular books on this subject are legion. Two approaches that have both practical and scientific credentials of considerable weight are *Pygmalion in the Classroom: Teacher Expectation and Pupils' Intellectual Development*, by Robert Rosenthal and Lenore Jacobson (New York: Irvington Publishers, 1992), and *Getting Well Again: A Step-by-Step, Self-Help Guide to Overcoming Cancer for Patients and Their Families*, by O. Carl Simonton, Stephanie Matthews-Simonton and James Creighton (Los Angeles: J. P. Tarcher, 1978). The first of these shows that the behavior of students in the classroom is powerfully influenced by the impressions teachers have of them, whether or not those impressions are based on anything "real." The second is based on medical research that shows how people can use their imaginations to cure serious illnesses like cancer.

4   Lev Vygotsky, *Thought and Language* (Cambridge: MIT Press, 1962).
    This is a seminal work on how children internalize their cultures. See also *Mind in Society* (Cambridge: Harvard University Press, 1978), which is a collection of essays to further develop the previous work.

Chapter 11

1   William Grey Walter, *The Living Brain* (New York: W. W. Norton, 1963).
2   A thoughtful, if overbearing, discussion of the aspects of this problem is to be found in J. Allan Hobson's *The Chemistry of Conscious States* (Boston: Little, Brown & Co., 1994). Other contributions to the conversation may be found in John Horgan, *The Undiscovered Mind: How the Human Brain Defies Replication, Medication, and Explanation* (New York: The Free Press, 1999); Nicholas Wade, ed., *The Science Times Book of the Brain* (New York: The Lyons Press, 1998), and V. S. Ramachandran, M.D., Ph.D., and Sandra Blakeslee, *Phantoms in the Brain: Probing the Mysteries of the*

Why America's Children Can't Think

Human Mind (New York: William Morrow, 1998). This last has some useful categories for different kinds of conscious activity: the embodied self, the passionate self, the executive self, the mnemonic self, the unified self—imposing consciousness, filling in and confabulation, the vigilant self, the conceptual self and the social self (see 246–57).

3 One of the things that makes Joyce's *Ulysses* arguably the greatest novel of the twentieth century is that it accepts and exploits this fact. Everything in it happens in one day. It is about the state of the stream of consciousness of several people on that day.

4 What I'm getting at here is a very basic element in the perception of reality. If you are one of the vast majority who have ten fingers, you are likely to know that your fingers are one example of those groups that have ten members. You can then generalize the number ten from many particular instances. This perception eventually becomes so automatic that you can't imagine not knowing it. That being so, anyone who has not generalized the number ten in this way might seem unbelievably stupid to you, and because you have forgotten even learning that generalization, you can't imagine how it should be taught to someone who hasn't learned it. It is in this area of what seems most obvious that many of the deepest conundrums about learning may be found. Indeed, they are so deep that they have seriously impeded the progress of developing artificial intelligence. So indeed, what seems most obvious is, in this sense, most mysterious.

One of the most startling discoveries I've made over the years is how very often a tiny misunderstanding that might easily be cleared up in less than five minutes can create a barrier to knowledge about some basic principle that can confuse a person for decades. For example, when I was trying to learn to sing part-songs, I somehow got the idea that in order to sing harmony you had to think of a particular note in the melody and then sing a note that was different from that one. This left me completely confused about part-singing until I was well over fifty. Then one day it occurred to me that harmony is just a different tune sung against the dominant one. If you learn that different tune, you can sing part-songs very easily. I suddenly understood the problem and became very good at part-singing. Since my life experience had frequently required me to sing part-songs in public and I had always done it badly, I could have saved myself enormous embarrassment, frustration and mediocrity by making that little discovery a few decades earlier than I did.

I mention this because such misunderstandings are legion in everyone's experience. They can be discovered only when a you begin to explore, in some depth, what's going on when you're trying to do something you can't do well. Under the right circumstances, it's then often possible to clear up lifetime confusions in a few minutes. But you can't solve a problem until you know what it is that you don't know or can identify what system of thinking is causing you to make the mistake you're making.

5 Pleasure is experienced differently by different people. I often derive profound excitement from studying the footnotes of the texts of obscure Shakespeare plays, or from reading record reviews of eighteenth-century operas practically no one has ever heard of. You

might derive the same kind of pleasure from examining a list of the batting averages of baseball players a century ago. Or perhaps the latest electronics catalog sends you into nirvana while the person next to you gets equal pleasure from the umpteenth Louis L'Amour western. It's this sort of diversity of taste that makes it rather difficult to decide in any objective way what constitutes a good book. In the end, as Shakespeare said, "There's nothing good or bad but thinking makes it so."

Chapter 12

1 George Bernard Shaw, *Immaturity* (New York: Wm. H. Wise, 1930), xxxii–xxxiii.

2 Jean-Paul Sartre, *Existentialism and Human Emotions* (New York: Wisdom Library, 1957).

3 Even in the most rigid forms of fundamentalism, each person decides which aspects of the accepted dogma to act on vigorously, and which to soft-pedal. Total unity of opinion among the members of any group is theoretically impossible if only because no individual can know everything about what some other individual thinks. We are, for this reason, condemned to intellectual freedom whether we like it or not.

4 Chapter 22 provides an explanation of why this is so.

5 Art Linkletter's *Kids Say the Darnedest Things* is funny and cute, and I enjoy it. But it completely fails to take into account the essential seriousness and depth of which childhood thought is capable. Our tendency to dismiss children's remarks as, at best, a form of light entertainment has a crippling effect on our ability to discover the profound insights they may have to offer. We need to learn to have serious discussions with children that bring out the depth of thought of which they are capable.

6 Jean Liedloff, *The Continuum Concept* (New York: Alfred A. Knopf, 1977).

7 Young children seem to know better than falling off a cliff or doing damage to themselves with a sharp knife because these are threats that have been around for hundreds of thousands of years. They could not be expected to know, however, to look both ways before crossing the street or to avoid touching live wires. Therefore this approach to child rearing couldn't work in modern society, because society has changed beyond the ability of small children to adapt to it. Still, the Yequana have much to teach us about child rearing. Their methods could be easily adapted for use in modern society. Such experiments as Summerhill were attempts to do this. There are a number of experts in early learning development who use such methods with outstanding results. (See *Preventing Early Learning Failure*, listed under my authorship in the bibliography. See also A. S. Neill, *Summerhill School: A New View of Childhood* [New York: St. Martin's Press, 1993].)

8 Cf. Richard Feynman.

9 Biography and autobiography are always open to question, though, most of the time, Shaw was remarkably consistent in his reports on his life. There were some inconsistencies, however, between different accounts of the same event as he gave them over the

years, and as some of his biographers did as well. B. C. Rosset bravely set out to reconcile these in a comprehensive study of his formative years (*Shaw of Dublin: The Formative Years* [University Park, PA: The Pennsylvania State University Press, 1964]). This particular episode is dealt with quite simply in this book, and replicates exactly Shaw's report of it in *Sixteen Self Sketches*. Shaw adds the comments about his family's reaction of mirth in the Preface to *Immaturity*, cited earlier.

10 Van Wyck Brooks did an intensive study of the writings of Mark Twain toward the end of his life when he had become completely undone by a series of personal tragedies. He found the great humorist spinning out thousands of pages that led nowhere and contained none of his richly ironic point of view. It was evident from this loss of creativity that Twain did not have the emotional resilience to deal with the tragic aspects of his life the way Shaw did.

11 This aspect of Newton's experience and its consequences for science and philosophy have been compellingly dealt with by Morris Berman in *The Reenchantment of the World* (New York: Bantam Books, 1984).

12 When the film *Jurassic Park* came out, there was much concern about whether children should be allowed to see it. Under duress I took seven-year-old Jonathan. The film scared me so much I couldn't sleep that night, but Jonathan never flinched and insisted on seeing it again at least a dozen times.

Chapter 13

1 *Kenyon Review*, XXI, no. 3 (Summer 1959).

2 An excellent example is William J. J. Gordon's system of Synectics, which has been used to increase greatly the productivity of innovators in industrial and scientific settings. The entire system is based on personal, biological and morphological analogies, and proceeds by making the familiar strange and the strange familiar.

3 This doesn't mean that many of his plays weren't historically inaccurate—often to an astonishing degree. It does mean that, like so many other great writers, he played with history as he saw fit and made many historical figures and events far more real for us than they could have been without him.

4 Recently in designing a computer-assisted learning program for a corporation, I was asked to produce a set of review questions on the highly technical material being taught, some of which is about the legal system. I had expected to write a series of multiple choice questions, but instead discovered that it made more sense to write questions that elicited precise information, but at the same time asked for a discussion of how this information would be applied. It's not possible, at present, for a computer to evaluate such answers, but they can be peer-evaluated in groups of students, or elicited in discussion with an instructor. The important thing is that in writing these questions I found myself thinking about the material in a much more powerful and useful way. Such ques-

tioning gets a student into the material more deeply and quickly. Through appropriate group process it could be used to replace much of the superficial standardized testing in use now.

Chapter 14

1 This is not unlike the concept developed in *The Inner Game of Tennis*, by Timothy Galway.
2 Ronald W. Clark, *Einstein: The Life and Times* (New York: World Publishing Company, 1971), 257.

Chapter 16

1 George Bernard Shaw, *London Music in 1888–89 as Heard by Corno di Bassetto (Later Known as Bernard Shaw) with Some Further Autobiographical Particulars* (New York: Vienna House, 1973), 85.
2 I have dealt with this work extensively in my book *The Everyday Genius*.
3 Evidence for this is in the writings of some of the people Shakespeare based his characters on. For example, Sir Andrew Aguecheek uses the same kinds of phrases, emotional expressions and ridiculous juxtapositions of emotion that Philip Sidney used in some of his private correspondence. Again, the private correspondence of Lord Burghley closely resembles the circuitous manner of speech used by Polonius, for whom Burghley was the model.
4 There's more science to this than you might think. Dr. Manfred Clynes developed a method called Sensics that allowed him to identify emotional patterns that defined the differences in composers' styles. He had concert pianists imagine themselves to be playing pieces by different composers while pressing a button that measured slight changes of pressure in an ongoing pattern. Many different pianists produced these patterns for composers such as Mozart, Beethoven, Chopin and so on. Regardless of the composition or the pianist playing it, the same pattern always emerged for each composer—a distinctive sort of emotional signature. We all know intuitively what this is, because we recognize the sounds of each of these composers almost instantly when we hear their music, and recognize it as easily in pieces we have never heard before as in those that are familiar to us. We have the same feeling about style in writing. Dickens, Joyce, Truman Capote, Hemingway, Fitzgerald (even, heaven help him, John Grisham) all have styles that we can recognize. Regardless of what they are writing about or describing, they have emotional signatures that show up throughout their work.
5 This rather unattractive word was introduced into the language (or at least popularized) by President Calvin Coolidge, who also said, "The business of America is business."

Why America's Children Can't Think

Chapter 17

1 The renowned plant physiologist Rupert Sheldrake has developed the concept of morphogenetic fields—an analogy to magnetic fields, except that the former are organized by the intelligent structure of organic systems. These fields are the storage area for memories and allow whole species to establish a collective memory and a collective consciousness. Many aspects of our collective experience that are otherwise unexplainable can be easily explained using Sheldrake's hypothesis. The mechanics by which this hypothesis might operate can be visualized in terms of a holographic field that interacts with the nervous system (or with other organic structures) as a storage mechanism for memory. Since no area of the brain has ever been found where memories are retained (as opposed to recorded or accessed), such a mechanism is needed. Fred Alan Wolf developed the model for a holographic memory, but I have seen no evidence that he and Sheldrake have communicated about this. See Rupert Sheldrake, *A New Science of Life: The Hypothesis of Formative Causation* (Los Angeles: J. P. Tarcher, 1987); Rupert Sheldrake, *The Presence of the Past: Morphic Resonance and the Habits of Nature* (New York: Vintage Books, 1989); and Fred Alan Wolf, *The Dreaming Universe: A Mind-Expanding Journey into the Realm Where Psyche and Physics Meet* (New York: Simon & Schuster, 1994).

2 In the 2000 presidential election, the concept of a trillion dollars was assumed in all the debates and most of the campaign speeches. Unfortunately a high percentage of the population has no mental model for a trillion dollars, so the argument was meaningless to them. This is one reason so few people vote: The candidates do not explain what they are talking about. It's as if a candidate said, "My opponent wants to take money out of your pocket and duodecasephalith it." Only the tone of voice would convey the slightest idea what the consequences of such a thing might be. The same problem arose in the O. J. Simpson trial. The prosecution spent many hours talking about DNA evidence with out ever explaining what DNA is. Most people don't know, and don't want to admit (even to themselves) that they don't. As a result, the jury may have tuned out the entire discussion and decided it was just an example of the double-talk white people have used to confuse and entrap black people ever since Thomas Jefferson (a slave holder) told everyone that it is a "self-evident truth" that "all men are created equal." If this truth was self-evident, how come Jefferson didn't know what it meant? One reason I often use the pronoun "she" in this book is that when Jefferson wrote "men" in that sentence, he never intended that it should include "women," so the argument that "men" means "people" is both false and ridiculous as everyone with any knowledge of history should know.

3 One would think this was self-evident, but it's only about as self-evident as Jefferson's utterly incomprehensible assertion of equality—for which there is no evidence either in physical reality or in the realm of abstract ideas. No two people have ever been equal to each other—not even identical twins. Nor were they created equal. Nor would they want

to be equal. So, in the light of slavery and everything that has happened since 1776, what do you think Jefferson "really" meant? (You have two hours to write your answer.) My point is, I have seldom seen anyone teach reading in a way that would invite students to form the habit of checking out all the unfamiliar concepts in their reading—which involves a great deal more than just looking words up in the dictionary. Though even inculcating *that* habit would be nothing short of a miracle. The resulting problems don't just afflict unsuccessful students. They afflict even presidential candidates. In the recent election I heard George W. Bush say something that made me think he didn't know social security is a federal program. (Don't be too hard on him—lots of people don't know that.) And I heard Al Gore say something that made me think he didn't know that if he said he had been somewhere, that meant he actually had to have been there. No wonder so many people have trouble reading.

4   Recently I have discovered that for many people this is not true. There are lots of intelligent people who literally have no mental constructs for even the simplest equations and are therefore completely befuddled by anything in the slightest degree mathematical.

Chapter 18

1   For example, the attacks on Pasteur by those who believed in spontaneous generation were so absurd that history has recorded only their absurdity. This overreaction in the other direction has made us overvalue Pasteur's discoveries at the expense of possible qualifications of them that might otherwise have developed in a more thoughtful atmosphere. Today many people realize that germs are not the entire explanation of disease. But the general public has bought the germ theory so completely that it is hard to get a hearing for qualifications of it that do not invalidate Pasteur's discoveries, but rather extend their implications and make their applications more precise and specific.

2   For example, those who have studied the ideas of the Iroquois Nation think they might have much to teach us. Unfortunately, we, who think we are not primitive savages, assume that we know better. There is, meanwhile, a body of evidence that strongly suggests the possibility that we are, in fact, really very primitive and very savage.

3   I have already aired the case of Sir Isaac Newton's difficulties in this regard. If there was ever a paragon of logical thinking, it was Newton. Too bad that, in so many respects, even the lord and master of all scientists made serious mistakes that have misdirected the scientific community ever since. As Shakespeare so aptly put it, "Madness in great ones must not unwatched go."

4   The saving grace of the U.S.A. is that it has so many unassimilated cultures that patriotic fervor, no matter what inspires it, is nearly always criticized if not condemned in some quarters.

5   The best account of this era in American history is *Dereliction of Duty: Lyndon Johnson, Robert McNamara, the Joint Chiefs of Staff and the Lies That Led to Vietnam,*

Why America's Children Can't Think

by H. R. McMaster (New York: Harper Collins, 1997).

6   A book that offers many examples of the need for this process in the political arena is Thomas Sowell's *The Vision of the Anointed: Self-Congratulation as a Basis for Social Policy* (New York: Basic Books, 1995). Though it focuses almost entirely on liberal political agendas, this book does a stunning job of revealing the way in which political action can make assumptions that are not valid without ever questioning their validity. Another book that is needed would tell the same story about conservative political agendas, which are no better in this respect.

7   A rare exception occurred on the "Today Show" on April 25, 2002, when Bernard Goldberg and Michael Moore, both of whom had recent bestsellers to their credit, admitted to positions at opposite ends of the political spectrum, while at the same time celebrating their agreement on many fundamental issues. Goldberg summed it up by saying, "We have one America but there are two cultures." See their books: Bernard Goldberg, *Bias: A CBS Insider Exposes How the Media Distorts the News* (Washington, DC: Regnery, 2001); and Michael Moore, *Stupid White Men* (New York: Regan Books, 2002).

8   Barry's thoughts on this subject are contained in the following Pendel Hill pamphlet: Barry Morley, *Beyond Consensus: Salvaging Sense of the Meeting* (Wallingford, PA: Pendle Hill, 1993).

9   For a typical example of this very common intellectual disaster, see chapter 22.

10   Even Leonard Bernstein, possibly the finest composer of the second half of the twentieth century, fell into a similar pitfall. Oversensitive to criticism, he was unable to bring many of his important projects to a conclusion. When, on occasion he had a partial failure (as in the case of *Candide*), he rewrote it continually for the rest of his life.

11   In strict mathematical terms, this is not correct, since because this infinity can be mapped onto other infinities it is therefore not different from them. (There is no difference between the infinity of whole numbers and the infinity of fractions. However, the infinity of irrational numbers is of a different order than the infinity of fractions, and in subdividing an inch, we need to decide which of these infinities we are implying. Once we imply it, however, there's no difference between this infinity and that which arises from subdividing a long series of inches.) My statement is, however, close enough to make the point I am after here.

12   You math buffs may be aware of Lakatos's criticisms of geometry and other types of mathematical reasoning that call into serious question most of the logic you learned in your math classes. (Imre Lakatos, *Proofs and Refutations: The Logic of Mathematical Discovery*, eds. John Worrall and Elie Zahar [New York: Cambridge University Press, 1976]).

13   A particularly mystifying confusion developed in the history of rocketry. As you know, in a jet engine fuel explodes, impacting the solidity of the end of the plane and pushing it forward. Every child is supposed to know that this happens because "every action

produces an equal and opposite reaction." Physicists who don't know that are roughly equivalent to preachers who have never heard of God. Yet much of the opposition to the development of rocketry came from physicists who were certain that this principle couldn't work in a vacuum, and so rockets couldn't be operated in interplanetary space. They can. What could possibly have made anyone think they couldn't?

14 Readers interested in a zany scenario for human extinction (albeit quite a believable one) might want to sample the last chapter of *Next: The Future Just Happened*, by Michael Lewis (New York: W. W. Norton, 2001).

Chapter 19

1 In Francis Fergusson, *The Human Dimension in Dramatic Literature* (Garden City: Doubleday, 1953).

2 In Cleanth Brooks, *The Well-Wrought Urn* (New York: Reynal and Hitchcock, 1947).

Chapter 21

1 Richard Daniel Altick, *The Art of Literary Research* (New York: Norton, 1963), 5.

Chapter 22

1 President, Chicago Bar Association, and editor of *The American Bar Association Journal*. Starting in 1959, Bentley wrote and sponsored an excellent series of articles on the Oxford theory in the *ABA Journal*.

2 Sylvester Jourdain was the author of *A Discovery of the Bermudas, Otherwise Called the Ile of Divels*. James Campbell's *Reader's Encyclopedia of Shakespeare* says only that "Shakespeare may have made use of this pamphlet for his description of the storm and the atmosphere of Prospero's island in *The Tempest*."

3 The following is quoted from the guidebook of Otley Hall, pages 23 and 24:

The Plahouse was an occasional theatre and served several purposes, rather like a school assembly hall where plays are put on, assemblies and parents meetings are held, and meals are eaten. It held a Banqueting Room on the first floor that was possibly used as a courtroom, and a ground-floor loggia for walking in on rainy days. The top floor was used for viewing, and there is evidence that a large number of people where taken up to it. Nevertheless as its name, long remembered within the Gosnold family, suggests, its playhouse function was paramount.

The wood for the Plahouse was not local. It was brought in from the "London area." Assuming that it had not been removed from a London playhouse that was dismantled, like the 1576 Theatre whose timbers were used in the building of the Globe, then the wood was brought in from a forest in the Greater London area. Either way, London involvement was likely, and it is possible that de Vere was involved in the planning of the building. He had become a widower in June. After fighting the Spanish Armada in the summer of 1588 and holding the canopy over the Queen in the procession in St. Paul's in November, he disappeared from Court, possibly to Otley Hall to stay with his cousins and help put the finishing touches to the Plahouse. Some Oxfordians (who believe that the Earl of Oxford was the author of Shakespeare's works) maintain that *Hamlet* was completed in the winter of 1588/9 and *Othello* in the spring of 1589, and it is fascinating to think that their author may have stayed at Otley Hall during these times, recovering from his wife's death and advising on the theatre.

4   This is how Laertes characterizes Hamlet when describing him to Ophelia. Like Anne Page and Fenton, Ophelia and Hamlet are based on Anne Cecil and Edward de Vere.

5   "*The Merry Wives* belongs to that small group of Shakespeare's plays that have no known source." Thus writes William Green in his introduction to the play in *The Complete Signet Classic Shakespeare*. It is clear from the events described here that the chief source is now known, and that it does not derive from some other play, but rather from the author's real-life experiences.

6   Eva Turner Clark (ed. Ruth Loyd Miller), *Hidden Allusions in Shakespeare's Plays* (Part Washington, NY: Kennikat Press, 1974).

7   William Plumer Fowler, *Shakespeare Revealed in Oxford's Letters* (Portsmouth, NH: Peter E. Randall, 1986).

8   The word "disfurnishing" appears in Oxford's novel (the first English novel) *The Adventures of Master F. I.*, but I have been unable to trace any variant of this word in any glossary of works published during Oxford's lifetime.

Another fascinating bit of literary DNA is the following: Oxford made frequent use of proverbs, as do most writers. Unlike them, however, he often made up his own pseudo-proverbs. That's certainly one reason he is the most often quoted writer in all of literature. Following is one of the made-up ones that I imagine comes from the experience of carpentry he would have had when as a lad he hung about the workmen who were building the wooden platforms for stages constructed in Hedingham Castle's great hall. Most carpenters know that if you drive a headless nail into a plank in the wrong place, one way to get it out is to use another nail to drive it through, leaving the second nail enough above the surface of the wood so you can pull it out.

Following are four proverb-like references to this phenomenon:

The proverb saith unminded oft are they that are unseen
And as out of a plank a nail [another nail] doth drive,

So novel love out of the mind the ancient love doth rive.

This is from *Romeus and Juliet*, by "Arthur Brooke" (actually, Lord Oxford).

F. I. hoping to drive out one nail with another, and thinking this a means most convenient to suppress all his jealous supposes . . .

This is from *The Adventures of Mr. F. I.*, by "Anonymous," later "George Gascoigne" (but in reality, Lord Oxford).

Even as one heat another heat expels,
Or as one nail by strength drives out another,
So the remembrance of my former love
Is by a new object quite forgotten.

This is from *The Two Gentlemen of Verona*, by "William Shakespeare."

One fire drives out one fire; one nail, one nail.

This is from *Coriolanus*, by "William Shakespeare."

All four of these works have been shown by other means to be by the Earl of Oxford. These quotations demonstrate his amazing propensity to reuse and develop certain ideas that are cross-referenced among his many works. As far as I know, no other writer of the period is as cross-referential and self-referential as "Shakespeare," and examples like this one can probably be gathered by the hundreds. Note that in all four cases the basic "Shakespearean" paradox is revealed: the virtue of a thing is its own undoing, and the force that drives it is the force that destroys it. Note also how the maturity of the writing advances as the boy of twelve becomes the man of twenty-three, and the mature writer emerges from the cocoon of juvenilia.

In addition to the above, *The Spanish Tragedy* includes a line stating that one ill drives out another. (Lord Oxford also wrote *The Spanish Tragedy*.) The most important quality in this play that links it with "Shakespeare's" style is that it keeps altering the position from which we view the action. Here, randomly selected, is the beginning of Hieronimo's soliloquy at the beginning of act 3, scene 2:

O eyes, no eyes, but fountains fraught with tears;
O life, no life, but lively form of death;
O world, no world, but mass of public wrongs,
Confused and filed with murder and misdeeds!

Why America's Children Can't Think

O sacred heavens! If this unhallowed deed,
If this inhuman and barb'rous attempt,
If this incomparable murder thus
Of mine, but now no more my son,
Shall unreveal'd and unrevengéd pass,
How should we term your dealings to be just,
If you unjustly deal with those that in your justice trust?
The night, sad secretary to my moans,
With direful visions wake my vexéd soul,
And with the wounds of my distressful son
Solicit me for notice of his death.
The ugly fiends do sally forth of hell,
And frame my steps to unfrequented paths,
And fear my heart with fierce inflaméd thoughts.
The cloudy day my discontents records,
Early begins to register my dreams
And drive me forth to seek the murderer.
Eyes, life, world, heavens, hell, night, and day,
See, search, show, send some man, some mean, that may—

This is more fustian than poetry, and will have far to go yet to reach the level of *Hamlet*. Still, fustian though it is, it's great fustian—any actor's dream of a powerful speech. No wonder this play remained a hit for several decades. What seems excessive to the eye, lightens like a heavenly storm in the ear, an exciting set of images that keep shifting the perspective as, in the first four words, the denial of what was said immediately before is established. The effect is of an army of paradoxes parading through the situation like a battalion that seems almost inexhaustible.

9 The Veritas Publishing Company will bring out my full-length book on this subject, entitled *The Shakespeare Mysteries*, in tandem with Syril Kline's historical novel on the same subject. In addition, the company is planning a complete new scholarly edition of all the works of Lord Oxford, to be edited by about sixty different scholars at many colleges and universities. My book is scheduled to appear in February 2003.

10 The reference to "impress of shipwrights" is from the first scene of *Hamlet*, and is one of the reasons that so many believe this scene was originally written in 1587, while the English were preparing for war against Spain by a huge increase in the rate of shipbuilding.

11 There is an almost exact parallel for this situation in recent American history, and this story, too, was completely hidden from the historical record for more than half a century and even now remains tucked away in obscure articles in a couple of journals. The Summer 1997 issue of *The Historical Review* contains an article by Thomas Howell,

entitled "U.S. Domestic Propaganda in World War II."

Its contents should become a chapter in every history book that covers twentieth-century America, for it is still unknown to most people. As evidence of this astonishing fact, Howell cites *A Democracy at War: America's Fight at Home and Abroad in World War II*, published in 1993 by William O'Neill. In it, O'Neill refers to "Washington's lack of interest in propaganda."

Nothing could be further from the truth. But to discover that truth, Howell had to comb government documents and the records of many private organizations, as well as numerous ancient articles in newspapers and magazines; for the story he had to tell was, without that effort, unknowable.

What emerges is a picture of a vast government propaganda machine that got its start on December 9, 1941, when "Secretary of the Treasury Henry Morganthau Jr. approved an initiative to seek civilian writers who would promote the war effort, and within a month the Writers' War Board was organized." Incidentally, the government was interested in the most commercially successful writers it could find, since they had the best access to the media.

Howell continues:

> While the organization utilized thousands of writers nationwide to develop and place subtle propaganda in all communications media, the board itself was a self-recruited group of about twenty authors from the New York City area, mainly involved with popular or commercial writing. The chairman, Rex Stout, wrote best sellers about fictional detective Nero Wolfe. Other well-known members included Clifton Fadiman, editor of the Book-of-the-Month Club and host of the highly rated radio show "Information Please"; Broadway lyricist Oscar Hammerstein II; Broadway dramatist Russell Crouse; novelists Paul Gallico, Pearl Buck, and John Marquand; Pulitzer Prize–winning historian Margaret Leech; journalist William Shirer; and radio commentator Elmer Davis. Only Stout devoted himself full time to board affairs, but all attended weekly meetings and used their time, talents and contacts extensively.

Note the close parallel with the Elizabethan situation, for once again the government formed an organization that was run by one of the most popular writers of the day and turned it loose to do its work.

And, again like the Elizabethan government, the U.S. government took the official position (still almost universally believed today) that it would not engage in propaganda, only an official "strategy of truth." However, this position was untenable, since most of the significant true information that might have been relevant was classified for security reasons.

In fact, it was not long before the Writers' War Board was subsidized by the government, with the result that thousands of writers began placing tens of thousands of literary efforts in high-profile popular journals, newspapers, radio shows, movies and plays.

Highlights included "War Script of the Month," one example of which was Steven Vincent Benet's "They Burned the Books" and eight hundred prepared speeches per month "on war-related subjects such as 'Our Enemy—Madame Butterfly.'"

By 1944 the WWB calculated that 85 percent of its work "was done at the request of the U.S. government."

A striking parallel with "Shakespeare" is "The Murder of Lidice" by Edna St. Vincent Millay, a dramatic poem inspired by Hitler's execution of men, women and children in Lidice, Czechoslovakia on June 10, 1942. The following lines from that poem are a reminder of Henry V's anger at the French troops' slaughter of the boys in his camp. They also hearken back to Lord Oxford's reaction to the St. Bartholomew's Day Massacre:

The whole world holds in its arms today
The murdered village of Lidice,
Like the murdered body of a little child,
Innocent, happy, surprised at play—
The murdered body, stained and defiled,
Tortured and mangled, of a helpless child.

Howell's article makes it seem likely that without the Writers' War Board, the Nazis might have won the war.

12 See Allan Keen and Roger Lubbock, *The Annotator* (New York: Macmillan, 1954), 11.
13 Ibid., 20.

Afterword

1 We still lack any but the most primitive notions of how the educational system affects the economy. Sophisticated mathematical analysis is possible, and would almost certainly produce many surprising insights. Until such work is done, however, we will remain a highly primitive culture with respect to our ability to understand what may be in store for us in the future.

John Nash won the Nobel Prize in economics for his work in extending the notion of how the market operates to include a human tendency toward altruism. Much of his work was in the field of calculating the most effective negotiating positions for two people in dissimilar circumstances. This work opens the door for a consideration of how education (as well as some other factors) affects the development of the economy. In fact it should be possible to show that education, economics, multiculturalism and technology are all inextricably linked in their effect on one another. Only when national planners and systems analysts take these relationships fully into account will we be able to make meaningful statements about the future of the economy, technology and cultural development.

2 Marian Diamond at U.C. Berkeley has been the leader in this powerful new discovery.

3 See Robert Kanigel, *Apprentice to Genius* (New York: Macmillan, 1986) for an example of the intellectually playful atmosphere in which four generations of geniuses in the field of pharmacology learned to operate.

4 Allan David Bloom, *The Closing of the American Mind: How Higher Education Has Failed Democracy and Impoverished the Souls of Today's Students* (New York: Simon and Schuster, 1987).

5 John Taylor Gatto, *Dumbing Us Down: The Hidden Curriculum of Compulsory Schooling* (Philadelphia: New Society Publishers, 1992).

6 In the last few hours before this book went to press, I was able to crystallize the following report on the current situation from sources I have just recently discovered.

For several decades the government bureaucracies, largely in the form of intermediate school districts, which exist in forty-five of the fifty states, have successfully protected the public schools against any meaningful innovation. The failure of the public schools is thus not due to the teachers, many of whom are heroes toiling thanklessly in dens of intellectual iniquity. It is due to a ridiculously top-heavy administrative process that needs either to be trimmed very significantly, or to be put to work to produce the results I am suggesting here. If the money spent on school administration were used instead for raising the salaries of teachers, creating extensive opportunities for them to improve their methodologies, and smaller classroom sizes, the result could be an educational renaissance unlike anything previously known.

An anonymous source who spent much of his career on the staff of a state department of education told me, "I could complete all my responsibilities for the entire year in fifteen days. The rest of the time I had no official duties. Because I was committed to bettering education I spent my time trying to help the clients I supervised do a better job. But whenever I did anything like that I was reprimanded. 'You're not supposed to work with those people, you're supposed to keep them in line,' my boss told me."

He went on to reveal that, at least in his state, the members of the intermediate school districts are paid more than anyone else in the system. Their primary activity is to filter out new ideas, since these would require them to do more work. Their laziness is legendary, and when my source requested that they call the principals in the various school systems to verify certain required information, their reply was, "That's too much work."

These people actually spend their time going to meetings where they meet with similar individuals from other districts, often in other states. There they sell their consulting services to each other, and arrange to make trips to each other's districts, so as to use up the funds allocated for school improvement. It's this sort of "activity" that engages the time of a legion of Ph.D.'s. Their existence costs the state well in excess of $10 million in salaries alone. In addition, their offices are richly furnished with fine leather chairs and the like. All this, my source believes, is one of the largest sinkholes for money that exists today in public education. For example, in a drug prevention program he administered, 85 percent of the money went to these folks, and only 15 percent ended up in the hands of the school districts. How much of it actually served to educate any of the students is anyone's guess.

A single law passed in Congress could eliminate all such organizations and require each state department of education to take on the challenge I've described above. In the process, the ratio of money spent on administration, as compared to teaching, could be significantly improved. This would reallocate funds for the purposes mentioned above.

Short of such measures, we are unlikely to see any more improvement in the schools than we have seen over the last century—virtually none at all. During the same period, the private sector has realized the most rapid innovative advances in history. Unfortunately, however, because of the failures in the schools, the workforce has not been well enough educated to sustain the technological advances now in existence. That is one of the reasons the bottom fell out of the "dot com" movement, bringing on a most unfortunate economic recession.

Had the average American been able to move comfortably into the information age economy (instead of, as actually happened, only 17 percent of the population), we would have seen an explosive growth in our economy. Thanks to Moore's law, it is now theoretically possible to develop an economy that never stops growing until every person on Earth is comfortably well-to-do. This can be accomplished even while helping to repair the damage to the environment that past excesses have wrought.

We might actually have been there now, but for an unfortunate failure to pass the ball from one administration to the next that took place in 1989.

In its final days, the Reagan administration attempted to establish the National Learning Foundation (NLF) as a White House initiative, intended as a legacy to the nation. Unfortunately, the Bush administration that followed quashed this initiative almost immediately. Thus the self-named "education president" began his administration by dealing a deathblow to a very significant source of potential educational reform.

The NLF was designed to bring to public attention the many alternative forms of education that produced successful results in education that far surpassed those produced by traditional education. It was the shared view of those who gathered to form the NLF that schools can actually teach about ten times as much material as they now teach, without adding to the stress of either teachers or students. In fact, the only way to accomplish such an apparently astonishing goal is to introduce a great deal of fun into the learning process.

Because this opportunity was missed and the NLF was never adequately funded (though it continues to exist), the great liberal ideal of educating the average citizen well enough to be able to make informed decisions about future governance as a basis for intelligent voting has largely been replaced by a well-documented "dumbing down" of the schools—an effect both ultraconservative and ultraliberal commentators agree on, as well as most people in between the two extremes.

By insisting on evaluating the success of the schools on the basis of student scores Ion standardized tests, the second Bush administration has virtually forced teachers to teach to those tests, a process that—as all really good teachers know (and will usually tell you)—significantly retards both the process and value of education.

Therefore, any successful attempt to improve the public schools will have to focus on a widespread reform of teacher education, on widespread high-quality in-service training for teachers, on the integration of computer technology into the educational process, and on the transformation both of the curriculum itself and the way it is taught. By fostering the best available curriculum materials and teaching methods, the goal of "leaving no child behind" can be accomplished quickly and with many positive side effects. The result would be teaching that takes into account the following description of good learning based on information put forward by the National Research Council and other scientific organizations.

We now have a more detailed understanding of how the various parts of the brain interact to collect, process, organize and store information gathered by the various senses, and then create meaning and develop appropriate responses to these inputs. The most important idea drawn from these research efforts is that although this complex organ is made up of basically the same components with essentially the same functions, each individual has unique configurations of these elements, and therefore responds differently to various stimuli. Therefore, learning must always be individualized.

The following principles derive from this general statement:

a. Information is best learned in contexts established through previous experience.

b. The brain is designed to organize chaotic situations for itself, not to memorize previously established structures.

c. Skills must be layered in, so that the learner is always responding on many levels simultaneously.

d. Learning that is not based on emotion does not compute as part of the total personality.

e. The brain is designed to process many different inputs simultaneously. This capacity is diminished under stress.

f. Challenge enhances thinking. Fear limits it. The difference is up to the interpretation of the learner.

g. It is never advisable to learn something solely for the purpose of being able to learn something else. All areas of learning should be significant in and of themselves.

h. Intelligence may be best defined as the ability to operate simultaneously in your own best interests as well as those of your community.

i. There are no parts without wholes and no wholes without parts. Seeing these in relation to one another is crucial to learning.

j. The learning pyramid builds from the simplest to the most complex meanings. Therefore the most powerful way to open up new levels of understanding is to build in simple root concepts that are new.

In addition, some people respond more to the written word, others to pictures and sound. Others may be more sensitive to music. Others are more responsive to activities. There is solid evidence supporting the notion that the brain functions optimally when it works as a whole unit, when various senses and processes are mobilized, and when it is stimulated to reflect and create new ideas.

Writing as a nonpartisan supporter of education reform, I can see this process developing in several possible ways. Though the process might be rather different, the results would be at least similar.

As a group, Republicans favor privatization of the schools. They have already initiated a process that forces public schools in many states to compete against charter schools. Charter schools, promising to do a better job than the public schools, take students away from them, thus decreasing their available budgets. Thus the public schools are forced to compete based on the quality and value of their offerings, just like department stores, telephone companies and insurance agencies. This would speed up the process of forcing the public schools either to compete effectively or go out of business.

To a large extent this system has worked at producing such things as better computers, automobiles, telephone systems and many other things. However, such an approach is vulnerable to Gresham's law, which states that "bad money drives out good." We have seen this in the newspaper business, the book publishing industry and any number of other examples of corporate monstrosities destroying small but highly effective quality enterprises. That might lead one to suspect that the same unfortunate development could occur in the transformation of the schools.

Meanwhile, the idea of public education is a noble ideal with a long history, and it can still be saved. An approach taken up by the Democratic party might begin by adopting the findings of the scientific community that are stated above, and systematically revising all curricula and teaching methods. This could result from oversight that would raise the quality of education in each state. Competent people in the intermediate school districts or the state school boards could administer programs able to guarantee that students are so well educated that the average high school graduate is prepared to think deeply about significant issues and act professionally in the pursuit of significant goals. All activities designed to improve the system would be results based and, if possible, research based as well. This could be accomplished by reeducating the staff of the intermediate school districts so they are able to understand such programs well enough to administer them effectively. Each state could then be required to deliver an education that leaves no child behind.

There are two other models capable of accomplishing much the same thing. One is a coalition of groups with a commitment to innovations capable of radically improving education. This could be funded by the National Science Foundation, as well as interested corporations, and transform carefully selected schools all over the country into Flagship Schools.

The second is the West Virginia Project, a plan now being considered by the National Learning Foundation, designed to raise the economic status of an entire state until it becomes the first modern utopia. West Virginia is, for a variety of interesting reasons, the best place in the world to carry out such a project. According to this plan, Flagship Schools would be created all around the state and their models gradually spread to all the other schools in the state. Thus West Virginia would have the best educational system in the world, a model not only for all other states in the country, but throughout the world as well. A major industry for West Virginia would then be exporting its educational system to the rest of the world.

Of course there will be numerous objections to such a plan, many of them political in nature. Not carrying through on such a project, however, would be as immoral as gassing a large population, simply because unless such measures are taken, many people continue to suffer inordinately and some die very prematurely, not only in West Virginia, but also in many other parts of the world that could learn from West Virginia's experience.

For that reason, I confidently expect that the West Virginia Project will be carried out, and that the media will properly expose all those who try to stop such an essential movement forward in the direction of a newly effective civilization.

7   Martin Mayer, *The Schools* (New York: Harper, 1961).

8   A case in point is the Milton Hershey School, the best-endowed public school in the country. This school has a budget requiring it to spend half a billion dollars every year. It provides a posh boarding school experience for a K-12 enrollment of indigent students projected to climb to fifteen hundred by 2006. It describes its offerings as follows: "Specialized programs in the School's standards-based curriculum, which prepares students for both continuing education and the world of work, include K-12 career and vocational education, as well as agricultural and environmental education."

Meanwhile, "60 Minutes" has aired a lawsuit initiated by graduates of the school against the school's administration. They claim the school's current admissions standards filter out students with academic records below a certain level. These graduates point out that such standards were not operative when they attended the school, since they themselves would not have been admitted if they had been.

In contrast, FocusHOPE, an educational environment funded by the National Science Foundation and operative with multimillion-dollar budgets in both Detroit and

Why America's Children Can't Think

Philadelphia, is successfully training adult high school dropouts with abysmal academic records to become well-educated, high-level industrial engineers and managers. Hiding behind the amorphous phrase "standards-based curriculum" the Milton Hershey School cannot hope to compete with this record.

School vice president Ronald W. Thompson has so far been unresponsive to my suggestion that the school add a new curriculum (possibly on a separate campus) especially adapted to the needs of students with poor academic records. I have shared with him evidence that such a school could produce outstanding results of the kind mentioned in this book. This would be responsive to the demands of the disgruntled graduates of the school.

It could go much further than that, however. Instead of improving young minds to the extent that current research makes possible, the school has invested its huge sums in absurdly expensive architectural structures like a rotunda constructed of nearly 1,550 tons of marble. Symbolic of the intellectual vacuity with which the school has been run, this is an inexcusable architectural eyesore, though for the same price it might have been as beautiful as the national monuments in Washington, D.C.

Much more to the point, this school has the endowment to become a Flagship School. It is my contention that by doing this, the school administration could handsomely fulfill the legacy left by Milton and Catherine Hershey. They wanted to provide otherwise inaccessible opportunities to indigent children so as to transform their opportunities to succeed as Milton Hershey himself succeeded.

A Flagship School would be designed to demonstrate to the fullest extent what is possible in education, showing the nation how (for example) a poor, illiterate ten year old from the inner city could be transformed in a few short years into a highly competent professional in almost any field. Such a school would develop models on which other schools could found their educational programs. These models, expensive to develop in the first place, would not be expensive to reproduce. In fact, the right models could drastically lower the cost of education nationwide, while very significantly increasing its effectiveness.

9 The Ebbinghaus curve of forgetting was explored in the nineteenth century by Hermann Ebbinghaus. Using nonsense syllables because they were free of identifiable meaning, he demonstrated that much information is forgotten in the first twenty minutes, more than half of it in an hour, and two-thirds in a day. After that, retention is quite good. By establishing this approach to learning, Ebbinghaus was responding to the lecture-read-memorize form of traditional education, which is actually the least effective way to learn. By contrast, with the proper emotional setting, meaningful information can be learned easily and quickly and retained for very long periods of time. That is why education should be made more emotional and also more meaningful to each individual.

10 "On Dream Theory in Malaya," by Kilton Stewart in *Altered States of Consciousness*, ed. Charles Tart (New York: Wiley, 1972).

Select Bibliography

Books relevant to discussions in particular chapters are referred to in the Notes, and not always replicated here. The annotations below should help you find the books that will be most helpful to you in a general sense.

Abbott, Edwin A. *Flatland*. New York: Dover, 1952.

Abt, Clark C. *Serious Games*. New York: Viking, 1970.

Adams, Marilyn Jager. *Beginning to Read: Thinking and Learning about Print*. Cambridge: The MIT Press, 1994.

Adler, Mortimer J., and Charles van Doren. *How to Read a Book*. New York: Simon and Schuster, 1972.

Allington, Richard. *What Really Matters for Struggling Readers: Designing Research-Based Programs*. New York: Longman, 2001.

Altick, Richard Daniel. *The Art of Literary Research*. New York: Norton, 1963.

Armstrong, Thomas. *In Their Own Way*. Los Angeles: Tarcher, 1987.

Arnheim, Rudolph. *Visual Thinking*. Berkeley, CA: University of California Press, 1969.

Asimov, Isaac. Various works.

Bandler, Richard. *Using Your Brain—For a Change*. Moab, UT: Real People Press, 1985.

Bandler, Richard, and John Grinder. *Reframing*. Moab, UT: Real People Press, 1982.

Bateson, Gregory. *Steps to an Ecology of Mind*. New York: Ballantine, 1972.

Berard, Guy, M.D. *Hearing Equals Behavior*. New Canaan, CT: Keats Publishing, Inc., 1993.

Berman, Morris. *The Reenchantment of the World*. Ithaca, NY: Cornell University Press, 1981.

Bettelheim, Bruno, and Karen Zelan. *On Learning to Read: The Child's Fascination with Meaning*. New York: Vintage Books, 1981.

Botkin, James W., et al. *No Limits to Learning: Bridging the Human Gap*. New York: Pergamon, 1979.

Brookes, Mona. *Drawing with Children*. Los Angeles: Tarcher, 1986.

Brooks, Cleanth. *The Well-Wrought Urn*. New York: Reynal and Hitchcock, 1947.

Brooks, Cleanth, and Robert Penn Warren, eds. *Understanding Fiction*. Englewood Cliffs, NJ: Prentice-Hall, 1979.

————. *Understanding Poetry*. Englewood Cliffs, NJ: Prentice-Hall, 1976.

————. *Understanding Drama: Twelve Plays*. Englewood Cliffs, NJ: Prentice-Hall, 1948.

Bryson, Lyman. *An Outline of Man's Knowledge of the Modern World*. New York: McGraw-Hill, 1960.

Buzan, Tony. *Use Both Sides of Your Brain*. New York: Dutton, 1983.

Cobb, Jennifer. *Cybergrace*. New York: Crown, 1998.

Conroy, Pat. *The Water Is Wide*. New York: Bantam, 1972.

Damasio, Antonio R. *Descarte's Error: Emotion, Reason, and the Human Brain*. New York: Grosset/Putnam, 1994.

de Bono, Edward. *Lateral Thinking*. New York: Harper, 1973.

Diamond, Marian Cleves. *Enriching Heredity*. New York: The Free Press, 1988.

Diamond, Marian Cleves, and Janet Hopson. *Magic Trees of the Mind*. New York: Dutton, 1998.

Eliot, T. S. *Selected Essays*. New York: Harcourt Brace, 1950.

Esslin, Martin. *The Theatre of the Absurd*. New York: Anchor Books, 1961.

Fader, Daniel N., and Morton H. Shaevitz. *Hooked on Books*. New York: Berkley Pub. Corp., 1966.

Fergusson, Francis. *The Human Dimension in Dramatic Literature*. Garden City: Doubleday, 1953.

Flesch, Rudolph. *Why Johnny Can't Read—And What You Can Do About It*. New York: Harper, 1955.

————. *Why Johnny Still Can't Read: A New Look at the Scandal of Our Schools*. New York: Harper & Row, 1981.

Fuller, R. Buckminster. *Critical Path*. New York: St. Martin's, 1981.

Fuller, Renee. *In Search of the I.Q. Correlation*. Stony Brook, NY: Ball-Stick-Bird Publications, Inc.

Gardner, Howard. *Frames of Mind: The Theory of Multiple Intelligences*. New York: Basic Books, 1983.

_____. *The Unschooled Mind*. New York: Basic Books, 1991.

Gesell, Arnold, et al. *Vision, Its Development in Infant and Child*. New York: Hoeber, 1949.

Glieck, James. *Chaos*. New York: Penguin, 1987.

Goldstein, Kurt. *The Organism*. Boston: Beacon Press, 1963.

Gordon, William J. J. *Synectics*. New York: Harper and Row, 1961.

Gregory, R. L. *Eye and Brain: The Psychology of Seeing*. New York: McGraw-Hill, 1969.

Hall, Edward T. *Beyond Culture, The Hidden Dimension* and *The Silent Language*. New York: Anchor Books.

Hart, Leslie. *How the Brain Works*. New York: Basic Books, 1975.

_____. *Human Brain, Human Learning*. New York: Longman, 1983.

Healy, Jane M. *Endangered Minds: Why Children Don't Think—And What We Can Do About It*. New York: Simon & Schuster, 1999.

Hebb, Donald O. *The Organization of Behavior*. New York: Wiley, 1949.

_____. *Essay on Mind*. Hillsdale, NJ: L. Erlbaum Associates, 1980.

Herrick, C. Judson. *The Evolution of Human Nature*. New York: Harper, 1956.

Hillyer, V. M. *A Child's History of the World*. Revised by Edward G. Huey and Archibald Hart. Baltimore: Calvert School, 1997.

Honig, Bill. "Research-Based Reading Instruction: The Right Way." *The School Administrator* (September 1997). Also condensed in *Education Digest* (December 1997).

Horowitz, Mardi J. *Image Formation and Cognition*. New York: Appleton Century Crofts, 1970.

Isen, Hal, and Peter Kline. *The Genesis Principle*. Arlington, VA: Great Ocean, 1998.

Jacobs, Harold R. *Mathematics, a Human Endeavor*. New York: W. H. Freeman, 1994.

James, William. *Principles of Psychology*. Various editions.

Jaynes, Julian. *The Origin of Consciousness in the Breakdown of the Bicameral Mind*. Boston: Houghton Mifflin, 1982.

Journal of the Society for Accelerative Learning and Teaching.

Kanigel, Robert. *Apprentice to Genius*. New York: Macmillan, 1986.

Kline, Morris. *Mathematics in Western Culture*. New York: Oxford University Press, 1953.

Kline, Peter. *The Everyday Genius*. Arlington, VA: Great Ocean, 1988.

Kline, Peter. "Teaching to All of a Child's Intelligences" in *Preventing Early Learning Failure*. Ed. Bob Sornson. Alexandria, VA: Association for Supervision and Curriculum Development, 2001.

Kline, Peter, and Syril Kline. *The Butterfly Dreams*. Arlington, VA: Great Ocean, 1998.

Kline, Peter, and Laurence Martel. *School Success: The Inside Story*. Arlington, VA: Great Ocean, 1992.

Kline, Peter, and Bernard Saunders. *Ten Steps to a Learning Organization*. Arlington, VA: Great Ocean, 1993.

Kline, Wendy. *Building a Better Race: Gender, Sexuality and Eugenics from the Turn of the Century to the Baby Boom*. Berkeley: University of California Press, 2001.

Kurzweil, Ray. *The Age of Spiritual Machines*. New York: Viking, 1999.

Lakatos, Imre. *Proofs and Refutations: The Logic of Mathematical Discovery*. Eds. John Worrall and Elie Zahar. New York: Cambridge University Press, 1976.

Liedloff, Jean. *The Continuum Concept*. New York: Alfred A. Knopf, 1977.

Lewin, Roger. *Complexity: Life at the Edge of Chaos*. New York: Collier Books, 1992.

Lozanov, Georgi. *Suggestology and Outlines of Suggestopedy*. New York: Gordon and Breach, 1979.

MacLean, Paul D. *The Triune Brain in Evolution*. New York: Plenum Press, 1990.

McClelland, David C., and David G. Winter. *Motivating Economic Achievement*. New York: Free Press, 1969.

_____. "Encouraging Excellence" in *Achievement in American Society*. Eds. B. C. Rosen, et. al. Cambridge, MA: Schenkman Publishing, 1969.

McGuinness, Diane. *Why Our Children Can't Read*. New York: The Free Press, 1997.

Morley, Barry. *Beyond Consensus: Salvaging Sense of the Meeting*. Wallingford, PA: Pendle Hill, 1993.

Muncy, Patricia. *Hooked on Books! Activities and Projects That Make Kids Love to Read*. Englewood Cliffs, NJ: Prentice Hall; West Nyack, NY: Center for Applied Research in Education, Career & Personal Development, 1995.

Ogburn, Charlton. *The Mysterious William Shakespeare* McLean VA: EPM Publications, 1984.

Orr, Eleanor Wilson. *Twice As Less: Black English and the Performance of Black Students in Math and Science*. New York: Norton, 1987.

Pearce, Joseph Chilton. *Evolution's End: Claiming the Potential of Our Intelligence*. San Francisco: Harper San Francisco, 1992.

_____. *Magical Child*. New York: Bantam Books, 1977.

Perrine, Laurence. *Literature: Structure, Sound, and Sense*. Ed. Thomas R. Arp. Fort Worth: Harcourt Brace Jovanovich College Publishers, 1993.

Pinker, Stephen. *The Language Instinct: How the Mind Creates Language*. New York: William Morrow, 1994.

Plimpton, George. *The Paris Review Interviews*. Penguin Books, various dates.

Bibliography

Pribram, Karl, and Joseph King, eds. *Learning As Self-Organization*. Mahwah, NJ: L. Erlbaum Associates, 1996.

_____. *Origins: Brain and Self Organization*. Hillsdale, NJ: L. Erlbaum Associates, 1994.

_____. *Origins: Brain and Perception: Holonomy and Structure in Figural Processing*. Hillsdale, NJ: L. Erlbaum Associates, 1991.

Prince, George M. *The Practice of Creativity*. New York: Harper and Row, 1970.

Pullman, Bernard. *The Atom in the History of Human Thought*. New York: Oxford University Press, 1998.

Quina, James. *Effective Secondary Teaching—Going Beyond the Bell Curve*. New York: Harper and Row, 1989.

Quinn, Daniel. *Beyond Civilization*. New York: Harmony Books, 1999.

Rico, Gabrielle L. *Writing the Natural Way: Using Right-Brain Techniques to Release Your Experience Powers*. Los Angeles: J. P. Tarcher, 1983.

Rosecrance, Richard. *The Rise of the Virtual State*. New York: Basic Books, 1999.

Rosenthal, Robert, and Lenore Jacobson. *Pygmalion in the Classroom*. New York: Holt, Rinehart and Winston, 1968.

Russell, Peter. *The Brain Book*. New York: E. P. Dutton, 1979.

Russell, Peter. *The Global Brain*. Los Angeles: J. P. Tarcher, 1983.

Schank, Roger C. *Tell Me a Story: A New Look at Real and Artificial Memory*. New York: Scribners, 1990.

Scheele, Paul. *The PhotoReading Whole Mind System*. Minneapolis: Learning Strategies, 1993.

_____. *Natural Brilliance: Move from Feeling Stuck to Achieving Success*. Wayzata, MN: Learning Strategies, 1997.

Schiffrin, André. *The Business of Books: How the International Conglomerates Took Over Publishing and Changed the Way We Read*. New York: Verso, 2000.

Schuster, Donald H., and Charles E. Gritton. *Suggestive Accelerative Learning Techniques*. New York: Gordon and Breach, 1986.

Sims, Pamela. *Awakening Brilliance: How to Inspire Children to Become Successful Learners*. Atlanta: Bayhampton Publications, 1997.

Springer, Sally, and Georg Deutsch. *Left Brain, Right Brain*. New York: W. H. Freeman, 1985.

Stehli, Annabel. *Dancing in the Rain*. Westport, CT: The Georgiana Organization, 1995.

_____. *Sound of a Miracle: A Child's Triumph over Autism*. New York: Doubleday, 1991.

Sternberg, Robert J. *Beyond I.Q.* New York: Cambridge, 1985.

Stewart, Kilton. "On Dream Theory in Malaya" in *Altered States of Consciousness*. Ed.

Charles Tart. New York: Wiley, 1972.

Talbot, Michael. *The Holographic Universe*. New York: Harper Collins, 1991.

Tame, David. *The Secret Power of Music*. New York: Destiny Books, 1984.

Thruelson, Richard, and John Kobler. *Adventures of the Mind*. New York: Knopf, various dates.

Vygotsky, Lev. *Thought and Language*. Cambridge: MIT Press, 1962.

_____. *Mind in Society*. Cambridge: Harvard University Press, 1978.

Waldrop, M. Mitchell. *Complexity: The Emerging Science at the Edge of Order and Chaos*. New York: Simon and Schuster, 1992.

Willinsky, John. *Empire of Words: The Reign of the OED*. Princeton: Princeton University Press, 1994.

Wills, Christopher. *The Runaway Brain: The Evolution of Human Uniqueness*. New York: Basic Books, 1993.

Index

INNER OCEAN PUBLISHING publishes in the genres of self-help, personal growth, lifestyle, conscious business, and inspirational nonfiction. Our goal is to publish books that touch the spirit and make a tangible difference in the lives of individuals, families, and their communities.

The five books in our Spring 2002 list reflect our company's goals, depict the process of personal growth and spiritual exploration that we cultivate in ourselves and others, and encourage a reassessment of personal success and its contribution to our greater welfare.
We invite you to visit us at:
www.innerocean.com
Aloha.

Toxic Success:
How to Stop Striving and Start Thriving
by Paul Pearsall, Ph.D.
Foreword by Matt Biondi

Why America's Children Can't Think:
Creating Independent Minds for the 21st Century
by Peter Kline

Web Thinking:
Connecting, not Competing, for Success
by Dr. Linda Seger

The Initiation
by Donald Schnell
Foreword by Marilyn Diamond

Swimming Where Madmen Drown:
Travelers' Tales from Inner Space
by Robert Masters, Ph.D.
Foreword by Stanley Krippner